MW01258900

The Search for a
Vanishing *B*eijing

舊京大觀

The Search for a
Vanishing Beijing

A Guide to China's Capital Through the Ages

M. A. Aldrich

香港大學出版社
HONG KONG UNIVERSITY PRESS

Hong Kong University Press
14/F Hing Wai Centre
7 Tin Wan Praya Road
Aberdeen
Hong Kong

Text © M. A. Aldrich 2006

ISBN 962 209 777 4

All rights reserved. No portion of this publication may be reproduced or transmitted in any form or by any means, electronic or mechanical, including photocopy, recording, or any information storage or retrieval system, without prior permission in writing from the publisher.

M. A. Aldrich has asserted his moral rights.

Secure On-line Ordering
http://www.hkupress.org

British Library Cataloguing-in-Publication Data
A catalogue record for this book is available from the British Library.

Printed and bound by United League Graphic & Printing Co. Ltd., in Hong Kong, China

To

Zhang Guo Lao

COMMENT ON THE NAME OF THE CITY

Isn't it called "Beijing"?

Sorry, but the capital of China had been known as Peking in the English language for over three hundred years. Even after the establishment of the People's Republic of China in 1949, the name "Peking" continued to adorn English language maps and official stationery printed in China. It was only in the mid-1970s that the Chinese government insisted upon the outside world replacing "Peking" with the modern *pin yin* spelling "Beijing."

It escapes me why the English-speaking world bent over backwards to accommodate this demand. "Peking" is a far more evocative name that reaches back through the centuries and conjures images of China's majestic culture. Nor does "Beijing" lend itself to a more accurate pronunciation of the capital's name by foreigners, who slur the "j" and wind up producing a grating sound like "beige-zhing," a city not yet identified in China.

And why should there be a change simply for change's sake? We all know that "Moscow" becomes "Moskva" in Russian, but there is no great rush for a revision of the English name. "Krung Thep" is a name puzzling to most, but everyone recognizes "Bangkok." In Chinese, "New York" becomes "*Niu Yue*," a name that sounds like something to do with Central Asian silk routes and not the Big Apple. Why not live and let live?

As an unreconstructed, unrepentant traditionalist, I believe that the time is ripe for the revival of the name "Peking." Sadly, a younger generation might not recognize the proper historical appellation for this wonderful city. For this reason, the title of the book bends its knee to contemporary usage. The rest of the text, however, defiantly stands up for tradition.

CONTENTS

LIST OF MAPS

PREFACE

IN THE 1930S, TWO FOREIGNERS collaborated on a guidebook that became a celebrated classic among travel books on China. Lewis Arlington, an American born in California after the Gold Rush, had arrived in China in the 1880s to accept an appointment as an officer in the newly established Qing Imperial Navy. He spent the next fifty years in China, moving from service in the imperial navy to customs and postal work. During his sojourn in China, Arlington witnessed the demise of the Qing empire and China's struggle to install a modern system of government. After his retirement in the late 1920s, he turned his attention to writing about traditional Chinese performing arts and architecture. Somehow, he made the acquaintance of William Lewisohn, a young English student attached to the British Legation in Peking. Lewisohn was later to become a journalist.

Arlington and Lewisohn were foreign witnesses to the decline of Peking. Indeed, in their view, the first third of the 20th century had been devastating to the Northern Capital. From the Boxer Debacle to the ensuing foreign occupation and pillage, from Yuan Shi Kai's royal misadventure to the warlordism of Feng Yu Xiang and Zhang Zuo Lin, and finally to the transfer of the national capital from Peking to Nanjing, the city had already gone through deeply traumatic cataclysms by the time the two men began their collaboration. Further, after northern China had been brought nominally under the control of Nanjing in the 1930s, the Nationalist government ignored Peking's patrimony. Temples, shrines and courtyard mansions were converted into municipal offices, schools and barracks. Without imperial patronage, monasteries were left to the care of a handful of elderly monks who were powerless to prevent their libraries of ancient sutras or their lacquered altars laden with deities from turning into dust. Compounding this neglect, Chinese intellectuals, seeking modernity and a revival of China's lost centrality, decried historical sites as relics of a political feudalism and superstition that had already run its course. In their view, these places could be lost without mourning.

Arlington and Lewisohn were eager to record the sights of Old Peking before neglect and disinterest erased them from the map. In 1935, Henri Vetch, whose French Book Store in the Peking Hotel specialized in works on China, published the results of their work, a book entitled *In Search of Old Peking*. The two men expressed a melancholy expectation that many of Peking's sights were about to disappear into the ether. With an overtone of autumnal nostalgia, the authors guided their readers through the alleys of the city.

Little did Arlington and Lewisohn foresee that one of the world's most beautiful and cultured cities would undergo even greater upheavals during the balance of the twentieth century. The Japanese occupation left Peking a brutalized and squalid city that suffered even further deprivation during the civil war between the Nationalists and the Communists. After the declaration of the People's Republic in October 1949, the clock measuring the lifespan for Old Peking began to tick faster. By the mid-nineteen fifties, the actual appearance of the city became an ideological battleground between conservationists, who favored the creation of a new capital near the Western Hills, and ideologues, who wanted to tear down the city walls and build a metropolis in honor of the newly enshrined gods of modernity and socialism. After an airing of these views, Mao Ze Dong sided with the ideologues. The walls and gates of the old city, as well as implicitly the soul of Old Peking, had been issued their death warrants.

The "Great" Proletarian Cultural Revolution intensified the assault upon the elegant vestiges of the city as Red Guards shattered, burned and trampled relics that had previously escaped plunder and neglect. Some well-known sites were able to avoid the blow, simply because the government needed to tolerate a few "harmless" tokens of the old order. Others sites became the homes of important *politicos* or military officials, creating unintentional sanctuaries of the old culture.

After Deng Xiao Ping had consolidated his power in the late 1970s, the government called off the assault, leaving Peking's historical sites with the protection afforded by benign neglect. Not for long, however. With the opening of China to foreign investment, the remnants of Old Peking were faced with a two-headed enemy: avarice and urban development. By the 1990s, an aficionado of Old Peking would have to work very hard indeed to locate the places described by Arlington and Lewisohn.

As for myself, I first moved to Peking in the spring of 1993 and found that my initial impressions of the city were far from favorable. However, one afternoon, I happened to come across a newly reprinted copy of *In Search of Old Peking* in a hotel bookshop. With nothing to lose, I decided to follow in the footsteps of Arlington and Lewisohn during that elusive commodity called spare time. With effort, and admittedly perhaps a touch of romantic eccentricity, I found that, for a moment or two, I could force the concrete apartment blocks to yield to Old Peking. Sometimes it felt as if a ghost stepped out from behind the smog and concrete and approached me, eager to bring back to human memory forgotten people and stories. He seemed to be delighted to find an audience, although a suspect one on account of the bridge of my nose. After this initial encounter, I sought this apparition with the assistance of the writings of long deceased Chinese and foreign authors as well as the work of living scholars and journalists.

Peking — I use the old name because of its classical resonance — has already entered a new stage of urban development for the 2008 Olympics. This raises the specter of the city finally succumbing to an entirely modern (that is to say, Western) appearance, with just a few antique touches here and there. Myself, I deeply lament this inevitable consequence. I also admit that I might very well be an unwitting Confucian, yearning for the return of a Golden Age that exists only in the past, or perhaps in the mind. Nevertheless, there is something disturbing about the final transmutation of one of the world's oldest cultural capitals into a physical parody of the West for something as transitory as an international sporting event.

I hope that my sense of resignation is unfounded. The Peking government has funded the renovation of previously closed landmarks and has opened them to the public. These days, the Pan Jia Yuan antique market caters to enormous crowds of clientele on the hunt for Chinese antiques and curios. Carpenters continue to revive the craftsmanship of earlier centuries. An artist community grows and produces everything from traditional ink scrolls to abstract oil paintings. More importantly, there seems to be a flickering revival of faith among the visitors to Peking's temples. Perhaps the city is on the verge of a renaissance, with its current citizens reclaiming and resurrecting the elegance of the past. I certainly hope so.

This book is not meant to be a "serious" work about Peking.* I have not attempted to sift fact from legend or make any new contribution to a body of scholarship. Rather, I have simply gathered miscellaneous stories recorded over the centuries and set them out alongside their original stage sets.

---

* For a "serious" work about the city, the reader is directed to Susan Naquin's *Peking: Temples and City Life 1400–1900*, which has set the standard for English language scholarship for some time to come.

I am indebted to Arlington and Lewisohn for this approach. And like them, I have not included information that is found in conventional guidebooks, such as hotels, bus schedules or nightlife. There are many other books that can provide that sort of guidance. My expectation is that the reader will not only be able to get his or her luggage off the airport carousel but that he or she can also handle the other incidentals of travel.

I hope that my Chinese friends will pardon me for many points of view and stories that are as foreign as I am. Peking has always been a cosmopolitan city, and this is a point that I have tried to underscore in these chapters. To my critics, I can only offer the defense that my goal has been to enhance the visitor's enjoyment of the city by giving voice to the ghosts of Old Peking.

M.A. Aldrich
Coloane Village, Macao

ACKNOWLEDGMENTS

I WISH TO ACKNOWLEDGE FRIENDS, colleagues and acquaintances who helped me along my way, in one way or the other, along the alleys and backstreets of Old Peking: Kevin Abikoff, Dmitri Alemasov, Annabel Allen, Andy Andreasen, Yuriko Aoyama, Brian Arendt, Susan Armour, Buddy Arnheim, Professor Michael Barnhart, Bob Barta and the Sunnyland Jazz Band, Beijing Five Star Brewery Co. Ltd., Tom Bell, Kylie Bolton, Clifford Borg-Marks, Sara and Joseph Bosco, James and Suzanne Callaghan, Cole Rudolf Capener, Christina Chan, the late Chang Da-chi, Gigi Cheah, Lucy Chen, Xiao Chen, Martin Childs, Mr. Cheng of the Bai Ta Si neighborhood, Soshan Cheung, Stephen Cheung, Wesley Chiu, Jeremie Chou, Old Chu, Julian Chung, Scott Cocker, Charles Conroy, Mark Connolly, Michael J. Coss, Nicola Cunningham, the Zvi Cohen family, Philip Dews, the late Rick Danko and the late Richard Manuel, my mentor Ding Mow Sung, the former chief abbess of the Dong Jiao Nunnery, Christopher and Paula Dorman, the jolly maintenance crew at the Duan Cheng, Jon Eichelberger, Sunny Eng and his family, Stuart Eunson, Joseph Fazio, Dr. Desmond Feng, Catherine Fox, Ge Xiang Yang, Bob Giles, the Globe, Brenda Green, Todd Greenspan, John V. Grobowski, the Honorable Jose Guerre and his wife Mercedes, Art Hillman, David Hind, Mr. He of Nan Chi Zi, Bradley Herrold, Victor Ho, Maurice Hoo, Old Hu, John Sin-ger Huang, Joan Jacobs, the elderly gentleman playing croquet near the tomb of the Ming emperor Jing Tai, Mary Johannes, Don Jones, John Jones IV, Saburo Kagei, Riaz and Sumbul Karamali, Kenneth Keung, Peter Kieler-Saietz and his family, John and Jodie Kuzmik, Veronica Kwan, the Lao Sichuan Restaurant in the Chongqing Hotel (may you have many years of prosperity!), Janice Law, Professor Robert Lee, the late Sir Harry Lauder, Nancy Leigh, Robert D. Lewis, Erik Leyssens, Xiao Li at the Eastern Qing Tombs, Youn Ling, Liang Feng, Professor

Liang Pao-shuo, Liu Chi, Lim Mei Yin, David and Jennifer Livingston, Mary Liu, Vienne Liu, Liu Yue Hua, Christine Lim, Andrew Lockhart, Peter Lovelock, Stefania Malpighi, Patrick McGonagle, Milo, Ming Lui, Betty Mak, Andrew McGinty, June McKenzie, Paul McKenzie, Bruce McLaughlin, Greg Markey, Alex May, George Mansho, Timothy Millea, Michael J. Moser, Buddy Neel, Stephen Nelson, Eric Nygard, the Old Parr (gone but not forgotten), Pan Wei-ta, Del and Joanne Parks, Richard and Amy Pascoe, Professor Sung-bae Park, Julie Peng, the Red Star Distillery (long may you distill!), Yunan Ren, Rong Peng, Alex Root, Rona Ross, Liesbeth Ruijter, Michael Scogna, David R. Shannon, Shao Zili, Geoffrey Shi, Joseph Simone, Chris and Ruoyu Smith, the late Michael Smith, Michelle Smith, Nicholas and Hui Smith, Roger and Anne Marie Smith, Song Yao Qun, Francis Sullivan, Josef ten Berge, Jacqueline Teoh, Gene Theroux, Doug Thorpe, Rita Tse, Kenny and Fannie Tung, the red-faced book clerk at the now-defunct Xin Beijing Book Store, Wang Dahong, Wang Yi Hua, Ed Wes, Jonathan Weiser, Fritz Weiss, Betty Wong, C.H. Wong, Yang Guang Jie, Malcolm Yang, Professor Catherine Yu, Kathy Yu, the former residents of Yu Qian's Shrine, Winston Zee, Andrew Zeng, Zhang Ning, Cindy Zhao, and many, many other nice folks in Peking.

My Peking *ge'mer* and teacher, Lao Yang, gave me the gift of his balance, perspective and companionship during our travels and provided me with constant encouragement during days of darkness and light.

Pat Fontaine, an old comrade from late night *hu tong* strolls, went over and above the duty of an old friend, reading the manuscript during difficult times and giving me his valuable comments (and corrections). Chris Smith graciously and enthusiastically responded to my request to photograph contemporary sites in Peking.

Dennis Cheung of Hong Kong University Press helped the editing process along with his usual personal warmth and professional guidance. Latie Wong and Yau Sau Lee helped type the manuscript, and Latie cheerfully undertook the task of correcting my numerous misspellings in *pin yin* and in Chinese. Janice Law helped me with the last stages of the publishing process.

Lastly, I am grateful to my wife Chuang Mei-Chih for putting up with a spouse who just cannot resist walking into every broken down temple in North China. Of course, the views expressed in this book, as well as its many mistakes, are all my own.

NOTES ON USING THIS BOOK

Layout of the Chapters

The first three chapters are a general survey of Peking's urban design, traditional religion and history. I believe that these chapters will help deepen the reader's appreciation of the sights of the city while on the road.

Following Arlington and Lewisohn, the subsequent chapters introduce Old Peking by geographical section in relation to the long-vanished walls of the city. We begin at the heart of the city, Tian An Men Square, and gradually expand our travels from urban to rural Peking. I have not included a chapter on Peking's southern suburbs since this area was traditionally an imperial hunting ground with few buildings of historical importance.

Lastly, I have included chapters that broadly treat the topics of food, drink and Peking opera. Each of these subjects easily merits a book rather than a chapter. However, they are essential for a satisfying visit to the city.

Getting Around

Chapters 4 to 9 are written with the expectation that the reader will cover this ground on foot, with the advisory that these large blocks of territory can be tiring. Chapters 10 to 13 cover more territory than can be comfortably covered on one outing by foot. The reader can divide these sections and tackle them as separate walks. Alternatively, a bicycle would be very useful for seeing more in a shorter period of time. Finally, the sights in Chapters 14 to 21 are best visited by motorcar.

When you are searching for a particularly hard-to-find site, you should make polite inquiries with elderly folks in the neighborhood. The younger generation is unlikely to have the presence of mind to note historically significant places. Old timers are always the best bet for accurate directions.

Getting In

Many of the sights are on standard tourist itineraries. However, I have also included quite a few sights that are not open to the public. Here, you will have to use your ingenuity, sense of humor and chutzpah to get past any caretakers. Sometimes, these caretakers are as pleased as punch to have a visit from a curious foreigner. Other times, a polite request to take a look will provoke a reaction of unparalleled rudeness. Your experiences will simply be the result of the luck of the road. Obviously, Mandarin speakers and foreigners accompanied by Chinese friends might have better luck. In any event, simply be mindful that you are a guest of the country and do your best to convey your respect for Peking history and culture.

Romanization of the Chinese Language

English is not widely spoken in Peking. For this reason, I have endeavored to set out the English translation for each sight and street name along with the original name in Chinese characters and the *pin yin* romanization system officially used by the Chinese government. Where I feel it to be appropriate, I have sometimes included only the name in Chinese characters and *pin yin*.

To an English speaker, no romanization system for the Chinese language is satisfactory simply because the spoken Chinese language includes sounds not represented by the Roman alphabet. The *pin yin* system, which was invented in the 1950s and later made the official romanization method in the 1970s, reflects Russian influence in its use of letters not commonly used in English, such as "x," "q" and "z."

Contemporary usage in the mainland sometimes produces a long string of *pin yin* words linked together without spaces. When the string of words includes a jumble of x's, z's and q's, the resulting phrase appears quite unpronounceable, let alone intimidating, to a non-Chinese speaker. I have usually dispensed with official practice and have inserted a space between each word written in *pin yin*.

Here is a list to help readers find the approximate sound of the *pin yin* lettering system. First, here are the unusual consonants

Q   as the "ch" in "chick"
X   an aspirated "sh" sound, between "ss" and "sh"
Z   as the "ts" in "its"
C   as the "ts" in "its" as an initial consonant
Z   as the "ds" in "suds"
Zh   as the "j" in "jiggle"

The rest of the consonants are as follows:

B   as the "b" in "bar"
Ch   as the "ch" in "cherry"
D   as the "d" in "dangle"
F   as the "f" in "fit"
G   as the "g" in "ghost"
H   as the "h" in "hot"
J   as the "j" in "jiggle"
K   as the "k" in "killer"
L   as the "l" in "lummox"
M   as the "m" in "mother"
N   as the "n" in "nun"
P   as the "p" in "pickled"
R   as an unrolled "r" in "rock and roll"
Sh   as the "sh" in "shiftless"
T   as the "t" in "tongue"
W   as the "w" in "wallop"
Y   as the "y" in "yank"

And now on to the vowels:

A   as the "a" in "bar"
Ai   as the "ai" in Ricky Ricardo's "ai yai yai yai ai"
Ao   as the "ow" in "pow, right on the nose"
E   as the "e" in "her"
Ei   as the "ay" in "bay watch"
I   as the "ee" in "see unless preceded by the consonants c, ch, r, s, shi, z, or zh
     where it is pronounced like the "e" in "her"
Ie   as the "yeah" in "yeah, yeah, yeah"
Iu   as in saying the letters "e" and "o" real quick
O   as the "or" in "Lordy"
Ou   as the "o" in "So, what's your story?"
U   as the "oo" in "you fool"
Ua   as the "wah" in "a guitar wah wah pedal"
Ue   as the "way" in "go away"
Ui   as the "way" as in "sway to the music"
Uo   as the "aw" in "aw, shucks, ma'am"

Here is a little riddle for graying hippies or rock fans to see if you have mastered the *pin yin* system

Hei, zhou, wei er yu gou ying we de gun yin you hen?
Hei, zhou, wei er yu gou ying we de gun yin you hen?
     Gun ne shu er te mai o lei di bi ke si ai fen de he er we e ne ter man

Hei, zhou, wei er yu gou ying nao?
Hei zhou wei er yu gou ying nao?
     Gun ne fen de mai o lei di en shu te er nao.

Hei zhou, wei er yu gou ying we de be lu si te fo ti fo
Hei zhou, wei er you gou ying we de be lu si tel fo ti fo
     Gun ne shu er te mai qi ke bi ke si she bin run ning ruan

Hei zhou, wei er you gou ying nao?
Hei zhou, wei er you gou ying nao?
     Ai ge si ai gun na gou tu mou xi ko tu bi fo li.

Personal and Dynastic Names

In Chinese names, a person's surname always precedes the personal name. Since I frequently refer to Chinese dynasties, here is a list, with corresponding years from the Gregorian calendar, for ease of reference.

Xia	2205–1766 B.C.
Shang	1766–1027 B.C.
Western Zhou	1027–770 B.C.
Eastern Zhou	770–256 B.C.
Warring States Period	403–221 B.C.
Qin (as a separate state)	473–221 B.C.
Qin (as unifier of China)	221–206 B.C.
Han	206 B.C.–221
Three Kingdoms Period	221–265
Chin	265–420
North – South dynasties	420–589
Sui	589–618
Tang	618–907
Five Dynasties	907–960
Song	960–1278
Liao (in N. China)	907–1120
Jin (in N. China)	1120–1234
Yuan (in N. China)	1234–1278
Yuan (in all China)	1278–1368

Ming	1368–1644
Qing	1644–1911
Republic of China	1911– present (since 1949 limited to the province of Taiwan)
People's Republic of China	1949– present

I have used traditional romanization systems for proper names which are more commonly known, like Sun Yat Sen, Chiang Kai Shek and Tsingtao beer.

Peking in the 1930s

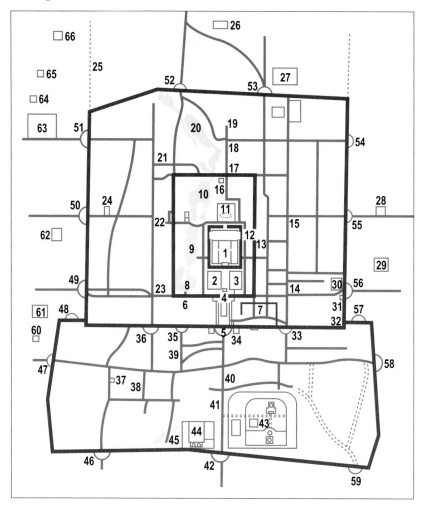

1. Forbidden City
2. Central Park
3. Imperial Ancestral Temple
4. Tian An Men
5. Zheng Yang Men
6. Chang An West Avenue
7. Legation District
8. Nan Hai
9. Zhong Hai
10. Bei Hai
11. Coal Hill
12. Bei He Yan
13. Wang Fu Jing
14. Dong Dan Arch
15. Dong Si Arches
16. Can Tan
17. Di An Men
18. Drum Tower
19. Bell Tower
20. Shi Cha Hai
21. Temple of the Protection of the Country
22. Xi Si Arches
23. Xi Dan Arch
24. White Pagoda
25. Mongol Earth Wall
26. Yellow Temple
27. Altar of the Earth
28. Dong Yue Temple
29. Altar of the Sun
30. Site of Examination Hall
31. Observatory
32. Fox Tower
33. Ha Ta Men
34. Railway Station
35. He Ping Men
36. Xuan Wu Men
37. Cow Street Mosque
38. Temple of the Origin of the Law
39. Glazed Tile Factory
40. Tian Qiao District
41. Qian Men Wai Avenue
42. Yong Ding Men
43. Altar of Heaven
44. Altar of Agriculture
45. Joyous Pavillion
46. Nan Xi Men
47. Chang Yi Men
48. Xi Bian Men
49. Chang An Men
50. Ping Zi Men
51. Xi Zhi Men
52. De Sheng Men
53. An Ding Men
54. Dong Zhi Men
55. Zhi Hua Men
56. Zhi Ming Men
57. Dong Bian Men
58. Sha Kuo Men
59. Jiang Zuo Men
60. Tian Ning Temple
61. White Cloud Temple
62. Altar of the Moon
63. Zoological Park
64. Temple of the Five Pagodas
65. Da Hui Temple
66. Big Bell Temple

1

THE PLAN OF OLD PEKING

THE URBAN DESIGN OF OLD PEKING is based on ancient Chinese theories of cosmology. When the Ming emperor Yong Le (永乐) chose Peking as his capital in the early 1400s, he ordered the city to be rebuilt according to the principles of the *Zhou Li* (周礼), an ancient Confucian text that propounded universal principles for the construction of homes and villages. The *Zhou Li* is one of the earliest essays on *feng shui* (风水 or literally, wind and water), a cosmological architectural theory that explained how to construct buildings so that they do not conflict with supernatural forces. Some aspects of *feng shui* are simply common sense notions for ventilation, water supply and solar heating. Other principles emphasize symmetry, proportion, and balance.

Old Peking was built on the basis of an imaginary central axis running from the south to the north of the city. This axis passed through the major southern gate Yong Ding Men (永定门) along Qian Men Nei Avenue (前门内大街), through Zheng Yang Gate (正阳门) and across Tian An Men Square (天安门广场) on its way north through the Forbidden City. The emperor's throne in the Hall of Supreme Harmony (太和殿) sat astride the central axis, which carried on through the Gate of Military Prowess (神武门), the central pavilion in Coal Hill and on out through the Gate of Earthly Peace (地安门) and to the Drum and Bell Towers beyond. Perhaps for both meteorological and historical reasons, the north was symbolically the source of bad fortune. For this reason, an artificial hill was built behind the Forbidden City with soil dredged from the imperial moats and lakes. There was no northern gate along the central axis since it would give harmful forces access to the emperor. When sitting upon his throne, the emperor faced south and accordingly the courtyards as well as Tian An Men Square were situated to the south of imperial buildings.

The *Zhou Li* also advocated the architectural principle of symmetrically placing boxes within boxes. In the precise center of Peking were the walls enclosing the rectangular-shaped Forbidden City, which functioned as the office and residence of the Son of Heaven and a graphic demonstration of the power and prestige of the empire. The Forbidden City itself was divided between the southern half, where official ceremonies were conducted, and the northern half, which was the personal home of the emperor and his retinue.

Around the Forbidden City, there was another wall, imperfectly rectangular in shape enclosing the Imperial City. Here lived the imperial attendants as well as officials, both civil and military, required for the day-to-day running of the Forbidden City. The Imperial City also was the location for a vast number of storehouses for the supplies of the Forbidden City. The current names of certain streets recall their former use, such as the Wax Storehouse Alley or the Pen and Paper Alley. A portion of the southern wall of the Imperial City still survives immediately to the west of the Grand Hotel on Chang An East Avenue.

Around the Imperial City was constructed yet another wall for the Northern City, which was the area for princely mansions and prestigious temples. Nearby are the beautiful imperial lakes that were nearly always used for the exclusive pleasure of the emperor.

In 1645, the Qing court, motivated by concerns of security, issued a decree ordering all Han Chinese residents to leave the Northern City and resettle in the Southern City, which, in those days, was a large portion of land enclosed by a rectangular shaped wall adjacent to the Northern City. Originally meant as a residence for commoners and merchants, the Southern City was redeveloped as wealthy or important Chinese citizens were forced to locate new homes there.

Under the principles of the *Zhou Li,* the outer city also ought to have enclosed the Northern City in a concentric pattern. One Peking legend maintains eunuchs or corrupt officials misappropriated the funds allocated for the construction of such a wall. Hence, the wall was never properly completed but simply finished off by connecting to the southern most walls of the Northern City. In actual fact, Yong Le never intended to create another outer wall for Peking. As the city grew, merchants and others spilled out from the main walls. In the 1550s, Mongol depredations forced the Ming court to wall off the southern flank. The eastern, northern and southern suburbs were too sparsely populated to be worth the expense.

From the 19th century, foreigners referred to the Northern City as the "Tartar City." "Tartar" is one of those maddeningly inaccurate terms that are applied helter skelter to nomadic groups east of the Urals. The word comes from *da dan* (韃靼), a Han Chinese term for a subgroup of Mongols. Eight groups of Manchu bannermen were posted in the neighborhoods of the Tartar City, each given the name of a color designed to offset the security risk posed by the other groups according to Taoist alchemy. The Southern City became the Chinese City, and one of the more lively areas in the old capital for entertainment and commerce since an imperial decree prohibited the construction of theatres and other establishments in the Tartar City that would lead the bannermen into soft living. By the end of the Qing, this racial segregation had fallen into disuse, though the terminology still stuck.

In keeping with the rites of the Zhou Li, the "right hand side facing the emperor" (namely, the east since the emperor always faced to the south during official functions) was an honored location while the "left hand side" was less respected. Given the Confucian emphasis upon rational persuasion over the rule of force, civilian officials used the honored eastern gates to enter the Forbidden City and stood in reverence to the emperor on the eastern side of courtyards. The less exalted western side was preserved for the military officials, which, in the views of Confucians, were a necessary but untutored evil.

The main courtyard in the Forbidden City

Before the 1980s, Old Peking was a capital city without a skyline. Chinese architecture did not favor tall buildings lest they interfere with the passage of spirits. Buildings in the Forbidden City and other royal mansions occasionally rose to two stories, as did pagodas erected with careful verification of their *feng shui* impact. Foreign residents, who were first granted the right to take the air from the city walls during the 1860s, remarked that from that vantage, the entire city looked like a forest since all courtyard and roadside trees were taller than the buildings. Only the yellow tiles of the Forbidden City, a white Tibetan pagoda and the blue tiles at the Temple for the Annual Harvest rose above the trees. You can catch a vague glimpse of Peking's disappeared forest canopy by looking at the Chao Yang (朝阳) diplomatic district from one of the office buildings in the area. Here you can see a small patch of greenery rising over the embassies, certainly the only place near Old Peking that rekindles memories of this former view.

In their day, the city walls encircled the city, thirty feet thick and about forty feet tall with crenellated borders and magnificent gates. Photographs provide only the slightest glimpse of what must have been a majestic sight. At the end of each day, the gates were closed with considerable ceremony. Both Chinese and foreign residents of the city commented on the sense of security that came about once the gates were closed for the evening.

The emperors constructed altars dedicated for ceremonies to revere the elements of nature. These altars were positioned in relation to the central axis and symmetrically with the Forbidden City at the center. In the eastern suburbs was the Altar of the Sun, while its counterpart, the Altar of the Moon stood outside the western wall. To the north was the Altar of the Earth, while the most magnificent of all, the Altar of Heaven was to be found in the south of the city. Directly to the east of Tian An Men Gate was the official temple for sacrifices to imperial ancestors. To the west was the Altar of Grains and directly to its south in the Chinese City was the Altar of Agriculture. No other Chinese city contained such monuments in honor of the constitutent components of Heaven. A trip taken across Old Peking immediately brought to mind mankind's place in relation to the sun, the moon, the planets, the stars and the earth.

Because Chinese architecture enshrines symmetry, Peking's main avenues ran north to south on each side of the central axis. Memorial arches or *pai lou* (牌楼) graced these avenues and gave them their names. A *pai lou* is a wooden or stone arch built over a street as a memorial to a noble citizen. Some arches were built in honor of nearby temples or altars. Others venerated "chaste widows" who refused to remarry and continued to perform rituals in memory of their husbands. Other arches were simply built as decoration, providing an elegant sense of location for people going about the city.

On the main thoroughfare to the east of the central axis was the Dong Dan (东单 or East Single Arch) and, slightly to the north of it, Dong Si (东四 or the East Four Arches). To the west and in perfect symmetry were, of course, Xi Dan

City walls and corner gate, circa 1860.

A surviving section of the city wall.

(西单 or West Single Arch) and Xi Si (西四 or the West Four Arches). Alas, these lovely structures could not accommodate the intrusion of modern traffic and disappeared in the 1950s, though their names linger indefinitely at their former sites.

In addition to the lakes of the imperial parks, moats surrounded the Forbidden City and the outer walls of the Chinese City. Within the city, sources of fresh water were important. Peking's water was traditionally brackish. Until the construction of the Mi Yun Reservoir in the 1950s, peddlers of sweet water roamed through the city streets hawking their precious wares. Neighborhoods developed around various fresh water springs, which might have been the origin of one of Peking's most distinctive landmarks. Peking's alleyways are called *hu tong* (胡同), a word possibly of Mongolian origin referring to a residential neighborhood centered around a well. Its precise origins are lost to us. The great British translator, Arthur Waley, tersely commented in a letter to his friend Osbert Sitwell: "Hu-t'ung is the transcription of a Mongol word, and has been in use in North Chinese since the fourteenth century. That is all that is known about it."[1]

To the casual visitor to Peking on a four-day package, smog-choked six lane thoroughfares and traffic jams will be the predominant memory of trips about the city. Such an oversight is lamentable and can only be compared to going to London without stopping off in a pub. Or, even worse, spending a weekend in Macao without dining at Fernando's. The congested, confusing *hu tong* are the heart of Old Peking, where you can glimpse the entrance to gray courtyard homes with richly carved door ways, see old men taking out their birds (in cages or anchored to sticks) for an airing, watch a late night peddler wave a fan over coals roasting a spiced lamb kebab, or simply enjoy the pleasure of walking down a street that has graced the maps of Peking for more than a thousand years.

The city of Peking is almost alone in the honor of having *hu tong*. (They exist in Tianjin and Kai Feng as well.) Unfortunately, if municipal planners and real property developers have their way, the *hu tong* are likely to go the way of the *pai lou*, or the covered bridges of Vermont for that matter. Thousands of hectares have already been torn down and replaced with white ceramic covered monstrosities, looking for all the world like gigantic wash rooms.

Amidst the *hu tong* you will find the traditional homes of Old Peking, called courtyard houses (四合院 or *si he yuan*). Ideally a courtyard house was built on a north-south axis, if this could be accommodated by the location of the land. A main door (with an ever-present doorman in the more well-to-do homes) admits residents and visitors to a courtyard with a hall facing the gate. (Like the Forbidden City, the proper place for a courtyard to receive guests is to the south of the main hall.) The main hall usually is the main living quarters if the courtyard house is

Memorial arches in 1930s Peking.

Memorial arches at the Alley of the Academy of the Sons of the Country.

Wintertime view of a *hu tong* neighborhood.

Courtyard home entrance, flanked by fading slogans from the Cultural Revolution.

a modest one. To the east and west are other rooms used for cooking, storage or bedrooms. The grander the courtyard house, the greater the number of courtyards. On each side of the first hall, there are passages (sometimes moon-shaped) that lead to another courtyard with a hall in front and side rooms to the east and west. Again, a third, a fourth or even a fifth courtyard might be found further back in the case of wealthy families.

In the courtyards grow local trees such as cypresses, willows, poplars, persimmons, oleanders and pomegranates. Glorious lilac bushes scent the air around man-made rockeries and grottoes, which were designed to achieve the highest aesthetic appeal by looking simply natural.

The Tartar City was the location for princely mansions (王府 or *wang fu*) for Manchu nobles. These mansions are built on the same principle as courtyard houses but on a grander scale, with artificial ponds, bridges, gardens, and pavilions. The main entrances are enormous red gates with brass door studs and wooden pillars, which can still be seen in some parts of Old Peking. The court allocated and confiscated these mansions as the fortunes of the resident officials ebbed and flowed.

In the 1950s and 1960s, courtyard houses and princely mansions were each parceled out among one or two dozen families who built new partitioned brick dwellings in the courtyards. Some have been turned over to research institutes or governmental agencies. Others are open to the public as museums. The most interesting are those that are private homes. Admittedly, it does take some pluck to sally forth into the backyards of unsuspecting Peking citizens. It is worth the effort to view the carvings of flowers, lions, false windows, clay pots containing fermenting cabbage or rice wine, auspicious signs on the walls amidst the jumble of bicycles, bird cages, flower pots, gate guardian pictures and tiled roofs. Some folks will respond with traditional Old Peking hospitality and offer you a cup of tea. Others might be, well, let's just say less charitable. Nevertheless it is always worth the gamble.

Buddhist (and Taoist) temples share a similar architectural design as the courtyard houses. Facing to the south, the temples will have a spirit screen to keep away malevolent spirits. (The retiring and dark nature of ghosts precluded them from making sudden spry turns. A screen to the south of the temple gate, usually an ornate work of art, prevents them from floating into the temple and causing mischief). A pair of stone lions guards the entrance way and two large poles flank the lions from which banners and lanterns were hung during festivals. The entrance usually leads to a hall with an effigy of the Maitreya Buddha, who, according to Mahayana tradition, represented the fifth and final incarnation of the Buddha, destined to arrive within the next 5,000 years. Guan Gong Di (关公

帝), represented in a mail outfit of the Han dynasty, stands guard in the first hall of a Taoist Temple. In the next courtyard, two square pavilions house a bronze bell and a wooden drum.

Next is the main hall, where the most significant images for the temple are kept. In Buddhist temples, it is the Sakyamuni Buddha in the center, and flanked on each side by Ananda and Kasyapa, his favorite disciples. Sometimes, in the sides of the main hall are statues of the 18 *lo han* (罗汉) or disciples of the Buddha. In Taoist temples, the main hall might house the Jade Emperor, a historical Taoist sage or another of the Taoist pantheon.

Beyond this main hall there is sometimes another courtyard dedicated to Guan Yin in the case of Buddhist temples, or other sages for a Taoist temple. Along the sides are additional shrines, libraries and study rooms. The courtyards contain enormous incense burners and the occasional rockery. If the temple also serves as a monastery, off to the back are the monk's quarters.

Unlike many residential buildings and shops, the temples were built with the intention that they would last for centuries and become local landmarks. The abbots of the temples hosted temple fairs, held every couple of weeks, in and around their temples, which became an integral part of Chinese life as merchants, entertainers and farmers congregated to sell their wares and swap gossip. Alas, this charming aspect of Old Peking lost ground after 1949 entirely, though you can catch a glimpse of the past at certain fairs held during the Chinese new year holidays.

Though far fewer than before 1949, Peking is a home for Buddhist pagodas (塔 or *ta*). These structures were not indigenous to China, but came from India with the sutras and the dharma. A pagoda generally served as a reliquary spot to mark the site of burial for a holy man. Most pagodas usually consist of five to seven stories while those erected under imperial decree have up to thirteen stories. Most are circular or octagonal in shape while some are built in the bottle shaped style of Tibet.

Another legend held that the city was based upon a schematic diagram of the legendary character No Cha (哪吒). He is a frequently mentioned hero in the annals of Chinese myths. Reputedly the son of Li Tian Wang (李天王), the so-called "pagoda-bearer" and one of the heavenly four gods of Taoism, No Cha was born with a large gold ring clutched in his right fist. He used the ring to right his enemies, such as the Dragon King when he was intent upon flooding. He also had magical powers to increase the size of his magical spear, which produced a set of fiery wheels, enabling him to travel far distances.

It is said that one of Yong Le's astrologers, a fellow named Liu Bai Wen (刘伯温), prepared a design for the construction of Old Peking on the basis of No

Pagoda in the Western Hills.

Cha's body. The main entrance gate of Old Peking corresponded to No Cha's head while his feet were depicted by two gates along the northern wall of the Tartar City. The other gates, imperial residences and lakes represented other parts of No Cha's body.

The urban design of Peking lasted until the 1950s. For a while, a debate raged among city planners over the future appearance of the city. Liang Si Cheng (梁思成), son of the Qing reformer Liang Qi Chao (梁启超) and an architect who studied at the University of Pennsylvania, strongly argued that a separate city should be built near the Western Hills as the capital of New China. He tirelessly advocated that Peking should be left as an open-air architectural museum. He lost that fight.

The city authorities began by transforming Chang An Avenue into a highway ramming its way from the east to the west in an obvious rejection of traditional Chinese urban theory. Pagodas, *pai lou,* and grand gingkoes gave way for a thoroughfare for political demonstrations.

Population growth also altered the face of Old Peking. In 1920, the population of Peking was about one million. Today, the city is home to 20 million people and has grown to the size of Belgium. Fearful of American bomb attacks on Chinese

The elegance of the past and the contrived modernity of the present.

factories, Mao ordered the decentralization of China's industry, resulting in factories springing up in Peking's residential districts. The spring dust, an age-old problem, was compounded by the constant presence of coal grit in the air. The beautiful azure skies of Peking's autumn were replaced by the yellow smog of the Shou Gang Steel Factory. The Western Hills, always a constant companion seen from the city, became a reclusive celebrity, only occasionally sighted by people downtown. City walls and gates were torn down in homage to the new feudalism of socialist modernity and the combustion engine.

In the 1980s, capitalist modernity made its way on the scene along with an intensified urbanization program. Gradually, golden arches moved into the vacuum left by memorial arches. The Dong An Market became Oriental Plaza, a sight more aptly called Occidental Hazard in light of its soul-less (but clean!) malls where the masses do their civic duty by being good consumers. Even such a reactionary as the Colonel from Kentucky stands guard before his many restaurants. Though the State's official histories venerate the memory of the Boxers, I think that they would be outraged about Peking becoming a citadel for a new breed of *er mao zi* and *san mao zi*[2] and probably disoriented by the disregard shown by the city's planners for age-old cosmological principles.

Be that as it may, we can spy some vestiges of the city's elegant past. If you know where to look.

2

TRADITIONAL BELIEFS

IN 1940, **H. Y. LOWE**, a Peking journalist of Manchu descent, wrote about a fictional family named Wu to depict the traditional rhythm of life in the capital. His stories first appeared in a Peking-based English newspaper in 1940 and 1941. Later, they were collected in a two-volume book called *The Adventures of Wu: A Life Cycle of a Peking Man*. Since the Pacific war had just broken out, Lowe's book did not enjoy wide circulation in the West and, regrettably, it soon disappeared from view.

Bodhisattva and saintly animals at the Five Pagoda Temple.

Mr. Lowe spun a tale of three generations living in a traditional courtyard house in the eastern Chinese city. The series began with the birth of a son and described the attendant rituals and ceremonies that celebrated such an event in Peking. In subsequent installments, Mr. Lowe recounted the details of annual rituals, festivals and customs in relation to the day-to-day life of the family Wu. The "hero" of the series was Little Bald Head, the nickname given to the Wus' son. The collected articles follow Little Bald Head from the first moments of life all the way through to school days, from days when he is playing traditional Peking children's games to his first attempts at a writing brush. The family embarks upon pilgrimages to temples in the Western Hills, raise pets such as grasshoppers, dragon flies and pigeons, and celebrates festivals marked on the old lunar calendar. The second volume is more somber as it relates the passing of Old Grandfather Wu and the necessary ceremonies to put him to rest with the propriety and reverence that he deserved as family patriarch. Perhaps Mr. Lowe was alluding to life in the capital as the Japanese occupation wore on. More than sixty years later, Lowe's book is marvelously evocative of traditional Peking.

Mr. Lowe inspired me to devise a different way to discuss Chinese traditional religion. Since religion affected every aspect of Chinese life, both tangible and intangible, these beliefs naturally shaped the design and motifs of every pre-modern sight described in this book. More precisely, the Qing emperor Qian Long (乾隆) indelibly left his imprint upon imperial Peking as nearly all surviving temples and parks were renovated during his 60 year reign in the 17th century and thus incorporate religious motifs and symbols of his era.

In order to explain the religious basis for these motifs and symbols to foreign visitors to Peking, I can think of no better literary tool than Mr. Lowe's. In this chapter, I introduce a fictional Peking citizen of Chinese heritage living and thriving in the year 1760, which is roughly the middle point of Qian Long's reign. His name is Old Wu. I will try to make a general sketch of the spiritual worldview of Old Wu, a convivial and good natured gentleman in his fifties with a taste for rice wine, pipe tobacco and Xin Jiang style fragrant roast lamb as well as a deep respect for tradition. In other words, someone after my own heart.

The core of Old Wu's world was the belief that the universe operated on a set of impersonal ethical principles that rewarded good behavior and punished evil deeds. Old Wu also accepted implicitly a spiritual realm beyond the tangible with spirits co-inhabiting this world side-by-side with its human inhabitants.

What was the origin of this universe? Nothing in Old Wu's cosmology pointed to a single deity as the divine creator. Instead, Old Wu would have said that once there was an undifferentiated mass of spirit and material called the *Tao* (道) or the way. After several eons of evolution, the components of the universe generally separated into *yin* (阴) and *yang* (阳) principles. In the mist of Chinese antiquity, the characters for these two words meant the shady and sunny sides of the same hill. Thus, the *yin* and *yang* principle meant to convey the notions of opposing spiritual forces of the same substance. *Yin* things were cold, wet, receding, female, cloudy, quiet, decaying, parsimonious, thin, inflexible, even-numbered and negative elements of the universe while *yang* things were hot, dry, expansive, male, sunny, boisterous, growing, rotund, effusive, flexible, odd-numbered and positive elements.

The Great Ultimate (太极 or *tai ji*) is the commonly known symbol of the *yin* interacting with the *yang*. It is represented by a circle divided by an S-shaped line. Within each of the two forces is a tiny dot representing the other force. The continual interaction of these two opposite components of the *Tao* in turn produced the myriad of things (万物 or *wan wu*), which can be somewhat analogous to 19th century notions of elements with positive and negative forces. Different aggregations of the myriad of things produced the physical and spiritual world around us. In a further refinement, the *yang* components were divided into the Five Elements (五行 or *wu xing*). The five elements were wood, fire, water, earth and metal, (air being a spiritual, rather than a material element). Old Wu recognized five senses of taste, five directions (inclusive of the center), five humors of the body, and five great founding emperors, among many others. This concept eventually encouraged the development of Chinese alchemy.

Old Wu believed that each person had a two-part soul as a consequence of this division of the cosmos into *yin* and *yang*. These parts were the *hun* (魂) and the *po* (魄). Upon death, the *hun* floated skyward and eventually disappeared into the ether overhead so long as its descendants carried out sacrificial rituals to provide sustenance to the *hun* in the afterworld. Old Wu believed that after five generations, the *hun* of an average person fused with the universe and lost its identity. If Old Wu skipped the rituals, then he would have committed a harmful act against the *hun* of his ancestors, who would respond by withholding their blessings from him and his family.

Old Wu believed that the *po* was more capable of posing an immediate risk because of its origins from the dark side of the *Tao*. If a person died peacefully and was venerated by his descendants, the *po* would contract and shrivel until it disappeared into nothingness. However, there was another view prevalent in Old Wu's time. The competing belief held that the *po* retained an individual identity for all eternity and went to a subterranean afterlife called the Yellow Springs. Here, rewards and punishments would be meted out in accordance with the deceased's behavior in life, as measured by the ethical standards of the universe. For instance, a failure of parental reverence (孝 or *xiao*) was held to be an especially glaring sin.

If someone died violently or was murdered, his *po* would be shattered and mutate into a ghost (鬼 or *gui*) that haunted the human realm in search of retribution. The *gui* would not necessarily attack their earthly tormentors. Rather, any mortal that wandered into their sights could be the victim of their malevolence. They would continue to seek revenge until they received sacrifices from mortals so as to provide comfort in their rootless wanderings.

Given the lack of stability in the days of Old Wu, the old boy believed that there was countless *gui* in the universe. Literally populations of tens of thousands of *gui* surrounded us in the mortal world, and any mis-step by a mere human could bring their awesome otherworldly strength against Old Wu and his family. For instances, if Old Wu hammered in a nail through a wall during his wife's pregnancy, he might inadvertently catch a passing *gui* by its foot. The *gui* might take revenge for this assault by giving Old Wu's newborn a club foot. A mis-applied needle by Mrs. Wu might result in her child disfigured by a harelip. The insertion of chopsticks into a bowl of rice during a meal would imitate a part of a funerary ceremony, thus bringing *gui* into Old Wu's home with the expectation of receiving homage. Such an inadvertent measure might provoke their displeasure and bring disaster upon the head of Old Wu. It was a world where the capriciousness of mortals was matched by the capriciousness of spirits.

The *yin* and *yang* principles are the recurring motif within the symphony of Chinese belief. Since *yin* elements could be pernicious, *yang* elements are associated with good fortune. Firecrackers set off at the New Year, or a celebration, or a funeral, served to chase away "pools" of *yin* forces, which could collect and threaten these events. While many foreigners find the omnipresent color red in Chinese settings to be garish, its brightness counteracts darker, and more harmful, influences.[1]

To perpetuate the family line and ensure that sacrifices would be made to the ancestors in future generations, Old Wu needed a son, preferably by birth though adoption could do as well. In this manner, Old Wu was aware that he was a link in time between those relatives who came before him and those who were to succeed him in this world.

It is probably worth confessing at this stage that Old Wu could have never comprehended, and probably would have expressed outrage, at a charge that these beliefs were gender biased. I do not believe that this is a basis for expressing moral triumph over Old Wu's worldview. There is something unseemly to my mind about kicking a belief system for reflecting the prevailing views of its time. Old Wu needed a son to perpetuate the family line, but that does not mean that Old Wu didn't love his wife and daughters or revere his mother.

Each year, Old Wu's foremost responsibility was to perform a ritual where cooked meats, fish, vegetables, fruit and wine were offered in front of small wooden tablets bearing the name of each ancestor. As the Chinese are a practical people, the "spiritual essence" of these dishes was offered to the ancestors while the family ate the "left-overs" later on. In addition, the family dispatched gifts to the ancestors by burning gold and silver ingot-shaped pieces of paper as well as daily goods and clothing made of paper. As I already mentioned, air was regarded as a spiritual substance, not a material one. Once set on fire, the spirits of these paper models were released and flew to the side of the deceased. Old Wu knew that Confucius venerated these sacrificial rituals for deceased relatives as a proper social ceremony. To forego them was perilous. The pervasiveness of this imperative could even be seen on the imperial level. Each year, the emperor conducted a sacrifice in honor of *shang di* (上帝), who was the progenitor of the Chinese people and the top of the line of all ancestors.

To provide an example of this concept from real life, I knew an overseas Chinese family in South Korea in the 1980s. While they had lived for a half-century outside China, they still held onto the traditional view of the world of spirits. During this sojourn in the Hermit Kingdom, the patriarch of the family had married many times. His second wife had passed away at an early age back in the early 1960s. Immediately after his second wife's death, the patriarch performed several sacrifices in her memory, though human nature being what it is, his attentions were soon drawn to another woman. The old fellow accumulated more ex-wives for the next thirty years or so, during which time, he failed to make any sacrifices to wife number two. Suddenly he found himself experiencing a persistent round of bad luck in both his professional and personal life. He retained a spirit medium to perform a séance to find out the causes of his bad fortune. Within a minute or two, the *gui* of his second wife entered the medium's body.

"Why have you forgotten me? I have been cold, hungry and penniless for all these years. Why oh why have you neglected me?"

Defensively, the patriarch blurted out that he did perform several sacrificial rituals after her death. The medium's voice rose to a shriek. "You only gave me *Korean clothes*! You know I only wore our traditional Shan Dong (山东) clothing. I have been walking through the cold for all these years with just my funeral shroud and burial clothes. You only gave me *Korean food*! You only offered me *Korean face powder and rouge*! In life, I was a Chinese and in death how can I be something else? I have walked these foreign lands for thirty years, gnawed by hunger and loneliness. My face is shrunken and my fingers bony. Why did you marry me if you were only going to neglect me in death?" The next day, the guilt-ridden patriarch complied with her request and his fortunes soon changed.

A story like this would have jolted every nerve in Old Wu as a timely reminder to scrupulously conduct sacrifices for the well being of his deceased relatives (especially expired wives). It would also cause him to recall stories from the Qing conquest of Peking. During the chaos, a rebel's army cut down many innocent civilians. The local Peking communities venerated a Buddhist monk who took it upon himself to bury abandoned bodies and hold rituals for them so as to prevent them from becoming ghosts haunting the city. Ceremonies were held in four suburbs for 49 days, providing offerings to those who died on land and sea. Once completed, "one no longer heard the ghosts crying."[2]

Old Wu was also keenly aware of other spirits as well. Some of these spirits were more august forms that evolved from the myriad of ten thousand things. In the 19th century, some scholars described this aspect of Old Wu's spiritual view as "animism," a term that drips with condescension. Old Wu believed that since the components of an ethical universe were present in all material things, there were spirits derived from the *Tao* in everything around him. In other words, he saw a spirituality that was woven through the very fabric of the universe and all of its elements. Spirits resided in trees, rocks,[3] and other important places, like cross roads or doorways. Old Wu would have pointed to the countless roadside shrines in Old Peking as evidence of the pervasiveness of the spirits. "Surely," Old Wu reasoned, "no one would build a shrine for a spirit that doesn't exist."

Old Wu would have also revered certain spirits whom Westerners might call "anthropomorphized forces of nature," a term that would have left Old Wu scratching his head. "How could these forceful spirits be based on humans?" In this vein, Old Wu believed in panoply of nature gods, ranging from the God of Earth to the God of Thunder, from the God of Fire to the God of the Wind. In each neighborhood, a God of the Earth would have jurisdiction of (and only of) his immediate vicinity. (As said in traditional Peking, one God of the Earth commanded one street and another one reigned on the next block.) A city god, based on a historical figure was worshiped in different neighborhoods to save the citizens from chaos or warfare (and to supervise the activities of the local Gods of the Earth).

In times of drought, Old Wu trudged to the temples of various rain deities to plead for a respite. If a fire threatened his neighborhood, Old Wu would scramble to the Temple of the God of Fire to beseech his help in saving his home. If he or someone in his family were suffering from illness, Old Wu would pray to the King of Medicine, actually a Tang dynasty Taoist mendicant priest, to restore health and peace of mind. He also believed that other practices essential to human life, such as agriculture or sericulture, had a spirit that discovered and promoted these activities to the human realm.

Likewise, each home had its own Kitchen God who appeared on a poster pasted over the cooking hearth. Old Wu would have been responsible to ensure that incense and other offerings were made to him throughout the year. Just a few days before the Chinese New Year, the family would bow to the image and burn the poster so that his spirit would be freed to report on the affairs of the family to the Jade Emperor, or the Buddha or the progenitor of the family line, or someone else, depending upon the religious procivilities of Wu's family. Before sending him off, Old Wu would smear the mouth of the god's picture with honey or gooey sweet sesame paste as an inducement to have the spirit report only the good deeds of the family. Or perhaps he was just aiming to gum up the mouth of the spirit. Interestingly, the old boy tended to pour a couple extra offerings of rice wine on the day of the send off.

Other deities were the spirits of historical or literary characters. Although their deification did not necessarily require a ceremony performed by a formal religious institution, individual acts of faith to these deities, especially if they resulted in the granting of wishes, would pave their way to enter the spiritual pantheon. For instance, someone might suddenly be inspired to pray to the spirit of a brave general killed in defense of the country. If his prayers were answered, the supplicant would build a shrine in gratitude, thus attracting more potential worshippers.

This is a custom that is still knocking about in some provincial backwaters. In the mid-1990s, a Hong Kong newspaper reported that a new Mao cult had sprung up in Wu Han. Seconds before a potentially lethal accident, a taxi driver beseeched the spirit of Chairman Mao to save him. Miraculously, the supplicant walked away from the wreckage unscathed. For a while, prayers for Mao's divine intervention were all the rage among Wu Han's taxi drivers.

Other legendary personages became deified and associated with various trades, depending upon the stories attached to their earthly lives. Every profession, from medicine to carpentry, from fortune-telling to pawn brokerage, had its patron saint for guidance and protection. If Old Wu were a carpenter, he would regularly show his respect for Lu Ban (鲁班), the patron saint of carpenters. If he operated a restaurant or was a wine merchant, Old Wu would revere Tu Kang (杜康) an expert vintner from the Zhou dynasty. If he was a butcher, Old Wu would pray to Zhang Fei (张飞) of the Han dynasty, who himself was a butcher before becoming a blood brother to Guan Gong Di in the epic *The Romance of the Three Kingdoms*.

There were certain religious practices that were reserved for women. Mrs. W (my name for Old Wu's wife) would have been responsible for harvest moon ceremonies, given the *yin* composition to the moon. By Mrs. W's time, the cult for the progenitor of sericulture had begun to diminish, though everyone would have acknowledged that prayers to the Empress of Sericulture, who discovered the method of silk manufacturing, would be properly performed by the woman of the house for families engaged in the silk trade.

With a welcome breath of fresh air, the religious view of Old Wu and Mrs. W shows a remarkable sense of tolerance compared to the gory history of Western religions. Old Wu would be astonished to hear that any one spirit insisted upon reverence to itself and none other. "How could such selfishness ever lead to harmony?" Intolerance was also alien to China's practicality. An illustration of this, and the practical bent of Chinese religion, occurred in June 1926, when the Chinese residents of Chang Chun (长春) asked the priest of the Russian Orthodox Church to pray for an end to a drought. Chinese city dwellers and country folk flocked to the Orthodox church in order to kow tow vigorously in the back of the cathedral as the Russian patriarch beseeched the Lord's blessing for rain, which duly arrived three days later.

As for "Taoism[4]," Old Wu would have paid only scant attention to the term. Among Western speakers, "Taoism" is sometimes used to distinguish between Taoist and Buddhist temples as places of worship. By Old Wu's time, popular Taoism had developed into different schools of thought that were propagated in monasteries while higher Taoist philosophy remained in the realm of the literati. Even if Old Wu had little education, he certainly would have been aware of the origins of Taoism as a philosophy advocated by the sages Lao Zi (老子) and Zhuang Zi (庄子).

Chinese legend says that Lao Zi was the author of *The Classic of the Way of Virtue* (道德经 or *dao de jing*), a poetic work written in the 5th century BC. A contemporary of Confucius, Lao Zi believed that society itself is the cause of national and personal strife. Misery arises because people no longer followed the *Tao* or the natural course of the universe. He advocated political leaders to adopt a philosophy of leading their citizens back to nature and away from artificial social conventions. His teachings were recorded in poetry filled with memorable analogies and enigmatic aphorisms. One of my favorites is "He who knows does not speak. He who speaks does not know." (Keep that one in mind at your next office meeting.)

Lao Zi believed that a perfect society was one where each family withdrew into self-sufficiency and harmony with nature. Lao Zi described this society as one of contented hermits where every farmer could see the smoke of the farm across the valley without ever having visited it.

While contemporary scholars might contend that Lao Zi never in fact existed, Old Wu would dismiss these bookish sophists with a wave of the hand. "In the Temple of the White Cloud there is a statue of Lao Zi and that proves that he lived! How else could it be?"

The *Classic of the Way of Virtue* sets out Lao Zi's practical philosophy for social harmony. Lao Zi advocated a mysticism whereby people align their behavior and desires with the all-embracing *Tao* and abandon individual extremes. He rejected social standards of success and their attendant ills of striving, acquisition, prideful knowledge, and righteous morality. Instead, by returning to a rustic life free from oppressive intellectualizations, people could find inner peace and tranquility. Lao Zi's ideal was a pre-industrial rural society where people obtained peace of mind through a mystical communion with the *Tao* and sagacious acceptance of a natural order.

In the *Classic of the Way of Virtue*, Lao Zi also offered advice about governance to would-be rulers. Because of these realpolitik suggestions, Westerners have dubbed Lao Zi's brand of philosophy purposeful Taoism. It also raises questions about the consistency of the author's philosophy because surely by assuming political control, a person lands in a world very different from Lao Zi's bucolic ideal. If it is true that he who knows does not speak, then why did Lao Zi write a book?

There are two answers to this riddle. The first is simple: there was more than one author, Lao Zi never existed, and some unnamed person just combined the verses with no concern for intellectual consistency. To top it off, the compiler slapped the name of a made-up philosopher on the cover of the book. I visualize Old Wu hurling his foot long pipe end- over-end at the iconoclast who suggests this heresy. The other answer is that the social chaos in China was so severe during the Spring and Autumn Period that Lao Zi felt compelled, like his contemporary Confucius, to offer some practical means to end the suffering that surrounded him. Therefore, he offered both practical and mystical advice. Old Wu would have responded more warmly to this second interpretation.

Retrieving his pipe that smacked against the head of the smart aleck iconoclast and lighting it once again, Old Wu would point out that Zhuang Zi was different from Lao Zi. Warming to the story, Old Wu would mention that Zhuang Zi was one of the first of a very long and venerable tradition of mad monks joyfully ridiculing society's inmates and all of their tortured intellectual abstractions. Rather than poems, Zhuang Zi wrote essays often presented as a discourse with his old friend, Hui Zi. Zhuang Zi was also a relativist who could not give a fig about finding "reality." In a celebrated quote, he observed that once he dreamed he was a butterfly. He asked whether he might not now be a butterfly dreaming about being Zhuang Zi?

Old Wu might recount a famous anecdote about Zhuang Zi's disregard for material, ill-conceived accomplishments. One day while Zhuang Zi was sitting beside a lake with his feet splashing in the cool water, several state officials came on the scene. In a show of pomposity twinged with the desire to get a distasteful deal done, they presented Zhuang Zi with a royal invitation to be the supreme councilor to the king.

Zhuang Zi became quiet for a while. While looking at the water, he recalled that the totem of the kingdom was a large dried turtle that had been caught by the king's ancestors. They killed the creature, smoked its flesh dry and hung it in the royal palace where all nobles and commoners paid homage to it as a symbol of state.

"Do you know of the royal turtle?" Zhuang Zi asked the court officials. But, of course they did. Zhuang Zi then paused and pointed out several turtles swimming in the lake in front of them.

"Do you see those little turtles?" he asked. "Who do you think is happier? The grand totem at court or these little turtles before us, wriggling their toes in the mud?" The officials admitted that the turtles in the lake were probably far happier than the hunk of desiccated meat at court. Zhuang Zi then turned his face away from the officials. "Then be gone! Leave me alone to wriggle my toes in the mud."

These Taoist principles would have colored Old Wu's thought even if he never learned to read. He certainly would have known the Taoist fable about the horse farmer.

It goes like this. In the northern border regions, there was a village where one of the farmers owned a white stallion that attracted both the admiration and envy of his neighbors. Suddenly one day, the horse broke out from its corral and ran away, causing a substantial loss for the farmer. His neighbors came forward to console him (or at least they wanted to be seen consoling him).

After several weeks, the horse, on its own, came galloping back to its corral, bringing with it a large herd of wild horses. In a single instant, the farmer's wealth multiplied many times. Once again, the neighbors came forward, this time to congratulate the farmer on his good fortune (or at least they wanted to appear to congratulate him). They marveled how this new wealth would not have arisen but for the misfortune of the horse's escape several weeks earlier.

Several days later, while the farmer's only son was taming one of the horses, he fell, shattering the bones of both legs, and became lame. Forgetting their prior envy and hiding a twinge of self-satisfaction, the neighbors came forward once more to offer their condolence again. Now, the farmer's future was uncertain since he had no able-bodied son to care for him in old age.

Three days later, war broke out. All able bodied young men in the village were drafted to fight on a distant battlefield. Because the lame son of the horse farmer was exempt from service, he remained in the village to care for his family as best as he could. Later, word arrived that all the young men drafted from the village were slaughtered in battle. From the carnage of the battlefield only a single white horse came back.

In the world of Old Wu, Buddhism carried a similar message. And certainly, as Old Wu would never slight any spirit, he would have revered the manifold deities of Buddhism. In the temples frequented by Old Wu, Taoist gods and legends usually mingled freely with Buddhas and the Jataka stories, just as they supposedly did in the spirit world.

Old Wu probably knew that the founder of Buddhism was a historical person, Siddharta Gautama, a prince born in the foothills of Nepal. At the time of his birth, fortunetellers warned that Siddharta was destined to be the founder of a new religion, a worrisome prediction for the prince's father, who simply wanted his son to be a nobleman. To thwart his son's destiny, Siddharta's father kept him inside a pleasure palace day and night, hoping that luxury might blunt his son's curiosity in spiritual matters.

The plan backfired. One day when he was in his twenties, Prince Siddharta wandered away from the palace and suddenly encountered, in quick succession and for the very first time, a corpse, a diseased person and a nearly starved beggar.

The revelation of death, disease and deprivation stunned the young prince, who abandoned the palace. At that time, various Hindu schools taught that a life of severe renunciation could lead to salvation. Following these doctrines, the prince adopted the strictest regime of any aesthetic school. He lived on only a few grains of rice each day and went without sleep. His only possession was a single tattered loincloth. Buddhist artwork often depicts the prince at this stage of his life as a mere skin-draped skeleton seated in meditation.

The path of austerity brought the prince no closer to understanding. He abandoned the life of renunciation and resolved to meditate beneath a Bohdi tree until he discovered the cause of worldly pain and salvation. After forty days of continual meditation, Siddharta experienced the jarring shock of "enlightenment," which is occasionally described as a piercing of the veil of subjective delusion. The prince went out to a deer park to preach his first sermon. He selected a deer park as a symbol of the sanctity of the lives of all sentient beings. From that point, he was known as the Enlightened One or the Buddha.

In a manner thoroughly satisfactory to Old Wu, the Buddha did not advocate partisanism. He said that his solution from the pain of life was not the only one, and those lashed to this mortal world might find other ways to enlightenment. His teachings were offered as a non-exclusive religion.

The Buddha taught that suffering arises because of our attraction, or "thirst," for tangible and intangible attachments. He explained that our intellectual and emotional clinging to subjective feelings and things plant the seeds of discontent.

Even the moment of the most exquisite happiness disappears to be soon replaced by longing for a return to that moment of transitory bliss.

A key aspect of the Buddha's teaching is reincarnation. The weariness of birth, age, death and the lack of fulfillment because of our attachments are sources of sorrow not just in this life but in countless future lives were we to seek no salvation.

In Old Wu's Peking, the belief in reincarnation of the *po* and *hun* existed concurrently with the contradictory notions of spirits and ghosts. Buddhists maintained that through kindness, a person's soul might transmigrate to a delightful spiritual sphere inhabited by heavenly deities and hosting immensely pleasing fields, streams and parks. Or, the wicked might be reborn as another sentient being, such as a rat or fish or even as a ghost. Since there was no single orthodox view of the afterlife, traditional Chinese society enabled Old Wu to pick and choose his beliefs from either Taoism or Buddhism, or both.

The Buddha also taught that actions, thoughts or omissions caused inevitable consequences that impact upon this life and the station of your next life. Karma is often pitched in terms that present deeds will be rewarded or punished in your next life. If Old Wu had read the sutras carefully he would have known that this view is incomplete. Rather, each act of volition or desire automatically bears consequences by placing you into one of the myriads of potential consequential paths in a manner reminiscent of chemical chain reactions.

To escape this cycle of consequences, Buddhism teaches us to engage in activities that do not yield karmic consequences. The Buddha advocated an Eight Fold Path, with principles governing mental disposition, emotional reactions and ethical conduct. The result of these practices is enlightenment, a total and clear perception that removes suffering.

Old Wu would certainly have known that the Buddha spent the rest of his life teaching and performing miracles. Upon his death, the Buddha entered into nirvana, a blissful state, free from reincarnation and subjective identity. It is said that nirvana cannot be described in language as it reflects a consciousness that surpasses any description.

Old Wu might have been aware that Buddhism evolved into three major branches. Theravada, or the Teachings of the Elders, is the prevalent doctrine in South East Asia. This school emphasizes the importance of the monastery as the sole means of achieving enlightenment and suggests that enlightenment may be obtained only after countless lifetimes spent as a monk.

As Buddhism spread through India, it absorbed many traditional Brahmic customs. The Indian sages Nagajuna and Ashovogosha are remembered as the founders of the Mahayana School of Buddhism (大乘佛教 or *da cheng fo jiao*), a term taken from the Sanskrit phrase Great Vehicle. As the second branch of the faith, Mahayana Buddhists believe that a Buddhist need not undergo countless lifetimes as a monk before reaching enlightenment. The Great Vehicle tradition dispenses with the centrality of the monastery and stresses individual effort that can result in enlightenment in this very life.

Mahayana tradition also re-interpreted the concept of the Buddha. Aside from the historical Siddharta (called the Sakyamuni Buddha), Mahayana Buddhists claimed that the Buddha appeared in the material world several times in the countless eons before the birth of Siddharta and that another emanation of the Buddha is to return once again in the far future.

Before its arrival in China, Mahayana Buddhism divided into two major schools. The Chan School of Buddhism (禪佛教 or *chan fo jiao*), known more commonly in the West by the Japanese word Zen, advocates meditation and dialectal argument to shatter subjectivity and its attendant chain of birth and rebirth. This branch of Buddhism embraced an iconoclastic and witty behavior and rejected linear logic. As the spiritual soul mates of the Taoists, Chan Buddhist monks, singing madly in mountains, turned convention upside down and engaged in playful riddles and conversations to break linear thought. These Chan inspired schools dissipated as institutional organizations in China over time. In Peking, ruins of a Jin era temple are one of the few tangible remnants of Chan Buddhism. However, the non-dualistic tenets of Chan remained as important teaching in Chinese Mahayana and would have equally and accurately availed itself of the fable of the horse farmer to make its point about danger of attachment to "subjective values."

The second major Mahayana school in China was the Pure Land School of Buddhism (地道佛教 or *di dao fo jiao*). Pure Land teaching picked up on the Hindu belief that religious devotion to a Buddhist deity can bring the devotee to enlightenment or at least a spiritual paradise called the Pure Land. The Buddha ruling over the Pure Land is the Enlightened One of Light, or Amida Buddha (阿弥陀佛 or *a ni tuo fo*). The Buddha of the Future, or Maitreya Buddha (弥勒佛 or *mi lo fo*) will come to bring salvation in the distant future. The Vairocana Buddha (毗卢遮那 or *pa lu zhe na*) was the Buddha that designed yoga meditation, an indispensable part of Buddhist practice. By devotion to one or more of these Buddhas, Old Wu might avoid this world of tears, or at least incur good karma for himself and his family.

Mahayana teachers maintained that enlightenment concurrently yields wisdom (*prajna* in Sanskrit) along with deep compassion (*karuna*). The Pure Land School also introduced the idea of *bodhisattvas* (菩萨 or *pu sa*), which are beings that have achieved enlightenment but elect to forego entering nirvana until all sentient beings are saved. The vow of the bodhisattvas arises from the compassion felt for the suffering of sentient beings.

Old Wu could accelerate his quest for enlightenment or seek divine assistance with an earthly problem, like hunger, grief, bareness, or persecution, by invoking the name of a bodhisattva. One of the most popular bodhisattvas is a deity called Avalokitasvara in Sanskrit (观世音 or *guan shi yin*). He is worshiped from Lake Baikal to the Volga river to Japan and Vietnam. In the Indian and Central Asian tradition, Avalokitasvara is a man with a thousand eyes and ears to hear and see the pleas of the suffering and a thousand arms to assist them. The Amida Buddha created him to propagate the prayer *om mani padme hum* (the jewel is in the lotus), which if chanted countless times, brings the devotee to the Pure Land. Avalokitasvara underwent a gender transformation at some point after his arrival in China and came to be called Guan Yin, usually depicted as a female deity woman wearing long robes and standing upon a lotus petal. Some believe that this compassionate woman was an existing feature of the local Chinese belief system and simply became associated with Avalokitasvara because of the compassionate nature of both deities.

Another important bodhisattva was Manjursi (文殊师利 or *wen zhu shi li*) who is usually represented holding an axe to split ignorance and suffering. He is the deity specifically sent by Siddharta to bring Buddhism to China.

Old Wu would have also revered the eighteen *lo han* (or *arhat* in Sanskrit) who were the Buddha's historical disciples. Since Indian records mention sixteen followers, another two disciples must have been picked up after the faith arrived in China. Old Wu would not have given a toss for this discrepancy. By Old Wu's time, devotion to Buddhist and Taoist deities had so permeated Chinese life that discrepancies in little facts could not overturn the basic premise of traditional Chinese spirituality: Old Wu would pick and chose those deities, prayers or beliefs that suited his own spiritual needs rather than ascribe to a religion that demands sole allegiance under the banner "One size fits all."

There is a sense from the literature about Old Peking that Mrs. W might have had a stronger attraction to Buddhism than Old Wu. The ritual practices of laypeople and the devotional elements of Buddhism could have appealed more to feminine nature (perhaps in the same way that Polish babaoshkas attend mass every Sunday while their men folk stayed at home and smoked their pipes). The compassionate kindness of Guan Yin, especially as the goddess who hears the cries of childless wives and children in pain, ensured her presence in every household altar, which would have been looked after by Mrs. W with especial reverence.

Old Wu would have been very aware of the third major branch of Buddhism given emperor Qian Long's military campaigns in Tibet. Vargryana Buddhism, more commonly called Lamaism (喇嘛教 or *la ma jiao*), is a Tibetan derivation of Mahayana Buddhism entwined with ancient beliefs from the Himalayas. In the

800s, Lamaism became the predominant religion in Tibet and arrived in China with Tibetans and Mongols during the reign of Kublai Khan. While regarded as a branch of Mahayana, Lamaism retained almost a Theravada dedication to the maintenance of monasteries. Meditation as well as acts of personal devotion to the pantheon of Buddhist and local deities would advance the adherent to salvation or temporary relief from suffering.

In the 14th century, a reformist monk named Tsong Kha Pa established the dominant Yellow Hat Sect of Lamaism. His features would be familiar to Old Wu as his statue graced Peking's lamaseries. In addition, paintings of Green Tara and White Tara, who were the deified Nepalese and Chinese wives of an 8th century Tibetan king, would have been very recognizable to Old Wu.

Since the 16th century, Lamaism has recognized the Dalai Lama (达赖喇嘛 or *da lai la ma*) as an emanation of the bodhisattva Avalokitsvara. The Lamaist theory holds that Avalokitesvara delegates his spiritual functions to a succession of earthly religious leaders, similar to the popes in Roman Catholicism. These Lamaist "popes" are perpetually reincarnated on earth as theological leaders while Avalokitsvara maintains a separate identity in the heavens. In the same manner, the Panchen Lama (班禅喇嘛) is the reincarnation of the Amida Buddha and holds the role as the second religious leader of Lamaism.

Many lesser Tibetan deities appear in the Lamaist pantheon as fierce or frightening apparitions, bearing weapons or wearing a necklace of skulls. The point is that these deities, ferocious as they appear, fight for goodness on behalf of other benevolent Tibetan gods and goddesses. While Old Wu might have held these fierce images in askance, he certainly would not have questioned their beneficial power, let alone their existence. For example, Mahalaka was the fierce tutelary god of the Mongolian people while Yamantaka was the conqueror of death, a ferocious emanation of Manjusri with a bull's head and multi-fisted fury.

Qian Long established many lamaseries throughout the city and hosted the Panchen Lama during his visit to Peking. Tibetan monks clad in purple robes would have been a common sight to Old Wu, who might recall the historic event of the visit of the Dalai Lama to the emperor Shun Zhi a century earlier. The Lamaist festivals would have become part of Old Wu's world. He would have clustered with the rest of the crowd at the Lama Temple to await the blessings during the Tibetan new year ceremony for "beating the devils." Old Wu would also have known that lamas were almost always Tibetans or Mongols and monks (和尚 or *he shang*) were almost always Chinese. However both groups were followers of the Dharma and thus entitled to Old Wu's respect.

Old Wu would not have favored fine distinctions being made between spiritual beliefs. However he might have agreed that Taoism seeks individual salvation in bodily or spiritual form through immortality while Mahayana Buddhism more so emphasizes compassion and salvation for all sentient beings. While both faiths promote mysticism, Buddhism in China was distinguished by its views regarding other worldly realms, reincarnation and the doctrine of karma, though Taoist monks did "borrow" some of these concepts by Old Wu's time.

Some folks complain that the principles of Buddhism are not easy to understand and require the dedication of time without logical proof of its efficacy. Like most people who revere a religion, Old Wu would not feel compelled to defend Buddhist theory. "Study it, and you will see how it makes sense," would be the stalwart advice of our old oak of Peking's citizenry. While lighting once again his foot long pipe, Old Wu would lean forward and forecast, "And as you see its ability to make sense of mundane things, then consider the parable of the arrow."

"Your spiritual self-awareness makes you aware of the pain of existence. This pain is like a poisoned arrow shot into your body. As you suffer from this wound, you really do not care about who shot the arrow, why he shot the arrow or from where he got the arrow in the first place. You do not care about the ingredients of the poison on the arrow's tip, or the angle at which it hit you. You don't care if the arrow has an iron or bronze tip. You simply want to take the arrow out. If you sense that you are wounded, Buddhism is the physician who will save you from suffering."

So far I have pictured Old Wu as a tradesman or laborer. If he were a member of the literati, he might have viewed devotional Buddhism and Taoism with skepticism and adhered strictly to the teachings of China's most famous sage, Confucius. In any event, Confucianism would have unquestionably been woven through the religious view of a Peking citizen of 1760 like Taoism and Buddhism.

Kong (孔), an underemployed bureaucrat from Shan Dong province, is better known to Westerners by his Latinized name Confucius. Born in 551 BC, he was a contemporary of Socrates and the Buddha.

Confucius advocated a behavioral philosophy that was woven from the customs and beliefs of the extinguished Western Zhou. He viewed self-cultivation as the way to achieve the indivisible goals of good government and social order. Self-cultivation meant that each person nurtures human-heartedness (仁 or *ren*) as a primary virtue. Once cultivated, *ren* is manifested through accepted social convention or rituals (礼 or *li*). *Li* encompassed a wide array of behavior, from music to speech to literature to the modes of social interaction. His interpretation of *li* reflects the social hierarchy of his age. Simply put, his social pecking order favors men over women, the older over the younger, the educated over the unlearned and, of course, the rulers over their subjects.

Confucius stressed that without human-heartedness all social custom was sterile, meaningless. Likewise, human-heartedness without propriety would descend into excessive individualism and misinterpretations of intent. The combination of the two, however, would result in social harmony. For myself, I understand *ren* and *li* by allusion to a classical quartet. Each musician must cultivate his talent, which is given voice through technique. Once talent and technique have been finely honed, each musician performs in harmony with the other musicians.

There was a strong spiritual underpinning to the theories of the Great Sage, as he came to be called. He saw the universe, or Heaven (天 or *tian*) as an ethical entity that rewarded good conduct and punished evil deeds impassively, almost mechanically. By cultivating *ren* and *li,* a person aligns himself with the ethical mandate of the cosmos and links himself harmoniously with the unseen world.

This concept of Heaven played an essential element in the Great Sage's political philosophy. A ruler was able to govern only so far as his conduct comported with the ethical demands of the universe. The Confucian title for the ruler of the State, the Son of Heaven, underscored the familial bond between government and the universe. Should an emperor fail the test of ethical government, Heaven would withdraw its mandate from the emperor and his ruling house would fall from power, much in the same way an all powerful father might turn his back on an errant son and his cohorts.

Confucius saw the proper functioning of government in both spiritual and social terms. Officials had to be properly educated before they could discharge their duties in an ethical manner. He warmly embraced the notion of administration as a counterweight to chaos. In order to preserve the wisdom of the ancients for use by subsequent officials, Confucius compiled the Thirteen Classics, which were Western Zhou era compendia of historical records, poetry, social customs, recommendations on governmental structure and other matters.

While Confucius placed a strong emphasis on officialdom, he also incorporated into his teaching the veneration of the rulers of the Western Zhou for the forces of nature. As we will see later on in our trips through Peking, these ceremonies were an integral part of the Peking calendar and wielded influence on day-to-day life in all of China well into this century.

Like Lao Zi and Zhuang Zi, Confucius spoke of the *Tao.* In the Confucian context, the *Tao* is the proper social and natural order required by an ethical universe. Rather than withdrawal, Confucius believed that every person ought to be educated in a manner suited to the proper order of society. The purpose of education was to instill a sense of human heartedness that could be manifested by *li.* The concept of benevolence required the sagacious man to reject extremes of emotion and to seek the "middle way." After cultivating the "middle way," a well-educated person ought to serve in government and advise rulers about the *Tao* of ethical government and be loyal (忠 or *zhong*) to the ruling house so long as that house adhered to the *Tao*.

Confucius also promoted the concept of the five personal relationships: emperor and subject, father and son, husband and wife, elder sibling and younger sibling, and older friend and younger friend. While Confucius did not believe in equality in the context of society and family, he emphasized that there were reciprocal obligations between the people in these relationships. Confucius enshrined filial piety as nearly religious reverence and affection for parents by their children. However, Confucius was an idealist and could not see that others might distort this principle into blind obedience, which certainly was the case for the authoritarian policies expounded by the Ming and Qing theoreticians. Confucius himself said that should a father engage in morally objectionable conduct, a son must respect Heaven's ethical order and remonstrate with his father to refrain from the corrupt conduct. If the father did not accept his son's remonstration, then true Confucianism requires the son to protest by abandoning his father until such time that the old man recovers his senses and returns to the right path.

Even though he is the most famous of China's philosophers, Confucius himself never claimed to have invented a new way of thought. Rather, he said that he was merely a public servant, struggling to keep the lamp of Western Zhou thought and ritual alight during the chaos of the Eastern Zhou. He said that he made no innovation but merely sought to preserve the glories of the past for the sake of social harmony. He did not seek to be a museum curator; rather he sought to preserve prior conduct in order to remedy China's ills.

By Old Wu's day, Confucianism had undergone nearly 15 centuries of refinement, including a varnish applied during the Ming to obscure the key concept of reciprocity. Obedience to the point of sycophancy had become the order of the day. Old Wu might have placed great stock in the hierarchies of his home and in his society. Frequently, the aspirations of offspring were suffocated on account of the demands of filial conduct. Confucianism was meant to be a moral force but its subsequent institutions redrafted its beliefs for the benefit of the ruling class.

I do not like to think of Old Wu as some inflexible doctrinarian who would have insisted upon complete obedience by his wife and children and taken offense at the slightest social mistake. I would rather think of him as a man who understood that reverence for the elderly and education for the young were the greatest accomplishments in this material world.

Unless he were a high ranking official, Old Wu probably never participated in the court ceremonies for the worship of Confucius and his line of scholars at the Confucian Temple in the north of the Tartar City. Rather, the Confucian touches of Old Wu's life could be discerned in the respect and care that he gave to his parents, his respect for the written word and his adherence to ceremonial politeness in social settings. He would revere the memory of any teacher and be strict about the education of his sons. If literate, he might have worked at one of the academies in Peking, providing Confucian instruction to examination hopefuls. On a more mundane level, he would have contributed to volunteers groups who collected loose scraps of paper with writing on them from the streets and burnt them. It was felt disrespectful to China's tradition of literature to leave such paper as loose trash.

Taoism, Buddhism and Confucianism were the three main religions of Old Wu's Peking and tended to be woven together in popular belief without regard to sectarianism. Old Wu probably embraced all three faiths at the same time.

In the middle of Qian Long's reign, Peking was not a purely Chinese city. Accordingly, Old Wu might have embraced additional beliefs and rituals from a different ethnic group. For example, a tiny percentage of Peking's population was Manchu. If Old Wu's family was of royal pedigree, he might have taken part in Manchu shamanist rituals performed inside the Forbidden City that recalled the misty origins of the Manchus in the forested mountains of the Great North East.

The term "shamanism" covers many types of beliefs from Central Asia to Central Africa. In this instance, shamanism is similar to the ancient Chinese belief that all natural elements possess spirits. The system originated somewhere in Central Asia and then expanded to Manchuria, Siberia, Korea and the Pacific Northwest, adapting to different cultures in the process. One essential aspect of Shamanist practice is the participation of a spiritually gifted person who, by training or supernatural phenomenon, becomes a medium for communication between the worlds of spirits and humans.

The rituals of Manchu shamanism became a state secret once the Qing dynasty brought them to China proper. Since Taoism and Buddhism were subject to occasional attack by Confucian scholars, the Manchus sensibly reasoned that their ancient and primitive rituals would be even more susceptible to political dispute. Shaman rituals were therefore practiced quietly and in secret in special temples in the Forbidden City and the Imperial City.

Similarly, if Old Wu were a Manchu, he would likely be a bannerman and actively involved with military matters or pensioned off as a reserve soldier. In either case, he would have felt a strong allegiance to various martial deities and heroes, such as Yue Fei (岳飞) or Yu Qian (于谦). His own ethnicity and the primacy placed upon equestrian skills would be reflected in a devotion to the God of the Horses (马神 or *ma shen*), a three eyed, multi-arm deity who had authority over all aspects of horsemanship and horse-rearing.

There are other "minority" religions, which existed in Old Wu's Peking. Catholicism first arrived with Jesuit priests in the early 1600s and made gradual inroads to convert nobles, eunuchs and court ladies. As late as the 1720s, the Jesuits were still making converts of Manchu princes even though the Qing court had officially banned conversion efforts. However, Chinese Catholics who had previously converted continued to worship at the four Roman Catholic churches built in various parts of the city.

If Old Wu had been a Roman Catholic, he probably would have taken a baptismal name, such as Luke. He also might have worked as a watchmaker since the Jesuits had previously introduced European clock-making technology, which remained primarily a Christian craft in Qian Long's Peking. By Old Luke's time there were about three hundred Catholic families in Peking attending mass on a weekly (if not daily) basis.

I do not believe that Old Luke could ever have had any seditious thoughts, just as many of the Peking members of sects were simply following their hearts and meeting spiritual needs. On the contrary, the Chinese Catholic tradition also reveres Confucius, Lao Zi, Zhung Zi and the Buddhist saints as precursors of the spirituality of the Catholic Church. Old Luke would have respected the sagaciousness of Chinese philosophers in the same way that St. Thomas Aquinas admired Aristotle and Cicero.

Were these Catholic sentiments something kept behind closed doors? Of course not. When Father Dominique Parrenin died in 1741 after spending 40 years in Peking in service to the Catholic community and to the imperial court, Chinese and foreign Catholics carried his coffin through the city on its way to the Jesuit graveyard in the western suburbs. Qing officials, who were non-converts but respectful of the man's contributions, accompanied the good father on his way to his final resting place. Mourners carried banners proclaiming Father Dominique's name in Chinese and Chinese Catholics reverentially carried images of Mary and St. Michael. Old Luke would have been among them, with reverence to his faith as well as pride in being Chinese.

Old Luke would not have known of Protestantism since missionaries of that faith did not arrive in Peking until well into the 19th century. However, Old Luke would have known of a brother community of Christians living in the far northeast corner of the city. Here were a small handful of mixed Chinese and Russian families that practiced the Eastern Orthodox faith.

Another great "minority religion" of Old Wu's Peking was Islam. The faith of the prophet has a history of more than 1,000 years in the capital. In this instance, I should morph Old Wu into Old Ma because Ma is a common Chinese Muslim surname, the Chinese equivalent of Mohamed.

A descendant of Old Wu enjoying an afternoon snooze in the winter sunshine.

Islam arrived with traders in South China and warriors from Central Asia. A mosque dating from the 10th century still stands in a predominantly Muslim neighborhood in the southwest corner of the city. Through intermarriage, an ethnically Chinese Muslim community developed with certain hallmarks of Islam; imams teaching the Koran in Arabic, hallal butchers and Muslim festivals. While Old Ma would not have wanted to discuss this issue too publicly, the Muslims' relations with the non-Muslim community waxed and waned. Despite imperial directives to embrace Muslims as "children of our empire," some Chinese were never able to overcome their suspicion of a "foreign" faith.

That said, the Muslim community made profound contributions to Peking. Chinese Muslims crammed and studied for the Metropolitan Examinations with some passing the grade and becoming highly placed officials in the Qing government. Poorer Muslims, facing destitution, ordered the castration of their sons, who were then able to find employment, and perhaps riches, in service at the imperial court. Muslim soldiers were regarded as superlative warriors and vied with Sino-Russians, Manchus and Mongols in terms of horsemanship. Muslim chefs produced innovations of northern Chinese cuisine with hallal ingredients, which in turn became as symbolic an element of Peking life as cypress trees.

Old Ma would have pointed out that there was no conflict between his faith and his patriotism. "See," he would say while pointing with a craggy finger, "see, our mosques are Chinese in style. We eat with chopsticks. Our teachings comply fully with those of Confucius. We are loyal to the emperor and we revere our families."

Old Wu would have applauded the synthesis implied by the views of Old Ma, who might have produced some ganja to share with Old Wu as they struck up their pipes. Further, Old Wu, with the self-confidence of tradition, would not have looked askance at Old Luke's faith. Rather, I can picture all three as good friends, thanks to the Confucian tradition of human heartedness.

So behold: here are my decidedly wistful, wildly optimistic and probably inaccurate views of Peking's religious beliefs at the time that Qian Long made the last round of truly grand renovations of the city's sights. Let us leave them, Old Wu, Old Luke and Old Ma, breaking bread at a roast lamb restaurant with cauldrons bubbling behind them, the old boys reciting classical verse, posing riddles, and enjoying an animating discussion about the greatness of Chinese thought amidst jars of rice wine and pipes of herbs.

3

HISTORICAL OVERVIEW

For the purposes of our wanderings, Peking first emerges in Chinese records of the Western Zhou dynasty (1027 to 770 BC). A walled Chinese village called the Reeds (薊 or *ji*) was built in the southwest suburbs of contemporary Peking. The Reeds was probably a Chinese colony of sorts, far from the center of political action along the Yellow River and governed by independent local princes. It came into existence during a dynasty remembered as a golden age of sagacious government and social stability.

Nonetheless, the security of the Western Zhou state dissipated in the long run. Around 770 BC, a non-Chinese people, perhaps with red-hair and fair skinned, ousted the Western Zhou rulers from their capital in the Yellow River valley. While the Zhou ruling house reestablished itself in a new capital city to the east, subsequent rulers were unable to reverse the loss of prestige caused by the invasion. For the next three hundred years, vassal states attempted to assert their independence and subvert their neighbors with increasing ruthlessness and violence. This was also the era that saw the rise of Confucianism and Taoism as both political and spiritual ideologies.

Starting in 403 BC, the Warring States Period marked the final collapse of the nominal authority of the Zhou dynasty. Its former fiefs broke into nine regional states waging constant warfare and political intrigue in a struggle for supremacy over all of China. Despotic rulers gambled with the lives and welfare of their subjects in desperate bids to defeat rival states. Warfare destroyed the harvest cycle, which in its turn ruined commerce and produced widespread poverty and famine. All forms of authority collapsed along with any certainty about the future. This era inculcated a deeply rooted fear of chaos in Chinese social thinking.

During this tumultuous time, the Reeds were spared from much of the suffering that afflicted the Yellow River valley. The city evolved from a settlement to the capital city of the State of Swallows (燕 or *yan*), which was one of the nine rival kingdoms. Accordingly, the walled city changed its name to the prosaic sounding Capital of the Swallows (燕京 or *yan jing*), which is still used as a poetic reference for Peking today. It is an apt name. Some two thousand years on, our wanderings will take us to palaces and temples where we can still encounter the sight and sound of swallows flying out from tiled roofs.

5,000 years of political history.

By 221 BC, the State of Qin, located in Shan Xi (山西) province, was able to overthrow Yan and the other seven states. The ruler of Qin, who is known by his reign name *Qin Shi Huang Di* (秦始皇帝) or the First Emperor of Qin, unified a nation whose history and culture were already over 2,000 years old *at that time*.

Qin Shi is well remembered in the Chinese annals as a bully, despite clucking and cooing that goes on these days about terracotta images of his Gestapo. He inaugurated an imperial system of government to consolidate his authority over the "world," meaning China. In order to thwart invasions from the north, he conceived of the construction of a tamped earth wall stretching from the Bohai Gulf to the deserts of Gan Su. He mobilized all of his subjects to support this awesome construction project, which took the lives of countless numbers of common people.

However, perhaps reflecting its fortunate *feng shui* location, the Capital of Swallows benefited from the social stability afforded by a unified nation. The city developed into a robust trade center for goods from He Bei (河北) and Shan Dong provinces as well as from Korea and Mongolia.

In a theme to be repeated throughout Chinese history, Qin Shi's onerous demands upon his people doomed his empire. Four years after his death, the Qin Empire, whose rule fell into the ineffective hands of Qin Shi's unstable son, collapsed with breath-taking speed. Exhausted by the emperor's ambitious and draconian rule, the people simply withdrew their support while the court faltered.

After a series of contending rulers, a bandit named Liu Bang (刘帮) re-unified the country and installed the Han Dynasty. His empire was a landmass that extended from the frosty mountains of Korea to the balmy rice fields of Vietnam and well into the heart of Central Asia. With a brief hiatus, the Han ruling house governed China for four centuries. It was a magnificent era for Chinese culture, philosophy and art. Chinese still refer to themselves as the people of Han while the spoken Chinese language is called the language of Han.

Like the Western Zhou, the Han dynasty began to dissolve after several centuries of rule. The breakdown had two causes. First, the local gentry inevitably resisted the nuisance of central authority. Second, the Han exhibited the symptoms of "dynastic decline," a term of art among Sinologists that refers to governmental weakness and drift arising from succeeding generations of loutish rulers "going soft" from luxurious living. On account of these problems the Han split into three kingdoms around 220 A.D.

During this period, Peking changed its identity again. Notwithstanding the dissipation of the Han, the settlement came to be called the Tranquil City (幽州 or *you zhou*). The name could have been a response to the arrival of Buddhism in North China, which took root during the middle period of the Han. Peking's oldest monastery, the Temple of the Clear Pools and Mulberry Trees (潭柘寺 or *tan jie si*), was founded in 230 in the Western Hills. A common Peking adage maintains that first there was Tan Jie Si and later came the Tranquil City (先有潭柘寺，后有幽州). It is easy to picture a city imbued with a reflective ambiance because of its closeness to mountain temples. While the monastery has been rebuilt countless times, there are, alas, no tangible sites in Peking that are from the day-to-day life of the Han dynasty.

At the end of the Three Kingdoms Period, China broke up again into numerous smaller states and then was unified by a short-lived dynasty called the Sui in 589. The Sui rulers quickly depleted their political capital through over-extended territorial ambitions. China became embroiled in a terrible war of attrition against the Spartan Koguryo kingdom in northern Korea. Having reached too far too soon, the house of Sui fell to the famous Tang dynasty in 619.

The Tranquil City turned into a strategic staging post for the Chinese wars fought in northern Korea. Some legends maintain that the popular sentiment turned against the Sui because of the countless bodies of Chinese soldiers left to rot on Korean battlefields with no proper burials or farewell ceremonies.

The first emperor of the Tang learned this lesson and set up the Temple of the Origin of the Law (法源寺 or *fa yuan si*) in You Zhou as a memorial and final resting place for the bones of new Chinese recruits killed in Korea. Other religious sites were established. Near the Western Hills, the Temple of the Sleeping Buddha (卧佛寺 or *wo fo si*) commemorates the Buddha's entrance into nirvana (and the implicit validation of his teachings). In the far southwest countryside, the Temple of the Cloud Place (云居寺 or *yun ju si*) is graced by several small Tang era pagodas, crafted with sweeping lines and a panache of understatement quite different from subsequent Chinese architecture

In 907, the Tang lost North China to a non-Chinese people, and Peking embarked upon a 450-year interlude of non-Chinese rule. In that year the Khitan,[1] a Sinified people related to the Mongols of the steppes, installed the Liao Dynasty in North China with Peking becoming one of their administrative capitals in 935. The Khitans had long ago adopted Chinese administrative methods, speech and costume while jealously safeguarding their monopoly on military power. Ironically, they renamed the city Nanjing (南京) or the Southern Capital since it was located to the south of their traditional homeland. In 1013, the Liao revived the name the Capital of Sparrows.

Here we come to a dynasty that left more tangible remains of its rule in the heart of the city. Old Liao maps depict alleys and streets, such as Xi Dan Avenue (西单) and the Brick Pagoda Alley (砖塔胡同 or *zhuan ta hu tong*), that still grace neighborhoods in Peking. The pagodas of Temple of Heavenly Tranquility (天宁寺) and the Old Man of the Ten Thousand Pines (万松老人), still standing on top of the graves of their monks, maintain a brave presence amidst concrete apartment blocks and over-passes. To the far east of the city in Tianjin Municipality, the Temple of Solitary Joy (独乐寺 or *du le si*) receives few visitors despite its outstanding Liao carpentry and woodcraft. Leaving the works of man aside, pine and gingko trees in the Western Hills are living traces of the Liao period.

The Liao ended in 1125 when another northern people, the Jurched, displaced them and took Peking. The Jurched people were a forest people from Manchuria who spoke a language curiously related to Finnish and Korean. The Jurched established the Jin (金 or Golden) dynasty and pursued more robust territorial goals than their Khitan predecessors. They fought the Song dynasty, successors to the Tang in 1179, and occupied China as far south as the Yang Tse River. Peking became the Middle Capital (中都 or *zhong du*), one of the administrative cities of the Jin dynasty.

The Jin did not leave us many physical structures. Aside from a few octagonal pillars in the Park of the Joyful Pavilion (陶然亭 or *tao ran ting*) in southern Peking,

and the magnificent pagodas of the Mountain of the Silver and Iron Wall (银铁
壁山 or *yin tie bi shan*), their primary legacy are Peking's parks and lakes, which
were renovated and expanded by subsequent dynasties. In the Western Hills, you
can also find a few funerary pagodas from their time.

In 1215, Peking's good luck ran out. In that year, Genghis Khan and his
Mongol armies burst out from Central Asia, displaced the Jin and captured the
city. It was a brutal conquest. Because Peking ventured to resist the Khan's army,
mounted Mongol warriors torched the city with incendiary arrows. Regardless of
race or class, every citizen was marked for death. A Central Asian envoy
commented that after the Mongol victory, nothing remained of the city but charred
frames. Not a living creature stirred, except for the vultures, and the city's broad
avenues were slippery with liquefied human flesh. The rest of China fell to the
Mongols under Kublai Khan in 1279.

In the years before the conquest of all of China, the Mongols gave Peking
the Mongolian name Khanbalik. Amongst Chinese, it was called Great Capital
(大都 or *da du*). The city was rebuilt entirely on the basis of traditional Chinese
designs, perhaps because the Mongols had no real interest in developing their
own urban planning and administration. The results of the reconstruction can
still be discerned in maps of contemporary Peking. In keeping with Chinese
architectural tradition, the Mongols used a chequer-board design to layout their
city and erected tamped earth walls in a rectangular shape, with the narrow ends
to the north and south. Traces of this earthen wall can be seen today near the
university district.

Kublai Khan was different from his nomadic forefathers. He developed a taste
for Chinese culture and appeared to enjoy urban life in Peking immensely. He
became taken with Chinese gardens, and at his instruction, Chinese engineers
dredged and enlarged the Jin's imperial lakes. A walled forbidden city was built
directly to the east of today's Bei Hai Park. Delightful city temples, such as the
Temple of the White Cloud, the White Pagoda Temple and the Temple of the
Eastern Peak, were built during the reign of Kublai and his descendants (though
each has undergone varying degrees of renovation in subsequent years).

In 1271, Kublai installed the Yuan dynasty. The choice of the name "Yuan"
(元), meaning "first" and possessing Chinese cosmological significance, underscored
the influence of Chinese culture upon Kublai. Because of the adoption of a Chinese
dynastic name along with the accoutrements of Chinese administration, the
Mongolian empire appears to be a native Chinese dynasty in historic records of
subsequent Chinese scholars. However, this Sino-centric view does not provide
the entire picture. During their reign, the Mongols conquered a territory that
stretched from Seoul to Hanoi, from Mandalay to Tibet, from Samarkand to

Baghdad, from Damascus to Moscow and even further on to the outskirts of Vienna.

Though rejected by historians as uncouth and barbaric, the Yuan rulers displayed grandeur and a breath of intellectual curiosity that appeals to my tastes. Kublai Khan once hosted a conference in Central Asia where Buddhists, Taoists, Christians, Manicheans and Muslims were invited to debate the "one true religion." One of Kublai's wives embraced Christianity while one of his daughters became a Buddhist nun in Tan Jie Temple. Kublai himself admired the teachings of a Taoist sage from Shan Dong who was permitted to set up a temple in the western suburbs of Khanbalik.

To Westerners, the Mongol dynasty is indelibly linked to a minor Venetian merchant called Marco Polo. Ever since the publication of his *Description of the World*, the truthfulness of his story and his alleged service to Kublai have been doubted. Some scholars believe that he simply cribbed his account from Persian guidebooks, especially since he omits many matters that fascinated subsequent travelers to China. For instance, he does not mention the Great Wall, chop sticks, or women with bound feet. Perhaps sensing a dubious reading public, Polo argued that what he saw was so exotic that he could not credibly present everything that he saw to his European readers. The debate, which is as old as his memoirs, is unlikely to have an authoritative resolution.

Nevertheless, Polo described a city that clearly comports with Yuan maps of Peking:

> All the plots of ground on which the houses of the city are built are four-square and laid out with straight lines; all the courts and gardens of proportionate size…. Each square plot is encompassed by handsome streets for traffic; and thus the whole city is arranged in squares just like a chess board … .In the middle of the city there is great clock — that is to say bell — which is struck at night. And after it has struck three times no one must go out of the city.[2]

By the middle of 1300s, the glue holding such a vast empire began to give way. In China, the end of the Yuan came about through a round of insurrections where Song pretenders and quasi-religious secret societies challenged Mongol authority.

Among these contenders, an ex-Buddhist monk turned adventurer and a native of An Hui (安徽) province finally succeeded in claiming the Mandate of Heaven. Zhu Yuan Cheng (朱元成) swept the Mongols from China and in 1368 established the last great Chinese dynasty, the Ming (明 or Bright). In the ensuing warfare, Khanbalik was set to the torch once again, but without the grim thoroughness of the Mongol conquest. The basic pattern of its streets and the sanctity of its temples remained amidst the ruins.

After adopting the reign name of Hong Wu (洪武)³, Zhu chose Nanjing as his capital. A fierce autocrat, he cowered his officials with threats of public humiliation, beatings or death. Taxation was regularized into the so-called "single whip system." Hong Wu also implemented a nation-wide surveillance and intelligence network that reached deeper into Chinese society than any prior dynasty.

Hong Wu intended to enshrine the principle of primogeniture for succeeding generations of Ming rulers. Since his first son died young, he anointed the first-born grandson of his first son, Jian Wen (建文), to be his successor. This decision put the chosen successor on a collision course with Hong Wu's fourth son, Yong Le. Upon Hong Wu's death in 1398, his grandson Jian Wen assumed the Ming throne. In response, Yong Le launched a military siege of Nanjing, which capitulated in 1402.

Despite his victory, Yong Le felt alienated by the court in Nanjing. Moreover, the dynasty was still under the threat of military invasion from the north as the Mongols had not entirely acquiesced in their lost empire. Logistically, a Ming army stationed in the north would suffer from tenuous supply lines should the capital remain in the center of the empire. In order to answer the threats from within and without, Yong Le concluded that the capital of Ming China had to be moved to his northern power base. In 1402, his court astrologers and geomancers confirmed that Yan Jing was an auspicious site for the Chinese capital. In the same year, Yong Le ordered a massive urban construction project that continued for nearly twenty years.

In 1403, the Ming court applied the name Northern Capital (北京 or *bei jing*) for the first time to the city. Upon the completion of construction work in 1421, the city became the capital of the Great Ming.⁴

Yong Le built his new city with all the architectural hallmarks of a traditional Chinese capital. It was a symmetrical and rectangular city facing to the south. Three sets of city walls were concentrically erected. Within the heart of the city stood the Forbidden City, the residence and office of the emperor, a site around which the entire city was designed to focus attention on the imperial presence within. Mountains to the north and west dispelled negative cosmological influences. An auspicious site for imperial tombs was found in a rustic valley outside the city walls and construction began on the first tomb of the Ming necropolis. In the Forbidden City, eunuchs compiled detailed reports on officials and suspicious citizens.

In order to eliminate lingering criticism about his ascension to power and create the illusion of historical continuity, Yong Le commissioned the literati to invent "eight great sites" of Peking, which were chosen to underscore the city's history and prestige. Revealingly, only two of the eight sites were to be found within the walls of the rebuilt city. Nevertheless, this sleight of hand worked. The sights worked their way into the folklore about Peking and were eagerly visited by subsequent generations of Chinese travelers.[5]

In 1424, Yong Le died during a military expedition beyond the Great Wall. He was buried in a grand tomb that had been constructed under his own supervision only a morning's ride away from his capital city. Yong Le's legacy was a Peking that was classically designed to reflect Chinese cosmology and built to entrench Chinese authority well to the north of the Yang Tse River. Over the next 100 years, more ceremonial and religious sites were built as the city's growing population spilled out beyond its walls. While Mongol invaders still thundered into the plains of Peking and caused havoc, they never were able to supplant Ming rule.

Since many aspects of daily life became highly ritualized, it is not surprising that the Ming bureaucracy stressed the performance of detailed rituals by the emperor to demonstrate his possession of the Mandate of Heaven. At this time, many of Peking's magnificent altars and temples were constructed as stages where the emperor revered and appealed to Heaven and the spirit world for harmony and blessings. Such rituals came to occupy a vast amount of the emperor's time and to consume a lion's share of the state's coffers. The rituals were timed to occur at auspicious times measured by the firmament. The solar solstices and equinoxes, the phases of the moon as well as the position of stars and planets dictated their timing. Nature indicated whether the emperor had the Mandate of Heaven through bountiful harvests and social stability. Catastrophes, such as floods and earthquakes, were taken as inauspicious omens that the emperor was losing his grip. The eclipse of the sun needed to be forecast in considerable detail so that the emperor could take the appropriate appeals to the celestial bodies for the return of the sun. The plan of Peking was Chinese cosmological metaphysics writ in stone and wood.

In 1603, Peking saw the arrival of Matteo Ricci, the first among many Roman Catholic priests, European, Chinese and Mongolian, who embarked on a mission to convert China to Christianity. Eschewing efforts at converting the lower end of society, Ricci understood that Christianity's only chance for acceptance was to incorporate the Chinese belief in China's centrality into missionary endeavors and to appeal to the literati. In particular, the Jesuits used their skills at astronomy in order to render valuable service in correcting Ming calendars (and thus ensuring that imperial ceremonies were performed at the right celestial moment).

Through his writings, Ricci introduced the European world to China. He confirmed that China was indeed Marco Polo's Cathay, which was an unsettled question in Europe at that time. He also invented a system to transliterate Chinese words into the Roman alphabet. Under his system of using Roman letters to spell Chinese names, the Ming capital became *Pequim* in Latin. Soon, other variations appeared in European languages: *Pequin* in Italian, *Pekin* in French, and then finally *Peking* in English.

At the end of the 16th century, the Ming once again faced an enemy from beyond the Great Wall. Ming officials had sought to conserve their military resources by appointing local warriors as military commanders in areas beyond Ming administration. The new threat was the Manchus, descendants of the Jurchen and the inhabitants of the mountains and forests to the northeast of Peking. Ultimately, a Manchu clansman named Nurhaci (奴尔哈赤) consolidated his tribesmen, retained Chinese advisors and bureaucrats and slowly exerted his control over Liao Dong (辽东), a territory outside Ming territory but with a population of three million Chinese settlers.

Nurhaci's selective absorption of Ming culture did not displace the sense of cultural identity of the Manchus. Though Chinese literature was esteemed, a Manchu script, based upon the Mongolian alphabet, was invented. Confucian classics were duly translated into Manchu and their philosophical principles embraced. In retrospect, it almost seemed as if the Manchus spent fifty years rehearsing the method of Chinese government before they struck.

At the same time, the Ming court exhibited the telltale signs of dynastic decline. The long reigning emperor Wan Li proved to be a disaster, as evidenced by the rise of corruption, factionalism and administrative incompetence. His successor managed to stay on the throne only for a month before dying, probably from a covertly administered dose of poison. From the 1620s to 1640s, Ming and Manchu armies battled constantly along the Great Wall.

In the end, the Ming was washed away by a domestic rebellion. A peasant named Li Zi Cheng (李自成) raised an army in the south that tumbled from victory to victory until they arrived at the gates of Peking. Court intrigue and political squabbling left the Ming incapable of resisting the bandit army, which took Peking in the April of 1644. With Peking in flames, Li Zi Cheng entered the Forbidden City and began preparation for a new dynasty to be called the Shun (顺).

According to Peking legend, Li's libido led to his downfall. While the city collapsed into chaos, Wu San Gui (吴三桂), a Ming military commander, stayed at his post in the Gu Bei Kou Pass (古北口) to prevent the Manchus from seizing the advantage of the chaos to invade China proper. When news of the fall of the city reached him, he re-evaluated his loyalties. Most disturbing of all, he heard that Li had kidnapped his favorite concubine and refused to release her. Because of his desire to reclaim his lover, Wu threw his hand in with the Manchus and opened the pass to Qing troops. Li fled the capital chased by Qing soldiers who finally hunted him down in Guang Xi province.

The conquering Manchus were fortunate in having a sagacious regent, Dorgon (多尔滚), ruling on behalf of his nephew, the emperor Shun Zhi (顺治). Dorgon engineered the transition of the Qing so as to win acceptance by the Chinese. Of all cities in China, Peking, as the capital, had to remain calm and orderly. He also understood that food and arms were the keys to success. Granaries were well stocked and the citizens of Peking given subsidized rations of rice. In Liao Dong, the Manchu army had been organized into different regiments, or "banners" which were designed to insert a measure of checks and balances so that no one regiment would become all powerful. The bannermen consisted primarily of Manchu soldiers though some Chinese residents from Liao Dong also served in separate regiments.

Most importantly, Dorgon understood the importance of continuity. Though the Dragon throne has passed from the Ming to the Manchus, the face of Peking did not change its appearance. Indeed, following the policy of Yong Le, the early Qing rulers sought to maintain the appearance of Peking and its sights to provide the comforting impression of continuity.

Under the careful instruction of Dorgon, Shun Zhi became the first Qing emperor to reside in Peking. Shun Zhi was a sickly and withdrawn child who took over the affairs of state when Dorgon died in 1657. Shun Zhi probably never wanted the burden of empire. In 1658, he suffered deeply on account of the death of his son and sought solace in Buddhism. In 1660, he endured more pain when his beloved empress passed away. These blows were too much to bear, and the grief stricken emperor soon caught small pox and died. His reclusive and melancholy tendencies led to a legend, unfounded, that he abdicated in favor of life as a Buddhist hermit in the Western Hills.

In 1661, Kang Xi (康熙) came to the Dragon throne and ruled for more than sixty glorious years. Kang Xi is remembered as one of the most intelligent and able monarchs that ever came to power. A contemporary of rulers like Louis 14th, Aurangzeb and Peter the Great, he consolidated his rule throughout China, ousted Ming loyalists and defeated rebellions waged from the south. He savored Chinese literature and philosophy while energetically leading military and hunting expeditions.

His writings reveal him to be a very likable man. He wrote of his delight in foods and wines and the joys of exercise and self-restraint, though he sometimes sounded like a doting father. ("The best thing for health is to eat and drink carefully and rise and retire at regular hours.")[6] In keeping with the nomadic origins of the Manchu, Kang Xi loved horseback riding, hunting and fishing. His intellectual curiosity ranged from mathematics, astronomy, geology, religion to music. He avidly collected specimens of rare animals and kept them on display in the Old Summer Palace. He tortured himself with worries that one of his sons might be homosexual. He showed a friendly collegiality in his letters to his servants. His conscience troubled him on account of the execution of political dissidents. In his personal records, he asserted, perhaps a little too defensively, that his compassion led him to reducing the degree of severity of capital punishment meted out to bandits and political dissidents. He indulgently listened to the Jesuits as they presumed to speak about Chinese culture, though his tendency to snicker in his sleeve suggests that the august emperor tended to overlook his own foreign roots.

Kang Xi died in 1722, leaving the Qing empire firmly in control of China. The next emperor was his son, Yong Zheng, a stubborn and guilt-ridden successor who lacked his father's interests, cosmopolitan flair and statesmanship. Yong Zheng seized the throne after violent intrigues against his brothers, five of whom were thrown into prison. His ascent to power tarnished his claim to the Mandate of Heaven. Accordingly, his undistinguished reign lasted for only 14 years.

Qian Long (乾隆) succeeded Yong Zheng with a reign that spanned 60 lunar years, from 1736 to 1795, and sat on the throne for the last glorious period of Qing rule. The length of his reign enhanced social stability though at the cost of an ingrained complacency against change and innovation. Though beginning with vigor and resolve, the reign of Qian Long planted the seeds for China's eclipse in the 19th century.

Like his grandfather Kang Xi, Qian Long was both a martial and literary emperor. Under his command, the Qing armies reasserted Chinese control over Xin Jiang and Tibet. Qian Long enthusiastically promoted Chinese poetry, especially his own as can be seen by the steles all over Peking. He was personally drawn to Tibetan Buddhism and generously supported lamaseries in Peking, whose monks in turn repaid the compliment and declared Qian Long to be a reincarnation of Manjursi Bodhisattva. In response to Confucian criticisms of the heterodox nature of Christianity, Qian Long proscribed Qing citizens, especially bannermen, from converting to Roman Catholicism while permitting Jesuits and priests of other denominations to use their technological and artistic skills for the court. The Jesuits developed a synthesis of the techniques of European painting with Chinese subjects, producing a three dimensional style of Chinese art that became the standard in Qian Long's court.

While preserving the overall design of the capital, Qian Long re-sculpted many sights of Old Peking. From the Forbidden City to the Western Hills, you will see that the vast majority of the city's surviving palaces, temples and parks bear Qian

Long's imprint. Qian Long relished traveling through his capital incognito and visiting restaurants, parks and temple fairs. It was his reign that cast the final appearance of Old Peking, which we will try to seek out in these pages.

Qian Long abdicated on his 80th birthday and retired to a separate palace inside the Forbidden City. However, the length of his reign had already begun to exhaust the country. While he is to be remembered warmly for restoring so many sights in Peking, his enthusiasm for renovation was a heavy burden of the state's coffers. Corruption began to be a significant problem throughout the empire. In his final years, Qian Long increasingly permitted a bannerman named He Shen (和珅), who might have been his lover, to govern the empire in all but name.

The successor of Qian Long, Jia Qing (嘉庆) ruled from 1796 to 1820 and ventured to revive the empire. Showing some of the vitality of his forbearers, he helped put down a rebellion that had broken out in north China. However, he lacked the vision and skills of his ancestors that were necessary for a full restoration of Qing glory and an effective adaptation to a changing world. Slowly, Qing authority collapsed while internal rebellions and foreign encroachments wrecked the country. Despite these upheavals, Peking still retained its age-old visage.

In 1850, Xian Feng (咸丰), an ineffectual and vice-ridden young man, ascended the dragon throne. His eleven-year reign saw the rapid descent of the Qing empire. Most significantly, Peking was invaded by a joint Anglo-French army seeking to enforce the terms of a treaty. Upon the arrival of Anglo-French troops in Peking, Xian Feng fled to the imperial summer resort at Jehol, where he died, a fugitive in the eyes of foreigners and a weakling to the dismay of his countrymen.

Xian Feng's most important legacy from his disaster-ridden reign was the political rise of one of his concubines, a Manchu woman born into a banner family and known by the name Yeholona. Her childhood was spent in alleyways immediately to the east of the Forbidden City. At the age of 15, Yeholona was selected for the imperial harem. She rapidly became Xian Feng's favorite consort because of her sexual dexterity, a talent that obscured her acute abilities at court intrigue. Her destiny and that of China were cast when she presented Xian Feng with his only son, a boy known to us as Tong Zhi (同治). Yeholona ensured that on the day of Xian Feng's death, an imperial decree anointed Tong Zhi as the new emperor with herself in the powerful role as regent.

At that time, foreigners better knew Yeholona as the Empress Dowager.[7] Photographs taken towards the end of her life depict a dour and unfriendly old crow, who was reported to be intensely superstitious as well as hateful of foreigners and their inventions. Chinese and foreign historians came to regard her as a cruel despot responsible for the prostration of China before foreign powers. Others such as eunuchs told foreign visitors of her grace and kindness, and she herself managed to charm those few foreigners whom she condescended to meet towards the end of her life.[8]

The Empress Dowager ruled as regent, *de facto* empress and paramount ruler during the reign of three emperors; her son Tong Zhi, from 1861 to 1875, her nephew Guang Xu (光绪) from 1875 to 1908, and Xuan Tong, better known to Westerners as Henry Pu Yi. Her son Tong Zhi died from small pox before reaching his maturity. Guang Xu formally assumed the throne though the Empress Dowager continued to exert ultimate control through Manchu factions and court eunuchs.[9]

The later part of the 19th century was tumultuous for Peking politics. As he matured, the emperor Guang Xu developed a deep concern for the fate of his country. In defiance of his aunt and her court factions, he summoned the courage to take the advice of a group of Chinese reformers and ushered in the One Hundred Days of Reform in the summer of 1898. Week after week, the throne issued decrees that embraced reforms in the fields of education, administration, technology and social welfare. The foreign community in Peking was thunderstruck by these moves. It appeared that during the summer of 1898 China was about to save itself the same way Japan had done so forty years earlier.

In September of 1898, Guang Xu derailed his reform program by taking into his confidence Yuan Shi Kai (袁世凯), a military governor general. Guang Xu had sought Yuan's help in arresting the Empress Dowager and displacing her court faction. Yuan promptly disclosed the emperor's plans to one of the loyalist friends of the Empress Dowager, who, in a rage, placed Guang Xu under house arrest. Several days later, he was forced to issue a humiliating decree, abandoning reform and announcing the reinstatement of the regency of the Empress Dowager.

At the same time, a rebellion broke out in Shan Dong province in protest over the surge of foreign products in China and the incompetency of the local officials. In this unrest, a sect called the Society of Harmonious Fists (义和团 or *yi he tuan*) came into existence advocating a philosophy vaguely based on local superstitions and curious extrapolations of Buddhism. The sect was dubbed the "Boxer Movement" because its adherents practiced a form of meditative exercise, which resembled shadow boxing to Westerners. Its adherents believed that through charms and spells, they were immune to bullets and could perform the feats of strength like Chow Yun Fat in *Crouching Tiger, Hidden Dragon*. They were anti-foreign and opposed to Manchu rule because of its perceived acquiescence to the foreigners. As the cult expanded beyond Shan Dong province, the Boxers killed Christian converts and missionaries, burned churches, tore up railways and telegraph lines and destroyed imported goods and their Chinese distributors.

As the Boxers approached Peking, various political factions debated the merits of the movement. Perhaps because of her superstitiousness the Empress Dowager agreed to support the Boxers, thinking perhaps that they could rid China of foreigners. The faction supporting the Empress Dowager accordingly encouraged the Boxers in their attacks on foreigners and stood by when the Boxers lay siege to Peking's embassy district. After a final meeting of contending court factions in June 1900, the Empress Dowager had Guang Xu issue a decree declaring war on the foreign powers. Thus began the "Siege of Peking" where a combination of imperial troops and Boxer rebels stormed the legations for a 55-day period.

In order to relieve the besieged embassies, the armies of eight foreign powers came together in a haphazard and poorly coordinated invasion. Foreign troops occupied the city and the surrounding countryside for about one year, looting cultural artifacts, terrorizing its citizens and breaching the sanctity of its imperial palaces and temples. Peking neither recovered from the trauma nor ever regained its imperial dignity and genteel refinement.

The Empress Dowager returned to Peking in 1902, made a token effort at reform, built up a modern army in north China under the command of Yuan Shi Kai, and kept Guang Xu in his cage. However, these cosmetic reforms were too late. For the next ten years, the Qing government crawled to its grave. In 1908, Guang Xu and the Empress Dowager died in extraordinarily rapid succession over two days. In her final moments the Empress Dowager issued a valedictory edict in the name of Guang Xu, in which Guang Xu reverently accepted the commands of the Empress Dowager to receive his nephew, Pu Yi (溥仪) as his successor with a pliable friend of the Empress Dowager's faction, a noble named Prince Chun and the boy's father, appointed as regent. Against a final backdrop of pageantry, a three-year-old boy became the Son of the Heaven, wailing and crying and being consoled by his father before an assembly of high Confucian officials.

When it all finally unraveled, it started in the south, (probably much to the satisfaction of the ghost of Zhu Yuan Cheng). In October 1911, a conspiracy between revolutionaries and imperial soldiers was uncovered in Wu Han. The local soldiers seized the initiative, forcing the Manchu governor and administration to flee Hu Bei province. Inspired by these events, revolutionary groups, local militia and provincial gentry declared their independence from Qing rule. By December, nearly every southern and central province had rejected the Qing. The revolutionary groups came together to form the Nationalist Party (国民党 or *guo min dang* in Peking *pin yin* and *kuo min t'ang* in an older romanization system), which became known by the initials "KMT." An opponent to Qing rule, a Southern revolutionary named Sun Yat Sen, became the provisional president of the newly established Republic of China while the Qing court clung to rule within the walls of Peking.

Finally, on February 12, 1912, Prince Chun, on behalf of the child emperor Xuan Tong, issued a decree acknowledging that Mandate of Heaven had passed sovereign authority to the Republic of China. Under the Articles of Agreement signed with the new government, the Qing regime was allowed to continue to exist, but only within the confines of the Forbidden City, the Summer Palace and the Imperial Resort in Jehol. In the words of Karl Marx, the Qing disintegrated like "mummified remains suddenly exposed to air."

Xuan Tong's abdication opened the door for a bewildering decade of factional maneuvering. Sun Yat Sen continued with his provisional government in the south. However, Yuan refused to leave his power base in Peking and courted foreign powers through their embassies for recognition and financial support. The provisional government agreed to install a Peking-based parliament of sorts, whose members were susceptible to Yuan's blandishments or threats, reflecting his prescient political philosophy that people "fear weapons and love gold."

In 1914, Yuan, maintaining the fiction of a national government in Peking, tried to install a new empire, the Grand Constitutional dynasty (洪宪 or *hong xian*) in Peking. He ventured to play the role of an emperor by performing traditional Confucian rites at various altars and temples in Peking as a prelude to the installation of a new dynasty. It is said that these rituals, shorn of their pageantry, were only a parody of China's past glory. For reasons that are still subject to speculation, Yuan gave up his plan of assuming the purple and died in despair in 1916. His legacy to Peking was a revolving door of small-time presidents from 1916 to 1924 and an impotent government that bought and sold votes in the Peking parliament, making a sham of constitutional government in the eyes of dispirited Chinese, and somehow bamboozling foreign governments to regard Peking as the representative government of all of China.

After its disillusionment with political reformation, Peking responded to the 1920s with a sense of desultory quietude. For a while, there was a popular belief that "only an emperor" could restore stability and there were no shortage of applicants. In February 1924, the warlord Feng Yu Xiang (冯玉祥) or the so-called "Christian General" occupied Peking. Feng was a convert to Christianity and, in a show of Chinese practicality, favored the baptism of his troops with a garden hose. He forced the cloistered Henry Pu Yi to leave the Forbidden City. In the same year, Sun Yat Sen went to Peking in order to seek a negotiated settlement with the northern warlords, dying suddenly in February 1925. Shortly thereafter, another warlord from Manchuria, Zhang Zuo Lin (张作霖), ousted Feng and took control of the city.

While these events transpired, a collection of intellectuals under the leadership of Li Da Zhao (李大钊) of Peking University established the Chinese

Communist Party ("CCP"). A youth from Hu Nan (湖南) province, Mao Ze Dong (毛泽东), and a patrician named Zhou En Lai (周恩来) were among the multinational group of founders, an event that was hidden from the hoi polloi of Peking.

After Sun's death, the party leadership of the KMT passed to a Zhe Jiang native and a graduate of the Whampoa Military Academy in Canton province. Chiang Kai Shek (蒋介石) was a soldier steeped in conservative Confucian tradition. He had lived in Japan, where he was both inspired and intimidated by Japanese material progress. He was also keenly devoted to the fight against Western imperialism and the restoration of Chinese prestige. As he consolidated his power base in south China, Chiang supported, on the surface, an alliance with the CCP. Behind the scenes, Chiang cashiered his wife, married the daughter of an influential Shanghai industrialist and cultivated ties with Shanghai bankers, entrepreneurs and gangsters.

The alliance between the CCP and the KMT ended in April 1927 when Chiang launched a successful and bloody pogrom against the Communists in Shanghai. With the CCP on the run, Chiang embarked upon the Northern Expedition, a campaign to bring China nominally under the control of a single government.

By 1928, Peking was under Nationalist control, and the city lost its capital status to Nanjing. For a period of 21 years, the capital was called Northern Peace (北平 or *bei ping*), which was a name that was belied by the Japanese threat growing in the former homelands of the Manchus.

As China entered the 1930s, foreigners were hard pressed to explain the Byzantine character of Chinese politics. However, Peter Quennell, a British writer and teacher, de-mystified Chinese politics in a simple masterpiece of elucidation:

> Any attempt to find a clue through Chinese politics seemed to lead direct into a small and airless room, crowded with the members of a single family … . Recent history is a warren of such rooms, the occupants of this room plotting against the occupants of that; while trap doors and secret passages and hidden stairs wind up and down and to and fro … . Events, which are utterly mysterious when considered from the Western point of view — the point of view that insists upon presupposing that politicians necessarily have policies and that even an ex-bandit may be a patriot — become simple as elucidated by a Chinese. Somebody or other has a nephew and somebody is heavily in debt to him. *Ergo*. A smile unweaves the mystery. It is just a big problem of family life, the politics of an overcrowded tenement, if you imagine the tenement as co-existing with, or being raised on the foundations of, a huge necropolis.[10]

While these tumultuous events were transpiring, the 1930s witnessed the last moments of a golden age for traditional Peking culture. While the Nationalist government neglected the city's heritage, the citizens of Peking still preserved customs and beliefs of an older era. Foreign visitors, like George Kates, John Blofeld, and Harold Acton left records of their passing participation in Old Peking life. H. Y. Lowe described the rhythms of daily life as Lao She chronicled the misery of the working class in their beloved city.

Karl Eskelund, a Danish journalist who later gained widespread popularity by punching Chiang Kai Shek's son in the nose, captured the affection that Peking engendered among foreign sojourners in the 1930s:

> I fell in love with the city from the first glimpse of the gray Tartar wall. I still love Peking better than any other place in the world. Nowhere else has the romantic past been blended so charmingly with the practical present. Peking has no tooting motorcars, no smoky factories, no ugly modern concrete buildings. The temples, the mysterious Forbidden City, the cozy dwelling houses with their intricate courtyards and gracefully slanting roofs, all stand today as they did when Peking was capital of the Middle Kingdom.[11]

On July 7, 1937, Japanese troops relied upon a trumped-up pretext to invade Peking and, from there, the entire Chinese seaboard. For the first time since 1368, a non-Sinified people ran the city with the intention of incorporating it into a wholly alien empire. Once Japan joined the Axis war in 1941, only foreigners who were the citizens of Axis or neutral nations were at liberty to carry on with their lives. By the time of Japan's defeat in 1945, the city was down-at-heel and unkempt.

Peace brought little breathing space for Peking since the struggle for the Mandate of Heaven broke out again between the Communists and the Nationalists. As the preeminent foreign power in Asia at the time, the United States, with little depth of understanding of domestic events, unsuccessfully mediated discussions between the two sides for a coalition government.

The KMT government failed to generate popular support against the Communists. After eight years of warfare, the rank and file in the Nationalist troops simply longed for peace and stability. As Nationalist troops were mobilized to fight the Communists, peasants withdrew their support. Strategically, Chiang made the fatal move of moving the majority of his best troops to Manchuria where they were overextended (like the armies of the Sui) and soon slaughtered or captured by the People's Liberation Army (the "PLA") under the command of Lin Biao (林彪).

In January 1949, the PLA took Peking without a fight. Several months later, the PLA crossed the Yang Tse River and swept the Nationalists from the mainland to the island of Taiwan. On October 1, 1949, Mao Ze Dong declared that the Chinese people had at long last stood up. He announced the establishment of the People's Republic of China from Tian An Gate. Peking had once again become the capital of China and the country's turmoil and humiliations seemed to be at an end.

Mao had given China prestige by installing a unified government. The first years of Communist rule were also an unqualified success for his government. Land reform gave ownership of the fields to the peasants who worked them. Inflation was brought to heel. Social ills, such as illiteracy, beggary, prostitution and opium addiction were tackled with a dedication that the Nationalists were never able to muster. Seeing these efforts at national reconstruction, thousands of patriotic overseas Chinese returned home to help.

Sadly, turmoil soon replaced the triumphs of the government's first years. In 1958, Mao initiated chaos through the Great Leap Forward, an industrial and agricultural program to "surpass England and catch up to America" in 15 years. All private properties — land, houses, livestock, and farm tools — were confiscated and the commune leadership performed all administrative functions. A utopia was promised where all property was collectively owned and private commerce and industry would disappear.

The face of Peking, mostly unchanged since the era of Yong Le, became a target for Mao's theories. During the Great Leap Forward, the city walls and gates were torn down to make way for highways. Soviet style architecture arrived in the capital at the Soviet Exhibition Center and the Museum of Military History. Roadside shrines, temples and pagodas were razed in the interests of modernity. These efforts intensified when the Cultural Revolution was unleashed in 1966.

As much as Yong Le wanted to demonstrate the continuity of his regime with the past in the 15th century, Mao ventured to erase all connection of Peking with its pedigree. Even the elderly themselves became targets of Red Guard violence. David Kidd recalls a discussion with his Chinese in-laws about the Cultural Revolution:

> Fifth Sister went on to tell me about the massacre of the residents of old Peking. The slaughter even had a name, *hong ba yue* — Bloody August. I was amazed that it had never been reported in the West and said so to her. "The government wouldn't like it," Fifth Sister said.
>
> Through the heat of that Bloody August, she told me, the young Red Guards had murdered the gentle citizens of old Peking. At night, the screams of the

beaten and dying made sleep impossible. Almost anything, even owning the photograph of a grandfather, could be cause for being beaten to death. Rather than guns or knives, the Red Guards wielded clubs and sticks, prolonged the agony as they wished, striking to kill on their blow or postponing the moment of death ten or fifteen minutes. It was said that as many as half a million people had died. She spoke of people covered with blood, women dragged by their hair through the streets, others hanging from trees, or drowned in Peking's lakes and moats. By the end of that month the dead were piled so high that they could not be burned fast enough in the huge new crematorium to the west that, then as today, is the last destination of all those who live and die in Peking.[12]

Where China stood up.

The year 1976 took Peking further along its path of misery. In July, an earthquake, a traditional harbinger of change, rocked Tianjin municipality, resulting in refugees flooding to Peking and being housed in quickly erected one story brick shacks (called 平房 or *ping fang*) throughout the city. In September, old, frail and speaking in unintelligible mutterings, a bed-ridden Mao "mounted the dragon and ascended the throne on high." Finally in November, Deng Xiao Ping (邓小平) staged a coup that removed the ideologues from government and brought much needed relief to the country.

To the historian, Chinese history seemed to slow down once Deng Xiao Ping inherited the Mandate of Heaven. Peking politics in the 1980s did not witness the dizzying volume of change as in prior years. However, by that time Peking's appearance turned into an inverted version of Eskelund's. The city walls were gone, the graceful palaces and temples obscured by concrete blocks, the silence of the alleyway shattered by traffic noise. On the positive side of things, traditional "old name" restaurants and stores (老字号 or *lao zi hao*), which had been unceremoniously turned into canteens and warehouses, resurrected their age-old names and revived their specialty products.

By the 1990s, Peking had begun to experience economic growth that raised people's standard of living but snuffed out the remnants of Old Peking that somehow survived the brutality of the 20th century. Over the past ten years, cranes and bulldozers invaded the back alleys of the old city, turning old neighborhoods into bombed-out wastelands and then monotonous, undistinguished housing flats and office buildings. However, concurrent with this material transformation, it also seemed that citizens of Old Peking began to return to the faiths of their ancestors. Tourists who once seemed to ignore the religious aspects of Buddhist and Taoist temples now returned to burn incense and beseech blessings from on high. Shrines that were eerily vacant now house statues, incense burners and prayer mats. While the city was undergoing the most pervasive reconstruction since Yong Le began his construction projects in 1402, it seems that a spiritual revival might also be in the wings as the last remnants of Old Peking are torn down in anticipation of China's coming of age for the Summer Olympics.

4

TIAN AN MEN SQUARE

WE BEGIN OUR TOUR OF Old Peking at the south end of Tian An Men Square (天安门广场). Standing back-to-back, as if they refuse to acknowledge each other's existence, are two large buildings. One was built by the emperor who gave Peking its imperial status and the other by the man who tore out that status, root and branch.

To the south stands the Gate of the Pure Sun (正阳门 or *zheng yang men*), now only consisting of the Main Gate and its outer Arrow Gate. The emperor Yong Le built the Gate of the Pure Sun as the first of many impressive barriers leading to his imperial presence in the Forbidden City. Straddling Peking's central axis, the gate originally contained five passageways leading into Tian An Men Square.

The Arrow Gate served as a first line of defense in the event of a siege while the Main Gate and its tower served to reinforce the prestige and power of the capital. After nine years of construction, Yong Le's engineers completed the gate in 1419. Two years later, Yong Le transferred his capital from Nanjing to Peking.

A semi-circular wall once connected the two remaining gates before the arrival of the combustion engine and mass transportation. Local sensitivities hindered any change to the appearance of the gate at first. For example, in the 19th century, Qing officials opposed the introduction of tramways, electricity and macadamized roads in the vicinity of Zheng Yang Gate on the grounds that such new innovations would wreck the *feng shui* of the city. When the Qing court at long last agreed to pave the area in front of Zheng Yang Gate, another debate broke out among the city's officials and citizens. How could the roadwork be done without offending the two stately lions by the entrance? A compromise was gradually eked out. The lions were blindfolded so they wouldn't know what was going on and thus could not be offended.

Tian An Men Square and Vicinity

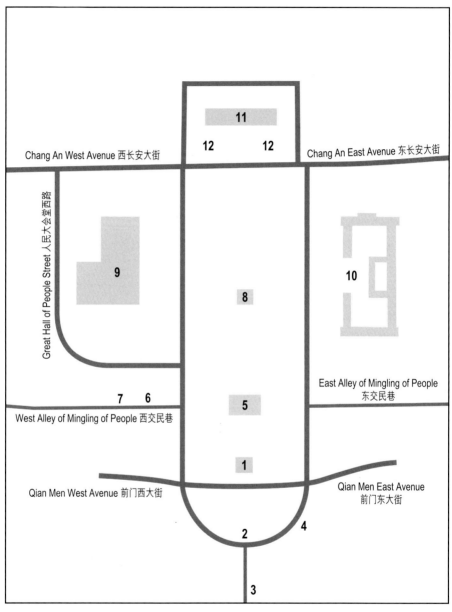

1. Gate of the Pure Sun（正阳门）
2. Arrow Gate（箭门）
3. Qian Men Wai Avenue（前门外大街）
4. former Peking Railway Station（北京火车站旧址）
5. Memorial Hall of Chairman Mao Ze Dong（毛泽东记念堂）
6. Bao Shang Bank（保商银行旧址）
7. Central Bank of China（中央银行旧址）
8. Monument to the People's Martyrs
9. Great Hall of the People（人民大会堂）
10. Museum of Chinese History（历史博物馆）
11. Gate of Heavenly Peace（天安门）
12. cloud pillars（华表）

Mid-Qing depiction of Zheng Yang Gate.

The Zheng Yang Gate in the 1920s.

A contemporary view of Zheng Yang Gate as seen from the north.

Such sensitivities disappeared with the Qing throne. Eventually, a road was rammed through the circular wall between the Main Gate and the Arrow Gate.

The post-liberation years irreversibly diminished the grandeur of the gate. The demolition of the city walls has given the Main Gate a reduced, truncated appearance that is a far cry from Yong Le's desired effect. Zheng Yang Gate now stands as a forgotten sentinel, gracing a trip through central Peking but otherwise not routinely visited.

Starting first with the Arrow Gate, we can view its gigantic dust-covered bolt lying in the tunnel. On the ends of the Arrow Gate are intricately carved marble crests and dragon rainspouts. With a little persuasion, the guard will permit the occasional foreign traveler to climb up the stairs for a nice view of the central axis down Qian Men Wai Avenue (前门外大街) on the south and the Main Gate on the north. Photographs from the 19th century depict a five passage way wooden *pai lou* over Qian Men Wai Avenue. Though the original was torn down in the 1950s, it is pleasing to see that the Peking authorities have erected a new *pai lou*, mildly revamped to accommodate the unyielding demands of modern traffic.

To the north, the central door of the Main Gate was opened twice a year for the emperor's procession to the Altar of Heaven and the Altar of Agriculture. The eastern portal was reserved for civilian officials while military officials passed through the western one. Commoners entered via the long vanished side gates in the linking walls.

During the 19th century, the Zheng Yang Gate was closed each day at dusk with considerable ceremony. A watchman methodically beat a gong, gradually increasing the tempo until he produced a continuous sound. Sudden silence was followed by the cries of the watchmen that all is well, and then the gates were closed and bolted with huge wooden beams and anchored in place with a huge Chinese lock. At the same time, all other gates in the city also closed. For a few minutes after midnight, the gates were briefly opened to accommodate government officials returning from a night's entertainment in the district directly to the south.

The towers on the gates are of relatively recent origin. In 1900, both towers were destroyed during the Boxer Debacle. In June of that year, Boxers, seeking to purge the country of any foreign taint, set fire to shops selling Western goods along the city wall. The ensuing conflagration spread to the tower of the Arrow Gate. After the occupation of Peking by foreign troops, Sepoys on guard duty around the Main Gate somehow managed to set the tower on fire. Upon the return of the Qing court to Peking, its citizens were keen to reconstruct the tower in order to restore the cosmological balance of the city. As part of the many concessions given to foreign countries in the aftermath of the Boxer Debacle, a German firm was hired to rebuild the towers, which explain such un-Chinese touches like the eyebrows over the windows in the tower of the Arrow Gate.

The Main Gate is open to the public. By climbing up the stairwell on the east side, we have a clear view of the Chinese City. Off to the southeast, the Temple of Heaven looks like a little thimble amidst the gray concrete high rises. Immediately in front of us to the southeast is the former Peking train station and clock tower, built in 1903 and now painted a garish silver color. The station was constructed adjacent to the legation district as a treaty obligation after the Boxer Debacle. In a manner strangely reminiscent of diplomatic evacuation plans after the June 4th Incident, foreign envoys insisted upon a close location for the train station in the event of any future upheavals. In the 1950s, the station was converted into the railway workers' club. It is now inartfully partitioned into small shops offering run of the mill consumer goods. It is easy to imagine an elegant restoration project, with fine restaurants and curio shops, transforming this neglected building.

Emperor Yong Le was the builder of Zheng Yang Gate. He was born in 1360, the fourth son of the founder of the Ming dynasty. During Yong Le's childhood, his mother and her siblings conspired to have him enthroned in place of the chosen heir, Hong Wu' grandson. The plot unraveled with the result that Yong Le spent seven years under house arrest. Upon his release, Yong Le was ordered to recover the north China plains from Mongolian invaders. In 1390, he was awarded the title the Prince of Yan (燕公) for his efforts at securing China's northern flank. When his father died in 1398, his nephew became emperor. This prompted Yong Le immediately to raise the standard of rebellion. Conquest quickly followed conquest. In 1402, Yong Le crossed the Yangtze River and captured Nanjing, thereby ousting his nephew from the throne and establishing his own reign.

Yong Le encountered resistance to his reign in Nanjing since many conservative officials viewed him as a usurper. In one instance, a functionary refused to bow to Yong Le, and reflecting the prevailing strain of Ming despotism, Yong Le ordered that the functionary be executed in boiling oil. In his final moments of agony, the functionary managed to turn his back on Yong Le, thus slighting (and enraging) him. The skin of another uncooperative official was torn from his body, tanned and hung outside a Nanjing city gate like a chamois. Later, a burst of wind snapped the skin into Yong Le's face as he rode underneath the gate, to the immense amusement of passers-by. Because of these and other countless snubs, Yong Le removed his court to the safer territory of Peking.

Directly across from Zheng Yang Gate is the Memorial Hall of Chairman Mao Ze Dong (毛泽东纪念堂), or in Frances Wood's delightful phrase, the "maosoleum." The memorial hall is a Stalinesque building with Chinese characteristics, constructed upon the site of an imperial gate in the Ming dynasty and lasting until the PRC. Originally, the gate carried the phrase the Great

Ming Gate (大明门). After the Manchus established themselves, the name was changed to the Great Qing Gate (大清门). The name was duly revised once again after the establishment of the Republic and was called the Great China Gate (中华门), and was then pulled down in the 1940s. The construction of the maosoleum began in November 1976, just two months after the chairman's death. It was completed in May 1977.

William Stevenson recalls that when the workers were installing the sign for the New China Gate in the 1910s, they had thought twice about throwing away the signage for the Qing, with practical concern that you never know what tomorrow may bring. Instead of consigning it to the garbage bin, they decided to put the sign in the attic of the gate where, in a dust-covered corner, they uncovered the Great Ming sign, placed there by long deceased workers who had the same second thoughts about the durability of the Manchus.

On both the northern entrance and the southern exit of the Memorial Hall are socialist era pink stone statues of the masses rising up with the inspiration of the Thought of Chairman Mao. After joining the queue at the entrance, it is hard not to notice that the Chinese masses in the flesh do not appear at all like these robust icons. Instead of the drab uniforms, the people in line are more comfortably dressed in casual clothes: shorts and sneakers, cotton shirts rolled up over men's torsos, sun dresses, sun glasses and Nike hats.

You enter through the entrance at the northeast. All parcels and cameras need to be checked with security, and a helpful man in green will snap to and accost you if you forget. No tickets are required. The queues are moved through with great speed while loudspeakers exhort the masses to refrain from spitting or littering, with feeble results. On the way in, flower vendors sell, well rent actually, artificial flowers to be left by the faithful.

You climb past two sets of marble balustrades carved wistfully with evergreen motifs. The maosoleum consists of two stories, though only the ground floor is open to the public. The second floor is presumably filled with mortuary equipment or basic ingredients from Madame Tussaud's. A large white marble statute of the Chairman greets us as we enter the North Hall. (Leave flowers here.) We are funneled into the Hall of Mourning where we can see the old boy in a crystal coffin on a black bier, draped with the flag of the Communist Party. Security guards hover as you shuffle past with the silent hope of catching glimpse of some faux pas, like the sudden detachment of the Great Helmsman's ear a few years go. The bier rests on an elevator that allows the remains to be removed like a dumb waiter for further cosmetic polishing. I wonder whether the guards keep their lunch pails in the deep freeze while the old boy is on view up on top.

A view from Zheng Yang Gate towards the former Peking Railway Station.

The "maosoleum" as seen from Zheng Yang Gate.

According to Mao's personal physician Li Zhi Sui (李志绥), the PRC Politburo began preparations for the Chairman's burial only several hours after his death. No prior preparations had been undertaken since speculative discussions of the Chairman's death was a taboo that could inflict dreadful consequences upon a career trajectory. The medical team was first informed that the body would lie in state for two weeks and then be cremated. Several hours later, the Politburo came back and informed a horrified medical staff that Mao's remains must be preserved for eternity, just like Lenin, Ho Chih Minh or Walt Disney. With this shocking news delivered in the early morning hours of September 9, 1976, they accidentally injected 16 liters of embalming fluid into the Chairman. The remains were so full of fluid that he looked like a Chinese Michelin Man. The doctor and his team worked frantically to siphon off the excess so that he could lie in state, though various body parts began to drop off during these frantic measures. Soviet technicians used to heap scorn upon the hatchet job done on Mao, which, in turn, fuels speculation that the remains are a wax replica.

Next is the South Hall where the marble wall is adorned by one of Mao's poems, a snappy number called "Reply to Comrade Guo Moruo":

A thunderstorm burst over the earth,

So a devil rose from a heap of white bones.

The deluded monk was not beyond the light,

But the malignant demon must wreak havoc.

The Golden Monkey wrathfully swung his massive cudgel

And the jade-like firmament was cleared of dust.

Today, a miasmal mist once more rising,

We hail Sun Wu-kung, the wonder worker.

O-kaaaye.

On our way, dozens of hawkers throng around the southern exit, selling Mao memorabilia, soft drinks, instant computerized portraits, and other tasteless consumer goods.

The Chairman makes an interesting study in contrasts when compared to Yong Le. In the 1930s, Mao exhibited an insightful talent for crafting military strategies and disrupting social order, which was the same talent that facilitated Yong Le's rise to power. Official history holds that Mao, like Yong Le more than five hundred years before him, personally planned the crossing of the Yang Tse that resulted in triumph. Like Yong Le, Mao, once in power, ordered the migration of millions of people to sparsely populated regions. The Chairman relied upon the talents of Kang Sheng (康生), the chief of the secret police, to establish a nationwide surveillance system that maintained detailed records on officials, soldiers and civilians, an achievement that far surpassed the espionage networks installed by Yong Le's eunuchs.

However, unlike Yong Le, the Chairman's military ability did not lend itself to administrative competence in a unified nation. His seasonal revolutionary campaigns disrupted Chinese society and led to the imprisonment and death of millions of innocent people. His unscientific ideologies stifled the agricultural sector, resulting in a famine that killed at least 20 million people. While Yong Le sent his vessels on diplomatic missions around the world, Mao closed the country from contact with the outside world, first shunning contact with the West and then the Soviet world. His advocacy of Third World solidarity, a shadowy reflection of the Zheng He's travels to overseas countries, was shown to be a hollow platitude in the aftermath of the Sino-Indian border war of 1962.

For both Yong Le and Mao, Peking was a tangible symbol of their respective reigns. While Yong Le strove to emphasize Peking's continuity with the past, Mao wanted to show that heaven and earth had been turned upside down. He extended Chang An Avenue in order to break the traditional north — south axis of the city. Buddhist and Taoist temples were ransacked and the monastic community driven out in contrast to Yong Le's cultivation of the clergy. Traditional architecture was squashed in favor of square concrete boxes.

Perhaps all of this happened because Mao had no great love for the city. He spent several months in 1918 and 1919 working at Peking University where he must have felt like an awkward outsider, speaking with a heavy southern accent, amidst the more worldly intellectuals of the capital. The city was no refuge for him, as it was for Yong Le.

I never apply the word "greatness" to politicians. It is a word more suitable for poets, artists, musicians, chefs and monks but never to the seekers and holders of political power. However, I acknowledge the point that he was the most successful Chinese politician in the 20th century. He was able to install central control over a vast continent that had fallen into disunity for more than a century. He secured the country's borders against threats of invasion. He fought the United States and its industrialized allies to a standstill in Korea. During the inaugural years of the PRC, Mao gave the Chinese people the prestige long denied them since the days of Qian Long's descent into senility. He undeniably met a given moment in Chinese history.

On the other hand, even by the calculations of the orthodoxy of the Communist Party, 70% of Mao's actions were correct while 30% were errors. Even accepting this grade school method for the evaluation of a national leader, a C-grade is not a laudatory achievement. Moreover, were we to factor in the lives lost in the Great Leap Forward, its resulting famine and the Cultural Revolution, it is easy to believe that the real liberation of the Chinese people began with the Chairman's death. Only then could normal life return to a unified China. Be that as it may, every nation needs its foundation myth where niceties like historical facts are shunted aside. As a symbol of national unity, the Chairman now serves a more constructive role in death than he ever did in life.

My favourite quote about the Chairman was a side comment tossed off by Jack Kerouac as he was musing about life and death, spirit and substance, and loss:

> When we buried my father, Mama insisted upon an expensive coffin which made me so goddamned mad, but not only that, though I was mad on that score, she had his old sweet body ambulated to New Hampshire for funeral and burial there by the side of his first son, Gerard, my holy brother, so that now as thunder breaks in Mexico City where I write, they're still there, side by side, 35 and 15 years in the earth, but I never visited their graves because I know what's there is not really Papa Emile or Gerard, only dung. For if the soul can't escape the body give the world to Mao Tse-tung. I know better than that....[1]

On the west side of Tian An Men Square near the Maosoleum is Xi Jiao Min Xiang (西文民巷), a small road that permits further sacrilegious sentiments in the face of a mummified orthodoxy. In the 1920s, government officials selected Xi Dong Min Xiang as site for the "Wall Street of China" and established various banking and financial institutions at this address. As is often the case with a government's explicit interference in commerce, Xi Dong Min Xiang never took off and slowly slid into obscurity. However, along this street are some interesting samples of western architecture from that era, well within a stone's throw of the Memorial Hall. The building on the corner with the clock tower is an office for the Bank of China. Along the northern side of the street are the former locations for the Bao Shang Bank (保商银行旧址) and the Central Bank of China (中央 银行旧址). The tree-lined street is a pleasant place to linger for a few minutes. Here the friendly beverage hawkers approach their potential customers in a more relaxed manner than their frenetic comrades on the square.

After retracing our steps, we return to the square and come to the Monument to the People's Martyrs, a thirty-meter tall obelisk with bas-reliefs of revolutionary scenes. A clumsy and unappealing monument, "this insignificant granite phallus receives all its enormous significance from the blasphemous stupidity of its location. In erecting this monument in the center of the sublime axis that reaches from the Front Gate to Tian An Men, the designer's idea was, of course, to use the advantage the ancient imperial planning of that space, to take over to the monument's advantage that mystical current, which carried along, rhythmically from city gate to city gate, goes from the outside world to the Forbidden City, the center of the Universe. The planner failed to realize that by inserting his revolutionary proletarian obscenity in the middle of that sacred way, he was neatly destroying precisely the perspective he wanted to capture for it."[2] I think the designer intended to do just that: the destruction of feudal notions of a sacred cosmological axis through brutal modern monuments. Leys wrote about eight years before the government tossed up the old boy's mausoleum. I wonder with pleasure what type of pyrotechnic Gallic fury Leys might have fired off if he had written *Chinese Shadows* ten year later.

The bas-reliefs were designed so that the most illiterate dullard could follow the story line. However, since I do not want to leave out any investment banker or lawyer or any other member of the five poisonous reptiles that we might have in tow, I will summarize the events depicted on the bas-reliefs after a slight digression.

In traditional China, the five poisonous reptiles appeared during the fifth lunar month as the spring weather warmed and these creatures awoke from hibernation. The traditional tally consists of the snake, the toad, the centipede, the scorpion and the lizard. On the Festival of the Excited Insects held in the fifth month, folks in Peking performed rituals to ensure that these creatures stay out of their homes. As to their modern day equivalents, I would add personal wealth managers, venture captialists, and advertising agents to the aforementioned list of reptiles. Alas, I know of no ceremony to keep these contemporary creatures at bay.

Starting from the eastern side of the panels and working our way chronologically, the first bas-relief depicts the "Burning of the Opium" on June 3, 1839 when Chinese in the southern port of Humen allegedly rose up and burned chests of opium imported by foreigners. Some creative license has been applied to this event since at the time, Chinese officials had been actively participating in the opium trade until the arrival of Commissioner Lin Ze Xun. Lin took imperial edicts at face value and tried to stop the trade, an action that was massively unpopular among foreigners, lower ranking officials, merchants and local consumers in south China. All of this devolved into the first Opium War of 1839 to 1842 in which Britain defeated China and demanded the opening of the country to the opium trade and the perpetual transfer of sovereignty over Hong Kong island.

Five poisonous reptiles or five ambitious upwardly mobile executive-types.

In an initial round of negotiations to end the hostilities, Lin and his British counterpart, Charles Elliot, met and hammered out a series of terms that failed to please both the Qing and British courts. As a rebuke for his over zealousness, Commissioner Lin was transferred to Ili in Xin Jiang province. Elliot became the chief British diplomat in the newly established independent Republic of Texas. I have heard that he is the source of the observation: "if I owned Texas and Hell, I would rent out Texas and live in Hell." Commissioner Lin probably had the same reaction to Xin Jiang (though to alleviate the monotony of the Ili landscape and provide a windbreak, he planted oak trees, which are still there and one of the few "sights" to be seen there).

The second relief depicts the Jintian Uprising of 1851, part of the disastrous Taiping Rebellion led by Hong Xiu Quan, a Guangdong man who repeatedly flunked the imperial examination and fancied himself to be Christ's younger brother. Hong took up arms against the Qing dynasty with the goal of establishing an egalitarian, classless society.

The third relief celebrates the Wuchang Uprising, which led to the 1911 revolution and the collapse of the Qing dynasty. The uprising started in the present city of Wu Han when the gentry classes rejected new demands for taxation from the central government. To everyone's surprise, the army in Peking under Yuan Shi Kai threw its lot in with the rebels and forced the abdication of the last Qing emperor. In this relief, soldiers and civilians attack the mansion of an imperial viceroy who high-tails it out of town.

We next come to a depiction of the May 1st Movement of 1919 where Peking students and citizens protested the terms of the Treaty of Versailles Conference. Next door, the May 30th Movement of 1925 is memorialized. On that date, British and Japanese troops shot and killed several Chinese protesters in the Shanghai Foreign Concession, an event which led to a nation-wide boycott of British and Japanese goods and increasing demands to an end of the unequal treaties.

Turning to the west side of the obelisk are depictions of the Nan Chang Uprising of 1927 against the Kuomintang along with scenes of the guerrilla war against the Japanese. Finally, the panels on the north side show the PLA's crossing of the Yang Tse River in 1949 to take Nanjing from the KMT. On the left and right hand sides of the north panel are representations of peasants supplying provisions to the communist guerrilla forces and common folk proclaiming "Long Live the Liberation Army."

The north face of the obelisk itself is decorated with Mao's calligraphy, proclaiming that "the people's heroes are invincible" while the south side expands this theme with a message authored by Mao and written in Zhou En Lai's handwriting.

The obelisk has served as the focal point for movements by other "peoples' heroes," not originally envisaged by the Communist Party. Indeed, as we continue our walks, we will see that Chinese history often reverses the immediate verdicts of prior Chinese governments. This reminds me of a quote by Stanislaw Lec: "When smashing monuments, save the pedestals — they always come in handy."

The first movement arose toward the end of March at the Ching Ming Festival (清明节) which is a traditional time for honoring the memory of deceased ancestors. During the festival that year, large numbers of Peking's citizens placed wreathes at the obelisk and held unofficial memorial services for Zhou En Lai, who had died two months earlier. After several days, the wreathes were removed, prompting an angry response from Peking's citizens, who heaped even more wreathes and penned eulogies for the premier as thinly veiled attacks on the Gang of Four. Crowds continued to gather as the First Tian An Men Incident picked up momentum. Mao apparently ordered the police to refrain from using firearms in quelling the demonstrations. The police are rumoured to have obeyed the letter of the law and, on the basis of supplementary orders from the Gang of Four, secretly beheaded demonstrators moments after they were arrested and taken to the courtyards behind the Gate of Heavenly Peace. By April 7, the demonstrations had been suppressed, though after the arrest of the Gang of Four, Deng Xiao Ping declared that the incident was a revolutionary one.

Since there were no foreign reporters in the square for the First Tian An Men Incident, it has fallen into a memory black hole for most foreigners. However, the Second Tian An Men Incident of 1989 is indelibly imprinted on foreign collective memory. After an initial ten-year honeymoon, the second incident woke up the foreign world to the reality of Chinese politics.

The second movement began because of the death of another high-level cadre, Hu Yao Bang (胡耀邦). In April 1989, university students held memorials for Hu, which gradually grew into a mass demonstration against corruption and for democratic reform. The demonstrations at first took on a festive feel, with government agencies, laborers and others petitioning the government for political and economic change. The demonstrations provoked spontaneous protests in every major Chinese city as well as paralysis on the part of the central government. In the rarefied air of Zhong Nan Hai, factions struggled to overcome opponents and defuse the government's inertia. The most potent symbol of the movement was a statue of the Goddess of Democracy, sculpted by the students of the Art Faculty at Peking University and placed directly across from the portrait of the Chairman on Tian An Men. As many noted that spring, "the statue looked like it belonged there."

The student demonstrations have become imbued with a mythical quality that has no bearing on the realities. Most of the student leaders were intoxicated with their own celebrity status and lost control over the demonstrations. They also showed an inexcusable immaturity in dealing with political power. In May of 1989, they turned a cold shoulder to the pleas of Zhao Zi Yang (赵紫阳)to leave the square. By rejecting Zhao, the students played into the hands of hard-liners like Li Peng (李鹏) and destroyed the political capital of Zhao, who was their primary patron in the central government. Some of the student leaders were intolerant of dissenting views and indifferent to the fate of their supporters. In their meetings with Communist officials, many student leaders were as arrogant as those whom they condemned.

The central government adopted an equally ham-fisted approach. By early June, demonstrators had begun to leave the square. The government might have been able to diffuse the crisis with ordinary crowd control techniques and non-lethal weapons. However, the central authorities believed that the risk of chaos compelled them to reassert their authority violently. Student demonstrators made their last stand here at the obelisk in the early morning hours of June 4th as tanks and armed personnel carriers, coming from the west side of Chang An Avenue, entered the square. Elsewhere in the city, inexperienced soldiers overreacted when confronted with discontented civilians and indiscriminately fired into crowds. In reaction to these unprovoked assaults, civilians in other parts of the city lynched and burned stray soldiers. In a move that simply compounded the government's suspicions about foreign participation in the movement, Western intelligence agencies were given the task of spiriting leading Tian An Men demonstrators out from the country in a project given the improbable name Operation Canary.

In the months after June 4th, the government erased all traces of damage save for one. Western journalists spoke of hearing an eerie rumbling rising from the tires of their cars whenever they passed over a certain section of Chang An East Avenue where scars from tank tracks proved to be intractable against efforts to erase them. The cries of wandering ghosts, or so said some elderly folks.

In the aftermath of all this pain, the central government declared the Tian An Men Incident to be a counterrevolutionary uprising, much to the grief of the families of those innocents shot down in the streets. The incident also irreversibly tainted the legacy of Deng Xiao Ping and ended the West's love affair with China.

You probably should not scowl back at the secret police who are out in force at the square. In 1992, an ABC television cameraman made the mistake of filming the police round up a solitary demonstrator. Something the cameraman did snapped something inside the police. They beat him up, detained him and released him after the lodging of predictably lame diplomatic protests. He returned to the United States in relative good health. However, after several weeks, he developed crippling pains throughout his body. His Western physicians diagnosed him as having fluids build up in his spine, a condition that they could not remedy. The poor fellow wound up in constant pain and could not sit upright for more than 15 minutes at a stretch.

There is a disturbing afterword to this story. The cameraman visited several traditional Chinese physicians to solicit their opinions. They were unanimous. The police had aimed each punch to cause the maximum degree of permanent damage while minimizing the immediate results of the beating. The physicians said that it was obvious that the police had been trained in traditional Chinese medicine so as to dole out such crippling beatings.

On this score, the plain-clothes police in golf shirts have something in common with the traditional governmental agencies that were arrayed around Tian An Men Square. The Ming and Qing Board of Punishments used to stand just a little to the north of the Bank of China on the west side of the square. Its cadres were trained in the art of inflicting pain and fear to their invitees, who were both criminal and political prisoners kept in basement cells within a large courtyard house. The functionaries at the Board of Punishments were taught how to execute prisoners by garroting, beheading, skinning and gradual slicing as well as punishments ranging from branding to castration. It was regarded as steady employment. It probably still is.

Moving a little to the north of the former Board of Punishments, you will find the Great Hall of the People, where the National People's Congress convenes annually and officials host foreign dignitaries. It was constructed in ten months with labor donated by the citizens of Peking in 1959 and was officially inaugurated for the tenth anniversary of the People's Republic. There are three main sections. The middle section is the Hall of Ten Thousand People, which consists of a huge auditorium for rallies and party congresses. The West Wing is a gold and white-pillared banquet hall. The East Wing contains 28 large rooms named after the provinces of China, decorated with art from each province.

The Great Hall conveys many memories of momentous events. It was in one of the confidential conference rooms during the national day celebration in 1959 that Mao and Khrushchev quarreled about nearly every aspect of Marxist development and foreign diplomacy, with the Russian wanting to take the road of peaceful coexistence and deployment of practical techniques and Mao arguing for world revolution and ideological purity at all costs. Sydney Rittenburg, an American communist who joined Mao in Yenan, described the scene:

> I was sitting in the balcony with a group of foreign experts, overlooking a sea of Chinese officials and delegations from other socialist states. At the intermission, a friend, an Indian professor from Singapore, and I walked out into the foyer to stretch our legs …. I saw the USSR's elder theoretician, Mikhail Suslove, walking about looking grave. Cambodia's Prince Sihanouk strolled by. The North Korean leader, Kim Il Sung was there too, and I was astounded by the sight. I have never seen a public figure so fat, his vast round stomach blending seamlessly into a thick jowly neck. He looked nothing like his pictures.
>
> My friend and I were enjoying ourselves milling about among the crowd of dignitaries when suddenly two great doors right by our side crashed opened and out strode Mao and Khrushchev. Khrushchev was on the left and Mao on the right, one short and fat, one tall and stately. The rage on the two men's faces was palpable. Khrushchev's was twisted into something between a scowl and a sneer, and he flashed a look at the people milling about him as if his anger took in every citizen in China. As for Mao, I had never seen him so angry. Usually, his anger was controlled, sarcastic, biting, needling. But at that moment, his fury was unchecked. His face was black and tense and the atmosphere all around him snapped and crackled at the force of his emotions. The two men strode side by side, but a million miles apart, back to the hall where they, unspeaking, resumed their seats.[3]

It was here that Zhou En Lai hosted Richard Nixon and Kakuèi Tanaka during their historic trips to China. Here was also the place that Mao's body laid in state in 1976 (after the hurried embalmment) and where student demonstrators kneeled holding petitions for the government in the spring of 1989.

These days, the Great Hall of People rents out its banquet rooms for signing ceremonies attended by CEOs, investment bankers, lawyers and other class enemies. The quality of the cuisine served during the banquet depends upon how much you are willing to shell out, as one Chinese acidly commented about the fare trotted out during a banquet hosted by my former employer. Even were the firm to have dug into its deep pockets, the cuisine on offer is at best second rate, and you can do far better for a gastronomic experience, plate for plate, at a dumpling stand in the Back Lakes district. Assuming a common language, dinner conversation still revolves around comparative meteorology as noted by Simon Leys thirty years ago. Foreign guests will go overboard about the tastiness of the dishes while lower ranking Chinese guests flatter existing or potential employers and important Chinese officials keep their own countenance and shovel away the rice. The banquet invariably ends promptly at 9:00 pm and as if by telepathic signal, Chinese guests leave clutching their gifts of electronic calculators, crystal name card holders and half-finished bottles of cognac while the foreigners smile stupidly, yawn and give impossible instructions in foreign languages to their mono-lingual drivers. At least you can get to sleep at a reasonable hour.

On the east side of the square is the Museum of Chinese History. The Museum is worth a visit as it is increasingly displaying arts and artifacts from the distant past. On my last trip, daily utensils from the Tang dynasty and artwork crafted during the Liao were on display (though no mention was made that the Liao governed Peking for a hundred years). Further upstairs is China's answer to Madame Tussaud's, with wax statues of both ancient and modern figures. In one room, Mao, Zhou, Zhu De and Liu Shao Qi, enjoy cigarettes while elsewhere the poet Li Bai (李白) looks a little shaky raising a wine cup. The model citizen, Lei Feng (雷锋),[4] looks as earnest and boring as a boy scout while Mao's favorite in-house academic and all round toady, Guo Moruo (郭沫若) has an appropriately sniveling demeanor. Confucius is here too, enjoying renewed popularity since the days that he was rubbished along with Lin Biao (who is not on display here). The figures here are quite vivid and I have to wonder who, or what, is actually in the crystal coffin in the mausoleum across the street. The museum is to be moved to some other prominent location as the Olympics draw near.

Next you should take one of the underpasses in order to cross Chang An Avenue. The underpass saves you crossing the street, but this is as good a juncture as any to bring up traffic direction. In China these days, people tend to drive on the right hand side of the road. Originally, traffic drove on the left hand side of the streets, but sometime between 1925 and 1930 a change was made for "scientific reasons" to adopt the American approach, perhaps in the hope of forestalling growing Japanese ambitions in the north. (Japan is a left-hand drive nation.)

At the very northern end of the square, we come to the Tian An Men (天安门) or the Gate of Heavenly Peace. Before the gate are two large Ming dynasty cloud pillars (华表 or *hua biao*) with stone lions enthroned on top. The mouths of these lions are open, symbolizing that they will report all events of importance to the emperor. (On the other side of the gate are two cloud pillars whose lions have closed mouths. They represent the need for discretion when the emperor travels incognito). The origins of these columns are in the Han dynasty, when common folk posted complaints and pleas for justice on an ornately carved wooden pole outside the emperor's palace. On each side of the southern entrance of the Gate are large marble lions, a typical motif outside the entranceways to palaces and temples. The lion on the right hand side is a male holding a globe while the lion on the left-hand side is a female with her paw over a lion cub.

The Gate of Heavenly Peace is regarded as one of the finest towered gates in the world. It began its existence in the early Ming years as a rather simple wooden memorial arch with the name the Gate For Receiving Heavenly Grace (承天门). The gate burned down twice, first in 1465 and again in 1644 during Li Zi Cheng's attempt to capture Peking. In 1651, emperor Shun Zhi rebuilt the gate in its current form.

In front of the Gate of Heavenly Peace, the top candidates in the imperial examination were honored while magistrates affirmed the death sentences of prisoners by placing a red check against their names on imperial edicts. Here also government officials read imperial proclamations for the enthronement of new emperors. The very last imperial edict was issued here on February 12, 1912. The regent for emperor Xuan Tong (Henry Pu Yi) exercised imperial authority on behalf of his six-year-old son and announced the cessation of the Great Qing Empire and the establishment of the Republic of China. In terms of constitutional law, few republics have come into existence by way of imperial fiat. The decree stated:

> "The Whole Country is tending towards a republican form of government. It is the Will of Heaven, and it is certain that we could not reject the people's desire for the sake of one family's honor and glory."

> "We, the Emperor, hand over the sovereignty to the people. We decide the form of government to be a constitutional republic."

> "In this time of transition, in order to unite the South and the North, We appoint Yuan Shi-kai to organize a provisional government, consulting the people's army regarding the union of the five peoples, Manchus, Chinese,

Mongolians, Mohammedans, and Tibetans. These peoples jointly constitute the great State of Chung Hwa Ming-Kuo [i.e., the Republic of China].

"We retire to a peaceful life and will enjoy the respectful treatment of the nation."

A wonderfully anomalous situation arose. In theory, a republican president governed the vast continent that made up China while, at the same moment, an emperor continued to reign in a territory that did not extend an inch beyond the Forbidden City.

As we pass under the gateway, the newest occupant of the place of honor, one of Mao's last official portraits, beams down on us. In the 1920s and 1930s, a blue pastel portrait of Sun Yat Sen graced the central entranceway of the gate. Later came a sign reading "New East Asian Order" posted by the Japanese occupation forces. In the late 1940s, a giant portrait of Chiang Kai Shek, also painted in light blue and made from crushed gasoline cans soldered together, was placed on the tower of the gate. It was not all that significant of a place.

This all changed on October 1, 1949 when Mao declared the establishment of the People's Republic of China here. From then on, it became a part of the national emblem of the People's Republic, and the tower would host Chinese and foreign dignitaries during the annual October 1st celebrations. It was also from this gate that Mao oversaw demonstrations by a million Red Guards in support of reorganizing society in accordance with his thought.

During the demonstrations of 1989, a couple of hooligans from Hunan province secretly made their way to the tower of Tian An Men and heaved paint-filled balloons on the benevolent features of Chairman Mao's portrait. Instantly a severe wind swept across the square, forcing people to take cover from the supposed wrath of the emperor.

For the payment of fifteen Renminbi, we can climb up to the sacred spot where Mao made his declaration and plain-clothes police snarl menacingly at the crowds. In all, this Chinese socialist Kabba is a bore and probably not worth the effort.

However, we can linger for a moment or two and reflect on a poem entitled *Chairman's Tomb and the Emperor's Palace.* It was originally posted on Democracy Wall, though it is fittingly recalled at this spot.

> Chairman's tomb and Emperor's palace
> > Face each other across the square.
>
> One great leader in his wisdom
> > Made our countless futures bare.

> Each and every marble stair case
> > Covers heaps of bone underneath.
>
> From the eaves of such fine buildings,
> > Fresh red blood drops everywhere.[5]

On the whole, Tian An Men Square has born witness to many dark and disturbing episodes in modern Chinese history. Before we leave the square, we should take note of a joyful Old Peking custom that can be observed from the gate: kite-flying. From this vantage point, we can see scores of people leaving worldly concerns aside by flying their kites to great heights far above the square.

Peking has always been China's kite capital, and the hobby enjoys an ancient pedigree in the Middle Kingdom. During the Eastern Zhou Dynasty, Mo Zi (墨子), a philosopher who advocated universal love among all people and a competitor of Confucius in the market place of ideas, describes a military engineer of his time who spent three years in perfecting a kite, which remained aloft for three days. Liu Bang's lieutenants excelled at designing and flying kites. At this time, kites were often used in warfare as secret codes to send messages from besieged cities to allied troops coming to their rescue. It appears that kites became a popular hobby around 900 A.D., because one of the Song emperors enjoyed flying them outside his palace gate. In the Ming and Qing dynasties, the best-crafted kites were sold to the imperial family and its retinue. The pastime was not relegated to children as many of the kites required years of experience in order to be flown expertly. The great Peking opera performer, Mei Lan Fang, was reputed to be the foremost kite-flier in Peking before the Japanese occupation.

Old photographs from the 1920s show a dazzling selection of kites made up as birds, butterflies, propeller-driven airplanes and dragons. The artistry in making Peking kites far surpassed the diamond-shaped Western kites made of newspaper and a white cloth tail. Then, as now, the most common were kites shaped like birds, and in particular the sand swallow, which mimics perfectly a bird in flight. The sand swallow kites are cheap and easily mastered. When flying them in the azure skies over Peking, the kite flier can savor several pleasurable hours where he will forget himself and his earth-borne worries. The most difficult to fly are the kites shaped like centipedes, in essence a collection of smaller kites linked together.

Kites are flown in the Square during all seasons except, sensibly, deep winter. The best times of year are early spring and mid autumn when strong columns of wind from central Asia pass high overhead. Of all the sights in Tian An Men Square, this wonderful pasttime of the common people predates all the tangible monuments of emperors old and new.

5

ZHONG SHAN PARK AND THE ANCESTRAL HALL

THERE ARE TWO PARKS, ORIGINALLY set up for imperial ceremonies, bordering each side of the Gate of Heavenly Peace. To the west is the main entrance for the Zhong Shan Park (中山公园), so named in 1927 as a memorial to Sun Yat Sen. At the beginning of his political career, he adopted the alias *Zhong Shan* taken from the Japanese name Nakayama. The *Guo Fu* (国父 or the Father of the Chinese Nation) picked up this *nom de plume* during his years in exile in Japan.

Upon entering the park from the south, we come across a white marble *pai lou* with blue glazed tiles. This monument has been recycled over the past

A 1930s view of the Imperial Ancestor Hall.

one hundred years. Originally, it was built on Chong Wen Men Nei Avenue at the precise spot where, in June 1900, a Boxer killed the doyen of the foreign diplomatic community, Baron Clement August von Kettler.

Zhong Shan Park and the Imperial Ancestral Hall

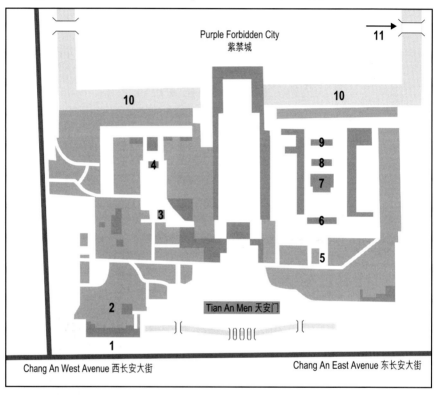

1. South Gate of Zhongshan Park （中山公园南门）
2. von Kettler Memorial Arch
3. Altar of Land and Grain （社稷坛）
4. Zhong Shan Hall （中山堂）
5. South Gate of Imperial Ancestral Hall
6. Halberd Gate （戟门）
7. Front Hall （前殿）
8. Central Hall （中殿）
9. Rear Hall （后殿）
10. Imperial Moat （护城河）
11. To the Courtyard

On that summer morning, the Baron was on his way to the Qing foreign affairs bureau to protest the rise of death threats by Boxers against foreigners. In keeping with the norms of his era, Von Kettler possessed an intense sense of rectitude and an imperialist scorn for non-whites. The day before his murder, he had beaten a local with his walking stick because the hapless Chinese had apparently "glowered" at foreigners while passing through the legation district in an ox cart. The poor fellow was sharpening a kitchen knife at the time, which the foreign community took as irrefutable justification for the Baron's assault. More despicably, Von Kettler also kidnapped a young boy traveling with the man and kept him hostage in the German Legation, where the youth later died of undetermined causes.

I cannot help but think that the creep von Kettler had it coming to him. The Kaiser's government had a different take of the incident. Howling in protest, the Germans insisted upon the construction of a *pai lou* by the Qing government as an act of contrition. Though long since erased, the *pai lou* once bore an imperial apology in Chinese, Latin and German, which reads in translation as:

> The monument is erected in order to point out that what is good, is good, and what is evil, evil. Let all Our subjects learn lessons from the past occurrence and never forget them. We order this.

The former von Kettler Memorial, now in Zhong Shan Park.

I admire the language selected by the Qing government. It can be read quite correctly as a condemnation of von Kettler. After China joined the allies in World War I, the memorial arch was cashiered and re-erected in Zhong Shan Park with a new inscription: "Right Triumphs Over Might" (公理战胜), a touchingly naïve sentiment from the heady days of Wilsonian idealism. Another metamorphosis occurred after 1949 when the arch was deployed to demonstrate the PRC's pacifist polices. The calligraphy of the Chairman's in-house intellectual and all round toady, Guo Mo Ruo, now graces the top of the arch with the inscription "defend peace" (保卫和平).

Carrying on to the north, we come to the Altar of Land and Grain (社稷坛 or *she ji tan*). Yong Le originally constructed these grounds as the site for two of the most important imperial ceremonies. Each spring as farmers began plowing throughout China, the emperor held a ceremony in reverence of the God of Soil (太神 or *tai shen*) and the God of the Harvest (社稷 or *she ji*) along with prayers for a bountiful harvest. In the autumn, the emperor returned to give thanks to these gods for the harvest. The origins of the ceremonies trace back to the Western Zhou dynasty. They consisted of imperial percussive music and a restrained dance performance for the pleasure of these ancient deities, whose favor was essential for the country's well-being. One aspect of the ceremony reflects the importance attached to the clarity of the emperor's prayers. Four men in official robes stood at each corner of the altar with long bamboo poles to shoo away any birds that might fly overhead and thus interfere with the heaven-ward transmission of these prayers to the two gods. Local versions of *she ji tan* were built in each provincial capital as well.

The altar is a white marble square containing soil of five different colors representing the five directions in which imperial authority stretched across the empire (white — west, green — east, black — north, red — south, and yellow — center). To the north of the altar is the *She Ji Dian* (社稷殿) where ceremonial instruments were kept. It is now called Zhong Shan Hall (中山堂 or *zhong shan tang*) in honor of Sun.

The hall as well as all other exhibits in Peking about Sun skip over an interesting fact about his fundraising skills. In the early 1890s, a Japanese intelligence agency called the Black Ocean Society funded Sun's revolutionary activities. Sun's goals were seen to coincide with those of the Society, which sought to expand Japanese influence in Korea. After the turn of the century, another shadowy quasi-official Japanese agency which took the name the Black Dragon Society (after a northern province in China) was founded to expel Russians from Manchuria and spread Japanese control throughout Asia. Once again, Sun knew where to go to get his bread generously buttered. Some writers speculated that only death prevented him from embracing Japan's theory of the Great East Asian Co-prosperous Sphere. This news about the Father of the Country tends to make propagandists on both sides of the Taiwan Straits uneasily shift their weight from one shoe to another.

Off to the east of the hall, there is a small collection of green wooden tubs filled with water and housing various types of goldfish. Little children rent fishing tackle in an unsporting attempt to hook the little fish. This scene brings to mind the many goldfish sellers who did business here during the 1920s. Goldfish are native to China and have been raised as pets since the 900s. The poet Su Shun Qin mentioned them in a poem written in the 11th century: "I stand on the bridge spanning the river/And enjoy watching the goldfish swim by (沿桥待金鲫／竟日独迟留)."

The varieties are bewildering at first. The most common is the red colored "grass fish" (草鱼) which commonly decorate residential courtyards. They thrive on mosquitoes and water fleas, the latter being sold by itinerant peddlers in Old Peking. Grass fish are hearty creatures that withstand manhandling by overly affectionate children. Another common type is the Dragon Eyes (龙眼 or *long yan*), with pop eyes and flowing tails in four branches. The Sky Gazers (望天儿 or *wang tian er*) are grotesque fish with two eyes perched on the top of their skulls.

There were also large fields full of green wooden tubs of goldfish to the north of the Temple of Heaven during the imperial era. Old Peking folk recall seeing Manchu nobles accompanied by their Manchu and Chinese wives, going for a stroll in the late afternoon, dressed in their finest robes. Numerous willows provided a pleasing backdrop of greenery. Goldfish Alley (金鱼胡同 or *jin yu hu tong*), now the address for the Palace Hotel and discos of dubious repute, also contained an extensive goldfish market. Alas, the only legacy of this custom appears to be in this quiet quarter of Zhong Shan Park.

We can leave the park by the western gate and make our way back to Chang An Avenue. On the east side of the Gate of Heavenly Peace we come to the extensive grounds of the second imperial park, now the Workers Cultural Palace, formerly the Imperial Ancestral Hall (太庙 or *tai miao*) for the Ming and then Qing ruling families. The grandeur of design and use of space is a good warm-up for the architecture of the Forbidden City.

The Imperial Ancestral Hall was built in 1420 as an exact replica of a similar temple in Nanjing. On account of natural and man-made accidents, the hall has been rebuilt countless times though it retains its original design. During the Ming, the Imperial Ancestral Hall housed the wooden ancestral tablets of the deceased members of the Ming imperial family. After the Manchus occupied Peking, the Ming tablets were replaced with those of the Qing ancestors.

The Imperial Ancestral Hall was the official site for ceremonies of ancestor worship by the emperor. However, given the importance of this ritual, there were other sites around the city where imperial predecessors were revered. For example, a separate "family" hall for more informal prayers to Ming and Qing ancestors was set up in the Forbidden City. To the north of Coal Hill is the Hall of Imperial Longevity (寿皇殿 or *shou huang dian*) for storage of portraits of deceased emperors. So as to take no chances of sabotage from an aggrieved imperial ghost from another dynasty, the Temple to the Successive Generations of Emperors (历代帝王庙 or *li dai di wang dian*) on the western side of the imperial city housed spirit tablets for emperors of extinguished dynasties.

In the 1970s, the hall was used to house the ashes of Zhou En Lai, Kang Sheng and other party luminaries before internment in Ba Bao Shan Cemetery. More recently, Giuseuppe Puccini's *Turnadot* was staged here in September 1998 in a stunning symbol of New China's entrepreneurial spirit with an opera almost comically steeped in Old Orientalism. The opera's plot revolves around a prince from "Tartary" who seeks to win the hand of Princess Turandot, a headstrong woman living in "ancient times."

Nowadays we need to make our way past a children's park by the southern entrance in order to enter the main part of the hall. Then you go over a marble bridge and through the Halberd Gate (戟门). The main section of the hall consists of three separate buildings set upon a three-tiered marble balustrade, a feature reserved solely for buildings of the highest imperial dignity. These buildings are the Front Hall (前殿), where the emperor offered sacrifices to his ancestors, the Middle Hall (中殿), where tablets were stored, and the Rear Hall (后殿) where the tablets of remote ancestors were stored. The supplementary halls to the east and west were used to house the tablets of Mongolian and Manchu nobles.

While the original contents of the Imperial Ancestor Hall have been scattered to the four winds, we can get a sense of the old custom by visiting the secondary hall to the west of the Front Hall. Here there is an exhibition of the spirit tablets for the emperor Qing Tai Zu (清太祖), Nurhaci, Shun Zhi and Kang Xi, each placed upon a miniature throne as befitting the spirit of a former Son of Heaven.

The emperor and his retinue came to the Imperial Ancestral Hall to report to his ancestors on the current state of affairs in the empire and to offer sacrifices in the form of incense, various cooked viands, grains and silk. The ceremonies in the hall were the imperial counterparts of ancestor reverence practiced by all Chinese. In each person's home, there was a household ancestral altar, set up in memory of three preceding generations of deceased ancestors. The more well to do might construct a separate building as an ancestral shrine to contain the tablets of long lines of deceased ancestors.

These ancestor rites were not empty rituals conducted for form's sake. Rather, it was believed that the actual spirits of the deceased returned to earth and entered the spirit tablets to attend these ceremonies. In this rather poignant fashion, the divide between the living and the dead was bridged. No one lost sight of the fact that every person is linked in a long chain of existence that imposes moral obligations on behavior.

David Kidd tells a moving story about a family ancestral shrine in his *Peking Story*, a memoir of his marriage to an aristocratic Peking woman and their life with her family. He recounts a trip to his wife's ancestral shrine on the side of a lake. Being once affluent, the family of Kidd's wife had maintained the temple's tablets for many generations along with the portraits of the deceased relatives. Kidd's wife could not recognize all of the relatives in the portraits but knew that they all shared her surname and that she was their descendant. The temple contained hundreds of tablets and paintings.

Shortly after 1949, Kidd took a second trip to the lake. While rowing a boat, he saw that a rather ugly concrete bulkhead had been tossed up between the temple and the lake. Citizens of the New China were sunning themselves on the embankment after a swim. Kidd did not row to the temple, but on his way to the shore, he passed floating tablets taken from the family temple and tossed into the lake, either for amusement or mindless vandalism by the interlopers. That evening, he was deeply troubled by a dream where he stood before all his wife's ancestors as they demanded why he did nothing to protect them from this ignoble treatment.

One foreign scholar foresaw the consequences of this type of material development and spiritual regression in 1910:

> If there is one statement about China that can be made with perfect assurance it is this: that if in the long process of reform she learns to despise and throw aside all the supports she has leaned upon thousands of years, if she exchanges for Western substitutes all her ideals, her philosophy of life, her ethics, her social system, she may indeed become rich, progressive, powerful in peace and war, perhaps a terror to the nations, but she will have left behind her very much that was good and great, she will have parted with much that was essential to her happiness and even to her self-respect, she will be a stranger to herself. And what will be the outward aspect of China of those days? Great industrial cities there may be; harbors thronged with ocean-liners and with great battleships flying the Dragon flag; miles of factories, barracks, arsenals and shipping-yards; railway trains, motor-cars and airships coming and going incessantly from province to province; warehouses, banks and stock-exchanges full of myriads of buyers and sellers, each straining every nerve to excel his neighbor in the race for wealth. And where, in this picture of China's possible future, are the thousands of ancestral temples where to-day members of every family meet to

do homage to their honored dead and to renew bonds of kinship one with another? They are to be seen no more. In their place stand thousands of village police stations.[1]

A walk along the imperial moat behind the Zhong Shan Park and the Imperial Ancestral Hall is especially enjoyable in mid-spring when the leaves of the willows have returned and the lilacs are in bloom. Here the old and young alike still perform scenes from the pageant of Old Peking life. Outdoor barbers clip the hair of customers seated on folding chairs on the sidewalk by the moat. In imperial times, these barbers played a secondary role as spies. They reported to the municipal guard any Chinese who had cut their queues, which was a crime of sedition during the Qing. On summer days, young children scamper along the street, dressed in loose smocks with their hair shaved into little round tufts on the forelocks. They look just like the children on the cover of a Chinese almanac or New Year posters. Vendors here sell pinwheels, an age-old Peking toy for young children who take delight in the spinning colors. Elderly men, usually dressed in blue cotton jackets and caps, enter into gentle but firm debates with rejoinders such as: 对不起，我的扣子没系好，把您露出来了 ("Excuse me sir, but I don't think my pant's buttons are done up and it seems that you have fallen out.") Other ancients squat on the sidewalk to enjoy a leisurely smoke with a long-stemmed pipe, probably filled with a blend of tobacco and marijuana that is favored by rural folks.

You might encounter the false hospitality of greetings shouted by passers-by. David Rennie noted that often foreigners were permitted residence in Peking, they frequently encountered children shouting "wei lo." Rennie, as well as Arlington seventy years later, could not figure out the meaning or origin of the term, as it is not standard Mandarin, though both felt that it was certainly not an honorific. I wonder if it was just early attempts by Chinese to say "hello." On that score, as we stroll around the area outside the Forbidden City, you might encounter the great-great grand children of Rennie's street youths, calling out "Hello," with a Peking *tu hua* addition of an "r" sound. The mocking salutation sounds like "Hellorrrr." A child only does this foreigner baiting in a group since there is no fun in badgering a bear if there is no audience applause.

In summer, you will see cricket vendors here as well as in other parts of the city. Properly called katydids in English, the rearing of crickets for pleasure is an age-old Peking past time. You will see a vendor with dozens of ball-shaped cages made of corn stalk that makes a prison for a grasshopper of two to three inches in length. There are many varieties of these little creatures. The Oil Gourd grasshoppers (油葫卢 or *you hu lu*) are a plump species that is renowned for its long-winded singing, which sounds somewhat like the quivering of a poorly dressed person in a stormy winter night. Golden Bells (金钟儿 or *jin zhong er*) are tiny grasshoppers that emit metallic chirps. Leisured people of Old Peking once kept them in little porcelain vases to magnify their music. Rattler Heads (梆儿头 or *bang er tou*) have a peculiar owl-shaped head. The most common are *guo guoer* (蝈蝈儿) who have oily black bodies, strong legs and bright green wings and a coloring of pink along their snouts and bellies.

People in Peking raise grasshoppers because of the sense of nostalgia invoked by their singing. The arrival of grasshoppers signals the harvest season and the advent of another winter, events that remind us of the passing nature of this world.

Grasshoppers are also kept for cricket matches, where the cricket owners provoke their proxies to wage battle against each other, which is a little bit like a couple senior partners of some international firm baiting two junior employees. When finally provoked enough to attack, the skirmish lasts about two minutes, with one of the grasshoppers being awarded the palm by either killing or maiming his competitor. Myself, I would rather just have the little guys sing.

One summer, I purchased three *guo guoer* and kept them until October. Old folks in Peking leave their grasshoppers in the corn stalk cages or, if feeling flush, will buy little wooden cages so that their grasshoppers can move about more freely. Though each one was of the same species, I found that my three grasshoppers had markedly different personalities. One was very withdrawn and usually quite reluctant to strike up a tune. Another had a penchant for striking dramatic poses, with his arms spread out as if to say "hark, who goes there?" whenever I jostled his cage. The third one just loved to eat and became visibly animated with joy whenever I placed vegetable scraps into his cage.

In summer afternoons, the three grasshoppers syncopated their chirping as if they were a jazz combo. One fellow would keep a steady beat as the other two took turns soloing on the offbeat. As the weather turned cooler, their jam sessions became less frequent. With the approach of cold weather, I turned them loose so that they could enjoy their final days in freedom. Once I opened the doors of the cages (or cut away part of the corn stalk cell), they were very reluctant to run away. Once they stepped outside their prison cells, they stayed by their cages for an hour or two before gradually wandering into the garden.

Around these back alleys behind the Imperial Ancestral Temple and Zhong Shan Park, you will also see people airing more substantive and long-lived pets. In Peking as well as throughout all of China, people love to raise birds. In the courtyards of many houses in the old neighborhoods, you can see one or more bird cages, hanging from the eaves to catch the sunshine. In order to give the birds a change of scene, elderly folks take the cages with them for a walk along the alleys or to the local park. The birds seem to enjoy the daily rocking and airing; they will go on strike and not sing if they are deprived of this daily perk. The birdcages are often delightful works of art with carvings of ancient noblemen and ladies enjoying a rustic setting. In keeping with Chinese emphasis on symmetry, little round birdcages house little round birds while pointy cages are reserved for pointy-headed birds.

The common birds in cages include the canary, the "Yellow Bird", the Mongolian Lark, the *Zi Zi Hei Er* (自自黑儿) and the *Tian Ke Er* (靛胲儿), who all are noted for their singing as well as their longevity. Since they are indigenous to northern China, they tend to live for many years, unlike transient birds, which are caught on their migration to the south and seldom survive the Peking winters.

Sometimes you will see a citizen of Peking strolling with a small bird poised on the end of a stick. These birds are those that have become accustomed to constant handling by humans and who learn to take their food from their master's hand. Later, a chain is attached to their foot or around their neck and then anchored to a stick. As they have given up dangerous thoughts like seeking freedom, they contently perch upon the stick while being taken on a stroll by the moat.

These are gentler days for Peking's birds. During the Cultural Revolution, some bright light hit upon the idea of an anti-bird campaign. In addition to attacks against bird-raising as a feudal pastime, the little creatures themselves were libeled as grain thieves and class enemies. In order to rid Peking of these so-called pests, every neighborhood was coordinated into groups that would bang pots and pans for an entire day. Frightened by this incessant din, the birds remained in constant flight until they dropped dead from exhaustion. There is film footage of tractors proudly pulling carts with mounds of dead birds past the Gate of Heavenly Peace. After the demise of the birds, an insect epidemic duly arrived on the scene in Peking.

Moving up the scale to mammals, you will also see in this neighborhood people walking their Pekingese dogs (叭狗儿 or *ba gou er*). It is written that the first Pekingese were brought to China from present day Turkmenistan during the reign of Tang Gao Zu. They were highly intelligent animals that were taught, among other things, to carry lanterns in their mouths to light the emperor's way at night. In the Song dynasty, emperor Tai Zong received a Pekingese dog named Peach Flower (桃花儿 or *tao hua er*) from an official in Si Chuan. It followed the emperor everywhere and would announce the emperor's arrival by entering a hall first and barking until all officials in audience had knelt down. After the emperor's death,

Peach Flower became despondent and refused to perform similar ceremonies for the new emperor. It is said that the dog died during Tai Zong's entombment and, in accordance with an imperial decree, was buried next to his master.

Leaping to the modern era, the Empress Dowager also adored Pekingese and kept nearly a hundred of them under her supervision. Her favorite dog was named Peony. Like Peach Flower from the Song dynasty, Peony was said to have died of sadness next to her mistress' tomb. It's a sweet story, but actually, a *doppelganger* was ginned up and put down while the eunuch Li Lian Ying sold off Peony to some hustler for a small fortune.

H. Y. Lowe noted that Pekingese dogs fell into two categories: longhairs and short hairs. The short hairs are pugs, like the alien Frank in *Men in Black II*. Longhaired Pekingese were called lion dogs (狮子狗 or *shi zi gou*) and fed rice mixed with sheep liver as well as handouts given by their masters throughout the day. The preferred Pekingese in those years were apricot colored creatures called Gold Silk Pekingese (金丝哈叭 or *jin si he ba*) while a black dog with white legs was called Black Clouds On White Snow (白雪黑云).

Peking connoisseurs had very specific criteria on which to judge a dog. The head should be rectangular without a pronounced snout and with the eyes as far apart as possible and "popped out" in appearance like a goldfish. Its ears should be thick, large and square shaped while its mouth should be long and the tip of the tongue protruding slightly to the left or right corner. (A protruding tongue in the middle of the mouth conjured images of the ghost of hanged persons.) The torso and legs of an ideal Pekingese would be short.

The presence of dog-fanciers reflects another aspect of the return of Old Peking culture. During the Cultural Revolution, dogs were looked upon as the legacy of bourgeoisie tastes and Peking's canines were dispatched without mercy. The ban persisted until the 1990s, when there were still special dog-catching (and killing) departments attached to local public security bureaus. Vendors furtively smuggled in dogs to be sold to Peking's rising middle class, who would pick up their pooches and run off if their paths crossed the police. (Interestingly, in the aftermath of the Anglo-French occupation of Peking in 1860, Peking dog fanciers had to do the same then too in order to keep foreign soldiers from confiscating their beloved pets.) By the mid-1990s, the Peking authorities sensibly concluded that there are more important problems to deal with.

As a parting observation, I have two evocative memories of this part of Old Peking. I once spent an idle hour sitting among the willows and looking across the moat as the setting sun staged a magnificent light show of purple, blue, rose, pink and amber hues. I then strolled off for dinner with friends at the Courtyard,

Imperial moat at night.

which is just around the corner from the moat at No. 95 Dong Hua Men Avenue (东华门大街95号). This makes for a lovely end to a day's wanderings.

Even more beautiful was a late night wintertime stroll with the moats on my left and the stern walls of the Forbidden City on my right. Peking's winter fog, illuminated by an occasional streetlight, and the echoes of my clacking footsteps against the wall and across the moat, erased all sense of troublesome modernity. Two policemen stared at me sullenly as I strolled past the empty Imperial Ancestral Temple on my way home.

6

THE PURPLE FORBIDDEN CITY

LOCATED IN THE HEART OF Old Peking, the Purple Forbidden City is inevitably included in every traveler's itinerary. For that reason, it loses much of its charm from the huge volume of sightseers that visit it each day. When constructing the Purple Forbidden City, the architects of emperor Yong Le never contemplated that thousands of people would traipse through the massive courtyards and up to the dragon throne each week.

There are two ways to avoid the crowds, though neither one is foolproof. I prefer to visit the Forbidden City during the coldest days of December when the winter light deepens the *sang beouf* red hue of the walls and the gray of the flagstones. In the alternative, a mid-afternoon start will enable you to visit a portion of the palaces as the crowds thin out. There may not be enough time to take in all of the Forbidden City with such a late start, but fewer sightseers will make up for that with an enhanced ambience.

These days, tour guides and taxi drivers commonly refer to the Forbidden City as the "Old Palace" (故宫 or *gu gong*). Its formal name is the Purple Forbidden City (紫禁城 or *zi jin cheng*). The palace was indeed forbidden in the sense that only the emperor and his immediate family and retinue could live inside its walls. The initial character (紫 or *zi*) refers to the North Star, which was thought by Chinese astronomers to have a purplish cast. This term inferred that the emperor was "as constant as the North Star" as well as the cosmological center around which all other beings revolved. Since the supreme deity of the Taoists lived on the North Star, it was an appropriate symmetry to have the Son of Heaven live in a palace that was its terrestrial counterpart.

Confucius compared a virtuous ruler with the North Star, which keeps its place while all other stars come to pay it homage. As other stars revolved about

Purple Forbidden City

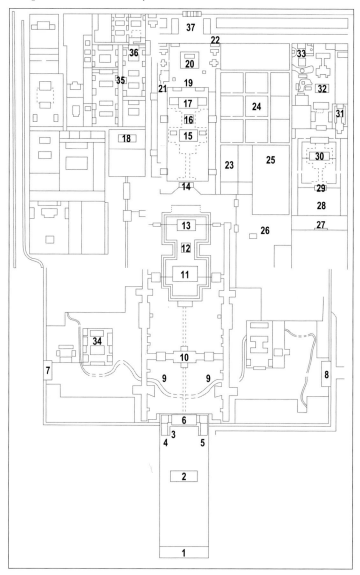

1. Gate of Heavenly Peace（天安门）
2. Gate of Correct Deportment（端门）
3. Moon Watching Site（老外观月角）
4. sun dial
5. gallon measure
6. Meridian Gate（午门）
7. Xi Hua Men（西华门）
8. Dong Hua Men（东华门）
9. Golden Waters（金水）
10. Gate of Supreme Harmony（太和门）
11. Hall of Supreme Harmony（太和殿）
12. Hall of Perfect Harmony（中和殿）
13. Hall of Preserving Harmony（保和殿）
14. Gate of Heavenly Purity（乾清门）
15. Palace of Heavenly Purity（乾清宫）
16. Hall of Union（交泰殿）
17. Palace of Earthly Tranquility（坤宁宫）
18. Hall of Mental Cultivation（养心殿）
19. Imperial Gardens（御花园）
20. First Heaven Gate（天一门）
21. Studio of Character Training（养性阁）
22. Silver Peace Temple（银安殿）
23. Hall of Abstinence（斋宫）
24. Six Eastern Palaces（东六宫）
25. Hall for Worshiping the Ancestors（奉先殿）
26. Arrow Pavilion（箭亭）
27. Nine Dragon Screen（九龙壁）
28. Palace of Tranquil Longevity（宁寿宫）
29. Gate of Imperial Supremacy（乾隆门）
30. Hall of Imperial Supremacy（乾隆殿）
31. Pavilion of Pleasant Sounds（畅音阁）
32. Hall of Pleasurable Old Age（东寿堂）
33. Well of the Pearl Concubine（珍妃井）
34. Hall of Military Eminence（武英殿）
35. Six Western Palaces（西六宫）
36. Palace of Gathering Excellence（储秀宫）
37. Gate of Military Prowess（神武门）

A view north of the Meridian Gate.

the Purple North Star, so too would lesser nobles, officials and foreign tribute bearers come to pay their respects to the Son of Heaven in the Forbidden City. Qian Long implicitly underscored the centrality of the emperor in Chinese cosmology when he replied to the diplomatic correspondence sent by King George III through Lord Macartney's embassy to Peking. Qian Long described China as the focal point around which all other quarters of the globe revolve, thus dismissing the request of the British monarch to open diplomatic relations on the basis of the equality of sovereigns.

We pass under the intimidating tunnel of the Gate of Heavenly Peace and then through the Gate of Correct Deportment (端门 or *duan men*). After several meters of souvenir hawkers and Coca-cola stands, we come to the Meridian Gate (午门 or *wu men*), which was built in 1420 as the official entrance into the Forbidden City. The Meridian Gate is unusual in Chinese architecture in that it has five towers set upon two wings extending to the south. For those traveling further a field, you can see a similar, but slightly contracted, entranceway for the imperial palace of the Nguyen dynasty in the Vietnamese city of Hue.

I strongly recommend that you bring along a well-chilled half liter bottle of Kuei Hua Chen Chiew (桂花陈酒), a sweet local wine, and sit under the western wing of the Meridian Gate some evening as the moon rises in the east. While the shadows extend across the flagstones and Peking settles down to evening song, a tipsy traveler can be lost in thought and float several leagues above earthly matters.

In front of the right and left wings of the Meridian Gate you will see a marble sundial and a marble stand with a traditional gallon measure (called 嘉量 or *jia liang*). These days, no one pays any attention to these silent sentinels that stood as solemn reminders for the court on the relentlessness of time and the exactitude of quantity.

The emperor appeared on a throne placed at the central tower of the Meridian Gate for only a handful of occasions, the imperial halls within being reserved for most other matters of state. From the Meridian Gate, the emperors received prisoners of war captured from border countries, announced the publication of the official almanac and punished errant officials. Since the Ming emperors relied upon public humiliation to coax loyalty from its officials, the Meridian Gate carried connotations of punishment in the minds of most Ming intellectuals. Here, before the Son of Heaven, officers of the Board of Punishments would beat disgraced officials with wooden rods.

Flanking the far eastern and western sides of the Meridian Gate are the Dong Hua Men (东华门 and Xi Hua Men (西华门, smaller lateral gates that were used for the visits of less august officials. Under the Dong Hua Men, the decapitated heads of treasonous capital criminals, including one hapless foreigner at the time of the Boxer Debacle, were hung in boxes as warnings to potential rebels or malefactors. A few meters from the Dong Hua Men and its symmetrical counterpart, the Xi Hua Men, there still stands, on the inner side of the bridges spanning the imperial moat, long forgotten steles written in Chinese, Manchu, Tibetan, Mongolian and Uighur, commanding all those on horse back to dismount before proceeding further into the Forbidden City. The emperor granted the right to proceed by horseback only to those officials who had rendered outstanding service.

From here we can also glimpse one of the elaborate corner towers of the Forbidden City. An Old Peking legend says that Yong Le's architects were at a loss to design towers that satisfied the emperor's demands for innovation. At last, inspiration came from an elderly man who strolled past an architect's home carrying a straw birdcage with an intricate roof. After a round of unsuccessful haggling between the architect and the old man, the birdcage mysteriously appeared on the architect's worktable later that day. Upon reflection, the architect realized that the old man was Lu Ban (鲁班), the patron saint of carpenters and architects and that he had intervened so as to assist his brethren in the craft.

A corner tower of the Forbidden City, illuminated at night.

It is said that Lu Ban was born in Shan Dong province in 606 BC and was a contemporary of Confucius. Legends abound about his carpentry skills, with claims that he built palaces for Taoist deities, invented a wooden self-propelled carriage and created a wooden bird with springs and feathers that could fly and act like a natural bird for three days (batteries not included).

Once past the Meridian Gate, we arrive at the most "public" area of the Forbidden City during imperial times. This section consists of three magnificent courtyards, each with a gate leading to an imperial hall. Using the same motif that we saw deployed for the central structures in the Imperial Ancestral Hall, a three-tiered marble terrace surrounds these three central halls. In order to approach them, we need to pass over five marble bridges spanning a small canal (the "Golden Waters") which flow through the courtyard.

This section of the Forbidden City was first opened to the public in 1914, two years after the prince regent for Xuan Tong issued the decree ending the Qing empire. However, something of the old autocratic spirit still remained in the minds of the palace guards. On the first day of the palace's life as a tourist attraction, the Italian diplomat Daniele Vare recorded the scene:

> The crowd pressed dangerously forward as it came to the bridges [before the Gate of Supreme Harmony], and the soldiers that were on guard pushed them back.

> In the distance we could see lifted sticks fall on the people's heads. [My wife] said something to [our secretary] about it.
>
> All his comment was "Those are not sticks. They are drawn swords." And they were."[1]

Beyond the marble bridges is the Gate of Supreme Harmony (太和门). As you approach the gate, you will walk past a central stairway with a sloping slab of marble, richly carved with dragons and phoenixes. These are motifs that you will encounter repeatedly during our visits to Old Peking's imperial buildings. The emperor was carried in a sedan chair over these carvings while his bearers clambered up the steps on each side of the carved marble. Following the footsteps of the bearers along the imperial path, you approach the Hall of Supreme Harmony (太和殿) in which you can view one of the lacquered wooden thrones of the last emperor, Xuan Tong, which still precisely straddles the central axis. On the marble terrace are eighteen incense tripods, each one representing one of the eighteen provinces of the Qing empire and modeled on ancient bronzes from the Western Zhou era. Two sets of bronze tortoises and cranes, representing longevity and loyalty respectively, stand silently facing south. Four large bronzes pots are placed on the terrace; these were filled with oil and were used for lighting. As prevention against fire from burning incense or oil lamps, iron pots filled with water were placed in strategic spots here and throughout the Forbidden City. I imagine that before electricity, the oil lamps gave the imperial halls a shimmering appearance at night.

Around the throne and on the terrace and courtyard in front of the Hall of Supreme Harmony, nobles and officials gathered to congratulate the emperor on the lunar New Year, the Winter Solstice, imperial birthdays, military victories and other august events. According to Qing protocol, these ceremonies were staged so as to reflect the emperor's centrality to the universe, once again like the North Star. Fifty high-ranking Manchu nobles stood around the throne on these occasions. On the first and second flight of the marble steps stood princes of the first and second rank, with lesser nobles positioned below. Finally, in the courtyard were the imperial military and civilian officials, standing in eighteen double rows according to their rank and dressed in their finest purple or dark blue robes. Clouds of incense billowed out from the hall, obscuring the imperial visage. Within the hall, countless bolts of yellow silk were draped along the walls and floors. Once the emperor ascended the throne, a Manchu noble called out commands, and all those in attendance bowed to the ground in nine prostrations.

In November 1908, the last official enthronement occurred here when ceremonies were held to congratulate a three-year-old Manchu boy named Pu Yi, whose reign name was Xuan Tong, on ascending the throne. Pu Yi called these years his "life in a yellow mist" because of the swirling yellow clouds of incense and yellow silks that attended all of his official functions.

The coronation ceremony for Xuan Tong turned out to be an ill omen for the Qing. Pu Yi was not happy and cried constantly. His father tried to soothe him by saying, over and over, "Don't cry, it will soon be over" (不要哭，快要完了). All officials and eunuchs in attendance took this as an inauspicious omen that the Qing would soon collapse. And it did.

By this time, you might have spied some curious sculptures on the eaves of the hall. These sculptures are elements of traditional Ming and Qing architecture, and a feature that you will encounter repeatedly on our journeys through Old Peking. The eaves host a series of tile beasts, consisting of dragons, phoenixes, scaled lions, sea horses, fire-eating beasts, scaled oxen and a winged animal with a human face leaning upon a sword. At the end of the eaves there often stands a human figure riding a chicken, which is said to be the tyrant Prince Min of the 2nd century B.C., who was lynched from an eave as a lesson to other tyrants.

The second hall is the Hall of Perfect Harmony (中和殿) where both Ming and Qing emperors participated in elaborate ceremonies for receiving nobles and officials. Here the emperors also reviewed the reports on the state of the empire to be read out to their ancestors at the Imperial Ancestral Hall. Again we can glimpse another of Xuan Tong's thrones, which is even more ornate than the one in the Hall of Supreme Harmony.

The last of the three halls is the Hall of Preserving Harmony (保和殿) where each emperor donned imperial robes and waited before leaving for ceremonies elsewhere in the Forbidden City. Here the emperor also held audiences with the highest scoring scholars in the Metropolitan Examinations. The emperor also personally proctored the last examination to determine the three top scoring scholars for that round of the Metropolitan Examinations. On the diplomatic front, Qian Long also held banquets here for Mongol and Uighur chieftains in a bid to gain their acceptance of his rule over their lands.

Behind the Hall of Preserving Harmony is the largest carved marble slab in the Forbidden City. It is decorated with dragons gambolling among clouds, mountains and waves, which are all symbols of the Son of Heaven's presence amidst the three components of the material world. The marble slab served as a bridge between the emperor's official world in the southern throne halls and his private life in the northern residence. This superbly carved marble slab was probably designed so that the emperor's thoughts would turn to the august duties of state as he was carted to the southern halls. Many tourists wander past this magnificent sculpture without taking time to appreciate its artistry.

Since the Great Within (内城 or *nei cheng*) or the emperor's residence is a veritable rabbit warren of palaces, halls, and pavilions, I will divide our tour of the Forbidden City at this point into three sections: the central approach, the east wings and the west wings. Let's carry on with the central approach.

Connected by a marble causeway with cloud and dragon balustrades, we pass through the Gate of Heavenly Purity (乾清门 or *qian qing men*) immediately north of the Hall of Preserving Harmony. On the borders of the Great Within, Manchu guards maintained a strict guard against intruders. In the evening hours, the only people permitted within these northern palaces were the emperor, his wives, concubines and daughters, sons aged less than 15 years and the eunuchs (dubbed "semi-men" by the Jesuit Matteo Ricci). No adult man with a complete firing pin could spend the night in the Great Within.

In these confines, the eunuchs numbered in the thousands. Traditionally, eunuchs were recruited from the ranks of convicts punished through castration or children whose parents entertained unusual notions of upward mobility. Since they socialized with the emperor during his "off duty" hours, many eunuchs found ample opportunities to ingratiate themselves.

The duties of the eunuchs were manifold: they acted as escorts for officials on their way to audiences with the emperor; they supervised the emperor's concubines; they oversaw deliveries of tribute gifts from the provinces and from foreigners; they were the curators of the art galleries and libraries in the Forbidden City; they delivered edicts for publication and distribution. As their salaries were low, they supplemented their income with kickbacks, bribes and proceeds from the sale of stolen imperial goods. If a royal prince wished to present a gift to the emperor, he needed to pay a "squeeze" to the eunuch delivering the gift. With the right incentive, a eunuch could misplace edicts viewed as inconvenient by well-heeled merchants. Eunuchs also often collaborated with concubines for mutual advancement. A eunuch could extol the virtues of a particular concubine, thus encouraging the emperor to spend more time with her. As the concubine's influence grew, she would reward the eunuch for his assistance and, inevitably, fling some imperial patronage in the direction of her family. If the concubine gave birth to a son, her status, and often the status of her eunuch co-conspirator, would undergo an astronomical rise. Some eunuchs siphoned off funds from the Qing treasury for the construction of Buddhist temples, an act that (hopefully) produced merit to offset such sins.

By the mid-19th century, most of the eunuchs in the Forbidden City had been recruited from the ranks of those volunteers who agreed to be castrated. To Westerners (and modern Chinese), this is a mind-boggling proposition. Harry Flashman, the hero of the series by George MacDonald Fraser, neatly summarizes our modern reaction to the phenomenon of court eunuchs in his novel, *Flashman and the Dragon*:

> These eunuchs, you see, are an extraordinary gang; in most eastern countries, they're prisoners or slaves who've been emasculated and given charge of the royal womenfolk. But not in China, where they're absolutely *volunteers*, I swear it. It's a most prestigious career, you see, offering huge opportunities of power and profit, and there are young chaps positively clamoring to be de-tinkled so that they can qualify for the job. Not a line of work that would appeal to me ... [2]

The Manchu guards did not always manage to provide strict security for the Great Within. Stories abound of men posing as eunuchs in order to seek the pleasures of concubines ignored by the emperor. Another legend holds that one of Qian Long's favorite daughters fell in love with a Manchu soldier. After duping the guards, she secreted him in her palace on many evenings until a eunuch revealed the affair to Qian Long. So as not to taint his rule with a reputation for laxness, Qian Long ordered his daughter and her lover walled up alive in a tomb in the Western Hills. The legend holds that country folk could hear the pitiful couple's dying cries for many days.

A nearly fatal breach of security occurred in 1813. A commoner named Lin Qing (林清) founded the Religion of Divine Justice (天理教), which was a sect that exacerbated the Manchu government's fears of popular revolt. Lin seemed to gather support in Peking by promising lower grain prices. With Lin as leader, one hundred cult members stormed the Forbidden City one night, assisted by two eunuchs, who had disclosed several underground passageways. The Manchu guards fled in panic and the rebels reached the causeway leading to the Great Within, intending to enter the palaces and slaughter the emperor Jia Qing and his family. Fortunately for Jia Qing, his young son, the crown prince Dao Guang, had not reached the age of 15 years and was still spending his nights in the Great Within. With the vigor of his ancestors, Dao Guang rallied some of the guards and overpowered the rebels after a day of fighting in the Forbidden City. Lin and his compatriots were executed and their heads put on display around the city.

Once past the Gate of Heavenly Purity, we come to, sequentially going north, the Palace of Heavenly Purity (乾清宮 or *qian qing gong*), the Hall of Union (交泰殿 or *jiao tai dian*) and the Palace of Earthly Tranquility (坤宁宫 or *kun ning gong*), all originally constructed in 1420. These three palaces were meant to be the symmetrical residential complement to the three ceremonial halls in the south of the Forbidden City. The Ming and early Qing emperors and their empresses lived and slept in these buildings specifically centered on the central axis. In the 1730s, Yong Zheng changed this protocol and moved his personal residence to the Hall of Mental Cultivation (养心殿 or *yang xin dian*) in the west wings.

Given his own rather messy and murderous ascent to the dragon throne, Yong Zheng wanted to avoid subsequent squabbles over succession. He implemented a procedure whereby the name of his chosen successor was placed in a gilded box behind the throne in the Palace of Heavenly Purity. Upon the emperor's death, the box was opened and the successor announced. This protocol broke down in the mid-19th century as Manchu factionalism increased in light of the decline of each subsequent emperor's capabilities.

The Palace of Heavenly Purity was the site of celebrated imperial banquets hosted by Kang Xi and Qian Long in a show of reverence for age. In 1722, Kang Xi held a "thousand old men" banquet to celebrate the sixty-first year of his reign. Over a thousand elderly scholars were feted during an evening that became a legend of conviviality and good taste among Peking folks of that era. In 1785, Qian Long imitated his grandfather and hosted a banquet for three thousand elderly scholars on the 50th year of his reign. Qian Long's own sons were detailed off to wait upon those guests over the age of 90.

The Hall of Heavenly Purity was the focus of political intrigues during the closing years of the Qing. In the western partition of the palace, Emperor Guang Xu held his ill-fated audiences with Kang You Wei in 1898. In the main audition hall, the emperor had his quiet discussion with Yuan Shi Kai for the coup d'etat against the Empress Dowager. Yuan promptly betrayed his master and on the orders of the Empress Dowager, arrested Guang Xu and imprisoned him for the remainder of his reign. Had the emperor's plan been successful, China's ensuing history might have avoided some of the misery of the 20th century.

Another throne is to be found in the Hall of Heavenly Purity. After his abdication in 1912, Xuan Tong continued to hold court here on the lunar New Year and his birthday. The imperial family and the remaining court officials assembled here on those occasions and bowed before the young man, a sovereign of three palaces and nothing more. Here, in miniature, continued the imperial ceremonies of the Great Qing until Xuan Tong was forced to flee from the Forbidden City in 1924.

The Palace of Union was originally constructed as the throne room for the empresses of the Ming. During Qian Long's reign, Manchu cosmology maintained that the palace was the central point in the Forbidden City for the convergence of the divine and earthly powers of the universe. Above the throne is a plaque with the Taoist words *wu wei* (无为). This term can be translated as "refrain from [egotistical] action." The underlying principle is to cultivate the self so that you do not need to act because everything will transpire in accordance with your self-cultivation. Here was a Taoist precept advising the emperors in a key hall amidst the Confucian orthodoxy.

As a tangible demonstration of the connection between earthly rule and heaven's blessing, Qian Long placed here the imperial seals of former dynasties, including reportedly those of Qin Shi. They can still be seen here wrapped in yellow cloth.

The Palace of Earthly Tranquility was constructed during Yong Le's reign. With the arrival of the Manchus, the palace was partitioned, and the western half was allocated to Manchu shaman rituals. Prior to their absorption of Chinese culture, the Manchus, like many northern Asia peoples, believed in shamanism. Manchu shamanism did not develop the complicated belief system of Chinese cosmology. Rather, the Manchus conducted rituals that visually depicted their creation beliefs, which bear parallels to rituals and legends from Korea, Siberia and the Pacific Northwest Indians.

Manchu shaman rites were secret, possibly because Chinese disdainfully regarded them as primitive or uncivilized superstitions. In those days, you simply didn't ask about them in Peking. The Manchu court performed these ceremonies in the early morning on imperial birthdays of the emperor and empress as well as on the lunar New Year. These ceremonies usually started with a Manchu soldier cracking a whip three times, followed by the sounding of a huge drum three times. Traditional Manchu music was played as the emperor entered the palace and ascended his throne. At that point, Manchu soldiers, wearing animal skins, animistic masks or costumes of ancient ancestors, began ceremonial dances depicting well-known legends. As the dances increased in pace and intensity, animals were sacrificed and the remains of their carcasses hoisted up a pole outside the palace. Led by a shaman priest, the Manchus chanted ancient songs and danced until sunrise.

In stark contrast (for most people at any rate), the eastern side of the Palace of Earthly Tranquility — richly decorated in red, the color of happiness and joy — was the imperial bridal chamber up through the 20th century. Later in his life, Henry Pu Yi described his less-than-blue ribbon performance during his wedding night in 1922:

> [This palace] was a peculiar room: it was unfurnished except for the bed-platform, which filled a quarter of it, and everything about it except the floor was red. When we had drunk the nuptial cup and eaten some sons-and-grandsons cakes and entered this dark red room I felt stifled. The bride sat on the bed, her head bent down. I look around me and saw that everything was red: red bed-curtains, red pillows, a red dress, a red skirt, red flowers, and a red face …. It all looked like a melted red wax candle. I did not know whether to stand or sit and decided that I preferred the Palace of Nurturing the Mind and went back there.[3]

Passing outside the Palace of Earthly Tranquility, we come to the Imperial Gardens (御花园), which supposedly retain their original appearance from the days of Yong Le. The central building in the Imperial Garden is the Hall of Imperial Peace. Before it stands the First Heaven Gate (天一门), flanked by two *qilin* (麒麟), a mythological beast commonly called "griffins" in pre-1949 China. Chinese legend held that *qilins* had the body of a deer, the hooves of a horse, and a single horn and only arrived in China when a wise and virtuous emperor was on the throne. While the presence of bronze *qilin* may have helped to soothe the ego of most emperors, one enterprising Ming official was able to gin up a *qilin* for Yong Le. On one of the imperial naval voyages to the Indian Ocean, a Ming admiral brought back a giraffe from East Africa and, presumably with a generous flow of fast talk, passed it off as a *qilin*. To the left and right of the First Heaven Gate are rockeries, bronze incense burners and a sizeable grove of cypress trees.

On the west side of the Imperial Gardens is the Studio of Character Training (养性阁 or *yang shen ge*), the former residence of Sir Reginald Johnston, a British official and China scholar who taught English to Henry Pu Yi from 1919 to 1923. You might recall that Peter O'Toole portrayed Johnston in the entertaining but historically inaccurate film, *The Last Emperor*.

Johnston was a fluent Mandarin speaker who spent many years in Her Majesty's government in Hong Kong and the leased territory of Wei Hai Wei in Shan Dong province. His books on China reflect a deep respect for Chinese tradition that was contrary to attitudes of imperial arrogance adopted by many Western officials of that era. On the topic of China's future, Johnston was a dedicated monarchist who felt that a revival of Confucian virtues coupled with the enthronement of a liberal emperor and the enactment of constitutional limitations were the only path for China, a view interestingly proposed by many Peking folks as the Republican era wore on. His insights into traditional Chinese thought and politics still make excellent reading today. He thought that Western proponents of democracy for China in the early 20th century made a common error: how can there be democracy when people do not understand, let alone embrace, democratic principles?

His book, *Twilight in the Forbidden City*, describes China's political situation in the early 20th century and recounts his years of service to the remnants of the Qing Court. It is a treasure trove of information about imperial protocol and the final workings of a system of government first set up in the early Han. Johnston so clung to his idea of a Qing restoration that he welcomed Japanese attempts to exploit Pu Yi for their goal of lopping off Manchuria from China. Sadly, he believed to the very end that Japan would revive the dignity and grandeur of the Qing throne. His book nevertheless makes compelling reading, especially if you seek aimless wandering rather than an orderly inspection of the historical sights at the Forbidden City.

Further to the north is the Silver Peace Temple (银安殿 or *yin an dian*), a Taoist temple first built in 1532 and one of the few structures dedicated to Taoist worship in the Forbidden City. Though Buddhists were in attendance at the court, it is interesting that there are no Buddhist temples here (possibly because of its connotations of a foreign religion). Nearby we come across a large rockery where the emperor and his concubines climbed to view the moon during the Mid-Autumn Festival.

At this point we retrace our steps to the Hall of Preserving Harmony and begin a tour of the east wings of the Forbidden City

Passing through the gate, we come to the Hall of Abstinence (斋宫 or *zhai gong*) where the emperor prepared himself for the imperial ceremonies at the Altars of Heaven, Earth or Agriculture by fasting. For emperors, fasting meant roughing it without wine, music, spicy foods, garlic or onions for a day or two. To the north are the Six Eastern Palaces (东共宫 or *dong liu gong*), formerly residences of concubines waiting to be summoned by the emperor. When the emperor prepared to retire for the evening, he would examine a set of jade tablets upon which were inscribed the names of his concubines. He selected his partner for that night by turning over the tablet bearing the name of a desired concubine, whereupon a eunuch scurried off to find the woman, scrub her down, perfume her up and dropped her off wrapped in silk or furs (depending upon the weather or current fashion) at the foot of the emperor's bed. A meticulous record was kept of which woman spent time with the emperor in case the union produced a child (and also as a means to screen out any by-blows). Phoenixes, the symbol of imperial feminity, abound in the Six Eastern Palaces.

Retracing our steps, we come back to the courtyard behind the Hall of the Preservation of Harmony and turn to the east in order to visit the Hall for Worshipping the Ancestors (奉先殿 or *feng xian dian*). This hall was used for monthly ceremonies for deceased ancestors while the Imperial Ancestral Hall in the southeast annex of the Forbidden City was reserved for the official annual ceremonies. Now the hall houses an extensive exhibit of clocks and watches from the 17th to 19th centuries, given by European monarchs or manufactured in China by the Jesuits.

There is a slightly mournful feeling that attends the display of these clocks and watches. Irreversibly focused on the past, the Ming and Qing rulers never grasped how these intricate little knick knacks were the precursors of a technological skill that morphed into the manufacture of Congreve rockets and rifled-bored repeating firearms.

To the south of the Hall for Worshipping Ancestors is the Arrow Pavilion, (箭亭 or *qian ting*) a Qing structure built in 1752 where the once nomadic Manchus held archery and horseback riding contests. On these grounds, the Manchus also tested the martial skills of the successful candidates of the Metropolitan Examinations. According to Manchu custom about archery, form in shooting was as important as the results at the target. As the Qing dynasty wore on, the ardent interests of the Manchus in such skills declined and the grounds fell into disuse. However, archery was still regarded as an appropriate military skill for national defense well into the 19th century, notwithstanding the contrary arguments sadly offered by Martini carbines.

Towards the northeast corner away from the Arrow Pavilion is one of the three great Nine Dragon Screens (九龙壁 or *jiu long bi*) of imperial China. (The other two are in Bei Hai Park in the Tartar City and in Dadong in He Bei Province.) In an era of interactive special effects and Dolby sound, it is difficult to appreciate the visual impact that these three-dimensional dragons had on people in the mid Qing. Seemingly in flight with each scale pulsating, the nine dragons span the three earthly spheres in a magnificent display of vigor and invincibility. Each dragon has five-fingered claws, a motif reserved as an exclusive symbol of the emperor.

While we are on the subject, "dragon" became a euphemism for the emperor himself. He was called the "dragon's person"; his appearance the "dragon's face"; his children the "dragon's seed"; his throne the "dragon seat." When an emperor died, it was euphemistically described as the emperor "having ascended the dragon to be a guest on high."

Unlike the West, the dragon was always considered a benevolent creature. There were many different types. Some were the rulers of the sea, like Neptune. Others lived in the sky, or among the clouds or deep in the earth. The dragon frequently depicted over doorways is the rain dragon, whose fancy could plunge the country into drought or floods. Dragons were believed to be omnipresent, and dinosaur bones and fossilized dinosaur eggs brought in from the Mongolian deserts were taken as proof of their existence (and then ground into medicine for their presumed restorative effect on virility). The Qing imperial printing office included two dragons circling in struggle for a pearl, in a manner reminiscent of the lion and unicorn at the head of all official British stationery. The flag of the Qing dynasty was an imperial dragon against a yellow background. An echo of this symbol could still be found in the 1990s, since the territorial flag of British Hong Kong depicted a dragon and a lion beside Hong Kong harbor.

Turning to the north, we come to the Palace of Tranquil Longevity (宁寿宫 or *ning shou gong*), which was Qian Long's residence after his abdication in 1795.

Qian Long did not wish to appear to be an unfilial grandson by having a reign period longer than his grandfather Kang Xi. For this reason, he abdicated after his sixtieth year on the throne and withdrew to this palace where he hoped to supervise the activities of his successor, Jia Qing. However, by the end of his reign, Qian Long had lost his authority to a bannerman named He Shen who was his closest advisor. For the last years of Qian Long's life, He Shen ruled the empire in the name of Qian Long, to the intense frustration of Jia Qing. Once Qian Long had ascended the dragon to be a guest on high, Jia Qing finally was able to cashier He Shen, who had reportedly acquired a personal wealth estimated at three hundred million pounds sterling at that time.

On the right, the Gate of Imperial Supremacy (乾隆门 or *qian long men*) leads to a causeway that takes us to the Hall of Imperial Supremacy (乾隆殿 or *qian long dian*). Further to the north is the Pavilion of the Ceremony of Purification, where the emperor and his guests used to conduct a drinking game that dates back to the poets of the late Han dynasty. Wang Xi Zhi (王羲之), a scholar noted for his calligraphy, invented a game where he floated wine cups down a maze-shaped brook. If the cup floated to one of the guests, he would have to compose a poem or drink the wine for the forfeit. The garden is evocative of something more elegant than the legions of XO cognac bottles that fill tumblers at banquets these days.

Further along, you will pass the Pavilion of Pleasant Sounds (畅音阁 or *chang yin ge*), a three-storied pavilion used for the performance of Peking opera. Although Qian Long built the Pavilion, the Empress Dowager, who was immensely fond of this art form, extensively used it for performances that occurred on certain key holidays of the lunar calendar or for special events, such as the Empress Dowager's 60th birthday. Far outstripping Bayreuth's marathon festival of stultifying boredom, these operatic performances were held everyday for six to seven hours for a two-week period.

Continuing to the north, we come to the Hall of Spiritual Cultivation (养性殿 or *yang xing dian)* and the Hall of Pleasurable Old Age (乐寿堂 or *le shou tang)*, both of which were formerly treasuries in the Qing era. Inside is an impressive selection of jade from the Western Zhou dynasty until the Qing dynasty.

Ancient Chinese treasured jade because its translucent appearance suggested that it was a suitable material for communicating with the spirit world. In the Western Zhou era, jade utensils were used for funerary rites and ancestor sacrifices. Zhou kings gave noblemen jade scepters as a symbol of their authority and as a reminder of their obligations to the unseen world. Later, charms and Buddhist deities were carved in jade to underscore the cosmological bond between the people in the material world and the invisible souls next to us in the ether.

The Chinese classify jade in three categories: the general type called *yu* (玉), the dark green variety called *bi yu* (碧玉), and the emerald green variety called *fei cui* (翡翠). These three descriptions are only the tip of lexographic ice berg, as illustrated by this quote from a Manchu author in 1777:

> There is a river in Yarkand in which are found jade pebbles. The largest are as big as round fruit dishes, or square peck measures, the smallest are the size of a fist or chestnut, and some of the boulders weigh more than five hundred pounds. There are many different colours, among which snow white, kingfisher green, beeswax yellow, cinnabar red, and ink black, and all considered valuable; but the most difficult to find are pieces of pure mutton fat texture with vermillion spots, and others of bright spinach green flecked with shinning points of gold, so that there two varieties rank as the rarest and most precious of jades.[4]

Given that a considerable amount of Qing jade came from the far western regions, Chinese Muslims specialized in the trade and carved exquisite masterpieces in the form of incense barriers, brush pots, vases, wines vessels, seals and plaques, some of which are on display in the Hall of Pleasurable Old Age.

As we leave the Hall of Pleasurable Old Age, we pass a small well cover, which is the Well of the Pearl Concubine (珍妃井 or *zhen fei jing*). In the last moments before the imperial court fled from the Allied armies in 1900, legend maintains that the Empress Dowager ordered the death of Guang Xu's "Pearl Concubine," the most beloved of his consorts. One story maintains that the Pearl Concubine encouraged Guang Xu to remain in Peking, face the Allied invasion and assert his own authority over the old witch. The Empress Dowager ordered her eunuchs to throw the concubine in to the well in the presence of the stricken Guang Xu.

The Empress Dowager had her own version of the incident. Perhaps fearful of the Pearl Concubine's ghost, the Empress Dowager wove a story of the concubine's heroism, claiming that the Pearl Concubine had virtuously committed suicide after being left behind accidentally when the court scurried off to Xian. By looking at the tiny size of the well, it strikes me that the Pearl Concubine must have avoided oils and sugars extensively used in the Manchu cuisine of those days. It isn't even large enough for a midget, let alone an imperial consort.

For our tour of the west wings of the Forbidden City, we return to the Hall of Preserving Harmony, either through the central approach or by retracing our steps.

At the time of this writing, the southwestern approach to the Hall of Military Eminence (英武殿 or *wu ying dian*) was blocked for repairs. The hall was originally constructed as a place where the emperor purified himself before battle by fasting and being apart from his concubines. In the final days of the Ming, the one-eyed rebel Li Zi Cheng directed the affairs of his short-lived Shun dynasty from here.

Turning to the northwest, we reach the Palace of Cultivating the Mind (养心宫 or *yang xin gong*), built in 1537, which was the residence of every Qing emperor from Yong Zheng to Henry Pu Yi. The palace is shaped in a horizontal H, with the southern hall formerly used as an office for the emperor and the northern hall as a living room. The front gate sports a jade tablet with a five-fingered dragon, and in the Hall, the western bay holds a painting by the great Jesuit painter, Giuseuppe Castiglione, executed in a manner to extend the impression of the room's depth.

The room to the east was where the Empress Dowager supervised or, less charitably, manipulated the official activities of the child emperors Tong Zhi and Guang Xu. Behind the emperor's throne in the eastern bay is a yellow curtain. Behind that is another throne where the Empress Dowager sat while the emperors gave an audience. Some argue that this is conclusive proof of the perfidy of the Empress Dowager. Actually such "eaves-dropping" settings were commonly used by Qing regents.

To the north are the Six Western Palaces (西六宫or *xi liu gong*) that served as the residences for the imperial family. The northernmost of the Six Western Palaces is the Palace of Gathering Excellence (储秀宫 or *chu xiu gong*), where the Empress Dowager celebrated her 50th birthday in lavish ceremonies that disgusted Sun Yat Sen who was visiting Peking at that time.

From here we can turn to the east and then approach the northern gate of the Forbidden City, the Gate of Military Prowess (神武门 or *shen wu men*). At the time of writing, the tower housed an exhibition of Japanese art work given as tribute gifts to the Ming and Qing emperors. The exhibition celebrated thirty years of diplomatic ties between China and Japan while tactfully ignoring other wrinkles in the modern diplomatic history of these two countries. (In 2005, a different note is struck on account of Japanese historical revisionism of school texts, with organized protestors heroically throwing stones at the Japanese embassy.)

While the Meridian Gate was the main entrance for official ceremonies, court officials usually entered the Forbidden City through the Gate of Military Prowess in order to attend more routine affairs of state. In the early morning hours, Manchu noblemen and court officials assembled for their imperial audiences outside this gate, beating their arms together to keep warm and purchasing warm roasted chestnuts from street side vendors. The practice of morning audiences carried on even in to the twilight years of Pu Yi's residence in the Forbidden City. Here is a recollection published in 1923:

Twists and turns among imperial balustrades.

In the bitter cold of early morning, while it is dark, the mandarins come in Peking carts or carriages, wearing their voluminous fur-lined official robes of dark plum-colored silk. Their basin-shaped or fur-faced hats, with black aigrettes and thick red fringe, are topped with jeweled buttons, the coloring indicate each one's rank; and their numerous outriders on shaggy ponies always accompany them. As they arrive without the gate, each is saluted by the gray line of soldiers guarding it, and enters into the palace courtyard through it, by sedan chair, on horseback or foot, according to his rank .... Along the sides [of the gate] are food venders, gathered with steaming caldrons where often the officials passing in and out will stop and take a hasty bite. The eunuchs from within the palace, too, constantly come and go; some with long shaggy queues are dressed in coolies' clothes and others with slender pipes and silken tobacco pouches hanging at their sides in richest satins, with precious jewels studding little round black silk hats; or still another group in long coats of brightest blue brocade.[5]

When considering the last years of the Qing court, the name "Gate of Military Prowess" is ironic. It was through this gate that Guang Xu and the Empress Dowager fled, disguised as commoners, from foreign invaders in 1900. In 1924, the "Christian General" Feng You Xiang forced Henry Pu Yi to leave the Forbidden City through this gate.

It had bitter memories for others as well. In 1923, as a response to corruption, theft and arson by the attendants of the imperial household, Pu Yi expelled hundreds of eunuchs from the Great Within. For most of these exiles, they had known of no home other than the Purple Forbidden City. For several days they loitered on the north side of the gate, somewhat like my freedom-stunned crickets when they came out of their small wooden cages, until they gradually drifted away to the Buddhist temples and specially created retirement homes outside the Great Within. Today gigantic Hino buses, foot-sore tourists and taxi touts congregate on this spot, obscuring the melancholy dramas that unfolded here.

7

THE EASTERN IMPERIAL CITY AND ENVIRONS

THE ORIGINAL EASTERN SECTION OF the Imperial City Wall ran along Bei He Yan Avenue (北河沿大街) and Nan He Yan Avenue (南河沿大街). A small sliver of the red wall with its yellow glazed tiles still stands near the intersection with Di An Men Avenue (地安门大街). I think it makes for a pleasant addition to expand the scope of this tour to include some sights that were actually in the section of the Eastern Tartar City that abutted the Imperial City.

We will start at the corner of Dong Dan Avenue (东单大街) and Jian Guo Men Nei Avenue (建国门内大街). Turning to the east on Wai Jiao Bu Street (外交部街), the first major entranceway on the north takes us into the pre-liberation era residential housing built for foreign doctors at the Peking Union Medical College Hospital. The hospital, like other institutions with a sense of taste and history, has elected to revive its original English name. During the Cultural Revolution, the hospital sported the name "Peking Anti-Imperialist Hospital." When a *New York Times* reporter fell ill in 1971 on one of the first visits to the New China by a team of American journalists, the hospital staff thoughtfully covered up all anti-imperialist slogans in the hospital in order to save the feelings of the journalist (who knew no Chinese anyway).

The buildings are lovely two storied brick houses with porches and chimneys, all in a park-like landscape. Hospital staff still live in these elegant remnants that were reportedly designed by a Dutch architect.

Carrying on further to the east, we come to No. 33 Wai Jiao Bu Street. Here we can see the baroque four-columned entranceway to the former Tsungli Yamen (总理衙门)or foreign affairs office of the Qing dynasty. Pictures from the late 19th century show that the Tsungli Yamen originally occupied a traditional courtyard house. In the 20th century, a large Western style building, complete with the

Eastern Imperial City and Environs

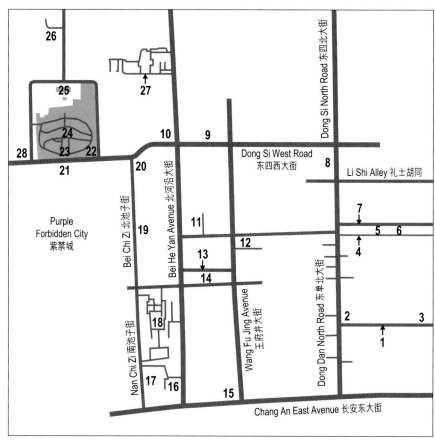

1. Wai Jiao Bu Street（外交部街）
2. former foreign doctors residence
3. former Tsungli Yamen（总理衙门）
4. Shi Jia Alley（史家胡同）
5. Luxembourg Embassy
6. Hao Yuan（好园）
7. Nei Wu Bu Alley（内务部胡同）
8. Dong Si Mosque（东四清真寺）
9. Art Exhibition Hall（美术馆）
10. Red Building（红楼）
11. former Residency of Lao She（老舍故居）
12. St. Joseph's Cathedral (Eastern Cathedral)（东堂）
13. Pewter Lane（锡拉胡同）
14. night vendors

15. Peking Hotel（北京酒店）
16. Returned Students Club
17. Imperial Archives（皇史宬）
18. Mahalaka Temple（玛哈喇嘎庙）
19. Temple of the Thunder God（凝和庙）
20. Temple of Cloud God（云神庙）
21. Prospect Park（景山公园）
22. Chong Zhen's tree
23. Tower of the Beautiful View（绮望楼）
24. Pavilion of the Thousand Springs（万春亭）
25. Hall of Imperial Longevity（寿皇殿）
26. You Qi Zuo Alley（油漆作胡同）
27. Wax Storehouse Alley（蜡藏胡同）
28. Hall of High Heaven（大高玄殿）

existing columns, replaced the courtyard house. To the west within the gate, we can see several traditional Chinese studios that might have been attached to the original building. The area now is an apartment complex for staff of the Ministry of Foreign Affairs.

Returning to Dong Dan Avenue and turning to the east on Shi Jia Alley (史家胡同), we pass the minute Luxemburg embassy, located in a spot within the former city walls and well away from the diplomatic compounds further east. I imagine that this might be the only legacy of the pre-liberation embassies that were located near the city center. Continuing further east, there are three preserved courtyard houses at Nos. 51, 53 and 55 Shi Jia Alley. The last address, called Hao Yuan (好园), now functions as a hotel with traditional style courtyard rooms comfortably renovated and furnished with modern conveniences.

As we continue north along Dong Si South Avenue, more classic courtyard houses can be seen at No. 11 Nei Wu Bu Alley (内务部胡同) and No. 129 Li Shi Alley. All of the side streets off Dong Si Avenue are wonderful for a winter evening stroll as the snowflakes gather upon the stone drums outside the doorways.

After emerging from the alleyways, we can circle back to Peking's largest mosque, which is at No. 13 Dong Si Avenue (东四大街). It was built in 1356 and reconstructed in 1447 with funds donated by the Ming Muslim general, Chen You (陈友). In 1450, the emperor Jing Tai (景泰) issued an imperial decree renaming the mosque the Temple of Purity and Truth (清真寺), a term that has become the standard Chinese name for all mosques in China. As is the case with nearly all ethnic Chinese Moslems in Peking, the imams are extremely courteous to foreign visitors, especially Mandarin speaking ones, though you should wear conservative clothing in respect of local sensitivities.

The Dong Si Mosque covers over 10,000 square meters and is said to combine Ming and Islamic architectural elements. The interior is richly engraved with gilded Koran quotations. Among other relics, the Mosque has a Yuan dynasty copy of the Koran, a stele inscribed in Chinese and Arabic recounting the restoration and a portion of the original bronze minaret cast in 1468. The mosque also served as a lodge for visiting Muslim tribute missions because of its close proximity to the Forbidden City.

The Muslim community in China can trace its origins back to the arrival of Arab traders in the early Tang dynasty. Broadly speaking, the community has two components: the *hui min* (回民), who are ethnic Chinese that have embraced the faith, and Uighurs, who are the original Turkish inhabitants of Xin Jiang. There are more than 200,000 Muslims in Peking and over 60 mosques to be found in back alleyways. The Dong Si Mosque gift shop sells quotations from the Koran, written in Arabic but executed with the brush techniques of Chinese calligraphy. They are intriguing samples of how Chinese Muslims intertwined faith and culture.

In 1729, Yong Zheng issued an edict proclaiming that Chinese Muslims were to be regarded as the children of the emperor because their customs were fundamentally the same as other Chinese. Later on, Qian Long took the same position. While Chinese Muslims in the city had a separate identity, they flatly rejected assertions about their fifth column status.

Turning west on Dong Wu Si Avenue (东五四大街), you will come to the Art Exhibition Hall (美术馆) built in 1962. While there are no permanent exhibitions, it is worthwhile to visit the museum from time to time to check on any new artwork on loan. For example, the museum once hosted a stunning collection of Chagall paintings. Across the street are shops selling art supplies at very reasonable prices for those wishing to dabble in (or deepen) new directions of expression. The sales folks in the shops are helpful.

Continuing to the west you come to the Red Building (红楼 or *hong lou*), the original home of Peking University. "Beida" (北大), as the university is called colloquially, grew from the Tung Wen School, founded in the 1870s by W.A.P. Martin, an American educator and missionary, as an institution to teach Western languages to Chinese students. In 1898 the school was reconstituted as the Imperial University. The university was constructed on the former site of the Temple to the God of Horses (马神庙 or *ma shen miao*), a deity who was of particular significance to the martial forbears of the Manchus. The God of Horses had three eyes and four arms, each of which brandished a sword. Perhaps as a distant recollection of the Arabian origin of China's finest horses, Peking folk believed that the God of Horses was a Muslim. Accordingly, broiled mutton was an essential offering and none but the most unlettered would offer pork to the august lord.

By the early 20th century, the adherents of the cult of the God of Horses had dwindled. Once members of a group enjoying imperial patronage, their numbers had dwindled to horse farmers, black smiths and stable keepers. By 1911, the temple was long gone and the grounds turned over to the Imperial University, now renamed as Peking University, where the institution remained until its removal from its cramped quarters to the spacious ground of the former Yen Ching University on the outskirts of town in 1952.

I am getting ahead of myself. Martin, the founder of the university's predecessor, arrived in Peking in the early 1870s. He quickly came to the conclusion that education was the best vehicle for propagating the Gospels in China. Martin disdained mere proselytizing and sought a way to be of use to the Qing government in order to demonstrate that Christians could be of benevolent assistance to China. It was in this spirit that he translated a standard textbook on international law and practice. At first, imperial officials dismissed the book as unintelligible because they could not make heads or tales out of foreign legal concepts. Later, during a protracted dispute with Germany over a Chinese vessel seized in Qingdao, the Tsungli Yamen resorted to Martin's book when all other avenues had failed. And presto! To the astonishment of the Yamen officials, Germany conceded to the position of the Chinese government, as argued on the basis of principles gleaned from Martin's book. From that point, official use of Martin's book skyrocketed, even though he received no acknowledgement, let alone royalties, from his contribution to China's fight against imperialism. He spent the rest of his life in China seeking a satisfactory synthesis between Chinese and Western culture. He was buried in Peking in 1915.

In May 1919, the Red Building, as Peking folks called it at that time, became the staging point for citywide demonstrations against the Treaty of Versailles. During the post war negotiations, the warlord government acquiesced to Japanese demands to acquire German concessions in Qingdao in exchange for a large loan, the proceeds of which predictably wound up in the pockets of the Peking authorities. These demonstrations grew into the May 4th Movement for the reform of Chinese politics and culture.

During these years, the librarian of Peking University was Li Da Zhao, a scholar, writer, economist and cofounder (with the now-disgraced Chen Du Xiu) of the Chinese Communist Party. In 1918, Li formed the New China Study Group to learn about new philosophies, such as Marxism and Darwinism. One of the members of the study group was Li's library assistant, a lad from Hunan province called Mao Zedong. It is easy to conjure up the image of petulant youth overcharging students for late fees or hiding the reserve reading from foreigners. Actually, Mao's job was to record the names of all people reading the library's newspapers, an experience that probably led him to believe in the efficacy of this type of surveillance in later years. He probably found the world of Peking intellectuals rather intimidating, with few scholars or students having time for a rustic youth. Real or perceived slights probably stung him and gave him a basis for his anti-intellectual policies in later life (not to mention his indifference to Peking's patrimony).

The first floor of the Red Building is open to visitors and contains an exhibit of documents from the New Culture Movement. Off on one side is Li Da Zhao's office. A few classrooms are restored to their original threadbare appearance. The "Beida" spittoons lend a nice homey touch and are enviable souvenirs.

At No. 19 Feng Fu Alley (丰富胡同) off Deng Shi Kou (灯市口), you will find the former Residence of Lao She (老舍故居), the 20th century author who depicted both the splendors and miseries of life in Old Peking. His most famous work is *Rickshaw*, which follows the tragic fortunes of a poverty-stricken rickshaw puller. *Mr. Ma and Son* describes the experiences of two Chinese sent to London during the 1920s and weaves a wonderfully bittersweet story about cross-cultural romance. In the 1930s, Lao She penned a science fiction novel called *Cat Country*. An indirect satire, his novel recounts a Chinese spaceman landing on a distant planet inhabited solely by cats. The political and social conventions of the cats are those of Chinese society in the 1930s, which appall the astronaut.

During the Cultural Revolution, the Red Guards relentlessly hounded this gentle man, one who took delight in the passage of seasons in Peking, the calls of its street peddlers and the sight of darting swallows. Refusing to sacrifice his integrity or his beliefs, he killed himself to escape his tormentors. His home is open as a memorial to his life, and it is rewarding just to sit in his courtyard and absorb some residual positive energy from this gentle author's home.

Retracing our steps, we turn south on Wang Fu Jing Avenue (王府井大街), which once was called the 5th Avenue of Peking. Originally called Ding Zi Jie (丁字街) during the Yuan Dynasty, the street was renamed Wang Fu Jie (王府街 or Princely Mansions Street) when ten Ming princes built their homes here in 1417. Geomancy principles of the time prevented any new wells being sunk, least they interfere with the *feng shui* of the Forbidden City. Since there was only one well of sweet water in the neighborhood, the name of the street changed once more to Wang Fu Jing Avenue or the Street of the Well for Princely Mansions. A bronze marker is placed upon the supposed site of the original well on the west side of the street.

In the 1920s, the street became Morrison Street, so named after the Australian journalist, George Morrison, who had his residence here at the turn of the last century. An intensely ambitious man, Morrison reported on Chinese events for *The Times* of London and zealously advocated an expansion of Britain's influence in the Far East. In keeping with his imperialist beliefs, he seldom hesitated to distort his reports so that Britain would appear in the best light. He despised Czarist Russia and was a tireless supporter of the Anglo-Japanese entente.

Morrison believed that China's political future lay in the hands of Western educated Chinese democrats, like Sun Yat Sen. However, sensing the sure bet of military power, he resigned from *The Times* in 1912 and became advisor and public relations spokesman for Yuan Shi Kai, a move that led to a loss of influence and prestige (as well as astonishment by Western observers that Morrison could so recklessly squander his reputation). Morrison later represented the Peking government during the Versailles Treaty negotiations and died in 1920, acknowledged as the most influential foreign journalist that had ever lived in the city and remembered as a rat by all who had personal contact with him. In later years, historians revealed the vainglorious and arrogant side of Morrison's career in Peking.

Now Wang Fu Jing Avenue has been turned into a gentrified pedestrian zone of Western-style consumer stores. It is difficult to imagine that it was on this street that Derk Bodde first saw the arrival of the People's Liberation Army into Peking in January 1949:

> At their head moved a sound truck from which blared the continuous refrain "Welcome to the Liberation Army on its arrival in Peiping" …. Beside and behind it, six abreast marched some two or three hundred Communist soldiers in full battle equipment. They moved briskly and seemed hot, as if they had been marching a long distance. All had a red-checked, healthy look and seemed in high spirits. As they marched up the street, the crowds lining the sidewalk burst into applause … .

> Behind the soldiers marched students carrying two large portraits, one of Mao Tse-tung and the other presumably of Chu Te, commander in chief of the People's Army. A military band came next and finally a long line of trucks carrying more soldiers, students and civilian employees of the telephone company, railroad administration and other semi-official organizations.[1]

On the east side of Wang Fu Jing Avenue, you can visit St. Joseph's Cathedral, also called the Eastern Cathedral (东堂 or *dong tang*). In the late 1600s, the Dutch Jesuit Ferdinand Verbiest lived here and after his death a church was constructed with the blessings of Kang Xi. The present church was built after the Boxer Debacle. For years it had been entirely inaccessible. In 1999, the Peking government took laudable measures to renovate the square in the front of the church, which now, unfortunately, attracts more than a reasonable flow of New Chinese Youth on skateboards and racing bikes. However, at night, it is a marvellous sight, worthy of the wings of St. Joseph.

On the west side of the street, we come to a non-descript alley called Pewter Lane (钖拉胡同 or *xi la hu tong*). Once the Park Avenue for Manchu aristocracy, the lane was the childhood home of the Empress Dowager before she was whisked away to the harem of Xian Feng. She returned home only once, after having achieved the honor of giving birth to Xian Feng's only son. During her visit, her parents prostrated themselves in front of their daughter, as she was now the Empress Regent. No one would have guessed that she was about to embark on a career of more than fifty years of court intrigue and political upheaval. I imagine that, when young, she looked very much like the children that play now in Pewter Lane and might have reflected nostalgically on her years here as a ruby-cheeked black eyed little girl playing amidst the rubbish and coal bricks.

Keep on your toes around the intersection of Wang Fu Jing Avenue and Dong An Jie. The numerous foreign hotels attract old crows who have learned enough English to chat up a foreigner to cadger some money. Conversations start off with a sucker line like "Oh, my daughter is studying child psychology in Boston" or some other kindly sounding opening. If Ma and Pa Kettle are slow to come across with the dough, the less than *sotto voce* comments, delivered in a rough Peking *tu hua*, by Pirate Jenny to her street side cohorts, grow with a furious intensity. Soon three or four cohorts join her and try to talk the pigeons into some scam. Mind you, not that this only happens at Wang Fu Jing Avenue.

Off Dong An Men Avenue (东安门大街), a night market of street vendors selling various regional Chinese snacks has become a much welcomed institution. The cuisines vary from Peking dumplings to Uighur kebabs to Shanghai noodle dishes. This is a wonderful place for a late night snack.

Carrying on down to the intersection of Wang Fu Jing Avenue and Tian An Men East Avenue, you will turn to the west and pass the oldest hotel in the city, the Peking Hotel. It was built in 1917 by a French consortium and immediately became the place of preference to stay in Peking. After 1949, the municipal government took over the management of the hotel and built two annexes, one immediately to the west of the hotel in 1954 and another to the east in 1973. Most recently, a five star luxury hotel was added to the western annex.

The main entranceway of the hotel once (long ago) housed the book shop of Henri Vetch, who published foreign language books on Chinese culture in the years of Old Peking elegance. After 1949, the hotel was the host for countless visitors on friendship or peace delegations from bellicose countries in the Communist block or the so-called Third World. In the early 1980s as China opened its door to Westerners again, the hotel housed offices of foreign businesses and news agencies. In the past several years, the hotel has been given a face-lift that has erased any sense of nostalgia but will appeal to the nouveau rich from Orange County or Peking's far flung villas.

After the completion of the 1973 annex, Peking officials were thunderstruck to learn that a hotel guest could draw a bead very easily into the Zhong Nan Hai compound from the top floors of the hotel. To solve this problem, a solely tactical structure was constructed on the west side of the Forbidden City to obscure the view.

As one of the few places where foreigners could buy a meal during the 1970s, the Peking Hotel saw interesting clashes between the outside world and the New China. One friend tells me of an occasion when a mixed group of foreigners were drinking beer on the rooftop café of the hotel. As the evening progressed, somebody knocked over an empty bottle, which shattered on the floor. A waiter stormed up and rudely insisted that the accidental culprit pay not only for the beer, but the deposit for the bottle. The waiter's tone struck a nerve that I recognize. It lies hidden in all expatriates in Peking and produces astonishing, unimagined bursts of fury over heavy-handed treatment doled out by Peking's apparatchiks. In a flash, every customer on the rooftop was picking up empty bottles and smashing them on the floor. This protest quickly devolved into a pitched battle between staff and foreigners, who, upon gaining the upper hand, burst out into the stairwells and down into the streets where they rioted and fought with pedestrians and automobiles. (Peking does have a way of gloriously sparking its long-term foreign residents into unusual and unpremeditated spectacles.)

Another foreign acquaintance tells of a different incident. While he was staying in the hotel sometime in the early 1980s, a spontaneous demonstration broke out one night. China's football team had just won a match against a Western team (perhaps Albania?). Hundreds of Peking folks marched to the hotel, long viewed as a foreign enclave, shaking their fists in hostile triumph and chanting "We beat you, we beat you, we beat you to death!" It would have taken a little more than a glass of buttermilk to stop the ruminations that night.

Walking out of the Peking Hotel, we can turn briefly down Nan He Yan Avenue (南河沿大街). On the west side of the street at No. 111 is the former Returned Students Club. Starting in the 1880s, the Chinese government sent students to Europe and North America to learn the ways of foreign devils in order to be able to navigate the world of diplomacy a bit better. In 1916, the club was established upon the site of an old temple called Pu Sheng Si (普胜寺) constructed in 1651 as a memorial to the conquest of China by the Manchus. A stele in Chinese, Manchu, and Mongolian still stands inside the club recording this fact (assuming, of course, that you can negotiate your way past the man in green at the gate).

Ambling back to Chang An Avenue, we take the next northern turn through an archway in the red wall. Nan Chi Zi (南池子) is another ancient street of Old Peking that carries many vestiges of the imperial past, including a recently installed park nestling on the north side of the Imperial City wall. On the east side of Nan Chi Zi we come to the Imperial Archives (皇史宬) originally built in 1534 with fire-proof walls in order to house imperial records. These records were invariably the official histories of events, rather than true ones. During the Qing era, the amount of paperwork doubled as documents had to be kept in both the Chinese and Manchu languages.

There are two sections to the Imperial Archives. The front section, close to the intersection with Chang An Avenue, has become private residences. It makes for a pleasant wander among the decrepit buildings and the little courtyards where the residents brighten up the scene with caged birds, bamboo stalks, and red-colored door posters. The main entrance to the Imperial Archives is further to the north and presently houses an art gallery.

Continuing to the north, you will plunge into the back alleys in order to come to the Mahalaka Temple (玛哈喇噶庙) also know as Pu Du Si (普度寺). At the time of writing, the temple had been renovated and the recently built brick *ping fang* cleared away leaving the temple in the midst of a square-shaped tier.

Since its construction, this site has been connected with non-Chinese border regions. It was originally the home of the Ming emperor Zheng Tong after his return from captivity in Mongolia. Shortly after the Qing conquest, a new courtyard house was built here for Dorgon (多尔滚), the regent for the emperor and the strategic visionary of the Manchus.

Dorgon was the grandson of Nurhaci and the regent for his nephew, the young Qing emperor Shun Zhi (who assumed the Qing throne in Mukden before the invasion). Upon the collapse of the Ming, Dorgon's troops entered the city unopposed. At one juncture, Dorgon himself, in great animation on a street corner, tried to explain to Peking's citizens in his broken Chinese that the Qing troops had entered Peking only in the benign interest of preserving order for its citizens. The crowd only imperfectly understood his Chinese and wondered who the foreigner was. They soon knew.

Though only a "partially-cooked barbarian" to use the happy Chinese phrase, Dorgon thoroughly understood the Chinese psyche. After governing Chinese in Liao Dong, he knew that the Manchus needed popular support. In a bid for legitimacy, Dorgon created a fiction premised on Confucian theory. The reckless actions of Li Zi Cheng compelled the Manchus, who were motivated only by ethical concerns, to occupy Peking in a bid to restore social order. Once the Manchus were installed in the capital, the Mandate of Heaven compelled them to govern in place of the Ming in the interests of social stability.

It worked. Dorgon shrewdly made a show of adopted Chinese customs and rule. The Confucian bureaucracy and the examination system were to continue. The Qing emperor performed the annual rites at the altars and temples throughout the city, thus comforting the populace with the knowledge that these new rulers were mindful of Heaven. The remains of the last Ming emperor were given a proper burial in an imperial tomb amidst those of his ancestors

Dorgon was killed in a hunting accident in 1657. In the 1930s, Arlington and Lewisohn reported that his armor and weaponry could still be seen, dust-laden and forgotten, in a corner of the temple.

After Shun Zhi's death, Kang Xi converted the palace into a Mongolian lama temple in 1691 with the unique distinction that the lamas there were obliged to recite the Buddhist scriptures in vernacular Mongolian rather than Tibetan.

Another legend about Lu Ban, the patron saint of carpenters, relates to this temple. Once again, an architect found himself in trouble with his imperial overlords because he had designed a temple whose roof was disproportionately small for the hall. The architect was on the verge of suicide. However, on that day, the chef who had been assigned to prepare meals for the workers became ill and was replaced by an unknown itinerant, who wound up cooking an over-salted meal. When confronted with this complaint, the substitute cook simply said over and over again "I put too much salt in" (加重盐 or *jia chung yan*). The architect pondered these words and suddenly realized that they were a pun meaning add another set of eaves (加重檐), whereupon the cook disappeared. The extra set of eaves was an innovation that remedied the defect and gave a distinguished appearance to the Mahalaka Temple. Once again, Lu Ban in disguise had saved the neck of another architect.

The Sanskrit word "Mahalaka" refers to the "Demon Protector" of Lamaism, a deity that corresponds to Siva of the Hindu pantheon. In past years, the temple housed a large statue of Mahalaka depicted as a blue skinned apparition, with a necklace of skulls and standing upon the crumbled bodies of corpses. The ferocious appearance was not meant to instill fear or connotate evil. On the contrary, Mahalaka's appearance testified to his strength as a defender of Buddhism and its adherents.

In the 1930s, foreigners leased courtyard homes in the vicinity of the Mahalaka Temple and recalled the sounds of the monks' chanting in the early mornings. With liberation, the temple was converted into a primary school. Mahalaka has long since hoofed it out of town.

Finding our way out of the Mahalaka Temple and back onto Nan Chi Zi, we carry on towards the north. On the east side of the street we pass two temples whose roots are in Chinese animism. The four halls of the Temple of the Thunder God (凝和庙 or *ning he miao*), built in 1770, now serve as a secondary school, though the Temple's popularity with local Peking residents had already entered into a steep decline in the 1920s. As Juliet Bredon noted, "it is rather pitiful and makes one feel as though a revered tragedian had suddenly lost favour with the public, since his most magnificent gestures no longer have the power to thrill the audience."[2] In its day, the "Ministry of Thunder" employed over 800 supernatural officials, ranging from the God of Thunder, who was the big cheese with a head in the shape of a bird, to little goblins with the endearing job title "cloud pushers."

At the intersection of Bei Chi Zi (北池子) and Wu Si Avenue (五四大街), we come across the Temple of the Cloud God (云神庙 or *yun shen miao*) built in 1730. The main entrance is to the south and can be visited by pushing open the old red doors so that we can see its run-down main gate along with the decaying Bell and Drum Towers. The main hall of the temple to the north now is a Senior Cadre Retirement Home.

An alternative route on Nan Chi Zi route is to turn west on Dong Hua Men for a stroll along the walls of the Forbidden City bordering the imperial moat. Late during a foggy night in winter, you can almost hear the wall's soul as moonlight glistens off the frozen waters of the imperial moats.

Both routes take you to Prospect Park (景山公园 or *jing shan gong yuan*) directly to the north of the Forbidden City. The more common English name for the park is Coal Hill (煤山 or *mei shan*). Since the principles of Chinese geomancy consider northern exposures to be a source of bad fortune, Ming engineers constructed hills with soil dredged from the moats and imperial lakes as geographic spirit screens against bad luck. Five separate hills were made, an odd number allied with *yang* forces. A pavilion adorns each hill in the park, each built in 1758. The central pavilion straddles the central axis of the city. While a Peking legend claims that the hills were built upon loads of charcoal left over from the Liao dynasty, there seems to be no physical evidence to support the name Coal Hill.

Entering the park from the east gate and circling to the south, we come to a sophora tree planted at the spot where the last emperor of the Ming, Chong Zhen (崇祯), hanged himself. At the time of his death, the Ming had been in slow collapse for several decades. While Chong Zhen attempted to combat corruption, his efforts amounted to "too little too late." Famines and floods ravaged the countryside in those parts where local authorities had misappropriated funds for disaster relief.

The immediate cause for the end of the Ming was Li Zi Cheng, the one-eyed bandit who raised the standard of rebellion from the south. Chong Zhen desperately sought a military commander who could repulse Li's invasion, though all of his generals had proved incompetent or unwilling to take on the challenge. When the time came for the bandit army to breach the city walls, Li Zi Cheng and his troops were surprised that the capital fell easily to them. Li led his troops through Fu Cheng Men on his way to the Forbidden City (along the same route, interestingly enough, used by the PLA in June 1989). His troops looted and burned as he made his way to the center of the city. As he approached the Gate of Heavenly Peace, Li shot an arrow at the character heaven (天) and missed, which must have made him pause to wonder whether the Mandate of Heaven was in his hands.

Looking north from Coal Hill.

In the Great Within, Chong Zhen heard that the rebels breached the city walls. Delirious with grief, he seized a sword and struck down his empress and concubines as his remaining troops abandoned the city. A fire broke out in the southern section of the Forbidden City, soiling the blue spring sky with black scars. Chong Zhen walked out the north gate, his hair disheveled, his clothes soiled with the blood of his family, and his gait hobbled as he had lost a shoe. In these last moments, his only company was his closest eunuch, Wang Zhen En (王真恩).

After entering Prospect Park, he knelt down and begged his ancestors to forgive him. On the lapel of his sleeve, he wrote his last edict:

> I, feeble and of small virtue, have offended against Heaven. The rebels have seized my capital because my ministers deceived me. Ashamed to face my ancestors, I die. Removing my Imperial cap and with my hair disheveled about my face, I leave to the rebels the dismemberment of my body. Let them not harm my people.

Wang Zhen En assisted the emperor's suicide and then followed him to the Yellow Springs.

Until the early 1900s, the chain with which Chong Zhen hanged himself was still to be found on the sophora tree. The original tree was chopped down during the Cultural Revolution. Now another grows in its place.

At the south gate of Prospect Park you will come to the Tower of the Beautiful View (绮望楼 or *qi wang lou*) built in memory of Confucius and now operating as a shop of non-descript goods. As you ascend the hills by way of the stone paths to the crest of Prospect Park, you might be lucky enough to spy hoof-prints in the stones. I have often wondered whether they were left by the horses of Jiang Qing (江清), the wife of Chairman Mao and the most reviled person of 20th century Chinese history. During the Cultural Revolution, Jiang Qing used the park as her private grounds for horseback riding. In 1976, she along with her three fellow ideologues, the so-called Gang of Four, were arrested and tried for crimes committed during the Cultural Revolution. She resolutely defended her actions by asserting (rightfully) that she had the Chairman's full approval. In 1993, she died in prison by her own hand. These hoof-prints might very well be the only tangible trace of her awful existence in Peking.

On the central hill is the Pavilion of Ten Thousand Springs (万春亭 or *wan chun ting*), where you can savor a panoramic view of Peking's palaces. The Buddha statute in the pavilion is one of a series of replicas that have sat here since the Germans hauled away the originals after the Boxer Debacle.

From the pavilion, I can point out other sites for our wanderings. You can select just the ones that are the most appealing or visit them all, if you are feeling robust after such a long walk.

Direct to the north of the pavilion is the Hall of Imperial Longevity (寿皇殿 or *shou huang dian*), which was built in the mid Ming. On each lunar New Year, the emperor came to the hall in order to offer sacrifice to portraits of China's priors rulers, from the legendary Fu Xi to the emperor's own predecessors. Off to the northeast of the enclosure is the site where emperors and empresses were lain in state before burial in the imperial tombs. The buildings are now part of a children's park where the guards use a military precision to shoo away any foreigner who has temerity to ask to see the historic sights inside. For more than a decade, I have consistently encountered the rudest behavior of all of Peking's gatekeepers, presumably because the administration here wishes to protect its children from foreign contamination. We will have to content ourselves with viewing the hall from the summit of Coal Park.

Looking further north, we can see apartment buildings with traditional Chinese roofs on both sides of the central axis. Liang Si Cheng, the unfortunate architect who dared to argue for the historical preservation of Peking, was the designer of these buildings. Off to the northwest, near Di An Men Nei Avenue and down You Qi Zuo Alley (油漆作胡同) is the former residence of Deng Xiao Ping and his grey office building.

To the northeast is Wax Storehouse Alley (now called 腊藏胡同 or *la cang hu tong*), which was the 1930s residence of author George Kates. Called the "Oyster" by Peking's foreign community, Kates spent seven years in the old city in pursuit of that delicious sin of "going native." He lived in a traditional courtyard house, learned classical Chinese and drank deeply of the elixir of Old Peking culture. His memoirs were entitled *The Years That Were Fat,* an allusion to the Book of Genesis. Kates resurrects the elegance of pre-Liberation life, from the cries of the street peddler to the political squabbling of his domestic staff. Nothing remains of Kate's courtyard home. Nevertheless, I like to stroll down this *hu tong* in homage to the man.

Finally, to the west of the summit at Coal Hill you can see the circular blue tile roof of a pavilion in the Hall of High Heaven (大高玄殿 or *da gao xuan dian*), a Taoist temple built in 1542 in honor of the Jade Emperor, the overlord of the Taoist world of spirits. Legend holds that the Jade Emperor was initially a normal mortal, though extremely kind and generous to the poor. After many years as a hermit, he ascended into heaven where he resides in the stars of the Big Dipper along with the Queen of Heaven (西王母 or *xi wang mu*), who maintains a second dwelling in the mythical Western mountains. Some believe that the Taoist schools invented the Jade Emperor as a counterpart and rival to Sakyamuni Buddha. Others say that he is the Chinese manifestation of the god Indra. Among common people, he was believed to be the human form of *shang di* or heaven itself. He is usually depicted in imperial robes with a flat shaped hat with beads hanging in front of his face from the rim. (This was a tool whereby emperors could shield their eyes from unpleasant sights.) Since the Jade Emperor also shared the power of making rain with the Dragon King, emperors came here to beseech his assistance during times of drought. The blue tiles of the pavilion were designed to reflect the sky overhead and can be seen from Coal Hill.

However, we must satisfy ourselves with only a view from a distance since the temple has been a recreational club for high cadres for many years. Interestingly, in his memoirs, Chairman Mao's personal physician, Li Zhi Sui, noted that Deng Xiao Ping was able to avoid the First Lu Shan (卢山) Conference because he somehow managed to break his leg while shooting pool at the club. The good doctor does not explain how this came to pass: whether the future paramount leader of China was trying to execute an especially tricky shot or whether he might have had on board too much *wu liang ye*, a potent distilled concoction from his native province of Si Chuan, the issue is left for our speculation. In any event, the story goes that Deng had to be confined to bed in

Peking Hospital, thus ducking the conference and the fireworks that attended the demise of Peng De Huai's career.

Li goes on to say that Deng, the old stoat, was nurtured back to health by a buxom nurse from Si Chuan whom he somehow managed to knock up despite the impediment of a plastered leg hanging in the air. I have always admired socialist health care.

8

THE WESTERN IMPERIAL CITY

THE TOUR OF THE WESTERN imperial city starts at a place that is strictly off limits for us commoners.

On the north side of Tian An Men Avenue, the New China Gate (新华门 or *xin hua men*) is the formal entrance to the Zhong Nan Hai Compound (中南海), which is the seat of the central government and home to many high-ranking government cadres. Originally, the Zhong Nan Hai Compound was an imperial park with two lakes, the Southern Sea and the Central Sea, connected to the North Sea (北海 or *bei hai*), all of which were built for the sole pleasure of the emperor. After the fall of the Qing, Zhong Nan Hai was partially opened to the public. In 1949, the Chinese Communist Party chose this location for the residence of Mao and other luminaries. Before 1989, Chinese citizens could apply for special permits to enter selected areas of the compound. Currently, only PRC officials with special authorization may enter the grounds.

The New China Gate itself was originally built as the Precious Moon Tower (宝月楼) in 1758. Qian Long ordered the construction of the gate to win the favors of a stubborn concubine.

Qian Long's armies reconquered Xin Jiang and incorporated the homeland of the Turkish Uighurs into the Qing Empire. During the war, the Manchu troops killed a Kashgari potentate and captured his widow, a stunningly beautiful princess with classic Roman features. The Chinese called her the Fragrant Concubine because she always emitted a perfumed fragrance (or maybe because she just washed regularly — the record is not clear). The princess was brought to Peking as prize for the emperor.

Although the Fragrant Concubine hated her captors, Qian Long became quite smitten with this exotic addition to his harem. In a show of reticence that must

Western Imperial City

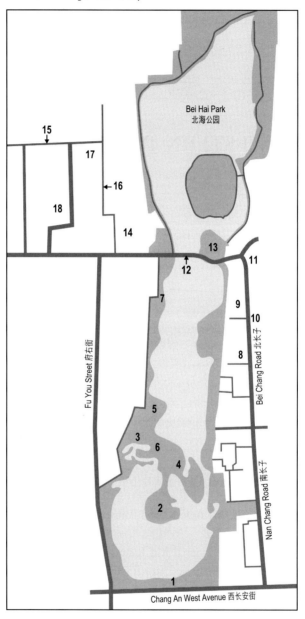

1. New China Gate（新华门）
2. Sea Terrace Island（瀛台岛）
3. Garden of Abundant Beneficence（丰泽园）
4. Longevity Hall（颐年殿）
5. Hall of Ceremonial Phoenixes（仪鸾殿）
6. Building 202
7. Tower of Purple Light（紫光阁）
8. Temple of Thunder God（雷神殿）
9. Temple of Prosperity for Ten Thousand Ages（万寿兴隆寺）
10. Temple for the God of Rain（福佑寺）
11. Office of Panchen Lama
12. Imperial River Bridge（御河桥）
13. Round City（团城）
14. Former National Library
15. Red Sandalwood Buddha Temple Street（栴檀寺街）
16. Grassy Mist Alley（草岚子胡同）
17. Grassy Mist Prison Site（草岚子胡同监狱旧址）
18. Northern Cathedral（北堂）

Bei Hai Park

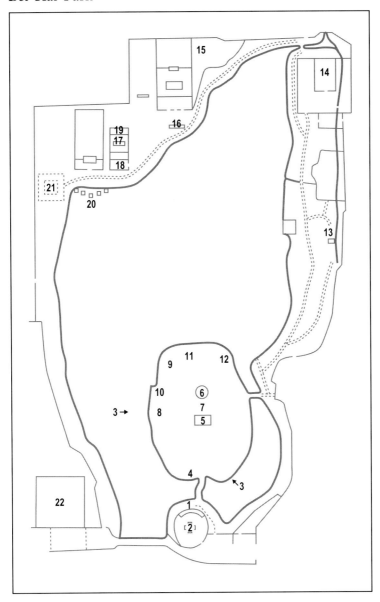

1. Round City（团城）
2. Jade Luster Hall（承光殿）
3. Hortensia Island
4. cultural desecration
5. Temple of Everlasting Peace（永安寺）
6. White Pagoda（白塔）
7. Temple for Cultivating Good Deeds（悦心殿）
8. Yi Fang Shan（一方山）
9. Tower for Inspecting Ancient Scripts（阅古楼）
10. Fang Shan Restaurant
11. Study to Ease the Mind（亩鉴室）
12. Stele with "Spring Warmth of Qing Dao"（琼岛春阳）
13. Pavilion of Freedom from Cares（濠濮阁）
14. Altar of Silkworms（先蚕坛）
15. Studio of Restful Mind（清心斋）
16. Gate of Heavenly Kings（天王殿）
17. Nine Dragon Screen（九龙壁）
18. Iron Shadow Screen（铁影壁）
19. Brief Snow Hall（快雪堂）
20. Five Dragon Pavilions（五龙亭）
21. Tower of Ten Thousand Buddhas（万佛楼）
22. former National Library

have been the talk of the Great Within, Qian Long refused to force himself upon the Fragrant Concubine. Instead, he tried to win her consent to his amorous advances by giving her all manner of precious gifts. For her part, the Fragrant Concubine had only one desire: to be given her freedom and return to Xin Jiang, presumably in order to lead a Uighur war against the Qing dynasty and avenge the death of her husband.

Qian Long spent his days dreaming up ways to please a woman who hated his guts and his empire. One of his gifts was the Precious Moon Tower, built so that the homesick concubine could look off to the west towards her homeland. Additionally, a mock Uighur village, with a mosque and market, were also built right outside the gate in the hope that the Fragrant Concubine would feel at home, soften up and uncross her legs.

Qian Long's infatuation with the Fragrant Concubine posed considerable concern for the government since her charms made him forget about affairs of state. According to one legend, the dilemma was settled by Qian Long's mother who, showing a deep maternal concern for her son's welfare, had the Fragrant Concubine strangled to death while Qian Long was busy with the annual ceremonies at the Altar of Heaven. Her remains were eventually interred in a beautiful Central Asian tomb in the suburbs of Kashgar.

As you peer into the gate, several men in green peer back and intensely watch your movements. From this vantage point, you can only see a spirit screen emblazoned with Mao's exhortation "Serve the People" and admonishing you to get back to work.

On each side of the gate are slogans, the western billboard declaring 伟大中国共产党万岁 (or "Long Live the Great Communist Party of China") and the eastern one with 战无不胜的毛泽东思想万岁 (or "Long Live the Ever-victorious Thought of Mao Ze Dong").

The eastern slogan recalls Mao's personality cult, which was greatly promoted by the now-reviled Lin Biao. Lin was catapulted into super-stardom in the heady days of the Cultural Revolution. While this particular slogan seems to have first appeared on a PRC postage stamp in 1967, it recalls Lin's campaign to deify the Chairman, which included Lin's editing and publication of the famed "little red book" of Mao's quotations.

Before 1949, Lin was the general that secured the Communist victory on the mainland by leading the PLA on its crossing of the Yang Tse River. An anemic looking fellow, Lin assumed entire control of the PLA after Mao ousted Peng De Huai in 1959. During the 1960s, Mao came to regard Lin as a potential successor as well as a collaborator in his ideological fight with the pragmatist faction of the CCP, represented by Liu Shao Qi and Deng Xiao Ping.

Through their devotion, Lin and the PLA became Mao's closest allies in the early years of the Cultural Revolution. Lin had captured the Great Helmsman's approval with an essay proclaiming that the poor countries should implement Mao's Thought by surrounding the capitalists countries in much the same manner that the rural PLA outflanked the urban-based Nationalists. From that time, Lin was regarded as Mao's heir apparent.

However, distrust creeped in, as it usually does in the world of Chinese politics. In 1970, Mao publicly humiliated Lin by repudiating his campaign to glorify Mao. Under the urging of his son, who had his own imperial ambitions, Lin decided that he needed to strike first if he did not want to go the way of Liu Shao Qi. Interestingly, it seems that a Mossad agent in the Kremlin learned of Lin's conspiracy. Tel Aviv passed this information to the Nixon administration, which, in turn, disclosed the plot to Zhou En Lai during Kissinger's secret trip to Peking in 1971. The official story in the PRC is that in September 1971, Lin unsuccessfully launched a coup and then fled the country. Since his plane was not sufficiently fueled, it crashed in Outer Mongolia, where Mao ordered Lin's remains to be buried.

The book, *The Conspiracy and Murder of Mao's Heir,* written by a Chinese author under the *nom de plume* Yao Ming-le and allegedly based upon classified PRC documents, claims that Lin and his family botched an assassination attempt against Mao during one of his inspection tours by train. It goes on to say that Lin and his family were killed by bazooka fire while being driven back from dinner with Mao and Zhou in the Western Hills. Yao suggests that Lin's flight to the Soviet Union was fabricated in order to ensure that his memory would be reviled for generations to come. Aside from his slogans on the gate, tangible traces of Lin Biao can be seen in yellowed 1960s political paraphernalia in the flea markets.

Moving on to recent times, the New China Gate was the focus of a significant protest during the Second Tian An Men Incident. In May 1989, huge crowds gathered outside the gate and taunted an official who happened to be one of China's hard-core torch bearers of the Stalinist line. An interlocuter in the crowd repeatedly hollered out the official's name and the crowds bellowed back the response *liu mang* (流氓 or punk) loud enough for the old darling to hear. It is a satisfying thought.

At the time of writing, Zhong Nan Hai is still a forbidden city in the literal meaning of the term. However, though it is a wistful suggestion, certain sites in Zhong Nan Hai might be opened to the public as China approaches the Olympics. For this reason, I will sketch a description of its sights, though I have never clapped eyes on them except through photographs or binoculars from Coal Hill.

Directly behind the spirit screen is the South Sea Lake, which is separated from the Central Sea Lake by the Sea Terrace Island (瀛台岛 or *ying tai dao*). The island is actually a peninsula, which was frequented by Kang Xi and Qian Long, who sometimes preferred to administer their empire from here because of the captivating scenery. After the 1898 Reform Movement, the Empress Dowager imprisoned Guang Xu on the island, which, ironically was suggested by Kang You Wei as a good prison for the old crow should the reform movement take root. Guang Xu once attempted an escape by fleeing over the frozen lake, probably with the goal of seeking sanctuary in the Foreign Legation district. This soon became a theme repeated by Chinese dissidents or those out of political favor in the 20th century. For example, Pu Yi sought refuge in the Japanese embassy in 1923. Li Da Zhao tried to avoid Nationalist troops by taking refuge in the Soviet Embassy in 1927. Professor Fang Li Zhi (方厉之) went to the American embassy in June 1989.

To the northwest of Sea Terrace Island is the Garden of Abundant Beneficence (丰泽园 or *feng ze yuan*) where the Qing emperors went into dress rehearsals for their ceremonies at the Altar of Agriculture in the Chinese City. Both Kang Xi and Qing Long took personal interest in the construction of this courtyard and the planting of mulberries, which was all well and good since this area became Mao's residence after 1949. Mao used Longevity Hall (颐年殿 or *yi nian dian*), which is a spacious building on the north side of the Garden, for meetings with foreign dignitaries. His private quarters, known as the Chrysanthemum Fragrance Study (菊香书屋) were in the second courtyard with magnificent pines and cypresses towering over wicker chairs and tables.

Carrying on towards the north, you will pass into the Central Lake Park and come to the Hall of Ceremonial Phoenixes (仪鸾殿 or *yi luan dian*). It was here that a dramatic council of war took place on June 20, 1900 when the Grand Council persuaded the Empress Dowager to issue a decree declaring war on the foreign powers. It was also from here that she issued her final decree on November 15, 1908 moments before her own death. She apparently died here while in audience with the 13th Dalai Lama, who was still on the run from the British invasion of Tibet.

Manchu soothsayers had once forewarned that should two living Buddhas meet face-to-face in this earthly world, one of the living Buddhas would have to die and take off for the spirit realm. This prediction was based on the belief that no one world could contain so much of the Buddha's essence. This legend probably first arose on account of the death of the sixth Panchen Lama during his visit to Qian Long, who was an ardent Buddhist and was also regarded as a living Buddha. As the Empress Dowager fancied herself to be a reincarnation of Guan Yin and was called the "Old Buddha" (老佛爷 or *lao fo ye*), her death after meeting the Dalai Lama did not come as a surprise to Peking's lamas.

However, the actual circumstances of her death are still shrouded in speculation. Some accounts say that Yuan Shi Kai, anxious to establish his own dynasty, shot her after her audience with the Dalai Lama. Others say that she was a misunderstood woman who probably died in grief over the death of her nephew, emperor Guang Xu, a story that strains credulity.

At the time of her death, the Empress Dowager had already been dressed in funeral robes embroidered with imperial phoenixes and was immediately placed in the coffin that she had always kept at the ready. Her body was moved from the Hall of Ceremonial Phoenixes to the Forbidden City to wait for an astrologically correct date for burial in the Eastern Qing Tombs.

In the 1920s, travel writers noted that in front of the hall were 12 bronze statues with animal heads and human torsos. The beasts depicted in these statues were the Twelve Animals of the Chinese Zodiac, about which there has been much scholarly debate. It seems that they represent an indigenous tradition that can be traced to the Han dynasty. In a ceremony held before the Winter Solstice, twelve palace attendants wore masks of these twelve animals in order to dispel malicious spirits. A similar ceremony continued at least to the 14th century in Korea.

To the northeast of the Hall of Ceremonial Phoenixes is Building 202, which was specifically constructed as an earthquake-proof residence for Chairman Mao in 1974. Coincidentally, a devastating earthquake hit Tang Shan in July 1976 on the very night that Mao was moved into Building 202, thus rekindling the belief that Heaven sends a signal on the eve of any dramatic political change.

It was also here on the evening of September 9, 1976 that the shadows overtook Mao. In his last moments, he was unable to speak. His sunken and lackluster eyes stared sightlessly at the members of the politburo gathered around his bed, such as Hua Guo Feng, Wang Dong Xing (汪东兴) and Yao Wen Yuan (姚文元). Just before Mao dropped off the twig, Jiang Qing burst into the room shrilly demanding why she hadn't been informed of the Chairman's deteriorating condition. He probably did not know if that was his last sound on earth or his first shriek in hell.

To the north of Building 202, we come to the Tower of Purple Light (紫光阁 or *zi guang ge*). In the 18th century, Qian Long received Mongolian tributary princes here. When the European powers along with Japan and the United States insisted upon a formal meeting with the emperor for the formal presentation of the credentials of their diplomats, Tong Zhi met them in this hall, reserved especially for envoys of lesser states, on June 29, 1873. In continuation with the old tradition, the PRC still receives foreign dignitaries here.

In the northwest corner of Zhong Nan Hai compound is the Hall of the Western Flowers, formerly used as a harem for the Qing emperors and later converted into the home of Premier Zhou En Lai.

If the Zhong Nan Hai compound remains closed to outsiders, you can take a look at the futuristic opera house built to the south of New China Gate. Designed by a French architect, the avant-garde building has been dubbed the "duck egg" by Peking's cab drivers, who know a con when they see one.

Alternatively, in search of Old Peking, you can make your way to the east for the corner of Tian An Men Avenue and Nan Chang Street (南长子 or *nan chang zi*) and turn northward into a beautiful tree lined street. On the west side of the street at No. 83, you will arrive at the Temple of the Thunder God (雷神庙 or *lei shen miao*) the counterpart of the Temple of the God of Thunder on the east side of the Forbidden City. These days, the temple is used as a primary school, with only a few of the original halls still in existence.

At No. 39 Bei Chang Street (北长子), you will come to the Temple of Prosperity for Ten Thousand Ages (万寿兴隆寺 or *wan shou xing long si*), which was a Ming armory that Kang Xi converted into a lamasery in 1700. Gradually, the lamasery evolved into a retirement home for elderly eunuchs. In the years before 1949, 70 eunuchs were still living in the temple. It is now a residential area for the military, so tread softly.

On some of the doors in this neighborhood and elsewhere in Peking, you can see that folks have pasted red papers with the Chinese character for fortune (福 or *fu*) written in black ink. This pleasant custom actually dates back to a King Herod-like event. In Nanjing shortly after the installation of the Ming throne, people used to celebrate the arrival of the New Year by hanging up pictures of a fertility goddess holding a lemon to her breast. Unfortunately, the goddess had unusually big feet. The Ming emperor Zhu Yuan Cheng took this as a personal pique since his empress had a great whacking pair of splayed toed flippers. One night, he ordered his soldiers to paste the character for fortune on all houses that had not posted the offensive picture. The rest were all slaughtered the next morning. Needless to say, this gave quite a boost to sales of red paper posters with the character fortune.

On the east side of the street, you can view the Temple for the God of Rain (福右寺 or *fu you si*) which was turned over to Yong Zheng's lamas in 1728. The temple also served as the temporary abode of Chairman Mao in his salad years during a brief return trip to Peking in 1922. To the north of the temple is a recently constructed office building with Tibetan motifs, such as white walls, brown roofing and rectangular windows. Now, the temple is the Peking Office of the Panchen Lama of Tibet. The restoration and construction of Tibetan style buildings clearly show that Peking has great expectations for their claimant.

At the intersection of Bei Chang Street and Wen Jin Street (文津街 or *wen jin jie*), we turn to the west and arrive at the south entrance to Bei Hai Park, the third of the great imperial seas constructed within the former city walls of Old Peking. The Imperial River Bridge (御河桥 or *yu he qiao*) has been expanded with time. Originally it was a simple two lane marble bridge. Local Peking folk once warned solitary travelers about an elderly man in a black cloak who loitered around the bridge with a donkey cart late at night. He offered his services for a reasonable fare to late night revelers on their way home. In truth, the cloaked figure was a malicious ghost, who sustained his otherworldly existence by drowning his customers in the lakes beside the bridge. Now for night time wanderers there is the more mundane risk of simply being mowed down by traffic.

The contours of the lake took their current form during the rule of Kublai Khan. Marco Polo recorded that:

> Between the two walls of the enclosure are fine parks and beautiful trees bearing a variety of fruits. There are beasts also of sundry kinds, such as white stages and fallow deer, gazelles and roebucks, and fine squirrels of various sorts, with numbers of the animal that gives the musk, and all manner of other beautiful creatures .... There extends a fine Lake, containing fish of different kind which the Emperor hath caused to be put in there, so that whenever he desires any he can have them at his pleasures. A river enters this lake and issues from it, but there is a grating of iron or brass put up so that the fish cannot escape in that way.[1]

At the southern entrance to Bei Hai Park, we come across the Round City (团城 or *tuan cheng*), a fortress-like structure that dates to the Yuan Dynasty. Some say that the fortress is built in the shape of a human skull, a common utensil in Tibetan ceremonies and an important symbol of Lamaism for Mongol Buddhists. Long before the Mongols constructed the walls of the Round City, the hill was part of a royal park built in the Liao Dynasty.

Ascending the stairs, we come across a small grove of ancient trees that were first planted during the Liao. In the 18th century, Qian Long conferred the title High Official for Providing Shade from the Sun (遮阳侯 or *zhe yang hou*) to a Chinese pine growing on the east side of Jade Luster Hall. Next to it, there is a lacebark pine that was bestowed the title White Robed General (白袍将军). Finally, another pine was given the title Sea Exploration Official (探海侯). I like the idea of having trees replace elected officials, especially those from Texas.

In the Jade Luster Hall (承光殿) sits a Burmese style white Buddha which was supposedly brought to Peking in 1890 by a wandering monk as a gift of tribute to the Empress Dowager from the Burmese King in Mandalay. Since the last Burmese king was sent into exile in India in 1885, some doubt lingers as to the

金鳌归里

A Qing impression of Bei Hai Park.

accuracy of the story. Perhaps the monk was simply seeking royal favor. In any event, the statue was well received by the Empress Dowager who bestowed honors upon the monk. The expression of the Buddha is one of extreme serenity, which is very characteristic of Burmese religious sculpture. Apparently the Buddha was "wounded" in the arm by troops during the 1900 occupation of Peking, though I have never been able to discern the scar.

In the south side of the courtyard, we can view a large black jade bowl carved during the Yuan dynasty and sporting an impressive array of sea creatures. One account maintains that the bowl was used as a wine vessel for imperial banquets and was somehow lost in the confusion at the end of the Yuan dynasty. During the early Qing years, the black jade bowl was found in a Buddhist monastery where it had been put to the less glamorous use of pickling vegetables.

According to some sources, black jade does not exist. Be that as it may, the fictional Harry Flashman poached a black jade chess set from the Old Summer Palace in 1860 and used the proceeds to buy his home in Leicester Square. I wonder what old Flash Harry would have gotten for the bowl. Or, for that matter, I wonder why the French forces occupying the park in 1900 didn't cart it away.

Bei Hai pagoda in the 1920s

A contemporary view of Bei Hai Park.

Finishing our tour of the Round City, we descend the stairs and move towards the marble bridge and two memorial arches. The bridge leads us to an island reconstructed in the Yuan dynasty. During the Ming and Qing, it was called Hortensia Island, after a herb that bestows immortality. The island, as well as the surrounding park, was originally created as a royal pleasure place in the 1100s, nearly three hundred years before Yong Le selected Peking for his capital.

Ancient records say that Hortensia Island was completely separated from the rest of the park. At sunset, the lake's barges were moored for the night, with the khans and their consorts left to the seclusion of the pavilions on the island. The Mongols were decidedly picky in their choice of companionship. All women brought to Hortensia Island had to pass muster first with a eunuch, who was commissioned to verify that the women were attractive, well mannered and free from any unpleasant odors that might detract a khan from lovemaking. I am tempted to picture this poor eunuch sitting on the edge of the lake as the barge is poled away at sunset, pondering where this career path led and wondering what lateral career moves could be made with this set of skills.

During the reconstruction of Peking, Yong Le enlarged the gardens and dredged the ponds. In 1651 the religious Shun Zhi constructed the white Tibetan pagoda on the top of the hill in commemoration of the first visit to Peking by a Dalai Lama.

If we cross the bridge to Hortensia Island in the summer time, the surrounding ponds will be adorned with lotus flowers in bloom, a traditional sight of a Peking summer for centuries. They are best viewed on an early August morning before the heat and humidity of the day rises. Buddhist art uses the lotus as a symbol of enlightenment, wisdom and compassion arising from the confusion of muddy darkness.

Once across the bridge, we come to the Temple of Everlasting Peace (永安寺 or *yong an si*). The name "everlasting peace" is a wistful euphemism given the loudspeakers that have plagued this part of the park since the days of Arlington and Lewisohn. Further sacrilege can be spied off to the left hand side where some forward-thinking entrepreneur set up a Kentucky Fried Chicken outlet.

Plunging headlong into the temple, we pass under a memorial arch whose adages are fortunately not a plug for deep-fried poultry parts. The front of the arch reads Imperial Brightness (御光). Ascending the south face of the hill, we pass various pavilions and a large rock carved with the words Kun Lun (昆仑), which happens to be the name of a mythical mountain in Tibet as well as a crummy Peking hotel infested with cockroaches and courtesans in equal measure.

Continuing upward, we come to a set of pavilions constructed by Qian Long in 1773 as a winter viewing stand for his mother to watch Manchu bannermen participate in skating competitions on the lake. Skating, as an imperial sport, has a very old pedigree in Peking such that by the time of Qing Long, the court had developed techniques of "ironing" the surface of the lake to make it smooth for skating. In 1795, Qian Long invited the members of a Dutch trade mission to watch bannermen stage a Qing version of Icecapades. Not having slight experience in the sport, the Dutch offered to give a demonstration of their skills. The ensuing competition that day soured relations between Dutch and Chinese as the sport became a struggle in making the other side lose face. I only hope that my spectacularly ungraceful forays on the ice in the 1990s might have assuaged the feelings of any Manchu spirits lingering around the frozen lake.

Again onward and upward, we take the broad stone path leading to the White Pagoda (白塔 or *bai ta*), not to be confused with another White Pagoda in the Western Tartar city. On the southern face of the pagoda is the Tibetan monogram for the "All Powerful Ten" written in the form of a Sanskrit character called Ranja. In classical times, the number "ten" (十) was regarded as a symbol of perfection. By twisting the ends in a counter-clockwise fashion, you produce the Buddhist swastika, a symbol of perfection transcending time and space.

In front of the pagoda is a small building faced with many glazed aqua and yellow tiles depicting a meditating Buddha. This building is the Temple for Cultivating Good Deeds (悦心殿 or *yue xin dian*), where once stood a statue of Yamantaka, a fierce Tibetan god of seven heads, thirty-four arms and sixteen legs. I assume that by building this temple, Shun Zhi wanted to demonstrate his patronage of all variants of Buddhism and would have revered this deity along with the rest of the Buddhist pantheon. Alas, the cosmopolitanism of Shun Zhi's reign was not long-lived. According to Arlington and Lewisohn, Chinese of the 1930s used to claim that only a horrible looking god like Yamantaka could keep wild people, like Tibetans and Mongols, in good behavior, a chauvinism that was to build to shocking levels as the century progressed. Apparently taking stock of the change of times and the decline of enlightened opinions, Yamanataka left the capital for destinations unknown at some point in the past sixty years. Perhaps he is in India.

For me, my fondest of memory of Bei Hai Park is standing at the top of White Pagoda Hill, clutching an umbrella and watching a thunderstorm sweep in from the west. The sudden gusts of wind seemed to blow away all the pedestrians far below while the rain deepened the hue from glazed tile roofs on the palaces. Within five minutes, I was alone on the summit, surrounded by pelting rain and once again sensing Peking's past all around me. I smiled as lightening and thunder reached a crescendo when the storm passed over the temples of their respective gods in Bei Chi Zi and Bei Chang Street. Maybe sometimes these old actors do come back to show children of a lesser age just how it's done.

Trotting down the north side of the hill, you will see a scattering of kiosks, pavilions and other ornamental structures. Before reaching the camelback bridge we pass a pile of rocks called Yi Fang Shan (一方山) referring to a mountain in He Bei province where a Taoist deity, the Royal Lady of the West (西皇母 or *xi huang mu*) is supposed to live in a magnificent palace surrounded by sacred peach orchards. Once every 3,000 years, the orchards yield peaches that confer immortality. The Royal Lady of the West is usually depicted in the attire of a Chinese princess riding a crane. Chronicles of the Zhou dynasty relate that the Royal Lady of the West used to visit dignitaries of that era. These days, she seems to make her living by lending her name to dubious restaurants in five star hotels that seem to have pinched a couple of stars from the firmament.

After crossing the bridge, you will come to the Tower for Inspecting Ancient Scripts (阅古楼), which refers to a collection of calligraphy set out in 400 steles of equal size. Among the specimens are works by Wang Xi Zhi (王羲之), Wang Nan Zhi (王南之) and Wang Xun (王珣) of the Later Han. Qian Long had ordered the Hanlin Academy to select the specimens for these monuments.

On the west side of the island, the double storied verandah was once regarded as the most beautiful structure in the park, though the wear and tear of the post-imperial world has left it a bit ratty. In the 1920s, restaurants were opened along the verandah, with Fang Shan Restaurant serving dishes based upon recipes from the imperial kitchens. Lao She penned the calligraphy for the sign outside the restaurant.

In a pavilion on the northwest section of the island, you can see a carved column with a kneeling figure holding a bronze plate over his head. While the column dates from Qian Long's reign, the statue alludes to a legend from the Early Han dynasty. Since 3,000-year-old peaches were scarce on the ground, Han Wu Di sought immortality by fermenting an elixir from the morning dew, which supposedly contains life-giving properties. Han Wu Di ordered his slaves to spend the night in the fields with their arms outstretched over their heads, holding receptacles to collect the dew. Regretfully, history fails to record the undoubtedly colorful observations of the slaves when they learned that they had drawn the straw for this duty.

Heading to the east side of the island, we pass a number of pavilions, rockeries and memorial arches. On the north side of the island stands a garden called the Study to Ease the Mind (庙鉴室), one of the favorite pleasure grounds of the Empress Dowager. Other adjacent buildings contain ponds, bubbling springs and pavilions specially built for musical entertainment. These grounds were preferred areas of pleasure, study and contemplation from the days of Qian Long until the Empress Dowager.

On the northeast side of the island is a marble stele, bearing Qian Long's calligraphy and memorializing that here is one of the Eight Great Sites of Old Peking invented by Yong Le; namely "the spring warmth of qing dao" (琼岛春阳). This spot has been a sight of classical allusions for over six hundred years.

Once across the bridge, we take the northbound path and pass the infrequently visited Pavilion of Freedom From Cares (濠濮间 or *hao pu jian*) consisting of rockeries, marble *pai lou* and arched bridges. Since this spot is secluded from the main paths, it is a lovely place to rest before continuing our tour.

Near the Di An Men entrance of the park, hidden behind the walls of a primary school is the Altar of Silkworm (先蚕坛 or *xian can tan*), constructed in 1742. The empress, rather than the emperor, conducted ceremonies in reverence of the goddesses of sericulture. Since he was probably run ragged conducting ceremonies throughout the lunar calendar, Qian Long insisted that the Altar of Silkworms be located in Bei Hai Park rather than its cosmologically correct position outside the city walls. Presumably, he wanted to save his empress from the wear and tear of traveling too far from the palace. The empress herself harvested leaves from sacred mulberry trees and passed these to her retinue who in turn fed the leaves to silk worms. In time, the worms were turned into silk used for the imperial ceremonies. Sometimes, upon polite inquiry, outsiders are admitted to see the altar when school is out of session.

Turning to the north west side of the lake, we arrive at assorted temples, pavilions and structures, most of which date from the time of Qian Long. The Studio of the Restful Mind (青心斋 or *qing xin ge*) was a favorite of the Empress Dowager, containing numerous pools, bridges, arbors and pavilions. After 1949, this "park within a park" was allocated for use by the Central Documentation History Research Institute and thus is another place where entry is forbidden. Adjacent to the studio is a glazed tile memorial arch called the Gate of Heavenly Kings (天王殿 or *tian wang dian*), which takes us to Small Western Heaven, formerly a collection of Buddhist temples now operating as the Peking Youth Science and Technology Hall.

Immediately to the west is another famous Nine Dragon Screen (九龙壁 or *jiu long bi*) built in 1417. Some connoisseurs consider that the specimen here in Bei Hai Park is the most exquisite in China. Originally, a Buddhist temple stood to the north of the screen, which served to obstruct malevolent spirits.

Returning to the lake, we come across the Iron Shadow Screen (铁影壁 or *tie ying bi*), which derives its name from the brown block of stone from which it is carved. The screen was made in the Yuan Dynasty and set outside the northern city walls as a preventive measure against harmful spirits arriving from hostile northern approaches. During the Ming, it was moved inside De Sheng Gate and placed in front of a foundry that cast bells for religious purposes. It was believed that the strong *yang* forces represented by the screen would frighten off any *ying* spirits that could despoil the sound of bells cast there. (Actually, the more persistent problem was the foundry's inability to pay its workers on a regular basis, thus prompting sit-down strikes throughout the Qing.) In 1947, the Iron Shadow Screen was brought to its current location in Bei Hai Park.

Returning to the lake, we come to the Pine Hill Library, containing various halls. The Brief Snow Hall (快雪堂 or *kuai xue tang*) takes its name from a poem written by Wang Xi Zhi of the Late Han Dynasty who, while composing a poem about a snowfall, suddenly found himself engulfed in a blizzard. The poem had been lost for decades until someone uncovered a stele and presented it to Qian Long. Wang is remembered as the "sage" of calligraphers whose style of brush stroke continues to inspire artists to this very day.

Next to the lakeshore are the Five Dragon Pavilions (五龙亭 or *wu long ting*) built on the lake and connected to the shore and each other by way of a stone causeway. The pavilions are built to resemble the curves in a dragon's body, with the dome of the central pavilion carved with many dragons to impress this point upon the unobservant stroller. From here, philistines can take a duck shaped boat back to Hortensia Island.

In 1949, Derk Bodde came across an incident that sparked some symbolic hope for the future of New China. During a stroll with his family along this side of the lake, Bodde came across two huge bronze incense burners that had been pushed off their marble pedestals. While they were sadly reflecting on this mindless vandalism, a small group of PLA soldiers walked by. Suddenly inspired, the soldiers decided to see if they could put the incense burners back on the pedestals. The bronzes were enormous, and the soldiers were not able to grasp them firmly. After several attempts, one of the soldiers hit upon the idea of rolling the bronzes to their pedestals and then rolling them up the side. This attempt proved successful and like playful youngsters the soldiers ran on to repeat this performance on each wayward bronzes.

> And we three foreigners, together with a small group of Chinese children which had by now assembled, applauded and shouted: "*Hao! Hao!*" ("Good! Good"). As we did so I thought to myself: This is probably the first time in decades — perhaps centuries — that a group of Chinese soldiers, undirected from above, and with no expectation of gain or praise for themselves, have spontaneously performed an act requiring initiative, effort, ingenuity and cooperation, simply in order to put to rights a monument belonging to the people.[2]

Continuing along the shore, we come to the Tower of the Ten Thousand Buddhas (万佛楼 or *wan fo lou*), which contains a myriad of plaster statues representing various Jataka stories. The temple was ransacked during the Cultural Revolution and has now been renovated in the tasteful style of a roadside trailer home in Florida at Christmas time. I imagine that the fellow who approved the KFC was given the job of renovating the tower. Adjacent to the western wall is the Great Western Heaven, formerly a temple now used as an open-air cinema. The temple still has glazed tiling inscribed with Buddhist texts and the construction of four memorial arches on each side.

Leaving from the south exit of Bei Hai Park, we point ourselves towards the west and pass the former National Library, originally established in 1910 and constructed in 1932 in an agreeable combination of Chinese and western motifs. To the north of the library once was Red Sandalwood Buddha Temple Street (旃檀寺街 or *zhan tan si jie*). The memory of this street's name is the only legacy of the temple that once stood here.

When Yong Le moved the capital to Peking, he wanted to ensure that the city had several symbols of antiquity. He brought to Peking the Red Sandalwood Buddha, which was one of the artistic and religious wonders of imperial China. It was said that the statue, five feet in height, had been carved in the Eastern Zhou dynasty in an accurate representation of the historical Buddha. The statue was also attributed with the ability to travel on its own accord, and thus it developed a reputation for having stayed at numerous monasteries throughout the centuries. Chinese writers in the Ming and Qing remarked on how the coloring of lacquer surface of the Buddha varied with the time of day and the temperature of the season. The sculptor depicted the Buddha in an unusual mudra, with his left arm on his side and his right arm raised as if beseeching heaven.

The Temple became one of the headquarters for Boxer troops during the assault on Peking's Legation District and nearby churches. In retaliation, French troops, who were assigned to occupy this section of Peking, destroyed the temple. The following year, Alicia Little, the wife of a British diplomat, tried to find out what happened to the statue:

> A Lama in another Temple, the Pa Tah ssu, on being asked about it, replied in the tone of a man heartbroken, and without even looking up. "Some people say it has been burnt. Some people say it has gone up to Heaven — and some people say it has begun travelling again."[3]

The Red Sandalwood Buddha has never been recovered. Perhaps it graces a private collection in Europe. Or perhaps its spirit was freed from its material body through the fires that ravaged this part of the city. Trying to track down the Red Sandalwood Buddha would make for a riveting historical detective story. It seems that this would be a far more valuable endeavor than all the fuss about several trashy Old Summer Palace relics recovered by a Chinese arms dealer.

Back along Wen Jian Street, you take a north turn into Grassy Mist Alley (草岚子胡同 or the *cao lan zi hu tong*). You will pass through an area razed for new construction until you come across the Downtown Student Dormitory of the Peking Medical School on the west side of the street. Here we can see a gate, the final remains of Grassy Mist Prison (草岚子监狱旧址), which was the incarceration center for political prisoners of the Nationalist government and later the Japanese occupation government. The concrete columns and heavy arch, along with the straggling pieces of barbed wire, were clearly designed to instill a sense of hopelessness in those brought here. In the early 1950s, the prison became redundant after the construction of Qin Cheng Prison in the suburbs between the Ming Tombs and the Great Wall.

Continuing to the west on Xi An Men Avenue (西安门大街), we take a north turn on Xi Shi Che Street (西什库街) and arrive at the entrance to the North Cathedral (北堂 or *bei tang*), a Gothic style Roman Catholic church painted in a light blue hue. In the long rectangular courtyard in front of the church, pavilions stand over weather beaten imperial steles and a Lourdes grotto that combines Chinese and Western themes.

The Northern Cathedral is of considerable historical importance. In gratitude for medical treatment that cured him of malaria, Kang Xi granted the Jesuits Gerbillon and Bouvet a parcel of land next to the Central Lake in 1693. Ten years later, a chapel was completed and opened with imperial permission. The Northern Cathedral continued to function until 1827 when Dao Guang deported all Roman Catholic missionaries. In accordance with the 1860 Sino-French Treaty, Peking restored the site to the Roman Catholic Church and a larger cathedral was erected there in 1867.

In 1885, the Empress Dowager, having taken up residence in the palaces in the Imperial Lakes, objected to the presence of the cathedral. Officially, she protested that the spires of the cathedral damaged the *feng shui* of the Imperial Parks. The Empress Dowager probably was annoyed that outsiders could peer at her from the tower of the cathedral in much the same way that the 1973 Peking Hotel annex afforded unauthorized views into the Zhong Nan Hai compound.

Since the Qing dynasty had just lost a bruising war with the French, most Manchu and Chinese ministers were reluctant to raise a new set of complications since the welfare of Catholic missions fell under French supervision. The matter was left to the capable hands of a minor official, a Mongol named En Yu who, through the assistance of a friendly Chinese priest, persuaded the church authorities to move to a new location called the Ten Storerooms (十庫), which is the current site for the cathedral.

The new cathedral was completed in 1887 and enjoyed an undisturbed existence until the Boxer Debacle. Nearly all contemporary recollections of the "Siege of Peking" focused upon the foreigners holed up in the Legation District in the southeast part of the Tartar City. In reality, the trials and tribulations of the survivors of the Legation siege were not all that bad. There were ample food stores, and factionalism between the Boxer and Qing imperial troops precluded any serious attempt to breach the defenses of the diplomats.

The experience of the defenders of the Northern Cathedral was a different story, however. Father Alphonse Favier was the bishop of the cathedral and assumed responsibility for its defense. Inside the grounds were 3,000 Chinese Christians, some only armed with spears and swords, together with thirteen foreign missionaries, some hundred seminarians and 11 Italian and 40 French marines under the command of Sub-lieutenant Paul Henry, who died just a day before the rescue.

The Boxers began their attacks on June 5, 1900 and continued without a truce until the Japanese troops relieved the cathedral on August 16. In contrast with the siege of the legations, the defenders of North Cathedral did not have sufficient rations. Moreover, if the Boxers breached the barricades, death was a certainty since the Boxers had already slaughtered foreigners and Chinese converts in other Peking churches. During the worst days, the Boxers turned 14 cannons on the defenses of the cathedral.

On Easter Sunday in 1901, Alicia Little visited the bullet ridden ruins of Bei Tang and recorded these recollections in her book *Round About My Peking Garden:*

> But now its façade riddled with shot, its aisles propped up by many beams, the trees behind with their bark gnawed off — one of the Sisters said 'by our mules' but higher surely than any mule could reach — the tumble down masses of brick and mortar behind the broken walls, the great pits where the mines exploded, engulfing children by the hundred, all recall memories of heroism and yet of suffering so long endured that the heart aches, the eyes brim over with tears and one sees all things through a mist. 'There,' says a young Portuguese Sister, her big brown eyes luminous with the recollection, 'there is where the Italian lieutenant was buried by a shell, and for three-quarters of an hour we could not dig him out. No, he was alive, and only bruised. Ah! The young French lieutenant that was sad!. He was so good. We could but grieve over his loss.'

Then we pause by the grave of the Sister Superior who lay dying as the relief came in, 'too late for me' as she wrote; her one thought for days past, 'What can I give them to eat to-morrow? What can I give them to eat? There is nothing left.' 'The poor soldiers,' said another Sister, 'they suffered so from hunger, although they tightened their belts every day. I tore all my letters into bits and made them into cigarettes. Burnt paper is better than nothing. And they had nothing to smoke. That is so hard for a solider.' Next we paused by the great pit where so many children lie buried, blown up by the mine. 'And we think there must be another mine over there not yet discovered,' said the new Sister Superior. 'If not, why should that house over there have been completely shattered at the time of the explosion, if there were no mine connecting it?' The Sisters are all great authorities upon mines and shells, now. They know too which trees' leaves are poisonous, and tell how the Chinese Christians swelled and suffered, trying to sustain life by eating them. They showed the remainder of their school children; three among them had before the siege lost both their feet through foot-binding. 'Surely you did not sleep here, whilst the cannonading was going on?" 'We always moved about with all our tail of children after us to where they seemed to be firing less,' said the young Portuguese Sister with the luminous brown eyes. Then came up an old Sister of seventy-six. She too had survived the siege. We visited the Bishop. 'Did any of your Chinese recant?' 'A few, very few.' 'I think 12,000 Christians have lost their lives,' said Monsignor Favier, 'three of our European priests, four Chinese and many of our Chinese Sisters. One priest hung on a crucifix, nailed for three days before he died. Monsignor Hamer they killed by cutting his arms and legs to the bone, filling the cuts with petroleum and setting them alight. What saved us? Oh, a series of miracles …. '"[4]

After 1949, the PRC established the Patriotic Catholic Association, a government appointed body that renounced the Vatican and took control of the religious activities of China's five million Roman Catholics. In the 1950s, the Australian journalist Dick Hughes attended mass at the Northern Cathedral and noticed that there were few Chinese in attendance. Most of the communicants were Africans residing in Peking, who were apparently unfazed by the official portrait of Chairman Mao that hung beside the altar. These days, most of the congregation consists of Chinese ancients with occasionally younger people in attendance.

The emotions stirred in the summer of 1900 are still strong, and the ghosts of its victims are under siege again. On October 1, 2000, Pope John Paul II canonized several Catholics martyred during the siege. The Chinese news agencies responded by declaring that they "deserved to die."

9

THE FORMER LEGATION DISTRICT

IN THE EARLY 20TH CENTURY, Peking had another walled district that was not built on the initiative of Yong Le or his successors. It enclosed a rectangular area running along the east side of Tian An Men Square and in an easterly direction along Chang An Avenue. At the intersection with Chong Wen Men Nei Avenue, the wall turned south. The old Tartar City wall served as the southern boundary. Within these walls, a wholly foreign city came into existence, only to disappear with the rise of the PRC. No traces remain of the wall of the former Legation District, though there are a few buildings scattered in this neighborhood that call to mind a long dead world.

In the Ming era, this area was known by the main street that ran along the north of the Tartar wall, the East Alley For Rice Exchange (东交米巷 or *dong jiao mi xiang*). Since the Grand Canal terminated near the southeast corner of the Tartar City, this neighborhood became an entrepot for deliveries of rice from the south. Later, the Ming built a hostel here for border people on tribute missions to the emperor, and thus its name was changed to the East Alley for the Mingling of People (东交民巷 or *dong jiao min xiang*). Mongols, Koreans and Japanese, among others, stayed at a courtyard house here but were severely restricted in their movement. (Tibetans were housed in the Lama Temple or in the West Yellow Temple, both lamaseries, in the north of the city.) In the early 1700s, a Russian mission was also set up here in accordance with a treaty between Kang Xi and Czar Peter the Great.[1] Although there was something of a "foreign" flavor to this district, both Manchus and Chinese lived here, especially court officials eager for a short commute to work at the Forbidden City and the surrounding ministries.

Former Legation District

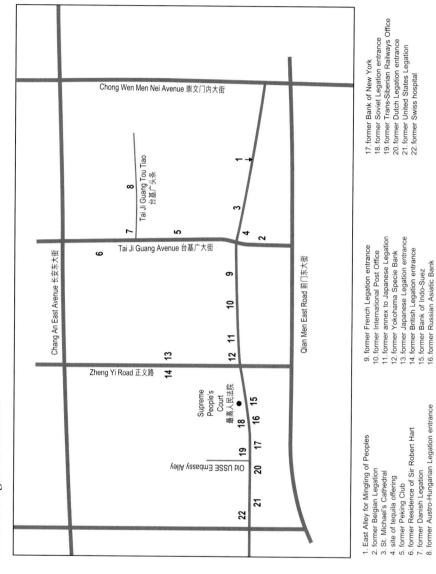

1. East Alley for Mingling of Peoples
2. former Belgian Legation
3. St. Michael's Cathedral
4. site of tequila offering
5. former Peking Club
6. former Residence of Sir Robert Hart
7. former Danish Legation
8. former Austro-Hungarian Legation entrance
9. former French Legation entrance
10. former International Post Office
11. former annex to Japanese Legation
12. former Yokohama Specie Bank
13. former Japanese Legation entrance
14. former British Legation entrance
15. former Bank of Indo-Suez
16. former Russian Asiatic Bank
17. former Bank of New York
18. former Soviet Legation entrance
19. former Trans-Siberian Railways Office
20. former Dutch Legation entrance
21. former United States Legation
22. former Swiss hospital

The burning of Zheng Yang Gate during the Boxer Debacle.

For over two hundred years, Western European countries periodically dispatched envoys to Peking in quest of the unwelcome concept of an exchange of permanent diplomatic missions. In the 19th century, under the threat of a British and French invasion, Xian Feng's representatives signed an agreement consenting to an exchange of envoys, along with onerous conditions that forced China into permitting relaxed rules for international trade. Once the treaty was signed, Xian Feng's court dragged its feet on ratification. In reaction, Britain and France dispatched a joint invasion force in order to compel ratification at bayonet point.

To satisfy national prestige, Britain insisted that the embassy of her Britannic Majesty's government must be located within Peking's city walls. The Dong Jiao Min Xiang neighborhood was offered up, presumably with the British unaware of its connotations of tribute missions. In short order, France, Russia, United States, Japan, Prussia, Italy and Portugal made the same request on the basis of most favorable treatment clauses in their respective treaties.[2]

The British leased the courtyard house of Prince Su, a Manchu official who had fallen upon hard times and needed the additional income. The French moved in around the corner in the home of Prince Yang. The Americans occupied an abandoned Taoist temple across the street from the hostel that was allocated to their then close allies, the Russians, in 1727. Within a decade, the other treaty powers opened embassies in and around this alley.

From 1860 to 1900, the Legation District was not exclusively Western in population. The diplomatic representations were interspersed among the homes of Manchu princes and hostels used for border tribute missions. David Rennie, the British legation physician, noted the arrival of a Korean tribute mission in 1861 and commented on their black horsehair hats and white *hanbok* clothing. Dr. Rennie favorably added, "there is a rough honesty of demeanour about the Coreans generally, not unlike that which characterizes the Mongolians." This roughness of manner was forcefully expressed when one of the members of the British legation wanted to observe their customs and habits at close quarters, with a Korean, apparently not appreciating a secondary role as a traveling zoo, throwing out the offending Britisher from the hostel. Mongolian princes arrived for stays in the hostel too. To cater to the needs of these steppe-dwellers, the Chinese set up a Mongolian market next to the British Legation, which bought and sold Mongol goods and foodstuffs.

Because the streets of Peking were unpaved quagmires in the rainy season, the Qing authorities extended to the foreigners the privilege of walking along the city walls. Later on, as a response to the absence of Western divertissements, the British built a racetrack on the outside of the city. All of the legations hosted soirees and struggled to find a common ground with their Chinese colleagues and servants. Western merchants also set up shops to sell imported goods to the foreign community while Christian missionaries sought converts through the rice dole or, in the next century, English language lessons.

The Boxer Debacle of 1900 suddenly put an end to this placid existence. The China experts in the Legation District dismissed this threat. (As an example of history repeating itself, I recall hearing a seasoned China expert in April 1989 assert that the on-going student demonstrations in Peking were going to blow over in another week or two.)

Beyond the gates of the Legation District, the Boxer Movement gained momentum. The sudden introduction of technological advances provoked a superstitious backlash, which played easily into the Boxers' hands. The Boxers stoked anti-foreign feeling by claiming that railways were an effrontery to the dignity of the earth dragons. They said that since rusted telegraph wires dripped reddish water on the ground, this also proved that ghosts were being cut to ribbons as they flew among the telegraph posts. Poor crop harvests were taken as evidence of the anger of the spirit world. These foreign intrusions had offended Heaven, which was, in turn, punishing China for its wayward behavior.

Foreigners were not alone as the focus for popular dissent in north China. In the provinces, people felt that Qing officials were thick as fleas with the foreigners and their offensive behavior. Some rural folk were also furious about Chinese Christians, who seemingly betrayed the way of the ancestors.

The movement initially alarmed the Qing court. However, conservative factions in Peking came to regard the Boxers as a potential ally against the threat posed by the foreign powers. By the spring of 1900, the Boxers had burst throughout north China, slaughtering foreign missionaries and Christian converts as well as destroying the offensive goods of the foreign devils, such as sewing machines, kerosene lanterns and blue cotton cloth. Because of their alleged spiritual powers, the Boxers mobilized large numbers of peasants, a skill at organization that appealed to conservative factions of nobles who loathed the presence of foreigners. When the Boxers appeared on the outskirts of Peking, debates broke out in earnest over the next step. In late June, the Grand Council met in Zhong Nan Hai and agreed to enlist the Boxers to throw out the foreigners. Shortly thereafter, an imperial decree was issued, declaring war on the foreigners in China.

This act of folly by the Qing court horrified the governors-general of the middle and southern provinces. Unlike people in the isolated north, these officials realized on account of their considerable contact with the outside world that such a war could only result in the humiliation of China. After consultations with Western representatives, these governors-general agreed to suppress any Boxer activities in their provinces in exchange for two sets of promises. First, the foreign powers would ignore the declaration of war. Second, Western forces would stay out of provinces where the Boxers had been brought to heel.

Other governors-general lacked such foresight and complied with the imperial decree. For example, the governor-general of Shan Xi province enthusiastically acted as the master of ceremonies for the execution of foreign missionaries and their families.

We will never have a complete and unbiased account of the Boxer Debacle. Qing court records were lost, or forged, in the ensuing chaos. Western accounts in the aftermath drip with a deep bias of national arrogance or personal agendas. Contemporary Chinese historians spare no spleen in the shrillness of their denunciations of the foreign invasion while Western scholars peck at different segments without trying to present the full picture.

No country comes away clean from the Boxer Debacle. It is best viewed as a morality tale about universal folly and stupidity that ought to silence any chowder head exposing thoughtless, senseless assertions of jingoistic patriotism.

By the middle of June, a joint force of Boxers and imperial troops laid an ineffective siege on the Legation District. From the very outset, all participants acted like spoiled children. Western writers recorded incidents of "insolent" provocation by the Boxers while failing to mention how their own soldiers beat and killed Chinese on the slightest suspicion of their association with Boxers. During our visit to the Zhong Shan Memorial Park, we have already mentioned the colossal arrogance of the German minister and super-bully, Baron Von Kettler.

For their part, the Boxers set fire to churches and shops selling Western goods. They aimed to kill three sets of "scoundrels": the *yi mao zi* (一毛子 or first hairy ones) meaning foreigners, the *er mao zi* (二毛子 or second hairy ones), referring to Chinese Christians; and the *san mao zi* (三毛子 or third hairy ones) being merchants who sold foreign goods. (These phrases can be usefully employed in contemporary Peking by the way.) The Boxers cut down hundreds of innocent Christian converts as well as ordinary Peking citizens whom they suspected of being secret Christians. (Some Boxers claimed that they had clairvoyant powers that enabled them to detect faint crosses on the foreheads of Peking's Christians.) Exploiting the paralysis of the central government, Peking's hoodlums joined the feast and looted the homes of wealthy nobles and the shops of merchants.

Many foreign witnesses believed that there was no unanimous agreement about the siege among the court factions of Manchu nobles. The basis for this belief is that the defense of the Legation District would have instantly crumbled if there had been a coordinated and sustained attack by imperial troops and the Boxers. Periodic truces unpredictably erupted throughout the summer. In one instance, a wagon of fresh fruit and ice was delivered to the besieged foreigners with, apparently, a note from the Empress Dowager wishing them well.

Within the Legation District itself, the ministers of different nationalities quarreled ceaselessly and failed to coordinate defense efforts. At the orders of agitated diplomats, legation troops retreated from strategic sites for no apparent tactical reason. On their own initiative, well-to-do Westerners exempted themselves from doing any manual work in support of the defenses. Hundreds of Chinese Christians sought refuge in the British and Japanese Legations, where they were treated as second-class allies and usually deprived of the same rations afforded to the "true blue" followers of Christ.

After fifty-five days of intermittent warfare, an "Eight Power Allied Army" — a hodgepodge of troops dispatched by six European countries, the United States and Japan — fought its way from Tianjin to Peking. As the foreign troops drew near to the outskirts of the city, the Empress Dowager, Guang Xu and the Qing court abandoned Peking and took up temporary shelter in Xi An. Once the foreign troops had occupied Peking, their commanders divided the city into different zones, much like Berlin after World War II. Russian, Japanese, British, German, French, Italian or American soldiers patrolled their respective districts and provided some administrative control in the vacuum created by the collapse of the government.

In the awful year 1900, the citizens of Old Peking experienced the most brutal carnage since Genghis Khan torched the Jin city in 1215. The flight of the court and the collapse of local administration inflicted a psychological scar on the city. The following account, written by the missionary Arthur D. Smith, brings back to memory the trauma:

When it was possible for foreigners again to traverse the streets of Peking, the desolation that met the eye was appalling. Dead bodies of soldiers lay in heaps, or singly, in some instances covered with a torn mat, but always a prey to the now well-fed dogs. Dead dogs and horses poisoned the air of every region. Huge pools of stagnant water were reeking with rotting corpses of man and beast; lean cats staring wildly at passers-by; gutted shops boasting such signs as "Perpetual Abundances," "Springs of Plenty," and so forth. Over the door of a place thrice looted and lying in utter ruin, one might see the cheerful motto "Peace and Tranquility." For miles upon miles of the busiest streets of the Northern and Southern Cities not a single shop was open for business, and scarcely a dozen persons were anywhere to be seen.

The arrival of foreign troops marked a new stage in Peking's ordeal. A fury for revenge possessed many of the defenders of the Legation District, leaving in the gutter any assumed Christian ethics. Diplomats and journalists succumbed to the temptation to loot homes and palaces, justified in their mind on account of their own financial loss from the siege. Foreign soldiers looted as an age-old spoil of victory.

While Chinese sources tend to lump all foreign imperialists into a single group, there were decided differences. Some missionaries took rice from the deserted markets for their congregation while others came back to pay for the rice once the merchants returned to the city.

All observers agreed that the most polite and efficient troops were the Japanese, who incidentally systematically looted their zone most thoroughly. French troops were agitated about *la gloire de France* and insisted that they should have the honor of occupying the Forbidden City, even to the point of firing at other "allies" who had wandered accidentally into the palace. The sepoys among the British troops treated the Chinese roughly and packed up all sorts of historical relics for delivery to the British Museum.

It was generally agreed that the worst soldiers were the Russians, who relentlessly harassed and beat Chinese in their zone. Because of the brutal discipline demanded by their officers, the Cossacks rigidly followed orders even to the point of severe cruelty, though foreigners found individual Cossacks to be kind and thoughtful whenever they were out from under the thumb of their officers.

The German troops arrived in a furor, intent upon humiliating China in revenge for the murder of Von Kettler. Kaiser Wilhelm's express instructions were to give no quarter and take no prisoners. It is rather disgusting language. "Let all who fall into your hand be at your mercy. Just as the Huns a thousand years ago under the leader Etzel, gained a reputation by virtue of which they still live in historical tradition, so may the name of Germany become known in such a manner in China ...." The German troops stripped the Jesuit Observatory of its astronomical equipment despite Berlin's full acknowledgment that the relics were clearly Chinese property to which Germany had no lawful right.

By most accounts, Italian and American troops were disciplined and well behaved. The Italian marines were dissuaded from looting religious relics from a fear that these were the work of the devil and any interest shown in his articles meant an additional term in purgatory. As for the Americans, they arrived after spending several months working on civil engineering projects in the Philippines. With no ax to grind, the Americans were more balanced in their reactions. The scholar Michael Hunt has written that in the American zone centered around Liu Li Chang, the American command enforced a ban on looting (to the point of arresting any of their own errant soldiers and sending them off to hard labor in chains), paved roads, improved sanitation and so impressed Chinese merchants in the Xuan Wu Men District that they petitioned the American troops to remain in Peking.

Notwithstanding the views expressed in contemporary Chinese history books, most of the foreign powers were eager to withdraw their troops from Peking as quickly as possible and deploy them in more pressing matters.[3] In the absence of any other viable government, the foreign powers realized that the imperial court of the Empress Dowager and Guang Xu would have to be reinstated. However, the foreign powers insisted that Boxers as well as certain reactionary Manchu nobles ought to be executed, usually with less due process than is currently available in the PRC or Guantanamo Bay. Others were sent into exile in Gan Su or Xin Jiang.

The Protocol of 1901, signed by the eight powers and the Qing court, set out onerous terms for reparations to be paid by China. It also stipulated that the foreign powers could administer and control the Legation District to the exclusion of the Chinese authorities. All Chinese were to move out of the district, and a defensive wall was built so that there could never be a repeat of the summer of 1900.

After the debacle, Britain's master spy, Sidney Reilly commented on the supine Qing court in a report to the British Secret Service: "the Manchus are finished. It is only a matter of time before China becomes the playground of the great powers. Their intelligence system, such as it is, for all practical purposes simply does not exist."[4]

Beginning in 1902, the Legation District became a reflection in miniature of the foreign world. Most countries rebuilt their legations according to the prevailing architectural styles in their home countries. An international police force patrolled the district and a French-run post office supervised the delivery (and misplacement) of mail. Foreign banks set up their Peking headquarters within its confines and foreign-run hospitals looked after the health of diplomats and other expatriates.

I imagine that by the 1930s, the Legation District had become an unbearably provincial enclave, at least for foreigners wanting to experience China. Writers like George Kates and John Blofeld ran a mile from any association with it. In his novel *Peonies and Ponies*, Harold Acton let out some steam about the sorts of Westerners that he encountered in the district. His Sinophilic protagonist reacts to a female example of the diplomatic community:

> What right had she here? She and her polypus type were profaning all his sanctuaries. Had he not seen her with a party of tourists, who had motored, actually hooting their horns, up to the very Temple of Heaven! When he thought of the spiritual isolation of those walled precincts, the lapis-lazuli tile above the cypresses, those marble circles of the altar where he had often stood alone in ecstasy, so close to earth yet in the very midst of heaven, — when he thought of all this and then, as with a nightmare jump, of the tartized teeth, the viscous stream of [her] still flowing saliva, while she sprinkled her vicinity with specks of chewed-up cheese, [he] sympathized whole-heartedly with the most ruthless and fanatical of Boxers.[5]

During World War II, the allied legations were shut down, though the Japanese respected the diplomatic immunity of the enclave for axis and neutral nations. Upon the establishment of the PRC, the Foreign Affairs Ministry redistributed the legations of capitalist countries to neutral nations like Burma, India and Indonesia. By the 1960s, a new diplomatic section was established outside Chao Yang Men. The district's wall was dismantled, though there is no cause for mourning in its case.

Starting on the northeast corner of Qian Men East Avenue (前门东大街) and Tai Ji Guang Avenue (太基广大街 or Rue Marco Polo as it was known in the pre-liberation days), we see in front of us the Zi Jin Hotel (紫金庄园). Here you can spy a series of European buildings with maroon bricks and steep green gabled roofs. Originally, this parcel of land was the residence of a Manchu prince named Xu Tong (徐桐), a strong proponent of massacring the foreigners in the Legation District in the summer of 1900. Xu seems to have been a thoroughly unpleasant character. Whenever going to the Forbidden City, he insisted that his sedan chair carriers take him out the least esteemed western gate rather than the north gate of his home. This was because he could not bear to set foot on Legation Street since foreigners had polluted it with their presence. He once boasted that he would have a sedan chair furnished with the leathered skins of foreigners. I suspect that the buffed pale hue might have been too ghostly for his taste.

Once the Legation District was besieged, Old Xu fell into the hands of the foreign defenders. However, through one of the countless mishaps that occurred during the Debacle, the French troops inadvertently released him, thus tossing away a valuable negotiation chip since Xu Tong was a favorite of the Empress Dowager. No matter, he expressed his gratitude for his release by egging on the Boxers to greater depths of violence. Just as pompous foreigners failed to foresee the outbreak of the Boxer Debacle, Xu Tong misjudged the end of the affair. As the eight-power army entered the city, Xu Tong and his entire family committed suicide. In another of history's delightful ironies, his former residence became a foreign legation.

The Belgians were granted the right to build an embassy here and erected a building that was reputedly modeled on the

St. Michael's Cathedral in the former Legation District.

chateau that his Excellency, the King of Belgium, gave to his favorite concubine.

These days, the former Belgian embassy operates as a cadres-only hotel whose little man in green by the main gate will officiously dismiss any curious outsiders. No matter since no one pays the least attention to the north gate, a place where I have loitered late at night with some of the usual suspects, taking swigs of Jose Cuervo tequila and leaving the empty bottle by the gate, just to show the ghost of Xu Tong that there are no hard feelings.

Across the street from this gate is St. Michael's Cathedral, a former Roman Catholic church now used by its government-sponsored successor. St. Michael's was built in 1903 and became a subject of ferocious vandalism during the Cultural Revolution. In the early 1980s, it opened again for services.

Turning to the north on Tai Ji Guang Road, you will pass the former Peking Club, which was once an exclusive domain of foreigners and now a recreational club for high-ranking cadres. Across the street is the Chinese Overseas Friendship Association, though the Chinese guards do not exhibit much friendliness to any overseas folks curious about the grounds. Perhaps this is because some analysts believe that the association is actually an espionage front for gathering intelligence from overseas. Be that as it may, if you are fortunate enough to be riding around in a black sedan, you might be able to drive past the guards and take a quick gander at the ornate two-storied stone mansion that was former residence of Sir Robert Hart (and some buildings to the north that once housed the Italian Legation).

At the turn of the century, Sir Robert Hart was a towering figure in the foreign community. He was an Ulsterman who came to China in 1857. After working for several years in the British consulate in Ningbo, he gained his fluency thanks to a Ningpo maiden who became his concubine. He had several children with this unnamed woman. Happily, Sir Robert provided for their welfare, unlike most Britishers. He left Ningbo once he assumed the all-important title of the Inspector General of the Imperial Maritime Customs, though he mentioned in his personal letters, with deep remorse, his regrets about leaving his common law wife.

In the aftermath of the Second Opium War, the Qing government admitted that it had problems paying reparations since it had a notoriously difficult time in policing the collection of customs duties by Chinese officials in distant ports. The British suggested a solution: the Chinese government should establish a separate bureau dedicated to the collection of customs duties from foreign traders and then staff that bureau with foreigners. Hart was the second foreigner to be appointed to the top post, the Inspector General (or "I.G." as he was commonly called). Hart held that post until he left China in 1908.

Hart hired a multinational team of foreigners and Chinese to be customs inspectors stationed across the breath of China. Without compelling reasons, no inspector could stay in any one city for more than three years. Hart's reputation for attention to detail was a terror even for the most conscientious foreign customs officials in the hinterlands of China. Chinese refused to work for him because of his exasperating attention to detail.

Chinese historians now denounce Hart as an insidious agent of British imperialism. There seems to be more emotion than dispassionate analysis in this condemnation. In his letters, Hart expressed, resolutely, his dual goal of serving the Qing government and enhancing a close friendship between Great Britain and China. He was ceaselessly aware that he was an official of the Qing government and forever reprimanded his employees who thought otherwise or showed disrespect to their employers. While he remained forever discreet in his opinions, he seemed to disdain bellicose Western imperialist officials and their xenophobic Qing counterparts in equal measures. Since Hart was straightforward, attentive to detail and beyond the pale of court politics, Qing officials trusted him.

Notwithstanding contemporary denunciations, I believe that this trust was not misplaced. For example, Hart was given the task of negotiating a treaty with the Portuguese concerning the future status of Macao. At that time, Lisbon was keen to pressure Peking into waiving its sovereign rights over the enclave. Hart was able to parry this demand and reached an ingenious compromise; namely that the Portuguese would exercise administrative control over Macao but not acquire it in perpetuity. This wording became the basis for the Portuguese custody of the enclave and its reversion to Chinese sovereignty in 1999.

By the end of the 19th century, Hart's prestige and influence among the foreign community had no parallel. Every Wednesday evening, he hosted an open house where foreigners and Qing officials gathered to listen to his brass band of Chinese musicians playing Western tunes.

However, like many other seasoned China hands, Hart did not see the virulence of the anti-foreignism that was lurking below the surface. He lost his home and nearly all of his possessions in the Boxer Debacle. Disillusioned and fatigued, he left China at age 73 and died in London in 1911, three weeks before the collapse of the government that he served so loyally.

Across the street from the entrance to his former residence, on the north side of the intersection of Tai Ji Guang Avenue (太基广大街) and Tai Ji Guang Tou Tiao (太基广头条), there is still an overlooked memorial to Sir Robert. Carved into the gray wall is a street sign reading "Rue Hart".

If we go down Rue Hart towards the east, we pass the former Danish legation at the first door on the north. Further down the street, the entranceway to the former Austro-Hungarian Legation can be found. After the Austro-Hungarian Empire disintegrated in 1918, the legation entered into a diplomatic limbo. Since China waived its rights over property in the Legation District, no Chinese governmental body could reclaim the site. Eventually, the foreign legations collectively took charge of these buildings and turned them into an old folks' home for stateless citizens. In the years between 1917 and 1949, elderly White Russians, down on their luck, sought refuge here. The original building remains splendidly landscaped in the middle of its grounds.

Retracing our steps to Dong Jiao Min Xiang, we carry on to the west and pass the former French Legation on north side of the street, which the French had first occupied in 1860. During the Boxer Debacle, the French Legation marked the area that was the eastern defense perimeter. All of the original buildings were destroyed with the exception of the two lions outside the entranceway.

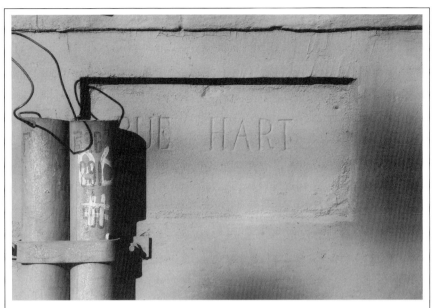

A forgotten testimonial to Sir Robert Hart.

The former French Legation.

In 1970, the PRC gave these buildings to Prince Norodom Sihanouk of Cambodia, who found himself in exile after being deposed while vacationing in a fat farm in France. Sihanouk lived here until his return to Phnom Penh under the Khmer Rouge in September 1975. When he fled Cambodia during the Vietnamese invasion of 1979, the prince bounced back to his villa and held diplomatic soirees here until the coast was clear for him to resume the title of King. I imagine that the PRC continued to hold King Sihanouk in such high regard as he consistently played the role of a tributary princeling.

The next building on the north side of the street is the former legation post office, built in the style of Western government structures of the 1920s. These days, it is a third rate Si Chuan restaurant made more dismal by nerve-racking karaoke music.

At the intersection of Dong Jiao Min Xiang and Zheng Yi Road (正义路) you can see that the People's Bank has moved into the former address of the Yokohama Specie Bank. Someone has attempted to restore, in a fashion, the site to its former elegance. Turning to the north on Zheng Yi Road, we eventually come to the former Japanese Legation on the east side of the street, now ironically the offices of the Peking Municipal Government. It was here in 1915 that Japan presented the Peking warlord government with the so-called Twenty One Demands, which in essence would have transformed China into a Japanese colony. It was also here that Henry Pu Yi fled after his expulsion from the Forbidden City in 1924.

Across the street, shorn of any indication of prior grandeur, is the main entrance to the former British Legation. Originally acquired in 1860, the British resisted the temptation of other countries to replicate "national architecture" and tastefully retained the traditional appearance of the palace. The large gate, which once sported a Lion and Unicorn, was briefly a storefront decorated with Christmas lights and selling surplus supplies from the Public Security Bureau, such as electric cattle prods, handcuffs and other knick-knacks in case you get caught short on your boss's birthday.

Before 1997, you could still find two large marble stones in front of the gates, which were used by British horse-riders to dismount from their horses. Regrettably, the stones have been dragged away.

During the Boxer Debacle, the British and Japanese legations were the northern barricades. Three thousand Chinese converts clustered in the Japanese legation. Foreign civilians were housed in the more secure British Legation, where they were able to sit out the siege on a diet of curried donkey meat, rice and champagne brought in from an early 20th century counterpart of Jenny Lu's.[6]

The sepoys were the first to enter the Legation District when the siege was lifted. Originally Zheng Yi Road was a canal draining fetid water from the Forbidden City. The sepoys came through the sewer drains under the Tartar City wall and marched directly to the British Legation. British Minister Claude MacDonald was immensely satisfied that his country's troops beat out all the others in the competition to liberate the Legation District. However, in the congratulatory mood of the moment, the Westerners forgot about the fate of other besieged allies. It was the Japanese who liberated the Northern Cathedral the next day.

Returning to Dong Jiao Min Xiang, we continue to the west and pass the former Bank of Indo-Suez. Next door is the former Russian Asiatic Bank, which later became the Bank of New York after the Bolshevik Revolution. These days, it is a police museum. Across the street, the marble columned gate for the former site of the embassy of the Soviet Union now leads the way to the Supreme People's Court, where indigent petitioners seek an audience and spend their nights on the street. Further to the west and marked by the horizontal yellow tiles running parallel with the roof is the former office of the Trans-Siberian Railways, which was operated first by the Czarist and then the communist governments of Russia. In 1950, Stalin finally waived all rights and transferred control over the railways to China. Behind the sentry box on the lane leading north you can still make out the sign "Union of Soviet Socialist Republics Embassy Lane."

In the summer of 1900, Russian and American troops maintained the western perimeter in this area. The troops of both nations were able to hold off Chinese troops by taking key vantage points on the Tartar Wall and the Mongolian Market. Alas, nothing concrete remains of this curious cooperation.

Continuing to the west, we come to the bricked up entranceway of the former Dutch Legation. We can see several Dutch burgher-style buildings in brick in the background. I recall one afternoon seeing the curious sight of posters of Churchill and DeGaulle from the Second World War on the walls inside the main building, though I was never able to find out how or why they continued to adorn the walls of this building well into the 1990s.

At the west end of Dong Jiao Min Xiang, we can just barely see over the wall of the former United States legation which, according to popular legend, was built on the basis of blueprints for a Washington DC post office. During the 1920s and 1930s, the legation grounds sported a baseball diamond. Across the street is a maroon painted brick building that served as a Swiss-run hospital.

As each year goes by, more and more of the sights in the former Legation District disappear. However, for those who would enjoy a fictionalized (and, admittedly biased) account of the siege of the legations, *Indiscreet Letters from*

Peking, written by L. Putnam Weale is a riveting read. Weale was the *nom de plume* of Bertrand Lennox-Simpson, a long-term resident of Peking and a widely published author on East Asian issues of that era. A friend of L.C. Arlington, Weale dabbled in many intrigues. An unknown assailant brutally butchered him in Tianjin in the 1920s, perhaps in revenge for prior indiscretions.

10

THE EASTERN TARTAR CITY

THE EASTERN TARTAR CITY IS home to several famous temples, city wall remnants and princely mansions. Alas, the character of this section of the city is under assault by the wrecking ball. All the places described below soon will become islands of antiquity surrounded by drab modern architecture.

The former Tartar City once curved in an inverted "u" shape along the northern walls of the city. The Second Ring Road now marks its borders. For this tour, you should start at the tower located at the corner of Chong Wen Men Avenue (崇文门大街) and the Second Ring Road.

The Fox Tower, as it once was called, was not one of the major conduits into the city. Rather, it was built primarily for use as a watchtower in 1439. Somehow it miraculously escaped demolition and merits a visit. Inside the building are three separate floors constructed of massive timber beams and housing the Red Gate Modern Art Gallery as well as an excellent exhibition of photographs of Old Peking. On the outside terrace, the gate's portal gives us a fleeting notion of the grandeur of the city walls. By the stairways leading to the ground, a sign in Chinese points to some barely visible graffiti, noting that these inscriptions were left by Russian and American soldiers and serves as "incontrovertible proof of their crimes" during the Boxer Debacle. I have visited the tower over the past ten years and have noticed that the English graffiti is of recent origin. In childish handwriting, "Dec. 16, 1900" and "U.S.A." can be discerned, though it is not clear what an American soldier would be doing in a watch tower in the Russian zone of occupation. Russian graffiti, if there ever had been any, has worn away with time. (I recall some Cyrillic script in the early 1990s). However, there is an abundance of graffiti in Chinese, helpfully dated June 15, 1949, July 8, 1960, and the year 1971, along with other dates, written by conscientious (and patriotic) scribblers.

Eastern Tartar City

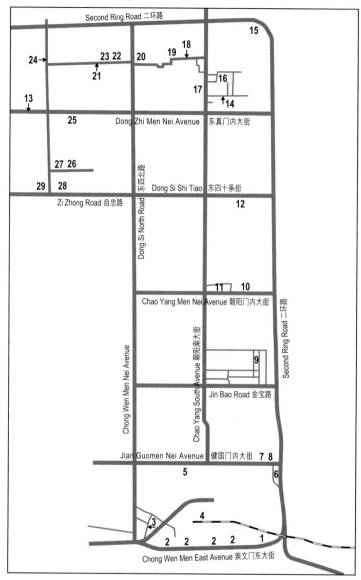

1. Fox Tower
2. Ruins of Tartar City Wall
3. Hou Gou Alley (后勾胡同)
4. Peking Railway Station
5. Shrine to Yu Qian (于谦祠)
6. Imperial Observatory (古观象)
7. Chinese Academy of Sciences
   (former site of Hall of Social Imperial Examination 贡院)
8. Memorial for Hong Kong's Return to Chinese Sovereignty
9. Temple of Wisdom Attained (智化寺)
10. Palace of Prince Fu (草王府)
11. Palace of Prince Duan
12. Southern Granary (南仓)
13. Dong Zhi Men Nei Avenue (东直门内大街)
14. Yang Guan Alley (羊管胡同)

15. Russian Embassy
16. Temple of Complete Teaching (通教庙)
17. Dong Zhi Men Xiao Jie (东直门小街)
18. Bao Ju Alley (炮局胡同)
19. Temple of the Cypress Grove (柏林寺)
20. Lama Temple (喇嘛庙)
21. Alley of the School for the Sons of the Nation (国子监胡同)
22. Confucian Temple (孔子庙)
23. School for the Sons of the Nation (国子监)
24. An Ding Men Nei Avenue (安定门内大街)
25. former Residence of Mao Dun (茅盾故居)
26. Memorial to Prime Minister Wen Tian Xiang (文天祥祠)
27. Palace of Prince Shun Tian (顺天府)
28. Memorial Site of the Passing of Sun Yat-Sen
29. Site of Duan Qi Rui's Government (段祺瑞政府旧址)

Turning westward on Chong Wen Men Avenue (崇文门大街), you can see the ruins of the Tartar City wall on the north side of the street. Previously, the view was obscured by hectares of badly designed houses and shops built between the ruins of the wall and the street. In a very encouraging move, the Peking government has decided to restore these walls and the surrounding area as a park.

Though long since demolished, the Gate of Excellent Scholarship (崇文门 or *chong wen men*) still lends its name to this district, which is also known by a more ancient name, Hata Men (哈德门). This colloquial name originates from the residence of the Mongol Prince Hata who lived in this vicinity during the Yuan dynasty.

By plunging into Hou Gou Alley (后勾胡同) off Bei Jing Zhan West Avenue (北京站西大街), we come across the Protestant Church formerly associated with the China Inland Mission. In 1864, Protestant missionary efforts in China had already been underway from Macao for nearly a century. In that year, Hudson Taylor, an Anglican lay-preacher, established a mission with the intention of spreading the gospel in the non-coastal parts of China. Taylor said that his commitment to China's conversion to Christianity took root one day when he was accosted by an elderly Chinese, repeatedly exclaiming, "Why have you taken so long to come here?" Taylor spent the rest of his life in China as a missionary addressing the query posed by the Chinese fellow (or so he thought).

Taylor followed the Jesuit approach by advocating that churches should be built in the Chinese style, missionaries should wear Chinese clothing and all missions should be "localized" as quickly as possible with Chinese converts. The China Inland Mission closed in 1950 because of accusations by the PRC government that it was engaging in intelligence services for imperialist powers. In another lovely irony, the church now is a local branch of the Ministry of Public Security, which undoubtedly gathers intelligence on comings and goings at the main Peking railway station around the corner.

The PRC's view of foreign missionaries obscures — and thus diminishes — a couple of valid points. Foreign missionaries introduced modern education into China, albeit in a culturally insensitive manner. In his book *China, The Pity of It* Nathaniel Peffer quotes the eminent British scholar J.O.P. Bland:

> Every Mission School was an instrument of denationalization. The pupils were taught, not as Chinese children preparing to share in the life of the Chinese life, but as American schoolchildren. Of literature, the Chinese learned English literature. Of history, they learned American history … . And it is not too much of a caricature to say that thousands of Chinese children grew to the age of sixteen without any clear knowledge that there had ever existed on this planet more than three men worthy of emulation: Christ, George Washington and Abraham Lincoln … .

The second valid reason for the Communist Party's belief that missionaries were spies is exemplified by a Georgia boy who came to China in 1940 to spread the gospel. His name was John Birch. After the Japanese attack on Pearl Harbor, Birch volunteered to act as a spy on behalf of the OSS and the KMT espionage agency, the Special Service (特务 or *te wu*). Birch reportedly had superior linguistic talents and could acquire the basics of several spoken dialects in an amazingly short time. It was Birch, disguised as a peasant, who took Jimmy Doolittle and his Tokyo raiders through Japanese occupied territory to the Nationalist wartime capital Chongqing. He also conducted countless information and surveillance missions on behalf of Claire Chennault and his Flying Tigers.

Birch had a close relationship with *te wu* agents who carried out cold-blooded assassinations against both Japanese occupation forces and Communist resistance fighters. The Chinese supervisor for these forays was Dai Li (戴笠), the ruthless head of the KMT espionage agency.

Chinese communist troops captured Birch ten days after Japan's surrender. For reasons that are still not clear, the communists tortured the preacher turned spy to death. In the 1950s, Robert Welch, a wealthy American industrialist, co-opted the dead man's name and founded the John Birch Society. Welch hailed Birch as the first American casualty in the Cold War, thus sadly giving further ammunition to the view of missionaries as a suspect group.

As mentioned above, the main railway station in Peking is right around the corner. Liang Si Cheng designed the building, which was completed in 1959 for the tenth anniversary of the People's Republic.

At No. 23 Biao Bei Alley (裱褙胡同), a gray courtyard house is the Shrine to Yu Qian (于谦祠), a Ming Minister of War and the general who defeated a Mongol attempt to recapture Peking in the 15th century.

In 1449, Mongol armies had occupied Datong (大同) and threatened to invade the capital. The emperor Zheng Tong (正统) was an indolent creature raised amidst court intrigues and palace backbiting. His closest advisor was a eunuch named Wang Zhen (王振) who had ingratiated himself with the emperor through flattery and gifts. Since Zheng Tong fancied himself as a military genius, he accepted the misguided advice of his eunuch and led his troops out beyond the northern passes. The battle resulted in a complete route of the Ming forces. Zheng Tong managed to get himself captured by the Mongols and held for ransom.

Peking fell into a panic, especially with the recollection of the carnage after the last Mongol siege in 1215. It fell to Yu Qian, a military official and former high scorer on the Metropolitan Examinations, to recover the initiative. Yu fortified the city's defenses by placing cannons on the walls. In the meantime, the Ming court selected Zheng Tong's younger brother, Jing Tai (景泰) to ascend the Dragon Throne and maintain administrative continuity. After several days of fruitless efforts to breach the city walls, the Mongols withdrew to the steppes, thanks to Yu Qian's tactical fortifications.

In a further humiliation to Zheng Tong, the Ming court rejected ransom demands sent by the Mongols, apparently content that Zheng Tong might never return. A year later, the Mongols returned Zheng Tong with the complaint that the *prima donna* was not worth the effort. For the next several years, Zheng Tong nurtured his resentments and plotted against Jing Tai.

Yu Qian became a hero to the people of Peking. They revered him in much the same way General Zhukov has been honored in Moscow. Yu continued in faithful service to Jing Tai until 1457, when Zheng Tong displaced his younger brother in a coup and recaptured the throne. Afterwards, Yu Qian was branded as a traitor and executed in Cai Shi Kou before a throng of silent, grief-stricken people.

Chinese history is full of reversals of verdicts. In 1466, Yu Qian was posthumously rehabilitated with his home converted into a shrine to his memory. Throughout the centuries, Confucian scholars, military officials and even Korean tribute bearers sought out the shrine and paid their respects to Yu Qian. Various Qing emperors allotted funds for restoration of the shrine, the last time being a gift granted by Guang Xu during the 1898 Reform Movement. After liberation, local people were housed in the shrine's courtyard.

Peking's contemporary urban planners have no time for Yu Qian. His shrine is located in a neighborhood that has been earmarked for "redevelopment". While I was researching this book, I visited Yu Qian's shrine at a fortuitous moment. The surrounding streets of courtyard houses were barren and abandoned, as if its residents had just fled an imminent invasion. Discarded belongings littered the street corners and everywhere people were loading crates and boxes onto trucks. I turned a corner and there was Yu Qian's Shrine. Workers had just loaded two large blue trucks with nylon canvass bags, crates and cardboard boxes. A semi-circle of morose people turned with a start to look at me.

"Isn't this Yu Qian's Shrine?" I asked. For a second, everyone seemed too shocked to answer this sudden apparition speaking *ren hua* (人话 or "human language").

"Yes, yes, yes," answered a small man with a flattop haircut, recovering his composure. His eyes had a look of unspeakable sorrow. "We have lived here for forty years," he said pointing to the entrance of Yu Qian's shrine. "And today the government is moving us away."

Suddenly, everyone began speaking at once, taking some solace in presenting their case to an outsider. The man with the sad eyes said that the people of his

天理何在 !!!
法律何存
我要居住权　抗议 强迁

Words of protest after a forced eviction.

neighborhood had never wanted to move, but they had no voice in the matter. Another man, dressed in a white t-shirt and shorts, waving a fan to cool himself, added heatedly, "Look over there. Those tall buildings? That's what the city wants to build here."

I looked into everyone's eyes. "But there's nothing beautiful or great about those boxes," I said. "Moreover, those types of buildings have nothing whatsoever to do with Chinese traditions. Or Peking traditions."

One of the residents was a tall goofy-looking guy who wore horn-rimmed glasses, a button-down shirt, shorts, black socks and black plastic "penny leather" shoes. He patted me on the shoulder and gave me a lop-sided grin. "Exactly right! To make money, the government wants us to give up our homes so they can make Western type skyscrapers. Peking will have nothing distinctively Chinese about it anymore."

The residents could not even look forward to preserving their community. Each family was assigned to different apartment blocks far away in north Peking. Instead of spending summer evenings gossiping with old friends on the street corners, they will be locked away in tiny cubicles of Western invention, not knowing their neighbors and having to ride elevators simply to go out to fetch a bottle of beer or yogurt.

An 1860s depiction of the Imperial Observatory.

When I told them that I was writing a book about Old Peking, they related, with communal sense of pride, the story of Yu Qian's heroism. They told me about a signboard that hung over the gate. It quoted one of Yu's poems on his quiet resolve to protect and defend the city and its citizens. Imperial stele once stood in the courtyard, but they are now long gone as was a cypress tree that Yu had planted. The shrine was an empty shell, and I arrived at the moment that its last shred of dignity — its people — was being carted away.

People in the remote back alleys do not always warm up when a foreigner barges into their world. However, my friends here found some solace in a foreigner sharing their sadness at the moment of their departure from the old neighborhood. It felt as if we were sharing a last communion at a requiem mass for Yu Qian.

As I said goodbye to them, the guy with the horn rims said, "Thank you so much, *ge'mer*." "Ge'mer" is a term that first appeared in China's prisons during the late 1950s. In Peking, it has become a counter-culture equivalent of word "comrade" (同志 or *tong zhi*). A *ge'mer* is an ally fighting the system with you. You will not find a *ge'mer* in respectable society, but only among those who no longer buy into the system. It has a pleasingly conspiratorial ring to it.

As I left, I told my friends, "Someday, the city will regret its actions here. Just like Wang Zhen."

觀　象　臺

The observatory during the Warlord Era.

A contemporary view.

"No," said Horn Rims. "Wang Zhen died in comfort with peace of mind. Same thing with those people. So long, *gemer*. I'm happy to have met you." Me too, *ge'mer*.

At the corner of Jian Guo Men Avenue and the Second Ring Road, a gray fortress recalls the role of stargazing technology in Chinese life. This is the Imperial Observatory (古观象 or *gu guan xiang*).

The Imperial Observatory played an essential role in the politics of Peking. According to ancient custom, imperial rituals had to be performed annually at a precise time during the earth's orbit of the sun. According to Confucian philosophy an ethical ruler who neglected to perform these rituals risked a disruption of harmony between this world and Heaven, which would send forth punishments in the form of natural or man-made disasters. Because of these beliefs, sometimes called chromonancy, an accurate calendar was not simply a way to track time. It was an essential tool in a bid to avoid calamity.

Over the centuries, this correlation between action and time resulted in an imperial astrology that dictated all of the emperor's activities. These rules were expanded to the lives of commoners as well. The imperial courts recorded the forecasts for the forthcoming year in an almanac that was printed by the imperial press, distributed throughout the country and had proscribed all activities for everyone in China.

And it controlled everything. Do you want to cut your hair? Well, you can do it without danger on Thursday or Saturday. Do you need to move house? Only on Monday or Wednesday. You are so reckless that you want to get married? Well, only on the first three weeks before the New Year. You cannot overemphasize the role of these almanacs in daily life.

There was even a meteorological aspect to these books. Just like the Old Farmer's Almanac in the United States, these almanacs included predictions for the weather in the New Year as well as advice on planting and harvesting crops.

Even after the collapse of the Qing dynasty, Chinese astrologers continued to publish almanacs. Reginald Johnston recorded his astonishment that even in 1918, the imperial retinue set Henry Pu Yi's daily agenda according to the traditional almanac. After assuming his duties as the imperial English tutor, Johnston checked into the Peking Hotel. Several imperial court nobles arrived to choose a date from the almanac for the commencement of classes. Johnston was put out when he was told the next auspicious date was some 45 days away, with the best day for such new endeavor two months away. The court officials tried to pressure Johnston to take the later of the two dates, though Johnston stuck to his guns and insisted upon the earlier date.

Accurate astronomy was the linchpin of the almanac system. During the Yuan dynasty, Kublai Khan built an observatory in the eastern part of Peking. When Yong Le moved the capital to Peking, he moved the Imperial Observatory to its current site. However, Yong Le faced a dilemma regarding the staffing of the observatory. In the confusion after the collapse of the Song, China had lost the technology required to calculate time. In the early days of the Ming, his imperial court relied upon two sets of astronomical calculations, one based upon the Mongol almanac — the Ta Tong (鞑同) and the other upon the Islamic calendar — the Hui Li (回历). Since Muslims were also concerned with astronomical expertise for religious celebrations, the skills of Muslim astronomers were welcomed at court.

In 1603, the arrival of Matteo Ricci in Peking turned this arrangement on its head. By European innovations in mathematics and astronomical calculations, Ricci proved both the inaccuracy and obsolescence of the Mongol and Muslim calendars. For the next century, the Jesuits gradually expanded their influence in the court by producing more accurate astronomic predictions. In 1623 they surpassed all other astronomers by accurately predicting the precise moment of a solar eclipse.

After the establishment of the Qing, the Manchus were keen to retain the Jesuits for their skills in astronomy (and, sadly, in cannon casting). Shun Zhi appointed Adam von Schall, a German Jesuit, to the position of chief astronomer, which outraged a Chinese Muslim astronomer, Yang Guang Xian (杨光先). Yang commenced an anti-foreign campaign to discredit the Jesuits by using the pretext of a two hundred year calendar prepared by Father Schall. Yang argued that Schall implicitly made the seditious assertion that the Qing would only exist for another 200 years. (It stood for another 247 years, but never mind.) The hapless priest was carted off to prison as Yang triumphantly resumed control of the Imperial Observatory and re-introduced the Muslim calendar.

In a *volte-face* common in China, Yang's calendar proved to be out of whack, and Yang was cashiered — a hollow victory for Father Schall, who was suffering from weakness and paralysis when he was released from prison. He died shortly after his release.

Yang was not to give up so easily. He wrote a treatise in defense of his calendar, entitled *I Could Not Do Otherwise* (不得已 or *bu de yi*). In his treatise, Yang declared that "he would rather have no good calendar than have foreigners in China," a xenophobia that foreshadowed Jiang Qing's cry that China "would rather eat socialist weeds than capitalist wheat." Yang also dismissed Western technology by declaring that it is precisely because of such technology that foreigners are potential enemies.

Poor old Yang's outburst is part of a never-ending chorus in China over the past seven centuries. In his case, he was probably unnerved by the sudden appearance of Western military and ideological control throughout the world — as demonstrated by Portuguese influence in Japan's internal affairs and the Spanish conquest of the New World and the Philippines.[1] Perhaps he was one of the first Chinese to see how little chime clocks could grow into Congreve rockets.

A Belgian Jesuit, Ferdinand Verbiest, took over the operation of the Imperial Observatory from Schall in 1669. From that year until 1838, Europeans were appointed to the position of chief astronomer, though not without complications.

After his appointment, Father Verbiest was charged with cleaning up Yang's shoddy calendar. In order to do so, Father Verbiest needed to cut out an entire month from the almanac, an excision that fanned the flames of anti-foreign feeling. Yang and his cohorts egged on another campaign in Peking, asking with outrage "What has become of that month and where has it been hidden away?" I can easily imagine Father Verbiest with his head in his hands, wondering what's going to happen next.

The Observatory is not a frequented site in Peking. By climbing up the stairs, we have a chance to examine some of the original, or perhaps replicated, astronomical instruments cast by the Jesuits. As I said before, German troops confiscated these instruments, which, given the continuing importance of the almanac in Chinese life, was a calculated insult of outrageous proportions. The instruments were returned in accordance with the Treaty of Versailles, which led Bernard Shaw to quip that this was the only good thing that ever came out of the treaty.

Across the street from the Jesuit Observatory is a coffee colored building that houses the Chinese Academy of Social Sciences. The building marks the site of the Hall of the Imperial Examination (贡院). The halls disappeared at the turn of the last century, but since they played such a significant role in the government of the Qing dynasty, it is worthwhile to reflect for a moment or two on the history of this site.

In order to select people worthy to govern the state, China's imperial dynasties implemented a civil examination system where aspirants to government office underwent a rigorous examination in the Confucian classics. During the Qing, the examinations were held in three stages, which can be simply described as local, provincial or Metropolitan Examinations. The latter, held for the *jin shi* (进士) degree, was administered every three years. This was the final examination before an applicant obtained highest public office (and with it the ability to squeeze public funds). In addition to orthodox Confucian principles, candidates were also marked on their knowledge of classical literature and their calligraphy. So much as a character missing a single stroke was sufficient basis for a candidate to be cashiered.

Confucian precepts held that since anyone could achieve spiritual and intellectual perfection, the examination were open to all, regardless of their station in life. In theory, even the son of the poorest peasant could, by knowledge of the classics, become one of the most senior officials of the empire. Of course, there were few commoners who had the wealth necessary for a son to spend his time in study rather than in the fields. Further, women were barred from sitting for the exam. Finally, during the Ming and Qing, official positions could also be bought, though they carried far less prestige.

During the late 19th century, the halls on this site consisted of some 8,000 tiny cubicles, each measuring ten feet in height and five feet square. The candidates were assigned a different character, which in turn was pasted upon the door of the allocated cubicle.

Before the examinations began, candidates had to change their clothes to ensure that no crib notes would be smuggled in. Then each candidate was walled into a cubicle for three days. Inside were a small table, a stool and writing implements. The candidates would remain walled up in their cubicles for three days and two nights, with deputies on watch to ensure that nothing would be brought in. Many cracked under the pressure, dying of exhaustion, committing suicide or going insane. The deceased were dragged out of the cubicles once the examinations had been completed, a preventive measure against distracting other candidates, which seems sensible.

Pressure undoubtedly was compounded by proctors patrolling among the lanes of cubicles waving a flag and calling out "Whoever has an enemy here may now take his revenge!" The deputies meant these words for any ghosts hovering overhead who would have a grievance against a candidate for a previous wrong. A candidate could console himself that the malevolence of an enemy's ghost was the cause of his failure of the examination. Peking legend had it that a hostile spirit could persuade a fly to land on a character, thus ruining the applicant's chances for passing by wrecking the strokes of a character. Or, in the case of a kind-hearted soul who never hurt a fly, the fly — apparently aware of the candidate's easy-going nature through the fly grapevine — landed on the examination paper and supplied a stroke missing from a character.

Human nature being what it is, candidates tended to conduct themselves with benevolence and charity in the days preceding the Metropolitan Examinations. Alms for the poor, incense for the deities, donations to public works and especially respective behavior to the elderly would all mark the behavior of an aspiring candidate, at least until the results were published.

The flag carried by the deputies depicted the Great Bear constellation, which was the symbol of the deity Kui Xing (魁星). According to legend Kui Xing was an ugly, but academically gifted dwarf, who surpassed all other candidates during a Tang dynasty Metropolitan Examination. When the emperor discovered the identity of the top-ranking candidate, he was appalled by the ugliness of the gold medal winner and refused to confer the degree. On cue, Kui Xing died of a broken heart but was then granted immortality and supernatural powers. His blessings were much sought after by examination candidates, both tall and short, good looking and ugly, in subsequent dynasties.

Kui Xing shared the title of God of Literature with Wen Chang (文昌), a deity who lives in the constellation of six stars of *Ursa Major*. Wen Chang appears to have been a scholar of the Tang era and a resident of Si Chuan province. Various legends are told about him. He was a general who defeated an invasion from Xin Jiang. Or he was a prophet who took mortal form through 17 incarnations, seeking to help mortals achieve bliss. He was depicted in a blue gown with scepter accompanied by two servants called "Deaf as Heaven" and "Dumb as Earth" as a reflection of the utmost discretion with which they served Wen Chang.

The last Metropolitan Examination was administered in 1900. In the aftermath of the Boxer Incident, foreign troops pulled down many of the cubicles for firewood. Because the foreign powers viewed the examination system as an institution that cultivated Qing anti-progressive policies, the Protocol of 1901 penalized the literary classes by forbidding the Metropolitan Examination for five years. However, the Confucian examination system was scrapped shortly before 1906, and the last of the cubicles were demolished in 1913. It is fitting that the site now hosts a similar institution, the China Academy of Social Sciences. On the anniversary of the Metropolitan Examinations, (i.e., the third month of every third lunar year), perhaps the scholars there might somehow sense the spirits of those who exerted so much energy and effort to demonstrate a stellar command of a forgotten philosophy.

Across Jian Guo Men Avenue is an electric rainbow-like contraption that was set up to celebrate the return of Hong Kong to Chinese sovereignty in 1997. This incredible eyesore will remain in place as a permanent memorial to the event, though it certainly does not look like something that will be a rock of ages. In keeping with the concept of geographical symmetry, there is another one of these abominations on Fu Xing Avenue on the west side of the city.

To the north of Jian Guo Men Nei Avenue on Lu Mi Cang Alley (禄米仓胡 同 or *lu mi cang hu tong*), we find the Temple of Wisdom Attained (智化寺 or *zhi hua si*). During our visit to the Yu Qian Memorial, we came across the misdeeds of the chief eunuch, Wang Zhen. This same man used his power and wealth to construct the Temple of Wisdom Attained in 1444. The temple is a marvelous example of Ming Buddhist architecture and was apparently built in the same style as a Song dynasty plan called "seven monastery buildings." The niches in the inner halls hold 9,000 small carved Buddhas, and the ceiling tiles have a Lamaist influence.

Wang Zhen built the Temple of Wisdom Attained in order to accumulate much needed merit and to establish a shrine where monks would perform ancestral rites in his memory. The temple held a statue of Wang Zhen for nearly two hundred years until Qian Long decreed that the statute should be destroyed and that the official records regarding Wang Zhen ought to cast him as one of the greatest villains of the Ming dynasty. Since that time, the temple has solely served the role of a center for Buddhist worship and study.

On No.137 Chao Yang Men Nei Avenue (朝阳门内大街) on the north side of the street from the Xin Jiang restaurant Afunti, is the former Palace of Prince Fu (孚王府 or *fu wang fu*), an enormous courtyard mansion built during the early years of Kang Xi's reign. Passing across the street, you will come across the grand main gate with two stone lions and come to the main hall of the palace. The Palace of Prince Fu originally consisted of many courtyards where *ping fang* now stands. Off on the east side of the main hall is the Chinese Portugal Historical Study Center.

On Shao Jiu Alley (烧酒胡同) further to the west of the Palace of Prince Fu, we find the Palace of Prince Duan, who was the fifth son of the Dao Guang Emperor. I think that he must have been a fabulously likable, rough-and-tumble sort, even though he threw his lot in with those who wanted to wipe out all foreigners in Peking during the Boxer Debacle.

According to Western accounts, Old Duan retained some of the straightforwardness of his Manchu ancestors. He was tall, stout and red-faced, with a considerable fondness for a dram of fire water and a taste for dog meat, which he specially bought in a shop near the Fox Tower. He enjoyed a reputation as an outspoken and honest prince who was not afraid of challenging the Empress Dowager. Being a direct descendant of an emperor, Prince Tuan looked upon the Empress Dowager as an interloper not worthy of holding the yellow. He did not feel constrained by court etiquette, which became increasingly debased during the Empress Dowager's reign.

One time, Old Duan wanted to give the Empress Dowager a specially prepared dish of salmon. The court eunuchs insisted upon the payment of a fairly large bribe before allowing gifts to be delivered to the Empress Dowager. Not one to be thwarted by eunuchs, the prince pushed his way past the court sycophants and personally presented the dish to the Empress Dowager, who needless to say was startled at the sudden appearance of Old Duan, barging his way into the inner chambers and cursing the eyes of the eunuchs and court attendants.

Since Old Duan endorsed Confucian concepts of propriety, he disapproved of the Empress Dowager's tastes for vulgar entertainment. Once, when the prince was at court, an "off-color" story was being told to the Empress Dowager. In the back of the pavilion, Old Duan jumped up, sang a popular obscene ditty, and generally behaved like a Qing version of Benny Hill. The Empress Dowager simply ordered him home, saying that the prince had too much to drink. However, his arrow had found its way home, and the Empress Dowager never again permitted such story telling at court.

Later, when an obscene play was being performed at the Forbidden City, Old Duan began applauding loudly, in contravention of imperial etiquette, which required silence and obeisance to the throne. The Empress Dowager sent another prince to scold Duan for a breach of etiquette. The prince exclaimed in a booming voice to be heard throughout the palace "Oh, I quite forgot. I was so taken with the play that I thought I was at one of those *public* theatres."

Regrettably, Old Duan took the wrong path during the Boxer Debacle. He personally commanded 1,400 Boxers in the siege on the Legation District. Initially the foreign powers insisted upon his execution, but later accepted permanent exile in Xin Jiang, where his taste probably graduated from dog meat to spiced lamb kebabs. It is said that the old spitfire came back to Peking in the early 1920s, just to rile the foreign powers, who raged, sputtered and insisted upon his return to the land of fine lamb and *bai jiu* (白酒 or moonshine).

Off the eastern side of Chao Yang Men North Street (朝阳门北街) are the walls of the former Southern Granary (南仓). One of Dorgon's policies to thwart revolts in the capital was to provide price-subsidized grain to its citizens. These granaries were strategically located in the Tartar City near the barracks of the bannermen.

The government's practice of annually filing the granaries produced a corresponding religious practice. On the 25th day of the first lunar month, the festival of filing the granaries entailed Peking families buying pork, mutton and beef for a daylong feast. Any guests stopping by on that day could not leave until they had stuffed themselves with roasted meats. Similarly, extravagant meals were given to house servants. The belief was that, as each household would invite friends and workers to eat freely and thus "fill their granaries," the gods of grain would be encouraged to do the same and ensure that the city's granaries were replete with rice, corn, millet and barley.

In the northeast corner of the Old Tartar City, there was a beautiful tree-lined road that passed through a traditional neighborhood, parallel to the East Second Ring Road. This street is called Dong Zhi Men Nei Avenue (东直门内大街). Unfortunately, this neighborhood also has been the subject of undistinguished urban redevelopment ruining its old appearance of grey tiled houses and tree shaded lanes.

Be that as it may, immediately to the west of the intersection with Dong Zhi Men Avenue, there is a hutong named Yang Guan Alley (洋管胡同). According to Reginald Johnston, the marquis Zhu Yu Xun (朱煜勋), a direct descent of the Ming emperors lived in great poverty on this street during the 1920s.

The Manchu emperor Yong Zheng had bestowed the hereditary title of marquis (廷恩侯 or literally, extended grace) on one of Zhu Yuan Cheng's descendants in a further display of the fiction of Qing "fealty" to the Ming. Yong Zheng also agreed to pay the Marquis and his descendants an honorarium in exchange for their performance of memorial rites at the Ming tombs.

In the months after the collapse of the Qing dynasty, gentry in He Bei (河北) and An Hui (安徽) provinces advocated a Ming reformation, a proposal that ran aground against the republican sentiments as well as the personal aspirations of Yuan Shi Kai. The Marquis Zhu lived in obscurity for the next decade. In 1924, Johnston learned that the reduced Qing court continued to pay a small honorarium to Marquis Zhu. Johnston arranged for Pu Yi to invite the Marquis for a visit to the Forbidden City.

On the specified day, the Marquis appeared in the traditional garb of a Qing official and kowtowed before his sovereign. Later, when Pu Yi moved to Tianjin after his exile from the Forbidden City, the Marquis paid a final tribute journey to the last emperor. Presumably he lived anonymously through the Japanese occupation and the establishment of the People's Republic.

At the end of Dong Zhi Men Nei Avenue, the Russian Embassy stands in socialist architectural majesty, nestled in the corner where the Second Ring Road swings from east to south. This plot of land and surrounding sites testify to a three hundred year tradition of Slavic culture in Peking.

During the middle of the 17th century, Russia was expanding its borders into Siberia. On the Amur River, the Russians established an outpost called Albazin. Within the log-walls of the fortress, Russian merchants conducted trade with Mongols and Chinese. Cossacks also launched raids into Qing territory to bring back much needed meat, mead and maidens. In 1685, Manchu forces successfully laid siege to Albazin fortress, bringing back to Peking forty-five Cossacks as prisoners of war. In subsequent border skirmishes, more captured Cossacks were brought to Peking, bringing the total number of Russian prisoners of war to around one hundred.

The martial skills and horsemanship of the Cossacks delighted Kang Xi, who granted them a pardon and organized them into a unit of the Qing army — the Eleventh Company of the Fourth Regiment of the Manchu Bordered Yellow

Banner. He also granted the Cossacks full religious freedom and gave them a Buddhist temple, which they converted into an Eastern Orthodox Church with the name the Church of St. Nicholas, later renamed the Church of the Assumption. The Cossacks married Manchu and Mongol wives and settled inside the city next to the northeast corner of the Tartar City Wall.

In 1685, Peking and St. Petersburg signed the Treaty of Nerchinsk, which had been negotiated with the linguistic assistance of the Jesuits. The treaty permitted Russian trade missions to come to Peking once every three years. While in Peking, Russian participants in the delegations were lodged in the Dong Jiao Min Xiang district in buildings reserved for tribute missions from border countries. Eventually, a separate building was allocated to the Russians, who built a second Eastern Orthodox Church, the Convent of Candlemass, which was later renamed the Church of the Purification of the Virgin, in the area that was to become the Legation District.

On the pretext of sending her congratulations to the Qing Court on Yong Zheng's succession, Catherine the Great dispatched a diplomatic mission to Peking, which eventually produced the Treaty of Kiakhta of 1727. In a departure from Chinese foreign policy, the treaty provided for an exchange of embassies without any Russian obligation to acknowledge the superiority of the Dragon Throne. This exception was most likely attributable to Peking's realization of the territorial threat posed by Russian expansion.

Another provision of the treaty granted the Russians the right to maintain an eccelestical mission so that resident Russians regularly could receive the sacraments of the Eastern Orthodox Church. The Russian priests sent to Peking did not attempt to recruit Chinese converts and thus sidestepped the political controversies arising from the Jesuits' participation in the Qing court. The treaty also provided for Russian youths to live in the mission and study the Chinese language. The ecclestical mission continued until 1954.

In the winter of 1948, Desmond Neil, a British language student, visited the Russian priests. At that time, a wall enclosed a monastery where the monks lived a bucolic life, raising dairy cattle and honeybees and growing grains and fruit. In the courtyard houses outside the monastery lived the descendants of the Albazin Cossacks, still fervent adherents of the Orthodox faith despite their Chinese features. In 1954, Peking evicted the Russian monks and turned the extensive grounds over to the Soviet Union as a new embassy. The Soviets built row upon row of apartment complexes to house their legions of technical advisors. By 1960, the relationship soured and many of the Soviet technicians were sent home. During the Cultural Revolution, Red Guards assaulted the Soviet embassy, with the Soviet diplomatic corps barricaded behind their desks and having to endure Red Guards rubbing mud (literally) into their faces. By point of reference, British diplomatic staff did not have to endure this effrontery. Some were simply bludgeoned to death.

Nowadays, the grounds of the Russian Embassy compound are a little Russian town enclosed in the heart of Peking. From the road, you can see numerous Western buildings while inside the greenery is home to rabbits, squirrels and birds. Russian residents have been so taken with these creatures that they are completely tame and unafraid of people. Inside the grounds are an orthodox church and a memorial cross for those killed during the Boxer Debacle.

There are still about several thousand descendants of the Albazin Cossacks in Peking. One of the descendants is a certain Mr. Du, a Russian-speaking Orthodox Christian Chinese who also calls himself Viktor Dubinin after his Ukrainian ancestor. The Orthodox community held its first Christmas celebration in fifty years at the embassy chapel in January 2002. The elders of the Russian Orthodox Church in Smolensk and Kalingrad especially sent a priest, Father Dionysis, to celebrate this special mass attended by Russo-Chinese.

At the time of the Christmas celebration, Mr. Dubinin expressed his concern that the Russo-Chinese community was on the verge of extinction. Until the spring of 2002, most of the Cossack descendants still lived in the neighborhood south of the Russian embassy. The area has since been razed and the Sino-Russians scattered to the four winds.

Since the 1990s, Moscow Patriarch Alexy II has been in discussions with Peking about the restoration of ecclestical ties and the recovery of remains of Russian nobility buried in Peking. Several relatives of Czar Nicholas II, including, for a time, the Grand Duchess Elizabeth, were buried in the former Russian Cemetery, previously located north of the city walls until it was submerged under the lake in Youth Park (年青公园 or *nian qing gong yuan*). Alexy II has requested Peking's assistance in recovering these holy relics, as they are viewed.

Turning left at the main gate of the Russian embassy, we continue down the street and take the next left hand turn amidst the rubble of the old neighborhood. On the west side of the Zhen Xian Alley (针线巷) is Dong Jiao Miao (通教庙 or the Temple of Complete Teaching). Originally the courtyard home of a eunuch of the Kang Xi era, the building was abandoned and in a ramshackle condition by the 1930s. In 1943, Buddhist nuns from Fu Jian province converted the ruins into a nunnery and, during the Cultural Revolution, the nunnery was turned into a factory.

The past ten years have seen something of a reversal of fortune for the nuns, and that gives me a cause for great joy. Peking municipality has allocated funds and Buddhist relics to the nunnery. These days, the nuns are willing to show the halls to foreigners. The mid-morning chanting, accompanied by clouds of incense, is particularly peaceful.

Turning north on Dong Zhi Men Bei Xiao Jie (东直门北小街) and then west of Bao Ju Alley (炮局胡同), we can take a serpentine short cut to the Temple of the Cypress Grove (柏林寺 or *bai lin si*), a Buddhist temple attached to the more famous Palace of Concord of Harmony (雍和宫 or *yong he gong,* also commonly called the Lama Temple). The Temple of the Cypress Grove was originally constructed in 1347 and was the largest temple complex in Yuan Peking. In subsequent years, the temple continued to be a notable Buddhist institution, having been selected for renovation in 1712 for the celebration of Kang Xi's sixtieth birthday. The temple also formerly housed a magnificent set of printing blocks for the Buddhist Tripitaka carved in the 18th century.

During the Qing dynasty, the lamas of the Lama Temple embarked upon summer retreats to the Temple of the Cypress Grove. In the 20th century, the temple was the temporary residence of the French Buddhist and Tibet-traveler, Alexandra David-Neel who claimed, despite the skeptical responses of Anglophones, to have visited Lhasa in the 1930s. At the time of this writing, the Temple of the Cypress Grove serves as the headquarters for the Peking Historical Site Preservation Bureau which, typically, forbids outsiders from entering the temple. A white-gloved, uniformed guard will officiously shoo away the curious.

On Yong He Gong Avenue (雍和宫大街) is the Lama Temple, originally constructed as a prince's mansion for Kang Xi's fourth son, Yong Zheng. According to Manchu custom, the home of a reigning emperor could not be used as the residence of his descendants and would (usually) be converted into a temple. In 1745, Qian Long renovated the palace as a Lamaist temple for use by Mongolian and Tibetan monks. During the Qing era, it significantly reflected Peking's cosmopolitan flavor. The ceremonies of the Lama Temple became integrated into the cycle of life in the city, and thus the temple became an integral part of Old Peking. On the diplomatic front, Manchu officials housed the emissaries of Tibetan or Mongolian tribute missions in the monks' quarters.

Before the 20th century, the Lama Temple was not open to the public, perhaps because of apparent hostility or duplicity of the lamas against foreigners. Even in the late 1920s, Western writers related unpleasant near-escapes from kidnap attempts of solitary sightseers by the lamas.

Perhaps with some coloration of the truth, Arlington relates an incident where a monk encouraged him to enter an empty quarter of the temple on the promise of showing him unusual Buddhist relics. The monk then tried to lock Arlington into a cell until the old war horse brandished a revolver and demanded his immediate release.

Desmond Neil also had a story to tell about his visit in 1948. A monk brought Neil to a back cubicle where a Mongolian woman, smelling strongly of sheep and grasslands, flashed at Neil, a sight and smell that sent him scurrying for safety back in the main temple grounds. Perhaps these writers were still under the spell of stories of Fu Manchu and the image of mysterious malevolent monks. These days, the solitary traveler needs only worry about being run down by the scores of Hino tourist buses in the parking lot or being driven deaf by the megaphones of flag-waving tour group leaders

You enter the temple at the south gate and find a walkway that leads to a memorial arch. Along the way, you come across a delightful selection of cypress and pine trees, as well as an occasional pomegranate tree, tantalizingly bringing to mind Central Asia. Walking under the Gate of Luminous Peace (昭泰门 or *zhao tai men*), we pass the first courtyard and arrive at the Hall of Heavenly Kings (天王殿 or *tian wang dian*).

The Four Heavenly Kings were action-heroes in the Buddhist pantheon. They were reputed to guard the sides of Mt. Meru in the Buddhist heaven. The oldest of the four is the Land-bearer (持国 or *chi guo*) who carries a jade ring, a spear and a magic sword called Blue Cloud. The sword had wonderful powers. With one swoop, it generates a black wind full of thousands of arrows and spears, which were then followed by a firestorm breathed out by thousands of golden fiery serpents. The Far-gazer (广目 or *guang mu*) holds a four stringed guitar that sets his enemies' camps on fire upon being strummed. The Lord of Growth (增长 or *zeng chang*) wields a supernatural umbrella that can plunge the world into darkness when opened or send lightening bolts thundering down on the earth if inverted. The Well-famed (多闻 or *duo wen*) carries a white rat that can transform itself into a man devouring white-winged elephant, or some other man-eating animal. He also sometimes carries a pearl that could be tossed like a supernatural hand grenade.

In the center of the Hall of the Heavenly Kings, there is the Maitreya Buddha (弥勒佛 or *ni le fo*), who is also colloquially called the Big Belly Buddha (大肚佛 or *da du fo*) because of his ample paunch. He is a favorite in China and Chinese communities in South East Asia as well as in Japan. Some scholars doubt that this obese figure represents a historically or theologically sound personage from the Buddhist tradition. A more likely explanation is that he was originally an indigenous god of wealth, who insinuated his way into the Buddhist pantheon. He is often shown with elongated ear lobes (a symbol of compassion) and surrounded by a group of small children, which represent fertility. There are more orthodox depictions of a trimmed down Maitreya Buddha, usually in a contemplative pose and wearing a crown as a symbol of his deeply compassionate wisdom. We will come across these shortly.

Leaving appearances to one side, the Maitreya Buddha is a bodhisattva who was a member of the Sakyamuni Buddha's retinue according to the Mahayana tradition. Legends are scarce about his origins or relationship with Sakyamuni, who supposedly appointed him as his successor to reappear and save the world after the lapse of 5,000 years.

Westerners have a habit of dismissing this form of Maitreya Buddha as if he was a paedophilic fat slob with big ears. This is terribly unjust. It is not the deity's fault if the sculptor's chisel fails him. I know of one story that illustrates the reason for his enduring popularity.

> [This bodhisattva] had no desire to call himself a [Buddhist] master or to gather many disciples about him. Instead he walked the streets with a big sack into which he would put gifts of candy, fruit or doughnuts. These he would give to children who gathered around him in play. He established a kindergarten of the streets.
>
> Whenever he met a [Buddhist] devotee he would extend his hand and say: "Give me one penny." And if anyone asked him to return to a temple to teach others, again he would reply: "Give me one penny."
>
> Once as he was about his play-work another [Buddhist] master happened along and inquired: "What is the significance of [Buddhism]?"
>
> [The bodhisattva] immediately plopped his sack down on the ground in silent answer.
>
> "Then," asked the other, "what is the actualization of [Buddhism]?"
>
> At once, [he] swung the sack over his shoulder and continued on his way."[2]

In the next courtyard, we see a Lamaist motif. On the east and west sides are temples dedicated to Tibetan deities along with Tibetan prayer wheels. Each prayer wheel contains volumes of Buddhist sutras written in Tibetan. A spin of the wheel yields the equivalent karmic merit of reciting the wheel's entire contents.

The large bronze incense burners, now dark green with age, were gifts of Qian Long. Occasionally you will smell the rich thick scent of Tibetan incense, composed of garood wood, sandalwood and sapan wood. Another scent is Tibetan juniper. The use of incense reflects the Chinese view that air was a spiritual, not material substance and a medium for offering gifts to the other world. It is for this reason that tobacco smoking is a taboo in a temple. It sends a disrespectfully awful scent to the gods.

Incense also represents the last great sense that has not been overtly commercialized in the West. Granted, perfume and colognes are big-ticket items, but traditional Chinese adored a scent for its own sake and bought very expensive incense for this reason. Incense also reputedly attracts spirits and ghosts and thus was shunned by those without a clean conscience.

In the third courtyard we find the Hall of Eternal Divine Protection (永和殿 or *yong he dian*) housing the trinity of Mahayana Buddhism. The central statue represents Sakayamuni (or the historical) Buddha, almost always seated in the "Calling the Earth To Bear Witness" *mudra* that symbolizes his rejection of temptation. On his right is the Amida Buddha who draws his name from the prayers "Hear us, O Amida Buddha" (南无阿弥陀佛). The Amida Buddha is the Buddha of boundless light, sometimes said to be the celestial reflection of the historical Buddha. On the left is the Manjursi Buddha, a bodhisattva of benevolence who, in the incarnate form of an Indian monk came to China to spread the *dharma* but left for Tibet, apparently appalled by the relentless intrigues of Chinese monks. The Manjursi Buddha supervises a Buddhist paradise where kind-hearted people (who refrain from factionalism) can be reborn for many ages.

The next courtyard leads to the Hall of the Wheel of the Law (法轮殿 or *fa lun dian*) where the high lamas taught theology to the monks. On the left-hand side is the teaching platform where the Dalai Lama elaborated upon Lamaist theology in 1952 to 1953 while the Panchen Lama used the platform on the right for religious instruction. In the middle stands a fifteen-meter statute of the founder of the Yellow Hat Sect of Lamaism, Tsong-kha Pa. In the skylight by Tsong-kha Pa's head are enormous thangkas, which are immeasurably beautiful and rival anything in the Cistine chapel.

Among Peking folks, the Tsong-kha Pa statue is associated with a story about Coppersmith Han, who was a gifted craftsman from the Qing dynasty. After other artisans delivered the final cast of Tsong-kha Pa, its expression displeased the head abbot of the Lama Temple. He felt that the bronze did not reflect the benevolence of the great lama. He approached Coppersmith Han with a request to recast the bronze for a "reasonable amount." The coppersmith asked for two pieces of silver, a cost far below the prevailing market price for such renovation work. Though mistrustful of Han's bid, the abbot retained the coppersmith who repaired the statue with two well-aimed blows of his hammer, thus giving the expression of Tsong-kha Pa a dimpled smile.

Going into one more courtyard to the north, we come to the fourth and final courtyard of the Lama Temple. Before us is the Pavilion of Ten Thousand Fortunes (万福阁 or *wan fu ge*). The two sky bridges connected the wings of the Pavilion are rare in Peking architecture. Inside the pavilion stands a 75-foot tall statute of the Maitreya Buddha, reportedly carved from a single trunk of cedar. The crown shows that the Maitreya Buddha has elected to stay within the world of sentient beings because of his compassion and wisdom. Like all other bodhisattvas, he vows to assist all with achieving enlightenment. In the days when an emperor visited the temple, a lantern above the statute's head was lit.

In the hall, the Maitreya Buddha is flanked by two large "incense sticks," which are about four meters long and 12 centimeters in diameter. They are called Phoenix-Eye Incense Sticks (风眼香 or *feng yen xiang*) because of the numerous little holes shaped like the eyes of the mythical bird. A Qing era legend relates the story about a group of Mongol merchants who discovered these poles in the middle of the Tenger desert.

After losing their way during a sandstorm, the merchants spent days travelling in circles, unable to relocate the trail. On the verge of despair, they suddenly spied these two poles. They believed that the poles were huge incense sticks that heaven sent to show them the path back to civilization. By walking in the direction indicated by the two parallel sticks, the Mongols were able to reorient themselves and successfully found the route to Peking. When a Peking prince heard about this story, he dispatched a team into the desert to recover the incense sticks, which were given to the emperor, who in turn, deposited them in the Lama Temple. The so-called incense sticks were two large prehistoric plants that lived in an inland sea. With the passage of time, the plants turned into stone fossils while the Tenger desert replaced the sea.

In the annual calendar of Peking's festivals, the Lama Temple was particularly famous because of the so-called "devil dances" (打鬼 or *da gui*) on the 30th day of the first lunar month. This terribly misnamed ritual entailed Mongol lamas dressed as various Tibetan deities dancing to traditional temple music. The ritual began with several lamas charging at the crowds with whips, much like guards for traveling Manchu princes, in order to clear a space. The purpose of the ritual was to have the lamas, in the guise of their deities, exorcise evil demons from the city. Several of the lamas wore skull masks as a joking reminder of the inevitability of death so as to take away the painful sting associated with the end of earthly life. In this regard, the ceremonies had something in common with the Festival of the Dead in Mexico. The folks of Peking came out in droves to attend the ceremony, which usually concluded with the abbot throwing coins into the crowd. Here was one example of the city's multicultural complexion, with Tibetan festivals becoming part of Peking's life cycle. Sometimes, the ceremony ended with the monks tearing up effigies made of dough and red dye and thus impliedly recalling the human sacrifices that once occurred in the Land of the Snows.

In prior years, I loathed the Lama Temple. It was a place of crass commercialism, with foreign and Chinese tourist hordes, herded like a gaggle of ducks, with loudspeakers blaring, noisy vendors of ice cream and Peking 2000 flags for sale. However, there was once a slight touch of spirituality. On one autumn afternoon, I slipped away from my office with a colleague, who was expecting his first son sometime that winter. Seeking a safe and healthy birth for the child, we went to the Lama Temple and knelt before one of the Tibetan deities to offer incense. A sudden hush fell over us, followed by a sense of grace and a sense that our request had been granted. As we stood up to leave, some one else heckled us in Peking *tu hua*. I grounded my teeth in anger and walked out of the temple. My colleague and I went out for a beer.

In the summer of 2005, I had no particularly optimistic expectations in visiting the Lama Temple. To my immense pleasure, many local folk were burning incense, offering prayers and bowing before the white-scarved statues. A Peking friend accompanied me to pick up a Buddha statute that the monks had blessed for her. The loudspeakers and ice cream vendors were still there, and perhaps people were just going through the religious motions for good luck. Nevertheless, I had the satisfactory feeling of an early and unexpected spring.

Taking our leave of the Lama Temple, we head for the Alley of the School for the Sons of the Nation (国子监胡同 or *guo zi jian hu tong*) across the way on Yong He Gong Avenue (雍和宫大街). Here is a fine oasis of calm and peace that contrasts sharply with the milling crowds of the Lama Temple. The Alley of the School for the Sons of the Nation is the only public street still graced with four *pai lou*. We pass the first of these on our way to the Confucian Temple (孔子庙 or *kong zi miao*) on the north side of the alley.

The Confucian temple is a Mongol era structure that was renovated by Kang Xi in 1689 and by Qian Long in 1737. In order to reflect reverence for the Great Sage, two multilingual marble steles instruct those on horseback to dismount from their horses as they traverse the temple's main gate.

The first courtyard contains over three hundred twenty steles inscribed with the names of successful candidates from the Metropolitan Examinations. "The granite register goes back for nearly six hundred years; but while intended to stimulate ambition and gratify pride, to the new graduate it represents a lesson in humility — showing him how remorselessly time consigns all human honors to oblivion."[3]

Several stone drums inscribed with poems sit at the first gateway.. These neglected carvings served as important badges of legitimacy from the Early Han through to subsequent dynasties. The stone drums were part of Yong Le's strategy to place various symbols of antiquity to shore up his bid for Peking's legitimacy as the Ming capital. The poems are quoted from Zhou classical literature that had been preserved by Confucius. In the early Han dynasty, the imperial court carved these poems into stone drums to represent symbolically the "sounding" of Confucian principles through the drums. They were taken by the Jin when they captured the Song capital of Kaifeng in 1126. Later on they were lost. During the Ming, new drums were carved and installed in the Confucian temple. These drums,

A ceremony in honor of the sage, circa 1920.

The Confucian Temple on a desolate snowy morning.

like the Red Sandalwood Buddha, were part of Yong Le's attempts to weave a connection between Peking and the virtuous golden age of the Zhou dynasty.

Entering the main courtyard, you first come across the Hall of Great Perfection (大成殿 or *da cheng dian*) with its broad "moon terrace." Traditionally, the main hall had no portrait of Confucius. Rather a simple memorial tablet bearing the sage's name sat in a center altar of honor upon a miniature throne. Other Confucian scholars remembered in tablets were also placed on the altar. Given the importance of music in the Great Sage's philosophy, the Hall of Great Perfection holds a collection of classical Chinese musical instruments.

In the early Republican days, New China scorned the memory of Confucius and the temple fell into neglect. Later, both Yuan Shi Kai and Chiang Kai Shek saw the value in reviving Confucian ceremonies here, much to the scorn of subsequent Western scholars, who claimed that they were only casting about for a political philosophy of popular acquiescence, a typically foreign perspective that captures only half of the picture.

H. G. Creel, the famous scholar of Chinese philosophy, presents a typically un-foreign view about the ceremonies at the temple:

> It was held at dawn and I had to get out of my bed at two A.M. — how willingly you can imagine. For most of the long ride to the temple, I felt very sorry for myself. Gradually, however, the impressiveness of the situation and the magnificence of my surroundings took me out of myself. The sky was a deep, luminous blue that was quite unbelievable. The temples and the pine trees had indeed passed before my eyes on other occasions, but my senses were so sharpened by the dawn that I now realized I had never before really seen, much less appreciated them. After many years I can still see the details of that ceremony much more clearly than I see the room about me. And I now understand why the Chinese held court at dawn. If it had been my business to deliberate upon affairs of state, I would have done a far better job of it that morning than I could ever do over a luncheon table or drowsing in the midafternoon.[4]

With China's liberation, Confucius took another plunge in popularity. On August 23, 1966, Red Guards staged a public humiliation of three hundred of Peking's finest literary and performing artists. The thugs built a bonfire of theatrical props stolen from Peking Opera troupes. Actresses were forced to kneel on the smoldering ash while men were beaten with the stage props. Lao She was one of the most persecuted victims that day. His physical weakness bolstered by his strong will drove the Red Guards to ever more savage beatings. He drowned himself the next day in Taiping Lake.

Now the temple might be experiencing a revival of sorts. Hong Kong newspapers have reported that the temple now hosts a school for pre-schoolers, where they learn to recite several Confucian classics, such as the Classic of Filial Piety (孝经 or *xiao jing*) whilst dressed in classical Chinese robes.

To the west of the Hall of Great Perfection, we find a modern hall containing carved stone copies of the Thirteen Classics created during Qian Long's reign. The emperor was concerned that another tyrant like Qin Shi would rise to power again to "burn books and bury scholars."

A little to the west of the Confucian temple is the School for the Sons of the Country (国子监 or *guo zi jian*). During the Yuan, the local gentry built a small school which was converted into an academy by Yong Le. The present buildings are Qian Long's renovation

The glazed *pai lou* in the Academy of the Sons of the Nation.

in 1783. Walking into the courtyards, you pass a beautiful ceramic memorial arch and come to the Palace of Concord Harmony (辟雍宫 or *bi yong gong*). Once in his life, every Qing emperor was obliged to come here to lecture on the Confucian classics, an event which was attended by court scholars and officials.

The prestige of the institution began to fail with the collapse of the Qing empire. By the late 19th century, the School sold low-grade academic scholarships and appointments to all comers, even those with mail orders, for the silver equivalent of two United States dollars. According to legend, the carp in the pools and flowers in the gardens of the Palace of Concord Harmony all disappeared in the same year of the establishment of the republic.

The School for the Children of the Country played an interesting role in China's relationship with the foreign world. During the Qing dynasty, the academy was assigned the task of teaching Chinese to students from tributary states, such as Korea, Mongolia, Vietnam, and Burma. In accordance with the Treaty of Kiathka, six Russian youths studied Chinese in order to facilitate communication between the two empires. I can imagine these children making their way, on Sunday mornings, from their dormitory to the Church of St. Nicholas for mass.

In the early days of the legation district, Arlington and Lewisohn recorded that Chinese would yell *wei lo* at foreign residents. Did they, these students, hear the same calls? Were they regarded with contempt or simple neglect? What did they think of the Tibetan chants emanating from the Lama Temple?

In the 1930s, a Russian arrived in Peking who might have spanned the breach between St. Nicholas and Tsong-kha Pa. Father Vassily fled from his homeland for Mongolia in the aftermath of the Russian Civil War. During his sojourn in Mongolia, the Russian priest learned Buddhist theology and meditation techniques. For the rest of his life, he claimed no home of his own, perhaps citing the Gospels and the sutras about the transience of life and wandered between Peking, Shenyang and Harbin. He administered to the spiritual needs of Russians and Mongolians, but was rebuffed by Chinese. Whenever he was in Peking, he stayed in the Lama Temple where the lamas called him the Ruski Lama. His brother monks at the Russian ecclestical mission would have nothing to do with him and dismissed him as a misled soul who had embraced the devil's tools.

The writer John Blofeld visited Father Vassily at the Lama Temple. He initially thought the priest had a noble bearing but became dubious, if not distrustful, because of Father Vassily's enthusiast advocacy of Buddhist meditation as a tool for producing supernatural tricks. While Lamaist Buddhism contains many legends about feats of supernatural *leger de main* performed by lamas, Buddhist orthodoxy rejects such tricks as a bagatelle that ultimately injures the conjurer. When Blofeld rose to take his leave of Father Vassily, he noticed a religious painting, partially obscured by shadows, on the wall. As Blofeld leaned forward to get a clearer view, the unlit lantern over their heads seemed to ignite by itself. The monk's cell filled with light. The father calmly noted to the astonished Blofeld that the picture was the Holy Mother, though he did not say whether he meant the Virgin Mary or Princess Tara of Tibet.

Father Vassily and Blofeld crossed paths once again at a "love-in" held for the expatriate Russian community. The evening commenced with a formal Russian dinner with invitees that could not be called glamorous. Some were lame and others elderly. Nearly everyone ignored Blofeld and did not feel compelled to translate dinner conversation for his benefit.

Around ten o'clock, a pale Russian youth picked up a guitar and began to strum one Russian melody after the other. The music slowly took possession of each Russian at the dinner table. Each person reached out in ecstasy and locked hands with a dance partner, regardless of age or gender. For the next two hours, the embittered and sour émigrés danced in euphoria with their ailments and age slipping away and their faces lit by an inner glow that turned them into cherubs. Father Vassily presided over the dance from the sidelines, looking at his countrymen benignly. One by one, they exhausted themselves and slipped into unconsciousness until Blofeld and Father Vassily were the last two people still awake in the room.

The Russian priest saw the puzzlement on Blofeld's face and challenged him. What did Blofeld expect, an orgy? Father Vassily had brought them a small piece of heaven for a few moments, a place of peaceful sanctuary away from the cares of their rootless world. The sense of bliss would fade away day by day until the next session with Father Vassily. But at least for a few minutes, these lost Russian souls felt a joy that did not fall neatly into Christian or Buddhist orthodoxy.

Leaving the academy, you will pass to the west and out from under the last *pai lou* to the street, turn south on An Ding Men Nei Avenue (安定门内大街) and then to the west on Drum Tower East Avenue (鼓楼东大街). The former residence of writer Mao Dun (茅盾故居) is located on No. 13 Hou Yuan'ensi Hu Tong (后圆恩寺胡同) in an attractive courtyard house. Mao embraced socialist themes early on in his career as a result of the New Culture Movement. His most famous novel, *Midnight* recounts the story of a Shanghai capitalist who faces ruin because of communist inspired strikes. Instead of throwing his lot in with communists, he speculates in the stock market only to be out-maneuvered by a Shanghai comprador with foreign backing.

Further to the south, on South Fu Xue Hu Tong near Bei Xin Qiao is the Memorial to Prime Minister Wen Tian Xiang (文天祥祠 or *wen tian xiang ci*) originally built in 1376 by the first Ming emperor Hong Wu in memory of Prince Minister Wen of the Song dynasty. Wen was born in 1236 in Jiangxi. In 1256, he won the highest honors for the Metropolitan Examination. After serving in a number of positions in the south of the country, he was ordered to negotiate a truce when Kublai Khan's armies began to move from northern China into Hang Zhou.

Eventually the Mongolian forces captured Wen and brought him to Peking in 1279 as a prisoner of war. For four years, he was held captive, and the Yuan government made repeated unsuccessful efforts to convert him to the Mongol cause. He was executed in 1282 at the age of 47. Peking legend holds that the site of Wen Tian Xiang's execution was near the present memorial.

Next door on the west, an elementary school now occupies the Palace of Shun Tian (顺天府 or *shun tian fu*), which was originally built in 1402 as a school for training officials in Confucian principles.

Coming down Yong He Gong Avenue (which turns into Dong Si Bei Avenue), we come to Zhang Zi Zhong Road (张自忠路) on the western intersection. This tiny street was originally called Iron Lion Street after a couple of long-disappeared cast-iron lions in front of a courtyard house and was renamed in memory of a Nationalist general, Zhang Zi Zhong (张自忠) who died in the war against Japan.

A red courtyard door leads into the Memorial Site of the Passing of Sun Yat Sen at No. 23 Zhang Zi Zhong Road. In early 1925, Sun was locked in negotiations with Peking's warlords for the formation of a coalition government. Sun's trip to Peking from Canton raised hopes that a single government could arise without a military solution. Sun was buoyed by the rapturous welcome given to him by 100,000 Peking citizens. However, the negotiations were not fruitful, and Sun grew gravely ill, finally passing away on March 12, 1925. His last words were reportedly "peace, struggle … save China." His body lay in state at the Temple of the Azure Clouds in the Western Hills before internment in Nanjing. These days, the memorial is yet another branch office of the public security authorities, and you will be waved on once again

Sun's last Peking residence was just down the street from the then-presidential palace, which is now officially registered as the Site of Duan Qi Rui's Government (段祺瑞政府阳址), located at No. 3 Zhang Zi Zhong Road. The buildings here are constructed in a Western neo-baroque style and nicely landscaped with trees and lawns. The central building has two floors with a main cathedral-like entrance while residential buildings in the back are Tudor-style houses. The area has the same feeling of a verdant oasis as we encountered at the residences attached to Peking Union Medical College.

The quietude of the grounds belies the pivotal political events that were played out here during Peking's tumultuous 20th century history. In 1912, Yuan Shi Kai installed his own presidential offices as well as the office of the executive branch of his government here. From Yuan's death in 1916, Peking's politicians became embroiled in power struggles that produced a series of revolving door governments. Duan held the position of premiership while various presidents competed with him in the distribution of bribes and the procurement of foreign loans. These buildings witnessed a bewildering array of presidential appointments, proclamations, declarations of war and even the restoration of the Qing throne for one month in 1917. By the early 1920s, the national government in Peking had become a charade with politicians allied with military warlords in civil war.

In 1924, warlords in north China invited Duan to assume the presidency of a provisional government for negotiations with Sun Yat-sen in order to create a unified government. Duan's uncooperative attitude vexed Sun to death, and he was able to retain the presidency until 1926 when the troops of the "Christian" warlord general Feng Yu Xiang besieged him in his presidential palace. After the Nationalist troops had entered Peking in 1927, these buildings were changed into the Peiping Garrison Command Headquarters.

In the years before 1937, the Nationalist 29th Army was headquartered here in an ineffectual attempt to resist Japanese encroachments. After the Marco Polo Bridge Incident, the Japanese government moved in its North China Army Command which, among other things, assumed control of municipal functions. In 1945, the Nationalist Army returned to Peking and claimed these grounds as its headquarters until being forced to leave again in 1949. Since then, the site became the annex classrooms for the People's University in Haidian district.

11

THE WESTERN TARTAR CITY

HERE WE CONTINUE WITH OUR visit to the Old Tartar City, which has a variety of sights, including scenic lakes and other landmarks.

The intersection at Di An Men West Avenue (地安门西大街) and Di An Men Wai Avenue (地安门外大街) is located right on the central axis of Old Peking. From here, you turn to the north and walk in the direction of the Drum Tower and Bell Tower.

While walking north, you will come across the Ming-era Back Door Bridge (后门桥 or *hou men qiao*) spanning the stream that drained the waters of Back Lakes District into the imperial canal flowing into the Legation District. Fortunately, the Peking authorities have dredged the canal and pulled down a number of the slipshod buildings that used to obscure the view from the bridge.

Immediately to the west of the Back Door Bridge you can see a moon doorway leading to the Temple of the God of Fire (火神庙 or *huo shen miao*), first built in 1605 and reconstructed in 1779. Peking once boasted eight temples dedicated to the God of Fire, who was probably a remnant of an ancient animism. Traditionally, the God of Fire was a red-faced deity with an oblong third eye centered in his forehead as an aid in seeing throughout the terrestrial world. He was primarily invoked as a protector against fires. When conflagration broke out in Old Peking, its citizens flocked to these temples, pleading with the god to spare their homes by reigning in his pet red crow that was reckoned to fly over the city looking for buildings to ignite. In recent years, the courtyard was filled with *ping fang* housing, though at the time of writing this book, the Peking authorities have begun to renovate the temple.

In the first days after the Chinese New Year, the citizens of Old Peking celebrated the Lantern Festival, which seems to have arisen in the dim past as a

Western Tartar City

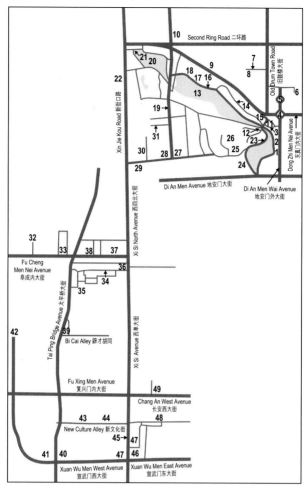

1. Back Door Bridge（后门桥）
2. Temple of the God of Fire（火神庙）
3. Yan Zhuang Ke Street（烟装科街）
4. Drum Tower（鼓楼）
5. Bell Tower（钟楼）
6. No.8 Ji An Suo You Xiang（吉安所胡同）
7. Xiao Shi Qiao Alley（小石桥胡同）
8. Bamboo Garden Hotel（竹园宾馆）
9. Guan Yue Temple（关岳庙）
10. Gate of Virtuous Victory（德胜门）
11. Temple of Broad Fortune（广福观）
12. Silver Ingot Bridge（银锭桥）
13. Shi Cha Lake（什刹海）
14. Ya'er Alley（鸦儿胡同）
15. Temple of the Grand Transformation（广化寺）
16. Hou Hai Bei Yan（后海北沿）
17. Palace of Prince Chun（醇亲王府）
18. former Residence of Song Qing Ling（宋庆龄故居）
19. De Sheng Men Nei Avenue（德胜门内大街）
20. Pond of Accumulated Waters（积水潭）
21. Hui Tong Si（汇通祠）
22. Museum to Xu Bei Hong（徐悲鸿博物馆）
23. Qian Hai Bei Yan（前海北沿）
24. former Residence of Guo Mo Ruo（郭沫若故居）
25. former Site of Fu Jen Catholic University
26. Mansion of Prince Gong（恭王府）
27. Mansion of Prince Qing（庆王府）
28. former Residence of Mei Lan Fang（梅兰芳故居）
29. People's Theatre（人民剧扬）
30. Temple for the Protection of the Nation（护国寺）
31. "Three Not Olds" Alley（三不老胡同）
32. Lu Xun Museum（鲁迅博物馆）
33. White Pagoda Temple（白塔寺）
34. Brick Pagoda Alley（砖塔寺胡同）
35. former Residence of Liu Shao Qi（刘少奇革命活动纪念地）
36. Pagoda of the Old Man of the Ten Thousand Pines（万松老人塔）
37. Temple of the Broad Meditation（广济寺）
38. Temple to the Successive Generations of Emperor（历代帝王庙）
39. former Residence of Qi Bai Shi（齐白石故居）
40. Temple to the City God（都皇城庙）
41. Central Conservatory（中央院）
42. Portion of Tartar City Wall
43. former Residence of Li Da Qiao
44. former Site of Peking's Women's University
45. Xuan Wu Men Nei Avenue（宣武门内大街）
46. Southern Cathedral（南堂）
47. former Site of Elephant Stables
48. Rong Xian Alley（绒线胡同）and former site of Sichuan Restaurant
49. former Site of Democracy Wall

celebration of the return of warmth and light. This street was once the center of the festival. People hung brightly colored lanterns from their homes and shops while a carnival atmosphere prevailed throughout the city. Wealthy families competed in commissioning the most attractive lanterns, which could be made of silk gauze, transparent horn, or stalks of wheat. Qing merchants used to set up ice sculptures, not unlike those in Harbin, for the amusement of the city's citizens. Young couples pursued romance, children shot off fireworks, and revelers would take snacks at roadside stalls and quaff thumb-sized glasses of firewater. Peking's women folk were permitted to wander about the town to see and be seen, an unusual liberty that was only countenanced because of the holiday.

Coming back out from the temple, we turn to the north and head in the direction of the Drum Tower. At the intersection of Di An Men Wai Avenue and Yan Zhuang Ke Street (烟装科街), there are two routes. The first route takes you to the Drum Tower in the north. Let's follow this one first.

In 1402, Yong Le built the Drum Tower (鼓楼), which stands in front of you to the north, as the primary timekeeper for the city. It was reconstructed in 1747, precisely 99 feet tall in accordance with geomantic principles against interfering with air-borne spirits who were said to cruise at 100 feet above the ground.

The traditional Chinese day consisted of twelve hours, each one symbolized by one of the twelve animals of Chinese astrology. The tower's timekeepers sounded the drum every 120 minutes, a new watch was set every day at 7:00 pm and the execution of official duties was timed by the beat of the drum. For instance, government officials attending a morning audience with the emperor would be awakened at the third hour (*viz.*, 1:00 am), gather at the Meridian Gate or the Gate of Military Prowess at the fourth hour (*viz.*, 3:00 am) and meet the emperor at the fifth hour (*viz.*, 5:00 am). When the watch was sounded, the timekeeper beat the drum 108 times in two rounds. These days, the Drum Tower makes a great place for photographing courtyard houses in the surrounding vicinity.

Further, to the north, we come across the Bell Tower (钟楼 or *zhong lou*) that was originally built at the same time as the Drum Tower but was destroyed by fire during the Qing Dynasty. In 1745, Qian Long had the tower rebuilt in stone. Timekeepers struck the bell in the tower immediately after each sounding of the drums. The first bell that was cast for the tower did not have a good resonance since it was made of iron. Yong Le ordered the casting of a new bell made of an alloy of brass and gold for a more melodious and impressive sound. The bell, still hanging in the tower and weighing 23,000 pounds, is the largest bell ever cast in China. Until the 1920s, the tolling of the bell could be heard twenty miles away.

A view of the drum tower and bell tower circa 1920s.

A contemporary view.

According to Peking tradition, the foundry had severe difficulties in alloying metals to produce a bell with the correct resonance. Frustrated by these repeated failures, Yong Le threatened to execute the bell smith if his next result ended in failure too. A soothsayer advised the bell smith that the components of the alloy, gold and brass, could never blend — they were both *yang* elements — without the balancing *yin* influence of the blood of a young woman.

After learning of the bell smith's predicament, his daughter persistently pleaded with him to let her be present at the next casting. Usually, women were prevented from attending the casting of a bell because their *yin* essence would hinder *yang* forces from consolidating in the molten metals. At length, the bell smith relented and permitted his daughter to be present. While the foundry hands poured the bronze into the cast, the daughter leapt into the mold. Her father make a desperate attempt to restrain her, but he was not quick enough. He was only able to lay his hands upon one of her shoes, which came off as she plunged into the molten metal.

The bell was perfectly cast and emitted the mournful sound *xie*, which is the Mandarin word for shoe. Whenever children could not sleep, mothers consoled them by saying that the tolling of the bell was simply the bell smith's daughter asking for the return of her embroidered shoe.

To the northeast of the Bell Tower, we can also visit the ramshackle courtyard house where Mao Ze Dong, the library assistant, stayed from 1918 to 1919. Here he lived in three rooms with seven other students. The entrance is on the east side of the street at No. 8 Ji An Suo You Xiang (吉安所右巷), where foreigners may visit only with prior notification.

On No. 24 Xiao Shi Qiao Alley (小石桥胡同) off the Old Bell Tower Street (旧鼓楼街), so named because it was the location of Yuan dynasty bell tower, we come across the Bamboo Garden Hotel (竹园宾馆), formerly the residence of Kang Sheng, the founder of the PRC's secret police. Originally from a wealthy land-owning family in Shan Dong, Kang Sheng joined the Chinese Communist Party in the 1930s and arrived in Yenan around 1936. He quickly insinuated his way into Mao's central committee and took responsibility for security and intelligence gathering. In the 1940s, he spent time in Moscow, learning the sadistic tricks of Stalin and his KGB. He designed a security system that ensured that every layer of society, down to the simplest neighborhood, was honeycombed with informers and spies. Though Kang Sheng was diagnosed as a schizophrenic in the early 1950s, Mao continued to rely upon him to instill terror and gather information. He was reportedly an accomplished ambidextirous calligrapher, a talent that awed, if not frightened, his colleagues. The hotel is a nice place to stay whilst rambling through Peking.

Returning to the south, you turn into Drum Tower West Avenue (鼓楼西大街). This is one of the most pleasant streets for a spring or autumn amble. The flavor of old China is wonderfully preserved here amidst the gray walls and cypress trees. It seems that Drum Tower Street has been able to keep modernity at bay for quite some time. Juliet Bredon observed in 1922 that this part of the city retained a medieval feeling, and, to a lesser extent, today it still does. The little sidewalk shops provide a nice resting place as well as tasty dumpling soups and Yanjing draft beer. In the early mornings, you can try a traditional Chinese breakfast of sweetened warm bean milk (热豆浆 or *ri dou jiang*) and deep-fried twisted cruller-like pastries (油条 or *you tiao*), which carry for me wonderful memories of early morning walks in the spring. The crullers are eaten all throughout China and should be dunked into the bean milk. Incidentally, since the crullers are somewhat slippery on account of being deep-fried, the Mandarin words *you tiao* have also come to be slang for an oily character of uncertain reputation.

At No. 149 Old Drum Tower Street, we come to the Guan Yue Temple (关岳庙), which is now the Peking Office of the Government of the Tibetan People's Autonomous Region. Depending upon the situation in Tibet, foreign visitors may have to report here to obtain a travel permit for a visit to the Land of the Snows.

The building was originally the mansion for Prince Yi Huan, the sixth son of emperor Dao Guang (and brother of Prince Duan, whom we met in the last chapter). Upon the prince's death in 1891, Guang Xu ordered the mansion to be turned into a memorial for his uncle. In 1914, Yuan Shi Kai's government appropriated the site and turned it into a temple in memory of Guan Yu (关羽) of the Later Han dynasty and Yue Fei (岳飞) of the Southern Song dynasty.

In the last years of the Han dynasty the young Guan Yu was a seller of bean curd who later decided to devote himself to study. After running away from home, he killed a magistrate who was forcing an aged couple to turn over their daughter (and only child) to him as a concubine. Guan fled to other provinces and later, at a village inn, met two men. One was a butcher named Zhang Fei and the other a seller of straw called Liu Bei. They fast became friends and in a peach orchard swore an oath to protect each other and live and die together. Guan Yu, with his compatriots, became a celebrated warrior general who dealt in fairness and kindness with the common people. Legend has him being executed at the age of 58 by his arch enemy Sun Quan (孙权).

Guan Yu is typically represented with a bright red face and a flowing beard. Because of his military success and code of honor, he was later worshipped as a god, Guan Di (关帝 or Emperor Guan). In south China, he typically can be found in restaurants since he also is the patron saint of caterers.

During the Song dynasty, Guan Di was singled out for exceptional honors and became a spiritual patriarch for the rulers of China well into the 20th century. In a Ming imperial decree in 1531, it was ordered that all events of national importance should be reported to Guan Di and that his birthday should be observed as a time of special reverence. The collapse of the Ming did not reduce the esteem that Guan Di enjoyed in official circles. Indeed, because of their emphasis upon military might, the Manchus adopted him as the patron saint of the Qing dynasty. On the popular level, he became one of the most widely worshipped deities in the Chinese pantheon. Foreign missionaries, groping for an analogy from Roman mythology, referred to him as the God of War, which is an inaccurate description. With the passage of the Qing dynasty, Guan Di's role again demonstrated his resistance to falling out of official favor. Yuan Shi Kai, feeling that the state should continue to promote military prowess as a means to strengthen the nation, created a cult of military heroes, with Guan Di as the leader of the pantheon.

Guan Di shared this honor with Yue Fei, a historical personage from the Song dynasty. Yue Fei distinguished himself by fighting the Golden Mongols who had forced the Song dynasty from the northern plains and captured the reigning emperor. Yue Fei uttered the famous motto *Huan Wo He Shan* (还我河山 or Return Our Land), which was revived as a call to arms by Chiang Kai Shek during the war against Japan. With the Song capital moved to the south, the new emperor was dubious of the benefits that Yue Fei provided to his reign, since if the north was recovered, the captured emperor would return and seek to replace him. In a manner foreshadowing the double-dealing that brought an end to Yu Qian, the Prime Minister of the Song, Qin Gui (秦桧) conspired to bring about Yue Fei's imprisonment and execution. In the manner now familiar to us, Yue Fei became rehabilitated with the passage of time and entered into the spiritual pantheon of the Chinese people.

In 1914, statues of Guan Di and Yue Fei were installed in the temple, which was then renamed Guan Yue Miao, along with 28 statutes of other lesser military heroes in the spirit world. In keeping with the code of architectural symmetry, the temple occupies a proportional site in the old city in relation to the Confucian Temple. Most famously in the pre-liberation era, Yuan Shi Kai led a deputation of Peking officials to the temple in 1915. Later, during the Japanese occupation of Peking, the pro-Han, anti-foreign associations of Yue Fei met with the predictable disfavor of the Japanese puppet government, which removed the statue of Yue Fei and changed the temple's name to the Temple for the Military Spirit (武神庙 or *wu shen miao*), another reference to Guan Di and one that was suggestive of the samurai code.

After the establishment of the People's Republic in 1949, the temple was converted into the Peking Office for the Dalai Lama who presumably worked here during his stay in the capital in 1953 and 1954. After the Dalai Lama fled Tibet in 1959, the building was turned over to the Government of the Tibetan Autonomous Region. While the building is not open to the public, you might be able to slip in and view some of the temple structures in the back.

At the end of the Drum Tower West Avenue, we can see the Gate of Virtuous Victory (德胜门 or *de sheng men*), another of the few mute surviving portions of the old city gates. Unfortunately, the only portion still standing is the arrow gate.

The Gate of Virtuous Victory was witness to two of the most important events in the life of the Empress Dowager. In 1860, the Empress Dowager came into the city through this gate in a successful bid to put her son on the dragon throne. Exactly forty years later, she had to embark upon an ignoble retreat through the same gate in the aftermath of the Boxer Debacle.

The second route through the Back Lakes District takes us on a westerly turn on Yan Zhuang Ke Street (烟装科街), a neighborhood that once sold tobacco products until the shops were nationalized in 1956. This entire area has been redeveloped as a bar and restaurant district. At No. 37 stands the Temple of Broad Fortune (广福观 or *guang fu guan*), a former Taoist shrine that now houses residential *ping fang* and a café. The street is adorned with Republican era shop fronts with detailed carvings in stone and wood. A quiet teahouse called Lotus provides a nice place to take shelter from the rain, cold, heat or thirst. By keeping to the south, you will come to the Silver Ingot Bridge (银锭桥 or *ying dian qiao*), where the view of the Western Hills was celebrated by Qian Long. The bridge, alas, is of recent construction and separates Shi Cha Lake (什刹海 or *shi cha hai*) from the Back Lake (后海 or *hou hai*). From this point, we will continue our walk along the north bank of the Shi Cha Lake.

In the Ming dynasty, this area was open to the public. The literati of that era left us accounts of banquets beneath flowering trees, fireworks, and eunuchs washing imperial horses. Odes were written about the joys of drinking warm wine in the snow and the fun of being pulled by a sled across the frozen lake. Lowe describes Grandfather Wu taking Little Bald Head to the neighborhood with the youngster captivated by all the things to see and do.

A brief detour off Ya'er Alley (鸦儿胡同) takes you to Temple of the Grand Transformation (广化寺 or *guang hua si*). The legend of the temple holds that a Yuan dynasty monk sat here in meditation for over twenty years, reading the Buddhist canon and living off rice given to him by his neighbors. After finishing each chapter of a sutra, the monk would save one kernel of rice. Periodically, he sold the surplus rice to raise funds to build the temple. Hence, he had transformed

(化 or *hua*) grains of rice into a place of worship. In 1634, a eunuch erected the stele in front of the temple, which relates this legend.

The temple's association with eunuchs carried on to contemporary times as it was the home of Sun Yao Ting (孙耀庭), the very last imperial eunuch. Sun was emasculated by his parents in 1911 and then went on to serve Pu Yi during the final years of his residence in the Forbidden City. Sun passed away in December 1996 after having spent his final years in residence here. After his death, Sun's family held a traditional ceremony for him at the temple, where they laid a gold cloth across his face, put ornate rings on his fingers and shrouded him in white silk embroidery with the dragon and phoenix emblems of China's imperial tradition. For his entire life, Sun lamented the end of the imperial way that thwarted the fulfillment of his destiny. He is buried in a dusty wind-blown graveyard beside the highway to Tianjin.

In prior years, an officious old man would promptly and rudely wave away any curious sight seekers. These days, the resident monks welcome visitors. On Sunday afternoons, the chanting from the main hall drifts across the neighborhood. The abbot, a congenial wisp of a fellow from Fu Jian province, is happy to show visitors some of the shrines as well as gifts donated by his temple's congregation.

Returning to Hou Hai Bei Yan (后海北沿), you can enjoy a wonderful stroll alongside Shi Cha Lake. During the summer season, throngs of Peking folk take in the scenery. In the wintertime, Peking's equivalent of the Polar Bear Club goes swimming in its icy waters. The present tranquility of the lake is inconsistent with its legend. During Qing times, people claimed that they could hear the plaintive cries of the spirits of those who drowned themselves in the lake. With this in mind, the duck-shaped boats on the lake add an inappropriate touch.

Further along Hou Hai Bei Yan, we come across the traditional courtyard home of Prince Chun, the father of Henry Pu Yi. Originally called *Qi Ye Fu* (七爷府 or Palace of the Seventh Son, after Prince Chun, who was the seventh son of Dao Guang), the residence has been divided with one part allocated to the China Association of Religions while the other is the former residence of Song Qing Ling (宋庆龄故居) .

The Palace of Prince Chun (醇亲王府) was known as the Northern Palace (北馆) during Pu Yi's reign. Prince Chun, Pu Yi's father and Prince Regent, is recalled as an amiable but ineffectual man who could not guide the Qing court past the intrigues of Yuan Shi Kai. The eunuchs of the Forbidden City used to say that the fate of the empire was sealed when Prince Chun breached Manchu custom by failing to move out of the palace where his son, a "dragon," had been born. When Pu Yi was ousted from the Forbidden City, the Northern Palace was his first stop on his flight to the Japanese Legation.

After 1949, Pu Yi's relatives sold the mansion to the Peking government. In the 1960s, a section was given to Song Qing Ling, the widow of Sun Yat Sen and sister of Madame Chiang Kai Shek. Its modern structures date from the time of her move-in.

Song Qing Ling was one of the three daughters of the Shanghai Methodist industrialist, Charlie Song. Like all of Charlie's daughters, Qing Ling was educated in the United States and returned to China seeking to lead the life of a modern Chinese woman in service to her country.

Charlie fell prey to the influence of Sun Yat Sen sometime around 1915. His second daughter, Song Mei Ling worked as a secretary for the Father of the Country until his roving eye scared her off. A few years later, Qing Ling, drawn by Dr. Sun's patriotic mission, took up the vacant position of secretary. Though already married, Sun seemed to carry a spark for much younger women. The old lecher arranged to cashier his current wife and marry Qing Ling in 1922, which caused something of a scandal in both traditional Chinese and Christian circles.

When Sun died in 1925, Qing Ling carried on as a public figure in the capacity of widow of "China's George Washington." Her leftist sentiments led her to drift away from her sisters Mei Ling, who married Chiang Kai Shek in 1927, and Ai Ling, who married T.V. Kong, a Shanghai financier and the Minister of Finance under the Nationalist government. Although she had benefited from her family's participation in the Nationalist government and various shady moneymaking schemes, Song Qing Ling's status as "Madame Sun Yat Sen" allowed her to escape the tar brush that subsequently sullied her sisters' reputations. She stayed on in the mainland after the Communist victory and sponsored assorted social welfare programs, joining the CCP on her deathbed.

Madame Sun was resilient as revealed by her shifting linguistic skills. In the 1930s and 1940s, reporters noticed that she preferred to speak in English, even with (or perhaps especially with) fellow Chinese. As the winds changed in the early 1950s, members of an Indian peace delegation recall her speaking exclusively in Chinese and relying upon the help of an interpreter. By the 1970s when the New York Times posted Fox Butterfield to Peking, she had rediscovered her English, still spoken with a slight southern accent from her school days in Georgia, and was enjoying a series of culinary delicacies and foreign motion pictures that were denied to the average Peking citizen.

Incidentally, her sister, Song Mei Ling (or perhaps I should call her Madame Chiang Kai Shek simply for the sake of symmetry) lived until 2004, celebrating her 106th birthday in New York before passing on. It is said that she was mentally alert, healthy and enjoying the intense satisfaction that Chinese have when they outlive all of their enemies and rivals.

At De Sheng Men Nei Avenue (德胜门内大街), you turn to the south and pass over a smallish marble bridge. It was here that the then revolutionary, Wang Jing Wei (汪精衛), placed a bomb in 1911 to blow up the regent, Prince Chun. Several howling dogs spoiled his plans, and he was later apprehended at the Peking Rail Station when several Qing secret agents noticed a man with a fake queue attached to his hat, which he had tipped to say good-bye to a few lady friends. The Manchus threw him into jail. His death sentence for attempted murder and sedition was thwarted by the October 1911 revolution. Wang's subsequent career was a checkered one that wound up as discredited as the ignoble Yuan Shi Kai. In 1920s, he joined leftist factions of the KMT against Chiang Kai Shek, but later switched to a right wing group. In the 1930s, he became active in Shanghai domestic politics and competed with Chiang Kai Shek for control of the KMT. In 1938, he negotiated an agreement with the Japanese government and became the head of a Chinese puppet government. Given his credentials as a former revolutionary, there always has been historical speculation, but no proof, on why he made his deal with the devil.

Further to the west, we come to Pond of Accumulated Waters (积水潭 or *ji shui tan*, also called the West Lake these days) in which once stood a solitary island. In the late 1930s, Blofeld came here to visit the Peach Garden Hermit, a Taoist recluse known for his unconventional behavior and rapacious embrace of life. The hermit lived on the top floor of a pavilion built on the island. Blofeld's friends gently warned him that the hermit might come across as an eccentric, "but this mild criticism had not prepared me to meet a glorious madman, drunk with *being!*"

> Lotus leaves lay so thickly upon the water between island and shore that it resembled solid ground. As soon as I reached the red zigzag wooden bridge spanning the space between the two, there burst from behind the willows on the island an astonishing young man who capered rather than ran toward me, waving his hand and letting forth peals of happy laughter. (This strange manner of welcoming me he chose to explain later by assuring me he had spent half the day attempting to conjure up a demon and that, at first, he mistook me for the fruit of his conjurations!) His tattered sky-blue robe had been thrown on so carelessly as to leave his chest and upper part of his stomach completely bare. His long hair, instead of being confined in a prim Taoist's bun atop his head, danced on his shoulders like the tresses of a forest nymph ….
>
> In response to my formal bow he laughingly seized my hand, and running backwards, dragged me across to the steps of his pavilion. Next, he pushed me into one of several chairs scattered about the open-sided lower story and began vigorously fanning me!

"Such exertion! Such exertion! All on a hot day, too! So, in response to my incantations, you have come all the way from the Western Regions to visit me. Come now, confess you rested on the way. Ha, ha, ha! So you speak jen hua [human speech] even though you are an Ocean Devil. I've had much to do with devils in my life. It is really pleasure to meet one like you."[1]

The Peach Garden Hermit carried on this banter, brewing a specially rare tea for Blofeld and boisterously discussing his expertise at exorcising demons, wrestling them from the bodies of patients and casting them away, often at great personal cost. The departing demon, having lost face, might suddenly fling the hermit to the wall. He claimed another demon beat him severely because the hermit forgot to fast beforehand, an important sign of respect demanded by citizens of the invisible world.

The exuberance of the Peach Garden Hermit overwhelmed Blofeld. Ten years later, he ran into the hermit near Wang Fu Jing. He right away invited Blofeld to share some wine fermented from small yellow flowers gathered from the Western Hills. Three cups slid down easily but potently. The hermit, though red in the face, seemed otherwise unaffected.

"You have an oceanic capacity," [Blofeld] laughed.

"Wrong again! A man born half-witted and kept intoxicated by too much sunshine and rain is impervious to wine. Take more to eat and you will feel better. You are not a Japanese to get drunk on three cups!"[2]

While the two drained the pot of wine and snacked on Peking delicacies, the Peach Garden Hermit admitted that Japanese soldiers sought him out to discuss Taoism. They dragged him to the courtesan houses and slowly drank themselves silly. The hermit took these opportunities to be whispered military intelligence collected by the courtesans. The next morning he sang impromptu verses about these secrets to Chinese boatmen passing by his island, who, in turn delivered them to the Chinese underground.

These days, there is no trace of the island refuge of the Peach Garden Hermit, which probably suits him right down to the ground. I can easily imagine that he discovered the elixir of life. In *Road to Heaven*, Bill Porter, an American writer and Buddhist, relates his encounters with hermits in the mountains in central China during the early 1990s and records that some hermits still believed that their masters achieved immortality. Perhaps the Peach Garden Hermit has taken up residence in the highlands. Or perhaps he continues his joyous life while earning a living as a dishwasher in North Beach, San Francisco and being a regular at Barry Melton's gigs at The Saloon.

On the north side of the lake is the Hui Tong Si (汇通祠), a Ming dynasty Buddhist temple originally known as the Temple of the Law's Transformation (法化寺 or *fa hua si*). Qian Long renovated the temple in 1761. Inside the temple is a memorial and exhibition for the Yuan era engineer Guo Shou Jing (郭守敬) who constructed Peking's waterways, including the nearby locks.

If you take a detour down Xin Jie Kou North Avenue (新街口北大街), you will come to a museum exhibiting paintings by Xu Bei Hong (徐悲鸿), an early 20th century painter who mastered both Chinese and Western motifs. In 1918, Xu lived in Paris, where he became one of the first Chinese to master oil techniques (something which his successors in the art produce at record levels, if the hotel art stores are anything to go by). In the 1940s, he developed his most famous theme, galloping horses in monochrome ink wash style. Another of his most famous paintings is "Chairman Mao Among the People."

Retracing our steps, we can continue the circuit by walking along the south side of the Back Lakes and arrive at the Silver Ingot Bridge. In this vicinity there are many inviting teahouses and bars attracting a broad collection of Chinese and foreigners.

Directly south of the bridge is the neighborhood where the adopted son and heir of the last emperor lived. Yu Yan was a nephew of Pu Yi, son of the Boxer leader Pu Chen and one of the retainers in Pu Yi's Manchukuo court in Chang Chun. With time, Yu became Pu Yi's most trusted servant, administering medicines and participating in intimate aspects of court life. For example, Yu Yan was allowed to tend to Pu Yi's wife as she was dying of typhoid. Pu Yi appointed Yu Yan as the chief mourner for her funeral. He was the only member of the imperial household permitted to wear traditional Manchu mourning clothes.

In his book *The Empty Throne*, Tony Scotland argues that by virtue of his lineage and by Pu Yi's express acts, Yu was selected by Pu Yi as his successor and would be the occupant of the Dragon Throne were the imperial tradition to be resurrected.

After the Second World War, Yu Yan was imprisoned with Pu Yi in Siberia and underwent re-education with him at Fushun in Jilin Province. In the 1990s he lived in a dilapidated courtyard house and sold his calligraphy, a skill at which most imperial Manchus excelled.

Continuing along Qian Hai Bei Yan (前海北沿) you will pass a delightfully traditional neighborhood with fine views of the Drum Tower, the Bell Tower and courtyard houses adjoining the Lakes. In wintertime, Peking folks come out to skate and huddle around small fires, eating roasted sweet potatoes and candied hawberries. The hawberries cost only RMB ¥2 a stick.

On the southern end of the west bank of the Front Lake, you will come to the former residence of Guo Mo Ruo (郭沫若故居), writer, archeologist, scholar, Chairman Mao's intellectual-in-residence and loyal sycophant of the Communist Party. While in Japan during the 1920s, Guo formed the Creation Society, which was initially dedicated to an all-out rebellious romanticism. The Creation Society published candid autobiographic confessions in which sexual desire and patriotic sentiment met with frustration and the hero was left guilt-ridden, morose and impotent, themes that later resurfaced with a venegence in *Shanghai Baby*. In the mid-1920s, Guo embraced Communism, writing that "I am able to impose order on all the ideas which I could not reconcile; I have the key to all problems which appeared to me self-contradictory and insoluble." He had a nice house, too.

By turning to the north on Long Tou Jing Street (龙头井街) you pass by what were the grounds of Fu Jen Catholic University until 1949. Going towards the north, you come to the Mansion of Prince Gong (恭王府 or *gong wang fu*). The extensive courtyard house was originally built sometime in the 1760s as the home of He Shen, the Manchu bannerman responsible for repressing Muslim rebellions in Yunnan province and the power behind the throne in Qian Long's declining years. He Shan was also responsible for overseeing the arrangements for the visit of the Macartney Mission to Peking in 1790. In the late 19th century, the mansion became the home of Prince Gong, one of the sons of the Guang Xu Emperor. It is also said that the mansion was the basis for the setting of Cao Xue Qin's 18th century novel, *Dream of Red Chambers*. In the 1960s, the site became a factory that was restored to its traditional appearance in the 1980s.

The courtyards in Prince Gong's palace contain delightful gardens, lakes, bridges and rockeries. Depending upon your fluency, this is a relaxing place to while away a summer afternoon working through a set of Chinese flash cards or the Poems of the Masters (千家詩) with English translations by the sage Red Pine.

Leaving the Palace of Prince Gong, there is another Manchu prince's home that invites comparison. On the north side of Ding Fu Avenue (定阜大街), a white marble plaque points out the Palace of Prince Qing (庆王府), which has been converted into *ping fang* residences and has come down considerably in the world, especially when compared to Prince Gong's residence. Prince Qing's home is not open to the public, though someone might show you around if you ask. Many of the gables and verandah decorations are originals.

By striking west on Hu Guo Si Road (护国寺) you will come to the former residence of Mei Lan Fang (梅兰芳故居), possibly the most accomplished performer of *dan* (旦) or female roles in Peking Opera during the 20th century. Many of the themes of Peking Opera go back to the Yuan Dynasty. In the later

1700s, the opera adapted to the tastes in the capital and developed a distinctive style, with the result that the city lent its name to the art form to distinguish it from other regional variations, such as Cantonese or He Nan opera. While Westerners find Peking Opera harsh to the ear and difficult to follow, it is an art form where time spent in study and exposure yields great pleasure.

In 1894, Mei Lan Fang was born into a family of traditional Peking Opera performers and became a nation-wide sensation in the 1920s, provoking the mass adulation that greeted other contemporaries like Enrico Caruso or Rudolph Valentino. In traditional Chinese society, women could not perform before an audience, and men played the roles of women characters, commencing their tutorship as a young boy and undergoing years of exacting, if not torturous training. Peking Opera is minimalist in that there are few props, and assorted gestures and mannerisms convey context as well as meaning. The exacting nature of Mei's art is demonstrated in the museum by a montage of various emotions conveyed by the gestures of a single hand.

At the height of his popularity, Mei Lan Fang performed in North America, Europe and the Soviet Union. In the courtyard memorial, you can see photographs of him with celebrities such as Charlie Chaplin, Paul Robeson, Sergei Eisenstein, Konstantin Stanislavsky and Berthold Brecht. A political and social progressive, he advocated an end to gender prejudice in China by training women to perform *dan* roles as well as revising traditional plays so that they would be sung in the popularly understood vernacular rather than classical Chinese. He remained in China after 1949 and enjoyed immense popularity in his later days. A colleague of mine once recalled that in the lucky event that her parents were able to get their hands on a pair of tickets to see Mei Lan Fang, they would be off like a shot, leaving her and her siblings locked up and alone in their apartment. Mei passed away in 1961 and thus missed the Cultural Revolution, which all but tore this performing art from its roots. The motion picture, *Farewell My Concubine*, recreates the power and tragedy of Peking opera.

The People's Theatre (人民剧场 or *ren min ju chang*) on the west end of Hu Guo Temple Street regularly presents performances, which, regrettably, are sparsely attended. The audience is mostly elderly folks who grew up with Peking Opera. I wholeheartedly recommend that you sit among the *lao tou*, or old folks with their caps and screw-top jars of tea because of their fine appreciation of properly performed opera. An electrical charge passes through the audience when a performer executes his role well, with the crowd unable to stifle the cries of *hao* (good) when their demanding standards are met.

In Peking Opera, the stage is usually bare except for one or two chairs and a table and is more like traditional Shakespearean theatre in its use of conventions.

At the back, two entrance ways on left and right of the stage serve for the actors' entrance and exit. The orchestra sits to the left of the stage.

Along the street between Mei Lan Fang's former residence and the People's Theatre, we come across an interesting slice of Old Peking street life, with open air markets, out-door barbers and small shops. At the intersection with Hu Guo Si East Alley (护国寺胡同), you can turn to the north and come across the ruins of the Temple for the Protection of the Nation (护国寺 or *hu guo si*).

The temple occupies the site of the home of Prince To To, a Mongol prince who rose to the position of minister of state during the Yuan dynasty. In accordance with the tried and true drill, Prince To To was accused of disloyalty, banished to Yunnan province in 1355 and died by poison, only to be exonerated ten years after his death (and three years before the Yuan dynasty came crashing down). His residence was then turned into a memorial shrine, which gradually evolved into a Buddhist temple and a public gathering place.

The temple was renovated in both the Ming and Qing dynasties, though by the Republican era, the eastern portion of the temple had disappeared. The remaining temple served as the site for monthly temple fairs where there would be found vendors of curios, calligraphy, flowers, birds, fish, pet insect, and food as well as storytellers, acrobats and fortune tellers. Up to 2004, all that remained was a single, inaccessible hall surrounded by lumber and other refuse.

In her *Blue Guide: China*, Frances Wood mentions that while in its prime the temple was renowned for its cultivated flowers. During a visit in November 1988, she could scarcely find it amidst heaps of Chinese cabbage, piled high by the temples. On one of my trips during a frosty winter night in 1995, the temple was also camouflaged with cabbages. They looked like a bundle of kittens, somehow immovably clinging to the wall of the temple, seeking the warmth or compassion of the gods who once lived inside. Alas, because of the development of hothouse farming in China, Peking is no longer deluged with cabbages at the outset of winter. However, on my last trip, an army of watermelons seemed to have laid siege to the temple. In May 2004, some dolt managed to set fire to the last surviving portion to the temple. Now only the temple's name remains on the street signs.

On the subject of watermelons (and trying to assuage my sense of loss), I should mention that in Chinese, the fruit is known as *xi gua* (西瓜), or "Western Melons." The name refers to the fact that the watermelon was first brought to China during the reign of Han Ming Di, two thousand years ago. The emperor had dispatched an envoy named Ban Chao (班超) to establish contact with the small kingdoms around Samarkand and Tashkent. After an extensive and arduous trip, Ban returned to China with a handful of seeds that introduced watermelons to China.

To the north of Hu Guo Temple Street, you come to the "Three Not Olds" Alley (三不老胡同 or *san bu lao hu tong*). While the street is quite ordinary, its name evokes the memory of a famous Ming dynasty admiral, Zheng He (郑和) who once lived here. Zheng He was a Chinese Muslim born in Yunnan Province. As a child, he was castrated so that he could serve the Ming court as a eunuch. On account of his intelligence and initiative, he rose in the military ranks of the Ming. However, unlike the last eunuch Sun, Zheng He's destiny led to fame and deification.

In 1402, Yong Le ordered Zheng He upon an unprecedented voyage. Zheng He was to sail a Ming imperial fleet to South East Asia and the regions further to the West, primarily in order to re-establish dormant contacts with the foreign world and to consolidate Yong Le's position as the emperor of the ruling house of China. Admiral Zheng took four voyages with an imperial fleet of several hundred ships throughout the islands of South East Asia, across the Indian Ocean to the Red Sea and the coast of Mozambique. Unlike the Portuguese and Spanish voyages of exploration, the Ming fleet was fully equipped to impress foreign lands with the power and wealth of China. Among the crew were warriors, artisans, and scholars as well as holds full of Chinese silk, jade and other goods to be given to local kings. The overseas Chinese community in Java and Malacca exuberantly received Zheng. Years after his arrival, Zheng rose to the ranks of a deity, like Guan Di and Yue Fei before him. His image can still be seen in the temples of old Malacca and Solo.

In Sri Lanka, the activities of the Ming fleet contradict the oft-quoted assertion that China has never dabbled in the affairs of foreign countries. Zheng threw himself into domestic political squabbles and led his warriors in battle supporting a political faction in Kandy. On subsequent trips, Zheng made a pilgrimage to Mecca and generally cultivated good relations with his co-religionists in the region. While in Africa, his troops captured a giraffe, which was shipped back to Peking and passed off as a *qilin*.

Yong Le granted Zheng the title "Three Protections Eunuch" (三保太监 or *san bao tai jian*) as a reward for his voyages. The *hu tong* where Zheng lived became known by a distorted version of the title, San Bu Lao.

From here, you can take a taxi or ride your bicycle to the Lu Xun Museum, which is located at the end of Fu Cheng Men Nei Bei Jie (阜成门内北街) near the West Second Ring Road. Lu Xun was one of the greatest writers in China during the 20th century. In the 1920s, he lived in a simple courtyard house here that in another astonishingly bad move on the part of the Peking authorities, has been razed. Lu's style was a sharp biting satirical view of both imperial Chinese society and the new society that was emerging during the Republican era.

His most famous work is probably "The True Story of Ah Q," which told the story of a crude country youth as a parable for China's problems in the 1930s. The story is set in a country village at the end of the Qing dynasty where the town folk ceaselessly bully Ah Q, who creates a dream world where any humiliation is transformed into a "spiritual victory." He starts thieving and declares his allegiance with the new revolutionaries in order to impress his townspeople. Eventually, the real revolutionaries come to the village and cooperate with the Mandarins and gentry to put Ah Q on trial where he is sentenced to death. On his way to the execution grounds, Ah Q still suffers from his delusions of spiritual victory and shouts slogans in praise of himself.

Returning to Fu Cheng Men Nei Avenue and heading east, you will come to the White Pagoda Temple (白塔寺 or *bai ta si*) which is also known as the Temple of the Marvelous Powers of Manifestation (妙应寺 or *miao ying si*). In 1092, a Liao emperor originally installed a pagoda here. In 1271, Kublai Khan totally reconstructed the pagoda in the Tibetan style, which is the structure that still adorns the neighborhood. The temple in front of the pagoda houses a magnificent selection of Tibetan bronze Buddhas and thangkas.

The White Pagoda presents something of a challenge to advocates of Han chauvinism since its pedigree is a lesson in Peking's longstanding cosmopolitanism. A Mongol emperor commissioned the pagoda, which was designed by a Nepalese architect Arginer in a Tibetan style (whose roots are in India) for a multi-ethnic congregation in an empire that spanned the Yang Tze River and the

The White Pagoda Temple.

Danube. The pagoda elegantly attests to the fusion of Han and non-Han cultures in past ages.

In past years, a popular Peking rhyme was associated with the pagoda: "At Bai Ta Temple/There is a white pagoda/On the pagoda there are bricks/But no tiles/On the pagoda's terrace there was/A great crack/Master Lu Ban came down/ and repaired the pagoda." In Chinese, the rhyme goes "白塔寺／有白塔／塔上有砖／没有瓦／塔台儿裂了／一道缝／鲁班下来."

The rhyme refers to a legend from the early days of the Qing dynasty when the terrace showed a wide crack that threatened to topple the structure and injure the residents of the neighborhood. While the residents pondered this dilemma, an elderly, slightly half-witted man in mason's clothing appeared from nowhere and circled the pagoda, shouting that he could repair it overnight. The next day, the crack had been filled in, and the job was duly attributed to Lu Ban, the patron saint of carpenters, who humbly appeared in disguise to preserve Arginer's handiwork.

Another legend maintains that a water dragon, whose capricious temperament was given to causing floods, inflicted considerable damage in this neighborhood about ten centuries ago. The monks, being knowledgeable in these matters, arranged through talismans and spells to imprison the water dragon in a well and built the pagoda on top of the well to ensure that the dragon would not cause any further disruption.

An interesting tour of the back streets of Old Peking can be had by taking the *hu tong* directly to the east of the entrance of the temple. From this street you will be able to glimpse a panoramic view of the pagoda. It is also fun to explore the neighborhood to the west of the temple. Here you will find courtyard residences with wooden monks' cells, now the homes of Peking senior citizens.

I have found the corner of the temple grounds near the pagoda to be a very tranquil spot to enjoy a bag lunch beside the cypress trees. Sometimes in this neighborhood, you will hear an unearthly hollow sound descending from the skies and then catch sight of a flock of pigeons overhead. The pigeons are pets of residents, who, in time-honored fashion, tie little bamboo whistles to their tails with a metal ring. The pigeon whistles take many shapes, some with as many as eleven little tubes. As the flock wheels overhead, wind courses through the whistle, which produce all five notes of the traditional Chinese music scale. Of course, you do not need to be at Bai Tai Si to hear them since this hobby is pursued throughout the city.

Returning to Fu Cheng Men Nei Avenue, we turn south on Tai Ping Qiao Xi Street (太平桥西街) and then turn into the second street on the east, the Brick Pagoda Temple Alley (砖塔寺胡同 or *zhuan ta si hu tong*). This alley is one of the oldest streets in Peking: city maps from 1050 depict it clearly. Unfortunately, the west side of this alley and its environs are under the wrecking ball at the time of writing.

There is a forgotten monument lost in alleyways at No. 2 Nan Si Yan Jing (南四眼井2号) off the Brick Pagoda Temple Alley. You locate it by asking folks in the neighborhood. This is the former residence of Liu Shao Qi (刘少奇革命活动纪念地), the Chairman of PRC and once second in command after Chairman Mao. Liu secretly lived in Peking for several months from 1937 to 1938 before returning to Yenan where he developed his skills as a master administrator and technician for the Communist Party.

After 1949, Mao picked Liu as his successor most likely on the basis of his administrative abilities. However, Mao grew uneasy with Liu's practical approach for solving social and economic problems and came to regard Liu as a "revisionist" without sufficient commitment to ideology. In 1967, the Red Guards surrounded the Zhong Nan Hai compound in an attempt to arrest and punish Liu. They smoked him out after Liu's wife had been tricked into leaving Zhong Nan Hai after receiving a false message that her children's lives were in danger. After three years of imprisonment and constant abuse, Liu died in an unheated inland prison, alone, naked and ill, without even a blanket for comfort during his final hours. After the purge of the Gang of Four and Deng's rise to power, Liu was posthumously rehabilitated, in a drill that must be wearily familiar to the reader by now. During the 1980s, the government issued 100 Renminbi notes ironically depicting Liu and Mao side by side (along with Zhou Enlai and Zhu De). Liu's former residence is completely run-down. An elderly woman residing in the courtyard patiently answers questions and points out the historical marker that once identified the house and now lies by the doorway.

Returning to the Brick Pagoda Alley, you will be pleased to see that the east side of the street still retains its traditional appearance and courtyard houses. As you amble down this curving street, we see in the distance the brick pagoda that gives the alley its name. The Brick Temple, or more properly, the Pagoda of the Old Man of the Ten Thousand Pines (万松老人塔 or *wan song lao ren ta*) marks the final resting place of a Jin dynasty Buddhist monk known by this sobriquet. In 1753, Qian Long constructed the current pagoda, which is now fronted by a shop selling Kodak film.

Coming out on Xi Si Bei Avenue (西四北大街) on the west side, there used to be a dumpling restaurant that gained notoriety in the 1970s as the lair of a serial killer. The owner invited transients to his restaurant with the bait of a free meal. There he would butcher them and use their flesh in the stuffing of his dumplings, which were very popular among both the foreign and Chinese communities. He was executed in 1980.

This neighborhood always seemed to have some association with death. Chinese cosmological symmetry perhaps played a role because after all, the Buddhist lands of paradise lay to the west of China. At Xi Dan, there used to be the Sunrise Coffin Bearers, an association of undertakers who staged one of the most widely viewed funerals for the late Peking opera actor Yang Xiao Lou (杨小楼) in 1937. Previously, the same company was able to wrangle the commission to carry Sun Yat Sen's remains from the Western Hills to the Forbidden City before onward delivery to his tomb in Nanjing.

Turning to the west on Fu Cheng Men Nei Avenue again, you will come to the Temple of the Broad Meditation (广济寺 or *guang ji si*), a Buddhist temple whose origins date to earlier Mongol dynasties before the first millennium. The temple was renovated in 1457 and again in 1699 and has experienced much devastation from fire, the most recent occurrence in 1934. The gateway is decorated with Sanskrit symbols and opens onto a large courtyard. In the main hall, there is a statue of the multi-eyed Avalakitosvera, the bodhisattva whose eminence is reflected in the Dalai Lama. The temple is one of the few that are still used for religious purposes and houses the Buddhist Association of China.

Down the street towards the west, we come to the monumental arches with green tiles, which are a part of the Temple to the Successive Generations of Emperors (万代帝王庙 or *li dai di wang miao*) first built in 1523. The temple formerly housed the spirit tablets of all past emperors, excluding tyrants, usurpers or those who were murdered or lost their throne, the latter two events being evidence of Heaven's disfavor.

At the time of writing, the temple was not open to the public, and the gatekeeper has a handy typed note in English explaining to stray foreigners that this historic site is closed and that "we have to stick to the rules," a phrase suggesting someone's education at a missionary school. This fellow beams merrily once you cave in and give up your attempt to visit the sight. At least the old gentleman smiles. I suggest that the reader give the old gentleman an orange or two, just to brighten his day.

Upon arriving at the intersection of Fu Cheng Men Nei Avenue and Tai Ping Qiao Avenue (太平桥大街), we turn to the south and go straight until we arrive at Bi Cai Alley (辟才胡同), where we turn to the west. At No. 13 Kua Che Alley (跨车胡同), we come to the former residence of Qi Bai Shi (齐白石故居), an artist who painted in traditional themes and eschewed the tawdry direct propaganda of sycophants like Xu Bei Hong.

There is an interesting account of Old China meeting with New India. The Indian journalist, Raja Huthessing called on Qi during a 1952 visit to China. At that time, Russian journalist Ilya Ehrenburg had "rediscovered" Qi. Copies of his work were selling well with visitors from socialist and neutral nations. Notwithstanding his concerns to the contrary, Huthessing found Qi to be an utterly unpretentious old man, living in a ramshackle splendor. A eunuch who was formerly attached to the imperial family acted as Qi's housekeeper and doorman.

Huthessing was impressed by the quiet and solitude, as well as the absence of slogans and loudspeakers, in the home of the artist. He was also struck by Qi's poverty. Qi's studio and home consisted of a few sticks of furniture. The Indian had previously seen Qi at a state banquet. "In his long black silk robe, high velvet cap, he was slowly coming up the steps leaning on the arms of the trusted woman whom he wanted to marry even at this age. In the other hand he carried a long red-lacquered staff. In the midst of the blue-uniformed men and women he looked out of place. He seemed to walk out of the ancient Confucian lore, a sage to lead the people back to filial piety and ancestral worship."[3] On the day of Huthessing's visit, he looked like he wanted no more than just to rest.

Qi belonged to a traditional school of painting with only flowers, birds, shrimps and lobsters as his primary subjects. However, Qi only gave his paintings a touch of political symbols. During the Japanese occupation of China, his favorite subject matter was crabs, symbols of tyrants. However, after 1949, when China required less subtle methods of politically correct artistic expression, Qi fell into oblivion until his rediscovery by the Russians. Rediscovery did not bring him material comfort. At that time, no one wanted his delicate pictures, which the master would roll up and put away into cupboards. His paintings sold for only a trifle, and he could afford no more than to give his guests boiled water instead of tea.

Huthessing had some tough sledding in communicating with Qi, who only spoke the Hunan dialect. Huthessing's questions were in English and translated into Mandarin and then from Mandarin to Hunanese and then back again.

Huthessing asked Qi to paint something for him at that very moment. The request revived the old master. When asked for a subject matter, Huthessing simply told Qi to paint anything that came to his mind. Qi painted a picture depicting two water buffalos, one walking away from the viewer, amidst a grove of bamboo and water.

"Why this picture?" asked Huthessing. "Does it represent the two ancient cultures of India and China." But no, Qi said that there is no political theme in this painting, or any of his paintings. And Huthessing did not know that China, be it Old or New, did not recognize India as a fellow traveler from antiquity.

"The cows remind me of my childhood," replied Qi. "Don't you know I was a cowherd till I was twelve years old? I have seldom drawn cows in my pictures,

Qi Bai Shi affixing his seal.

but today I remembered my childhood." One day, when Qi was taking the cows out, one of them wandered away and could not be found. Qi's grandfather beat him so badly that he ran away and became a carpenter's apprentice in a nearby village.

Huthessing understood that the picture showed an event that led to so much unhappiness. His departure from home some eighty years earlier was also the beginning of Qi's creative period.

These days, Qi's former residence is still ramshackle and unkempt. On the doorway, a sign warns in English "No Interruptions." Qi's legacy does not enjoy a shrine like a socialist museum, though somehow I sense that his spirit is probably on a corner near City Lights Books in North Beach, waiting in full throated impatience for the Peach Garden Hermit to get off work so they can go to The Saloon.

If you strike to the south, you will find the remains of a temple of the city god (都皇城庙 or *du huang cheng miao*) at No. 33 Cheng Fang Street (成方街). In this instance, a small portion of the temple, which had been rebuilt many times during the Ming and Qing dynasties, awaits you if you can talk your way past the guards. During the Ming and Qing dynasties, there was some confusion as to which historical being actually held the post of Peking's guardian deity. While some maintained that Yu Qian was the municipal patron, others claimed the post for another Ming era military hero and martyr, Yang Ji Sheng (杨继盛) who was murdered in 1555. Over time, the City God came to be worshipped by emperors, scholars, and the citizens of Peking, with his persona attributed with multiple meanings, such as protector of the capital against foreigners, the righteous voice of reason and the supernatural official responsible for the city and its communal ghosts.

Each city district had a temple for its "city god," usually a deified historical person, along with its God of the Earth (土地公 or *tu di gong*), a squat deity with a long Maltese beard and a staff. (The maxim was that the jurisdiction of each earth god was as finite as the street in front of his shrine.) Each district's city gods were annually taken from their temples and placed upon a sedan chair in order to be taken out for an inspection of his district. During these processions, people who had previously called on the god for help inflicted self-punishments as an offering of gratitude. "Pay-back" would take the form of hooks inserted in their arms or the wearing of cangues and chains. While long gone from the streets of Peking, these ceremonies can still be seen in Taiwan, although usually offered as tribute to other deities. Similarly, every district celebrates its own God of the Earth, usually housed in a small roadside shrine no taller than a meter and accompanied with a statue of his wife.

From here you can go to the north side of the Central Conservatory (中央音院) nestled in the corner of the Second Ring Road and Xuan Wu Men Nei Avenue (宣武门内大街). The conservatory occupies the former residence of another Prince Chun who, in this case, was the father of Guang Xu and brother-in-law of the Empress Dowager. It was from here that Guang Xu was spirited away on a cold winter evening after the untimely death of his cousin. I wonder if he had any "Rosebud" recollections of the days before his enthronement.

For those with enthusiasm for mummified remains of the city spirits, you can take a taxi to the Second Ring Road and head north in order to see a portion of the city wall that is entombed in between flyovers and concrete blocks. There really is nothing for you to linger over.

We now head further south. On No. 24 New Culture Alley (新文化胡同 or *xin wen hua hu tong*) stands the former residence of Li Da Zhao, co-founder of the Chinese Communist Party, in a run-down courtyard house. At No. 45 is the former site of Peking's Women's University, set up in the 1920s and poignantly, if indirectly, mentioned at the beginning of Zheng Yi Mou's *Raise the Red Lantern*.

Moving on to the intersection of Xuan Wu Men West Avenue (宣武门西大街) and Xuan Wu Men Nei Avenue (宣武门内大街), you will come to the former site of Peking's elephant stables (象房). Alas, there is nothing that remains of

賜塋來象

Peking's elephants out for an airing.

this institution of imperial Peking. However, it is a yarn too good to resist telling.

Starting in the Ming dynasty, elephants were quartered in Peking as an adjunct for the performance of imperial ceremonies. Most of the elephants arrived as tribute gifts from South East Asian kingdoms such as those in northern Vietnam or central Burma. The stables were enormous structures, consisting of six rows of eight stables, 36 feet by 18 feet and separated by massive walls lit by a skylight in the roof. The entranceway was a heavy iron bound door that spanned a deep trench into which the elephant keepers would leap whenever the elephants were aggressive.

Unlike their brethren in South East Asia, elephants in Old Peking were not compelled to perform heavy labor, like moving teak logs. Rather, they were used for ceremonial purposes to enhance the prestige of the emperor. For instance, elephants lined both sides of the entrance of the Meriden Gate in the Forbidden City when imperial officials came to report to the emperor. Once the officials had passed through the gate, the elephants would step forward and interlock their trucks as if to prevent any official from leaving without imperial permission. The beasts were also used to pull the imperial chariot when the emperor attended the annual prayers to the harvest at the Altar of Agriculture or his genuflections to his ancestors at the Imperial Ancestral Hall.

During the Qing era, the elephant keepers were from Vietnam and I can easily picture them shivering during the cold winter nights, wondering how on earth did they manage to get stationed this far north. As classic books of pre-World War II vintage like *Elephant Bill* and *Burmese Timber Elephant* explain, a mahout needed both extensive learning on elephant care and training as well as an intuitive understanding of the personality of his own elephant. All of these skills had to be, in turn, fine-tuned to fit the needs of the Peking court. You could have called the process "elephants with Chinese characteristics," the later part bringing a level of bureaucracy that must have stunned the poor packyderms. For example, if an elephant caught a cold, his mahout would be obliged to submit a memorial to the throne, whereupon the emperor wrote out one order instructing the elephant to return to the stables and another order commanding another elephant to trundle over as his replacement. Legend has it that the elephants would have to have the order read to them; otherwise, they remained immovable.

If an elephant harmed any member of the public, the emperor would order a punishment, such as a whipping, which presumably had no effect on its thick hind. Two other elephants would wind their trunks around the offender, forcing him to his knees. When the whipping was completed, the elephant would kowtow several times as if thanking the emperor for the punishment and putting him back on the straight and narrow. Elephants, like trees, would also enjoy imperial honors and titles, though they seemed to be free of the scheming that characterized the human bearers of such honors.

Rations were given on the basis of their duties, with more food provided to those who engaged in more onerous work; guard duty being regarded as tougher than chariot pulling. Dishonest mahouts sometimes raked off a portion of the rice allocated to their elephants and sold it on the black market to earn some extra copper, a sleight of hand that did not go unnoticed by the beasts, who would weigh their rations with their trunks and go on a rampage if they found themselves short changed.

Another means for the mahouts to augment their wages was the sale of elephant shit, which was purchased by Peking ladies as a hair wash bestowing a bright and shiny gloss that now would be the pride of the Body Shop. Environmentally safe too. Recalling the logo "a little dab will do you," men applied the elephant shit on nicks and scrapes left by the barber's razor upon their crown of their skull. These customs led to the term *xiang la zi* (象拉子), or giving the English translation a contemporary flavor, Elephant Dungsters, as a description of people who put on airs. It is a term ripe for revival.

The elephants were allowed once a year to take a stroll in the city, on the 6th of the sixth lunar month, when they were taken for a bath in the moat by the Tartar city. This day was a Peking holiday, with people taking the day to watch the elephants bathing.

In 1884, one of the elephants was being put through his paces training to pull the imperial chariot for the ceremonies at the Altar of Heaven. I suspect that the creature was thoroughly sick of the drill. As soon as he saw his chance, he escaped from the quarters and went on a rampage. His escapade caused a tremendous panic throughout the southeast corner of the city, overturning vendor carts (and presumably vendors), breaking through wooden gates of courtyard homes and generally raising merry hell (pleasant to imagine). It all ended in tears when some Manchu hero tried to bring the elephant to heal but only succeeded in getting himself stomped on. After that event, the court banned the elephants from participating in the imperial ceremonies. Without being on the payroll of the Forbidden Court, the elephants were out of work and soon died of starvation a few years later. The stables collapsed in the early 20th century. Xinhua News Agency now occupies the site of one of the former elephant stables. Dynastic decline, indeed.

In the mid-1990s, elephants were suddenly revived as tribute gifts from South East Asia. In order to oust its competitors for a Peking telecommunications project, a Thai company gave the Peking Zoo a gift of two elephants, named "Unicom" and "Jiang Ze Min." The creatures knelt down when called by their respective names. While the tribute present opened doors for the short term, the Thais proved to be a white elephant when it came to technical expertise. Whenever someone asks me what does it take to win a bid in China, my stock reply is "elephants."

Coming to the northeast corner of the intersection of Xuan Wu Men Avenue West and Xuan Wu Men Nei Avenue, you come to the Southern Cathedral (南堂), formerly a Roman Catholic church but now used by the Catholic Patriotic Association. This site marks the residence of Matteo Ricci during the first decade of the 17th century. Adam Schall built a Catholic church here in 1650 in accordance with an imperial order honoring Father Matteo. A tablet in the courtyard is barely legible though it once read "Cathedral Built By Imperial Order." In 1827, Dao Guang ordered all Roman Catholic priests to leave the capital, and the Southern Cathedral was conveyed by deed to the Russian Ecclestical Mission, who owned the property until the Anglo-French Treaty of 1860 forced the Qing government to return Church properties. In that year, the South Church was a ruin, with great rents in the roof, and grass growing on the floor. Inside, every decoration and pew had been carted away while the courtyard outside was occupied by hawkers.[4] A "Te Deum" was performed here in October 1860 after the French priests completed the restoration, with Catholic converts slowly and cautiously emerging from hiding and returning to attend Mass. Alas, once again, the Southern Cathedral was destroyed during the Boxer Debacle and was rebuilt in baroque style in 1904. Masses are held every day.

Turning to the north on Xuan Wu Men Nei Avenue (宣武门内大街 and turning east on Rong Xian Alley (绒绒胡同), you will come across the China Club of Peking located in a courtyard house. This site originally housed the Si Chuan Restaurant, established in 1952, and frequented by Si Chuan native Deng Xiao Ping. For security reasons, the restaurant removed the spirit step of the main gate in order to facilitate Deng's caravan of limousines. The club offers overnight rooms for those holding a club membership, which starts at a wholloping US$15,000 admission fee, *plus* an additional monthly hit of US$100. This, mind you, is for a club whose English-speaking local management uncouthly refer to foreign visitors as *lao wai* in their presence, nonetheless! On principle alone, should you wish to stay in a Peking courtyard house, go to the Bamboo Garden Hotel or Hao Yuan, whose staff are impeccably polite in the best tradition of Old Peking and give this reverse discrimination relic a deserving miss.

After five-figured rudeness, let's draw our tour to a close at a vacant lot. On the corner of Xi Dan Avenue and Tian An Men West Avenue is a nondescript park where once stood Democracy Wall, Peking's Hyde Park from 1977 to 1979. The tradition of big character posters and essays had taken root in Peking during the May 4th Movement and has come alive again from time to time afterwards. In the aftermath of the arrest of the Gang of Four, Deng Xiao Ping allowed the citizens of the capital, up to a certain point, to have some breathing space to air thoughts and ideas without censorship. On Sunday afternoons, new posters and articles were posted on the wall. It was this generation of Chinese, having been suppressed for so long and cherishing the opportunity for educational advancement that proved to be the most talented and capable of any generation in China. Foreign experts teaching at universities in those early days speak glowingly about the first class of students allowed back for studies after the Cultural Revolution. This was the generation of creative and talented men and women who had been denied a voice for self-expression and were keen to make up for lost time.

As a first step to strangle the movement, Deng relocated Democracy Wall to the Park of the Altar of the Moon in a remote portion of the city to the west. Finally, in 1979, it was shut down in its entirety.

One Peking poet wrote a final farewell:

My friend,
Parting time is pending.
Farewell - Democracy Wall.

What can I briefly say to you?
Should I speak of spring's frigidity?
Should I say that you are like the withered wintersweet?

No, I should instead talk of happiness,
Tomorrow's happiness,
Of pure orchid skies,
Of golden wild flowers,
Of a child's bright eyes.
In sum, we ought
To part with dignity,
Don't you agree?[5]

The poetry of Democracy Wall captured the imaginations of a special generation of Peking's citizens. While Westerners, and Americans in particular, tend to interpret such aspirations these days as the cries of a downtrodden people, they are actually the voice of a nation that wishes to reclaim its country's dignity and prestige without being remolded in the image of any country, let alone the United States.

But there was indeed a time when China's intellectuals regarded the United States as a source of idealism and benevolence, and in turn, Americans could not resist the temptation of clinging to this ideal even as their government's external actions undermined it. This image of the United States as a guiding light was irretrievably shattered in the aftermath of the bombing of the Chinese embassy in Belgrade and the ludicrous explanations proffered by Clinton and the Pentagon. Worse was to come. To the minds of many, the image of American hypocrisy deepened tenfold because of the Second Gulf War and the Bush Administration's lame justifications for its misadventure. Perhaps the present state of the Democracy Wall is a fitting end to Chinese idealism about the United States. Now, nothing is left.

12

THE EASTERN CHINESE CITY

LET'S START THIS TOUR BY going to Dragon Pool Park (龙潭公园 or *long tan gong yuan*) in the southeast corner of the former Eastern Chinese city. Here you will find a beautifully landscaped park where the Peking authorities have revived lunar New Year temple fairs. In the middle of the park stands a single rectangular brick structure. This is all that remains of a memorial to Commander Yuan Chong Huan (袁崇焕) of the Ming dynasty. Commander Yuan fought the Manchus in the early 17th century but was eventually sabotaged through a combination of court intrigue and misinformation spread about him. In 1630, the Ming emperor Chong Zheng sentenced him to death by a 1,000 cuts on account of reports that he was on the verge of defecting to the enemy. Qian Long posthumously exonerated Yuan's name and had this temple built in his honor. On one side of the temple is a stele erected on Confucius' birthday in 1887. We will visit Commander Yuan's grave in a little while at a separate location in this part of the city.

From here, you turn to the north to Bai Qiao Nan Li (百桥南里) for the remains of the Temple of Prosperous Peace (隆安寺 or *long an si*), a Buddhist temple first built in 1454. The temple was once a thriving center of worship and a landmark for the surrounding neighborhoods. Now it functions as a school and the location of the Peking Youth Training School. It is well kept, though nowhere near possessing its former importance to the neighborhood.

By traveling to the west from the temple, you will come to No. 59 Middle School on Wo Fo Si Street (卧佛寺街). In the southeast corner of the schoolyard you will find the final resting spot of Commander Yuan. After Yuan had been torn to pieces, one of his footmen, a soldier named She, collected his commander's head from the execution grounds and secretly buried it in the courtyard of his

Eastern Chinese City

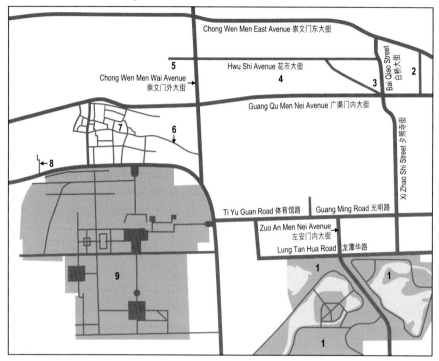

1. Dragon Pool Park（龙潭公园）
2. Temple of Prosperous Peace（隆安寺）
3. Memorial to Yuan Chong Huan（哀崇焕祠）
4. Former Location of Bamboo Wattle Street
5. Dong Hua Shi Mosque（东花市清真寺）
6. East Dawn Market Street（东晓市街）
7. Golden Terrace Study（金台书店）
8. Alley of True Loyalty（清忠胡同）
9. Altar of Heaven Park（天坛公园）

home. If She had been caught, he could only expect the same treatment as that doled out to Yuan. She vowed that he would protect the general's resting place and declared that all of his descendants would do likewise.

Interestingly enough, She's descendants *did* continue to guard the commander's grave from the late Ming to the present day. Qian Long issued a posthumous pardon and later, Chairman Mao declared the tomb to be a historic site. Descendants of She continue to look after the memorial, which underwent renovation in the summer of 2002.

Altar of Heaven Park

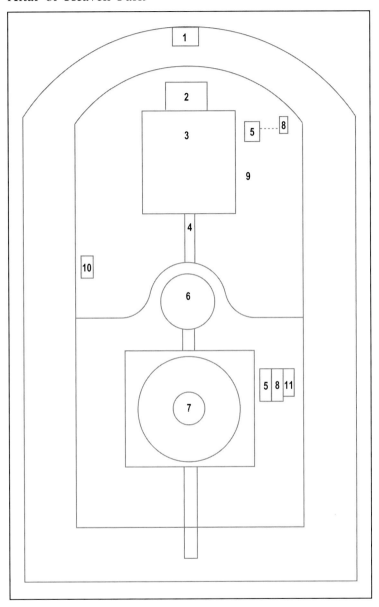

1. North Gate
2. Hall of Imperial Heaven （皇乾殿）
3. Hall of Prayer for Good Harvest （祁年殿）
4. Stone Causeway
5. Sacred Kitchens
6. Temple of the God of the Universe （皇穹宇）
7. Altar of Heaven
8. Storage for Sacred Utensils
9. Seven Star Rocks （七皇石）
10. Hall of Abstinence （斋宫）
11. Slaughterhouse

Turning to East Flower Street (东花市大街 or *dong hua shi da jie*) and heading west, you will come to a neighborhood that once boasted of an interesting side street called the Bamboo Wattle Lane (竹篱笆 or *zhu li ba*). In imperial times, the people on this street raised pigeons but not as pets as Peking folks do these days. By artificially expanding the pigeon's crops, the residents of this street trained the birds to steal rice from the Imperial Granaries. It worked like this. When the pigeons were released from their cages in the early morning hours, they flew to the granaries and gorged themselves, usually on the best quality rice in storage. When they returned to their homes, their owners forced them to drink a solution that caused the birds to cough out the rice, which the owners then sold on a retail basis. It was said that with a flock of 100 pigeons, an entrepreneur could rake in about 50 pounds of high quality rice per day. Typically, the owners starved their pigeons during the night to ensure a good haul the following morning.

The owners were always concerned about the welfare of their unpaid workers. To make sure that the neighborhood cats could not get at their little gray money making machines, the pigeons were locked up in bamboo wattle cages, which in turn gave the street its name. Alas, the street has been erased from the face of Peking's maps, but it is a marvelous story to think about while looking at these nondescript modern monstrosities.

Just a little to the west of East Flower Street, there is a marvelous Ming Chinese style mosque (东花市清真寺 or *dong hua shi qing zhen si*). The entrance is through a gate with two stylized minarets while the courtyards are built in traditional Chinese themes and decorated with Arabic quotations. The mosque is supposed to hold plaques given by Kang Xi and Qian Long, the latter praising Islam with the phrase "With Islam first, there is no second" (真一无二 or *zhen yi wu er*). There are rolling tiles, looking like waves, along the wall bordering the street. I have encountered occasional reluctance of the gate keepers here in letting non-Muslims in for a look. At the very least, you might be able to get to the main courtyard for a quick glance.

The immediate vicinity of the Mosque has been utterly razed. I am afraid that in these environs there will be nothing more than charmless high risers bearing such stomach churning names as "Wealthy Estates." Billboard advertisements for these luxury homes usually depict very fashionable Chinese or Westerners embracing a life of high-end consumerism. It makes you wonder how these clowns stole *their* rice.

From here, you can head to the East Dawn Market Street (东晓市街 or *dong xiao shi jie*), a delightfully medieval part of the city that is worth a morning in directionless wandering. On the north side of the street you will come to the Golden Terrace Study (金台书院 or *jin tai shu yuan*), currently an elementary school but formerly a school for students from the capital and the provinces to learn how to conduct imperial ceremonies. The current structure dates from 1750 and was renovated several times during Dao Guang's reign.

The Alley of True Loyalty (清忠胡同 or *qing zhong hu tong*) recalls to mind a temple that stood here in honor of the Song patriot Yue Fei, whom we have already tripped over in our travels in the Back Lakes district. Many shrines were built to his memory and the one down this lane, called the Temple of True Loyalty, was especially important in that it was both a patriotic and religious site as well as a meeting place for Peking's many guildhalls.

In the days before commercial hotels, travelers from the provinces stayed in regional guildhalls that were operated along the lines of the hostels in Dong Jiao Min Xiang for tribute missions. The guildhalls were set up on the basis of regional loyalties as a place in the capital where people up from the same province could speak their own dialect, eat their own cuisine and commiserate about the difficulties of life in Peking. The guildhalls tended to be fully occupied at the time of the Metropolitan Examinations when thousands of candidates took up residence before working their hearts out on the exam. Once these candidates left the city, a regional guildhall carried on its function as a gathering point for the merchants from their home province. In a parallel with the past, China's provincial governments these days build hotels that cater to their fellow locals.

In pre-1949 Peking, another kind of guildhall was built for merchants engaged in the same industry. These professional guilds set market prices and quality standards, produced a code of rules for transactions and supplied a forum for the resolution of professional disputes. These types of guilds ranged from lantern makers to coffin bearers to grain and oil salesmen. Some had their own halls, but a great many rented the facilities at the Temple of True Loyalty for seasonal meetings and banquets. Here they would also retain a Peking Opera troupe to put on a performance for their patron saint.

The most interesting guild to hold its meetings on these grounds was the Blind Men Guild, which consisted of sight-challenged entertainers. A foreign observer described a convention of blind people arriving at the temple, wielding their bamboo canes and hollering across the hall to find old friends. The guild boasted a management council of 48 positions, ranging from general manager to judge to inspector to witness to doorkeeper. The guild worshipped the San Guan (三官), or the Emperor of Heaven, the Emperor of Earth and the Emperor of Sea as their patron saints. Each year, the guild sent an annual report to the patron saints by burning a memorial before the altar. Punishments were meted out to those who broke the rules in the form of a prohibition against performing for a certain number of days.

These days, the alley is a scruffy scene without any tangible remains of the old temple. However, it still has the deep feeling of an unvarnished slice of Peking life.

Crossing the street to the south, you will next arrive at the northern entrance of the Altar of Heaven (天坛 or *tian tan*), which, in the view of many scholars, writers and travelers, excels all other temples in Peking. From the north to south exits is a walk of 6.5 kilometers. The grounds were built in 1420 with the southern border shaped like a square and the northern border curving to symbolize the meeting of heaven (the circle) and earth (the square). Surrounding the outer parameters are many delightful groves of cypress trees.

Heading south from the north entrance, you will first come across the Hall of Imperial Heaven (皇乾殿 or *huang qian dian*) where the tablets of Heaven and the Imperial Ancestors were enshrined. Before us, the entrance leads to a marble causeway linking the Hall of Prayer for Good Harvest (祈年殿 or *qin nian dian*), the Imperial Heavenly Vault (皇穹宇 or *huang qiong yu*) and the three-terraced white marble Altar of Heaven (天坛 or *tian tan*).

The Hall of Prayer for Good Harvest is a triple roofed circular building covered with exquisite blue tiles. It is built upon a white foundation with three terraces, the number which alludes to the Son of Heaven. On the very top of the Hall is a ball in fine gold leaf. Because of its majestic appearance, this hall is often mistakenly referred to as the Temple of Heaven. In imperial times, the building was actually less significant as it had nothing to do with the imperial ceremonies for Heaven. Rather the emperor came here in the spring to beseech Heaven to make sure that the emperor's subjects toiled diligently during the growing season.

The story goes that in 1889 a presumptuous centipede irritated Heaven by climbing up on the gold ball on the very top of the roof. In response to this pique, Heaven threw down a thunderbolt that incinerated the hall. (It was rebuilt over a period of ten years with Oregon pine, which was the closest wood that approximated the durable timbers first used in Yong Le's era). The accident was also interpreted to mean that Heaven was not likely to bless emperor Guang Xu, who had taken over the reigns of government that year.

Inside the Hall, there are four main central columns (symbolizing the four seasons) and twenty-four supporting pillars (representing the twelve months and the twelve hours of the traditional Chinese clock). The Hall has become a symbol of Peking as well as the entire country, and of no less significance, the registered trademark for Tsingtao beer.

Off to the east are a number of buildings used for the preparation of sacrifices. There are seven large stones here that are called meteorites and which gave occasion for the emperor to come here to pray for rain during droughts. Actually, they are nothing more exotic than building materials left over from the original construction in 1420.

I came to this section of the park on a bitterly cold Christmas morning ten years ago. There was a group of elderly men, bundled up in bulky cotton blue clothing but otherwise energetic and in good spirits. Three gentlemen in the group were playing traditional string and percussion instruments. One by one, each of the old fellows took a turn singing an aria from Peking Opera. This select group of connosieurs became animated with appreciation as each new singer delivered a song with an ever-increasing panache during the impromptu performance. The early morning winter light gave a vivid azure hue to the scene.

By retracing your steps to the marble causeway, you will arrive at the Hall of the Imperial Vault, a smaller circular temple with blue tiles. The hall was built in 1520 and restored in 1752. It is said that the circular wall produces an unusual acoustic effect: if you speak to the wall, someone on the other side of the courtyard can hear you as if he were standing next to you. I have no idea if this is true. On each trip here, I find that there are always too many rubes hollering at the wall and creating such a ruckus that I cannot hear my own thoughts, let alone the muttering of someone on the other side of the hall. You will notice a black circle running around the wall, exactly at the height of the average Peking citizen. I wonder if the purveyors of Vitalis have considered the potential of the China market.

Leaving the profane for the sacred, you return to the causeway and move further south. Here you come to the Altar of Heaven, the holy structure where each year, just before sunrise on the winter solstice, the emperor would pray to heaven. The altar, built in 1530, is made in three terraces of white marble representing heaven, earth and man. The circular balustrades are carved with cloud design and surround each of the terraces.

One day before the Winter Solstice, the emperor came to the altar from the Forbidden City in an imperial carriage pulled by an elephant. His route led him through the Gate of Heavenly Peace and then through the Front Gate and onto Qian Men Wai Avenue. For this occasion, all commoners were ordered to remain indoors on the pain of death, and the roadway was sprinkled with yellow dirt. Accompanying the emperor were over two thousand civilian and military officials. The emperor entered the compound through the northern-most of the western gates and went straight to the inner enclosure. He then withdrew to the Hall of Abstinence (斋宫 or *zhai gong*) located to the west of the altar and spent the night in fasting and meditation. Within the hall was a bronze statute of a Ming eunuch who, according to legend, had transformed his earthly form into a spirit so as to implore Heaven for blessings. The right index finger of the bronze statue was placed in front of its mouth to symbolize the need for silence and concentration on the part of the emperor.

At one hour and forty-five minutes before sunrise, the emperor donned a robe of imperial purple with a black satin hat and satin boots. He then rode in a chariot to the southern stairway of the altar. After resting for several moments in a yellow tent, the emperor then took hold of a blue gem symbolizing Heaven, faced the north and walked to the middle terrace. Two officials, one who directed the proceedings and the other who called out the next step in the ceremony, preceded the emperor. The spirit tablet of the Supreme Lord (上帝 or *shang di*) and the deceased emperors were placed on the top tier of the altar. Food offerings such as beef, pork, mutton, venison, rabbit, rice, sorghum, chestnuts, beetroots, celery, bamboo shoots and cakes were placed behind the tablets. Upon two tables sat carcasses of bullocks, cleaned and dressed for the ceremony. Enormous braziers and lanterns lit up the scene in the darkness of the frosty morning.

The ceremony consisted of nine stages. At the beginning, the emperor respectfully invited the souls of the Supreme Lord and the deceased emperors to enter the spirit tablets and observe the ceremony. Once the spirits were installed in their tablet thrones, the emperor offered them samples of the highest quality silk and jade. Next he offered one of the bullocks.

At that point, eight groups of dancers with halberds and shields came forward to perform a martial dance. After that, the emperor prostrated himself in the center of the altar while his prayer was read out:

> "The reigning Son of Heaven, subject (followed by Emperor's own name, which was taboo even to his nearest relatives), ventures to lift up the following prayer …."[1]

The prayer consisted of a request for blessings along with a report on the state of the empire. Upon the conclusion of the prayer, dancers holding long feathers and flutes performed the "dance of the blessings of civil administration." The emperor then offered the second bullock and the martial dance was repeated. At that point, the emperor ate a portion of the meat and drank some of the wine offered to the shades. Then, the Supreme Lord and the spirits of the deceased emperors were invited to return to the spirit world.

The last step consisted of the emperor supervising the burning of the offerings in the ovens built outside the altar. As the fires consumed the offerings, the spirits of these gifts were released to the realm of the Supreme Lord and the ancestors.

This ceremony, which traces its origins back to the Western Zhou, was performed for the very last time in 1899. The Boxer Rebellion and subsequent political instability prevented any subsequent ceremonies during the twilight years of the Qing. In 1914, Yuan Shi Kai, in his attempt to create a dynasty, performed an abbreviated version of the ritual, though it was regarded as a paltry affair when compared to the pageantry of past ceremonies.

The Chinese were not the only nation to have an Altar of Heaven. Since Confucianism hugely influenced Vietnamese and Korean culture, the kings of these two countries constructed circular altars for Heaven in Hue and Seoul.

In his memoirs, John Blofeld describes a wintertime visit to the altar in the 1930s. His Chinese friends made a special effort to come to the altar before going on to a banquet south of the Zheng Yang Gate. While Blofeld had visited the altar many times before, he was surprised on this trip:

> No imaginable effect of sunshine or storm could mar or enhance its perfection. Cloudless skies could not add to its mirror-like tranquility, nor gold-rimmed black and purple storm clouds vie with its awesome majesty. But snow! This feathery edifice of spotless white rising from a wide expanse of hard smooth now, and framed by the tracery of snow-laden branches in the surrounding forest, seemed lost — pure whiteness lost in white purity!
>
> I turned towards my friends, expecting their faces to reflect my disappointment. Instead, they were like men entranced. Motionless, oblivious now of the cold, they gazed in silence until at last the spell was broken by excited exclamations ….
>
> "I do not understand. Why are you all so moved. I love the altar as you do, but today it is lost, swallowed in a white brilliance equal to its own."
>
> "That," he answered, "is what we came to admire. Do you not see? Artists struggle all their lives to capture the infinite in works either great or small. At other times, the Altar reflects the infinite perfection, except that it cannot suggest the concept of infinite space. Now, void rising from void, it has become a true mirror of the universe's real form." [Turning to another of the group who did not share these Taoist conceptions], I asked him if he shared his friends' delight.
>
> "Of course," was his unexpected answer. "It is superb. Last time I came here, the marble was solid. Now it has liquefied and overflows the park."

As for myself, I have two fond memories of my own of the altar. One year, on the morning of the Winter Solstice, I trundled to the Altar of Heaven before sunrise. As the sun slowly peeked over the horizon, the white marble reflected the pink and yellow rays cast from the eastern sky and the ink black to light blue hues from the west. On another visit during the full moon, the altar appeared to float in the air because of the reflections of the moonbeams.

13

THE WESTERN CHINESE CITY

WE WILL START OFF THIS tour by walking south of the Zheng Yang Gate towards the commercial and entertainment district of Old Peking called the Great Bamboo Fence (大栅兰儿 or *da sha lar* in the Peking dialect), so named because the merchants used to set up a fence every night to keep out prowlers, riff raff, and the odd foreigner. The district lost a good deal of its verve during the Cultural Revolution. Nowadays, it is humming again during the daytime. In the back alleys, you can see bits and pieces of traditional Peking commerce markets, shops, restaurants and theatres that recall an older flavor of life in the capital. These neighborhoods also balance impressions of Old Peking as a place with a preponderance of otherworldly temples and refined palaces.

By turning into Rou Shi Street (肉市街) to the east for a quick look-see, you will pass the Former Fu Jian Ding Zhou Guildhall (福建汀州会馆 or *fu jian ding zhou hui guan*). Nearby on Xiao Jiang Alley (小江胡同 or *xiao jiang hu tong*) is the former Yang Ping Guildhall (阳平会馆 or *yang ping hui guan*), originally constructed during Qian Long's reign. Both buildings are now private residences. Here travelers from Fu Jian and Yang Ping could feast themselves on home-cooking and speak in their local dialects, probably decrying how their accents placed them at a disadvantage in dealing with Peking's sharp witted merchants. In memoirs written by southern Chinese visiting the capital, there are frequent complaints about the ever present scent of raw garlic and the inwardness of the northern Chinese. Others were enamoured with the city's sights and rose above these petty annoyances.

Cross the main street and turn west into Great Bamboo Fence Street (大栅兰街 or *da sha lan jie*). Jade Street (宝玉市街 or *bao yu shi jie*) runs parallel to Qian Men Wai Avenue. As its name indicates, the street was formerly a market for jade merchants. Today, as in the past, the neighborhood is home to numerous

Western Chinese City

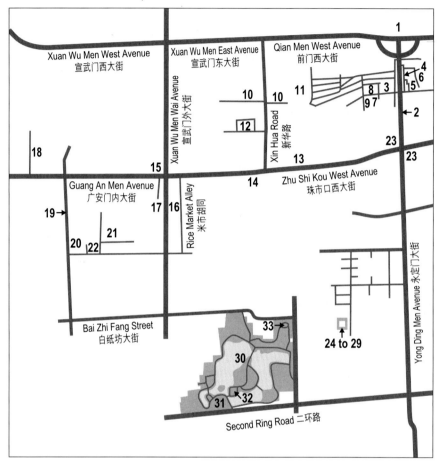

1. Zheng Yang Gate（正阳门）
2. Qian Men Nei Avenue（前门内大街）
3. Great Bamboo Fence（大栅兰儿）
4. Rou Shi Street（肉市街）
5. Fujian Ding Zhou Guild Hall（福建汀州会馆）
6. Yang Ping Guild Hall（阳平会馆）
7. House of Six Obligations（六必居）
8. Rui Fu Xiang（瑞蚨祥）
9. Hall of the Same Benevolence（同仁堂）
10. Glazed Tile Factory（琉璃厂）
11. Temple of the Fire God（火神庙）
12. An Hui Guild Hall（安徽会馆）
13. Jin Yang Fan Zhuang（安徽会庄）
14. Hunan and Hubei Guild Hall（湖广会馆）
15. Vegetable Market（菜市口）
16. Former Residence of Kang You Wei（康有为故居）
17. Former Residence of Tan Si Tong（谭嗣同故居）
18. Temple for the Protection of the Country（报国寺）
19. Ox Street（牛街）
20. Ox Street Mosque（牛街清真寺）
21. Temple of the Origin of the Law（法原寺）
22. Temple of Saintly Peace（神安寺）
23. Heavenly Bridge District（天桥）
24. Altar of Agriculture（先农坛）
25. Hall of Jupiter（太岁殿）
26. Hall of Propriety（礼殿）
27. Hall of the Four Seasons（四季殿）
28. Hall of the Twelve Months（月将殿）
29. Altar for Watching the Plowing（观耕台）
30. Joyful Pavilion Park（陶然亭公园）
31. Temple of Mercy（慈悲庵）
32. three graves
33. Mid-Autumn Festival site

shops selling a bounty of Chinese day goods and groceries: fresh meats such as beef, pork, pheasants, quails, ducks, chickens; squirming fish, aggressive crabs, and skittish prawns; vegetables and fruit, platoons of cabbage, an array of nuts from almonds to walnuts, wrinkled turnips, mounds of beans, apples in hues from dark red to light yellow, fat rosy autumn peaches, bright and cheerful orange colored persimmons, dried fruits and juicy melons along with locally produced sorghum, millet and wheat. Salt, sesame oil, soy sauce, vinegars and traditional firewater are all on hand in tiny bottles to five gallon vessels. From further regions within

Entrance way to the Big Bamboo Fence.

China are all types of green tea, exotic fruit, pearls, sweet wine, Central Asian silk, and southern hardwood furniture. Kites, diablos, pinwheels and other toys await the delight of young children.

By the end of the 19th century, the Great Bamboo Fence merchants also offered western goods, such as medicines, tobacco, kerosene lamps, and matches. The area also became known for its antiquities, jade, ink sticks, seals as well as literary services such as bookbinding and printing, scroll mounting, and stele carving. In the 19th century, a Western traveler reported seeing a local dentist trying his hand at English advertising: "Insertion false teeth and eyes, latest Methodists".[1]

The House of the Six Obligations (六必居 or *liu bi ju*), located near the intersection of Big Bamboo Street (大栅兰儿) and Grain and Rice Street (粮食街 or *liang shi jie*), began its existence as a shop set up in 1530 by six merchants from Shan Xi province. The storefront plaque is said to be in the calligraphy of an infamous Ming official Yan Song (严嵩). Later on, the store specialized in traditional Chinese medicines and, these days, stocks a wide array of Chinese vegetables, fruit, wines, spices and other groceries as well as a famed assortment of pickled vegetables.

There are two legends about how the store acquired its name. The original choice was the House of the Six Hearts (六心居 or *liu xin ju*), a direct reference to the six founding partners. While Yan Song is remembered as a knave, he did understand human nature and argued that it is impossible that six hearts could manage a single enterprise. By adding a stroke to the character for heart, he came back with a name that alludes to the discipline that the six partners must have for their store to be a success. It seems that Yan Song's advice worked. The store is still open for business after the two dynasties, countless warlord governments, a Nationalist administration, the Japanese occupation, the Communist victory and assorted campaigns during the Cultural Revolution.

Another legend maintains that the shop started its life as a spirits shop. Therefore, the origin of its name is said to relate to the six essential aspects of distilling spirit: purity of water, quality of the ceramic pots, temperature of the fire, cleanliness of the still, quality of the grain and the type of yeast used for fermentation. Here are distilling tips that are familiar to moonshiners everywhere.

A little further down on Great Bamboo Fence Street is Rui Fu Xiang (瑞蚨祥), an emporium established in 1860 by a eunuch for silk and textiles. The shop maintains an ornate two-storey green copper storefront from its imperial days. Across the street is the Hall of the Same Benevolence (同仁堂 or *dong ren tang*), which had been selling traditional Chinese medicines since 1669. As you stroll around the neighborhood, you will see various buildings constructed in the neo-baroque style that was popular in Peking during the 1920s.

Before the fall of the Qing, carved wooden posts towered outside their doorways, identifying stores that were patronized by the court. Each shop had its own distinctive sign to indicate its specialty.

Teashops in the Great Bamboo Fence helped spawn the birth of Peking Opera. In the 19th century, actors in need of a rehearsal studio practiced in the teashops during the afternoon lull in business. The teashop managers were pleased with any novelty that might increase trade. These "rehearsal-performances" became hugely popular, and gradually teashops evolved into opera theatres. The "chatty" nature of audiences watching Peking Opera can be traced back to the time when performers acted amidst the comings and goings of customers looking for light snacks and beverages. I am very pleased to see several teashops in today's Great Bamboo Fence advertise afternoon performances of Peking Opera. These are not formal productions but rather individual actors out of costume who sing their favorite arias.

Kang Xi issued a decree forbidding the construction of theatres in the Tartar City lest bannermen went soft from idle entertainments. This was poor strategic planning as bannermen flocked to this district for fun and song before the midnight curfew. At least the decree provided steady work for rickshaw pullers.

In the late 19th century, "drum girls" also became a part of the nocturnal pursuits of Peking's men folk. Borrowing from bannermen customs, entrepreneurs set up theatres where attractive young women played traditional Chinese drums and danced for an appreciative all male audience. The drummers usually doubled as courtesans.

As you continue on through this neighborhood, you might spy the picture of two bearded guardians pasted on doorways of residential buildings. These two guards usually appear in military attire, though they also have a less frequently seen civilian appearance as well. These stalwart door gods are two generals from the Tang dynasty. It is said that sleeplessness and bad dreams plagued emperor Tai Zong, thus fueling speculation that ghosts had decided to rob the emperor of his peace of mind. While everyone was a twitter about this supernatural problem, General Qin Shu Bao (秦叔宝) stepped forward and offered to keep watch each night outside the emperor's bedroom with his compadre Xu Jing De (徐敬德). From that point on, ghosts and sleeplessness no longer troubled the emperor. However, Tai Zong soon realized that the health of his generals would suffer if they were to stand watch each night. Accordingly, Emperor Tai Zong ordered that paintings of the two generals be placed outside his room. This proved to be equally efficacious and common folk throughout China soon picked up the custom. Fourteen centuries later, they still stand guard to protect Peking's residents from the "things that gae bump in the nicht."

So long as you continue to the west, generally taking the right hand route in any forks in the road, you will come out on New China North Road (新华北街 or *xin hua bei jie*) in the vicinity of the antique district called Glazed Tile Factory (琉璃厂 or *liu li chang*). The name of the district is derived from an early Ming tile kiln that supplied the court with glazed tiles during the construction of the capital. The name has remained even though the kiln closed for business some five hundred years ago.

Around the mid-Qing, the Glazed Tile Factory had become known for its antiques and antiquarian books. Manchu nobles, browsing while dressed in their best robes, were keen collectors. Even Kang Xi took delight in showing his collection of antique porcelain to visiting Jesuits. In the early years, it seems that the shops here were run by Chinese Muslims because they were master carvers of jade. From the sale of carved jade, the merchants branched into antique jade and from there into other antiques and books. By the end of the 19th century, the shops sold all manner of curios as well as calligraphy and paintings, paper, books and stone rubbings so that a person of letters could easily roam about here for many hours. The Chinese Muslim merchants were able to continue their business in the 1950s, but the Cultural Revolution closed the market (except for a trickle that still went on sale overseas for foreign exchange). In the 1980s, the neighborhood was revived and tarted up to look like a motion picture set.

Antiques are very expensive at the Glazed Tile Factory and you should have several trips before making a purchase here. You can easily spend half a day wandering in and out of the shops. In the tumbled down hostels to the south, itinerant peddlers from the countryside sometimes come to town with their discoveries, which portends an interesting round of negotiations for Mandarin speakers.

In 1930s, Osbert Sitwell recorded an interesting incident. A Xin Jiang peddler arrived in the Glazed Tile Factory to sell some curios found in China's Far West to a foreign friend of Sitwell's. After several rounds of negotiations, the foreigner engaged the wizened peddler in some small talk. It turned out that the fellow was named "King" (an obsolete Romanization for a Chinese transliteration of "Koenig"). Despite his Chinese appearance, Mr. King said that he was a Jew whose ancestors came to Central Asia fleeing a pogrom in Eastern Europe. He went on to relate how the Jewish community in Xin Jiang had been absorbed through intermarriage with Chinese, though they still maintained some religious observances. It had been known in the West for centuries that there was a small Jewish community in Kai Feng, but not one along China's inner borders. The anecdote confirms that every nation, race, and creed has come and lived in Peking at some point.

To the east side of the main thoroughfare at No 29 East Glazed Tile Factory Street (琉璃厂东街 or *liu li chang dong jie*) is the former Temple of the Fire God built sometime during the middle of Qian Long's reign. Since so much of their stock was flammable, the merchants of the neighborhood had a strong incentive to maintain a temple to beseech this deity's protection against fire. It has been converted into a "workers' cultural palace."

Continuing back to New China North Road, you can find the former An Hui Guild Hall (安徽会馆 or *an hui hui guan*) on the Alley of the Back of Sun's Garden (后孙园胡同 or *hou sun gong yuan hu tong*). The original site was the home of Sun Cheng Ze (孙承泽), a late Ming author who wrote many accounts of life in Old Peking. In 1871, the brother of Li Hong Zhang (李鸿章) converted the site into a provincial guildhall for people from An Hui province.

Returning to New China North Road, you turn east on Pearl Market Avenue (珠市口大街 or *zhu shi kou da jie*), which has been widened with considerable destruction to the surrounding neighborhood. At No. 241 Pearl Market Avenue, you will find Jin Yang Fan Zhuang (晋阳饭庄), a wonderful Shan Xi (山西) restaurant housed next to a mid Qing courtyard. This was the residence of the scholar Ji Yun (纪昀). Ji fared well in the Metropolitan Examinations and became a high-ranking official during Qian Long's reign. He was known for a humorous disposition and assiduous literary essays compiled in the Yue Wei Cottage Sketchbook. Because of court struggles and corrupt relatives, he was banished to Xin Jiang for several years.

There is a story about Ji that captures his ingenuity (and explains how he got into trouble). While at court, Ji got wind of rumors that his cousin, a provincial governor, was about to be investigated for embezzling revenue from the state salt monopoly. Ji Yun wanted to warn his cousin of the pending investigation but was fearful of leaving any incriminating correspondence. Ji solved the problem by sending his cousin an envelope containing salt and tea leaves. In Mandarin Chinese, the word for tea (茶 or *cha*) is a homonym for the word investigation (查). Alas, the Qing equivalent of the state auditors figured out the riddle and sent Ji up for several years of reform through labor in Xin Jiang, though his sentence was reduced because of the good will he enjoyed at court. He was eventually pardoned and returned to a high position in the school of the Sons of the Nation. While his official career never recovered, he did not seem to mind that much.

In the courtyard in the main part of the restaurant, there is a Chinese wisteria that was planted by Ji Yun over two hundred years ago. In 1963, Chen Yun Gao (陈云高), a former member of the Han Lin Academy during the last days of the Qing dynasty, was dining at the restaurant when the old tree caught his eye. It inspired Chen to write a poem:

> The place is now a restaurant
>> It was once the residence of Ji Tian
> Two hundred years after Qian Long's reign
>> The building is still here, after many owners
> The wisteria planted by Ji still remains
>> Pity that no more rock comes from Genyue Hill.

(The last line refers to a quarry that supplied a rockery in Ji's courtyard.)

In the early 1930s, Mei Lan Fang acquired the site as a training studio for Peking Opera students. The inner courtyard, which has five floors towering above it, reflects the well-blended combination of traditional and modern architecture that Mei sought when he renovated the building.

The restaurant occupies a peculiar island amid a sea of asphalt, the surrounding area having been razed for the widening of the road and the construction of new high-rises.

Returning to the intersection of Pearl Market Avenue and New China North Road, the former Hunan and Hubei Guild Hall (湖广会馆 or *hu guang hui guan*) now houses a museum dedicated to the history of Peking Opera. It was first built in 1808 and converted into a Peking Opera theatre in the last years of the Qing. The site has been well renovated and opera performances still take place here.

Continuing due west on Broad Peace Avenue (广安大街 or *guang an da jie*) you come to the district known as the Vegetable Market (菜市口 or *cai shi kou*). Today, the market exists in name only. At the end of the Qing, this was Peking's execution ground. In *feng shui* terms, southwest corners are considered to be unlucky. As a consequence, executions took place near the southwest gates of Chinese cities. It was also hoped that by dispatching the condemned there, their ghosts would get a head start on their way to the Western Paradise rather than linger in mortal neighborhoods.

The Qing executioner was something of a celebrity on account of the crowds that gathered to watch the gory spectacle. A prisoner was obliged to pay the executioner an appropriate tip to ensure a clean cut. If an unfortunate prisoner did not have friends or family that could buy a merciful death for him, the executioner might slowly saw through the neck of the condemned. In all other instances, the executioner's skills were subject to imperial scrutiny as well as punishment for any haphazard use of the sword. However, the professional executioners were experts in the field. Even when execution cases piled up due to a magistrate's illness or in the annual run-up to settling all outstanding criminal cases by the autumn, the executioners seldom failed to make their kill with one stroke of the sword.

The executioner had his choice of several swords, each one supposedly had a separate and distinct personality, a little like vintage wines for wine bores. It was believed that these swords sang to each other at night about their ghastly deeds, though this is more likely attributable to the fondness of the executioner and his gang for (non-vintage) wines.

Around the Vegetable Market are a number of historic sites. At No. 43 Rice Market Alley (米市胡同 or *mi shi hu tong*) is the Peking residence of Kang You Wei (康有为故居 or *kang you wei gu ju*), the Cantonese Confucian scholar associated with the 1898 Reform Movement. Kang lived here in a room he dubbed the "sweat-soaked boat" while advising emperor Guang Xu in the summer of 1898. In the aftermath of the military crack down, Kang fled to Hong Kong where he sought British protection from Qing assassins. Since Kang had never advocated the overthrow of the Qing monarchy, he was quite appalled by the republicanism that arose after 1912. He died in 1927, still insisting that a constitutional monarchy was the only viable government for China.

His former residence is definitely the worse for wear. 107 families live in a structure that had only 20 families in 1949. The spirit screen across the main gate, the gates themselves and the courtyard houses have all gone to seed.

The immediate vicinity of Kang's former residence is worth exploration, however. Here you will see shop-front restaurants cooking up a variety of onion pancakes and aromatic dumplings. In little cafes you can sit on a wobbly three-legged stool and tuck into a bowl of beef noodle soup and a Yanjing beer. Be ready to give big smiles and nods of acknowledgment to passers-by.

One of Kang's compadres, Tan Si Tong (谭嗣同), lived nearby in the Liu Yang Guild Hall at No. 41 Bei Ban Hu Tong (北截胡同), a place that he called the "Misty Room." Tan enjoyed a reputation as a poet prior to the 1898 Reform Movement. These days, there is not much that distinguishes Tan's residence from the other ill-repaired courtyard houses in the neighborhood.

Tan was an effective reformer. He secretly circulated a heterodox Ming essay that criticized autocracy and advocated democracy, industry and commerce. Guang Xu was pleased with his talents and had hoped that he would join his reform cabinet. When Yuan Shi Kai betrayed the reformers, Tan did not seek refuge overseas. He stood his ground and was executed at the Vegetable Market on September 28, 1898.

On October 3, 1898, the English language China Gazette, published in Shanghai, carried the following obituary:

> A touching story is told of young Tan Sitong …. who was arrested and decapitated Friday in Peking. Young Tan was very famous among the Chinese as a partisan of the China Reform Party. He was said to have been of an exceptionally high spirit and profound learning. His political views were very bold; so much so indeed, that his father had warned him more than once but the young man would not listen to the cautions of his parent, who had long regarded his son as a man destined to end in some fatal calamity….The other day, given the seriousness of Tan's situation, a member of one of the foreign embassies offered him the legation as an asylum. It is said that Tan replied that no fundamental reform of government could ever be exacted without bloodshed, a fact which he added could be seen in histories of many foreign countries. He, therefore, declared that he was prepared to die for the great cause he had adopted, of lifting China up, believing by his own and his companions' death that the influence of the Reform Party would be rather increased than injured by his fall. For this reason, he declined to seek shelter in a foreign legation, and even continued his propaganda in a more open and decisive manner. At the last, the coup d'etat came and he and his five friends fell the first victims to the storm in which the

triumph of the Empress Dowager and her party engulfed the luckless but dauntless few who made a late but desperate effort to do something towards saving China.

Tan's former residence is covered in shoddy fake red brick linoleum and has few visitors. On my last trip, I heard the melody of the Grateful Dead's "Trucking" floating out from one of the *ping fang*. The lyrics about a warrant and being busted on Bourbon Street along with the song's sense of resignation somehow seem fitting for a memorial to Old Tan.

Carrying on to the west on Broad Peace Avenue (大安大街 or *guang an da jie*), you come to the Temple for the Protection of the Country (报国寺 or *bao guo si*) on the north side of the street. Originally a Buddhist temple built in 1466, the temple now hosts a daily flea market where you can purchase relics from the Cultural Revolution, stamps, coins, jade and other reasonably priced curios. The temple is an example of a pleasant and constructive use of an Old Peking building.

Chinese Muslim curio dealer.

Turning to the south on Ox Street (牛街 or *niu jie*) at the corner with Broad Peace Avenue, you will come to the Ox Street Mosque (牛街清真寺 or *niu jie qing zhen si*). This neighborhood has undergone considerable renovation in recent years, with its attractive blue-gray ambiance replaced by a boring wide boulevard. According to legend, Kang Xi had his Muslim subjects quartered in this area because of the Ox Street Mosque, supposedly built during the Liao dynasty but whose current buildings are all of the Qing era. The mosque has a tower for astronomical calculations on the inside of the wall bordering the street. Once inside, you can peer into (but not enter unless you are Muslim) the prayer hall built facing Mecca. On the beams of the temples are quotations from the Koran in stylized Arabic calligraphy. Off to the southeast corner are the graves of two Muslin clerics who came to bring Islam to China during the 11th century.

There is a Chinese Muslim legend that shows how Chinese culture absorbed Islam. Chinese Muslims maintain that the founder of the Tang dynasty had a dream that a great man in the West had established a highly developed set of ethics. Intrigued by this dream, the emperor sent a delegation to see if there was any truth to it. During their travels, they supposedly met Mohammed and invited several of his followers to China.

In Peking, Chinese Muslims number approximately 200,000. Sadly, their Han neighbors regard them as a fractious and insular people. I find this to be utterly untrue. Rather, I am pleased to report that I have always been treated to the highest hospitality and friendliness. Despite their prejudices, the Han do recognize that the Hui are gifted chefs who are masters at preparing fabulous dishes like lamb hotpot (涮羊肉 or *shuang yang rou*) and lamb dumplings.

Ambling to the east along the street by the same name you come across one of the most beautiful Buddhist temples in Peking: the Temple of the Origin of the Law (法源寺 or *fa yuan si*). The temple dates back to the early Tang dynasty, though its roots are in the Sui dynasty. China had been in a state of turmoil and disunion for nearly three hundred years when the Sui dynasty finally unified the nation under one banner in 578. The Sui was not to last beyond the life of its founder, partially because of his ever-present desire for domination. The emperor elected to wage war against the Koguryo dynasty in northern Korea. Since the Koreans proved to be a worthy foe, the wars came to an ignoble draw that damaged the credibility of the Sui. The corpses of Chinese troops lay rotting on the fields of Northern Korea, with only half-hearted attempts at bringing their bodies back for a proper burial, as demanded by Confucian etiquette. This was the match that set the tinder on fire, and within fifty years of its creation, the Sui dynasty collapsed and the Tang began its splendid reign.

After emperor Tang Tai Zu inaugurated his new dynasty, he still had to address the problem of disturbances on his border with the Koreans. However, taking a page from the history of the prior regime, Tang Tai Zu was mindful of Confucian funeral etiquette. There would be no lost souls in his empire, raising havoc on account of the misguided sacrifice of their mortal lives to the state.

Tang Tai Zu oversaw the construction of the Temple of the Origin of the Law in the heart of Tranquil City, as Peking was then known. Legend holds that the bones of Chinese warriors killed in Korea were brought to the temple for internment beneath memorial stele, partially in order to honor their memory and partially to demonstrate that the Tang was not callous about its fallen heroes. Skeptics (or the clear-sighted, as I prefer to call us) can discern the cynicism common to all such memorials.

The earliest steles in the front courtyard of the temple date from the Tang dynasty. In some instances, the names of officials who later turned against the dynasty have been chiseled out. Most of the buildings date from the middle of the Qing.

A legend holds that Qian Long once showed up incognito for one of the annual vegetarian feasts held by the temple. Perhaps forgetting proper etiquette, Qian Long slapped his chopsticks down on the table any old way, much in the presumptuous manner of a host than the respectful mien of a guest. This breach of etiquette infuriated the abbot, who had already detected the imperial visage, but nevertheless threw out Qian Long from the banquet.

Another Qing legends holds that Qian Long's mother could hear the ringing of the bell in this temple even though it was about two miles away from her courtyard in the Forbidden City. Clearly, some supernatural spirit was at work, or, at the very least, someone who took a (Harpo) Marxist pride in stirring up the ruling classes.

The second and third courtyards are planted with purple and white lilac plants, which blossom in the middle of April and perfume the neighborhood. Apparently, the Red Guards dug out the original lilac bushes during the Cultural Revolution. The plants before you are nonchalantly redressing the wrongs of thirty years ago.

In her Blue Guide to China, Frances Wood notes that her copy of Arlington and Lewisohn's book contained a 1930s newspaper clipping, mentioning that the high point of the spring social season was the vegetarian banquet held for foreigners and Chinese alike, ostensibly to praise the view of the full moon through the lilac bushes. Perhaps that was just an excuse for some merriment by the monks with their foreign and Chinese friends. I imagine that much plum wine was consumed during the evening, along with tasty Lenten fair offered by the monks of the kitchen. There is no more spectacular time to visit the Temple of the Origin of the Law than when the lilacs are in bloom.

The wonderful open-mindedness of the monks of the temple has been recorded throughout the 20th century. During a visit in 1920s, Juliet Bredon was led to a side altar with tablets for the deceased:

> "These tablets," [the monk] explains, "are to commemorate the soldiers who died in the Great War and the offerings are for the comfort of their souls."
>
> "But no Chinese soldiers were killed on those dreadful European battlefields?" you suggest.

"Certainly, we know that. They are for the foreign soldiers."

"Of course you realize that none of those dead are Buddhists?"

"Yes, but may you not admire the beauty of their sacrifice? And are not all faiths fundamentally alike in that they desire the good of all mortals? In your Christian churches, do you not pray for the salvation of all and believe in it?"

At a loss to admit that immense kindly toleration such as this is not universal, you remain silent ....[2]

You can go south and turn to the west at South Huang Street (南橫西街). In the middle of this Muslim district, two Buddhist halls stand on a parcel of land that had seen all its other buildings razed. These two structures belonged to the Temple of Saintly Peace (神安寺 or *shen an si*), originally a Jin era temple but reconstructed in 1446 and again by Qian Long in 1776. The two buildings are bricked up and make a forlorn sight amidst the surrounding rubble.

From here, you need to retrace your steps by taxi or bicycle and return to the intersection of Qian Men Wai Avenue (前门外大街) and Pearl Market Avenue (珠市口大街). This district, called the Heavenly Bridge (天桥 or *tian qiao*), takes its name from a Ming stone bridge that has long since disappeared. Before 1949, the Heavenly Bridge was Peking's main entertainment sector. Throughout this neighborhood were street performers, jugglers, storytellers, acrobats, courtesans and street hawkers. Its street theatre ambiance and the pleas of professional beggars dissuaded the well-to-do and the socially pretentious from lingering here.

The Heavenly Bridge was also the heart of legitimate theatre in Peking. In the final years of the Qing, there were eight theatrical companies specializing in Peking Opera. Each theatrical season would open with a performance of "Conferring Happiness" (滋福 or *zi fu*) so as to bring in a new year of tranquility. In those days, there were different styles of music. For example, *kun* (昆), which originated during the Ming, was a slow and plaintive type of music. From Xian Feng's time, two flute operas (二黄 or *er huang*) were popular but later in the 1930s were only used for weddings and funerals. The *qin* (秦) type of performance, frequently using two pieces of wood struck against each other, took its name from Shan Xi province where both the Qin dynasty and this style of music originated.

Acting troupes dressed as famous historical figures entertained the crowds while walking about in stilts. Some street performers trained mice to run through a series of ladders, swings and tunnels on a miniature obstacle course. Monkeys were trained to don official robes and sit as if in attendance at court. Village boys also performed the "boat that runs on land." Dressed as women, the boys used a mock boat built of cloth and manipulated it so that it appeared to be rocking across the waves of a lake. This was usually accompanied by an obscene doggerel.

Another form of entertainment was shadow-puppet plays. These puppets were cut from donkey hide and dyed so that shadows, thrown upon a sheet illuminated from behind, appeared in color. The characters and motifs took their lead from Peking Opera. Dun Li Chen wrote that shadow puppet shows reached the height of their popularity during the reigns of Xian Feng and Tong Zhi.

There were countless other forms of entertainment, much of it similar to American vaudeville, with comics and singers. Some street performers presented feats of agility in the military arts, like sword dancing and archery. Others demonstrated their strength by pulling a Manchu bow with their teeth. Impressionists recreated a cacophony of sounds ranging from birds to animals, to dialects of spoken Chinese to cries simulating joy, laughter and sorrow. In contrast to our electronic world of interactive entertainment, a storyteller used no props to bring back to life long deceased heroes and villains before an entranced audience. "Strong men" would place a stack of bricks on their chest or back and lie down while their colleagues would smash the bricks with one blow of a sledgehammer. Others used false bladed axes filled with chicken blood to simulate the execution of a clumsy stagehand. Commenting on a piece of street theatre that could be seen all throughout mid-19th century China, Dr. Rennie records a street performer placing several needles and a string in his mouth. This conjurer continued to talk and sing to the audience once the deadly needles were in place. At the end of his performance he produced the needles from his mouth all neatly threaded together.

These entertainers of the Heavenly Bridge have all disappeared into the ether. You can see their black and white ghosts in picture books like *Tianqiao of Old Beijing*, which can be found in some of the bookshops and markets in Peking.

From here, turn to the south and take a west turn on Nan Wei Street (南纬路). Then go to the south when the street turns in that direction. In front of you is a large red gate that leads into the Altar of Agriculture (先农坛 or *xian nong tan*). Actually, the term "Altar of Agriculture" is something of a misnomer. Originally these grounds contained altars for several different ceremonies in an area almost as large as the Temple of Heaven. However, the park has fallen victim to Peking's urban sprawl, leaving only little bits of the old site.

The Peking Museum of Traditional Architecture is housed in the Hall of Jupiter (太岁殿 or *tai sui dian*), which was first constructed in 1532 and renovated in 1754. By ascending the marble terrace, you first past through the Hall of Propriety (礼殿 or *li dian*) and enter into a vast enclosed courtyard similar to those in the Forbidden City. To the north is the Hall of Jupiter, now housing exhibits on traditional Chinese construction techniques.

In Chinese cosmology, Jupiter was revered as the God of Time. The planet passes from one house of the twelve constellations to another every year on its twelve-year orbit of the sun. These houses were called "Palaces of the Moon." Although Jupiter's celestial travels impressed ancient Chinese astronomers, the imperial court came to adopt ceremonies for the formal worship of Jupiter only in the late Ming and the Qing. The emperor came to this temple to carry out a ceremony in honor of Jupiter on the last day of the lunar year as the God of Time moved into a new Palace of the Moon.

In day-to-day life, Chinese equated the happiness of the empire with Jupiter's solicitude. Each household sacrificed to the God of Time from fear rather than affection. Jupiter was dangerous. To invoke his wrath was to risk pestilence and misfortune. In Chinese, the word for a year in terms of human life is the same as Jupiter.

The other, less powerful time units were also worshipped here. On east wall is the Hall of the Four Seasons (四季殿 or *si ji dian*) and on the west the Hall of the Twelve Months (月将殿 or *yue jiang dian*).

The enclosure on the west hand side of the Hall of Jupiter contains two wells, the hall for storage of the spirit tablets to Jupiter, the God of Agriculture and other deities.

Directly to the south is the Altar to the God of Agriculture (先农坛 or *xian nong tan*), a simple single tiered square shaped altar in gray marble. The altar was built in 1530 in commemoration of the ancient emperor Shen Nong, who is reputed to have invented agriculture. To its east are small shrines for lesser deities such as the gods of earth, sea and wind, the gods of the five sacred mountains of China, the gods of the four seas and four rivers. These small shrines are part of the cult of nature whose origins stretch to the Zhou dynasty. Each shrine is decorated with carvings of clouds, mountains or waves.

Further to the southeast, you will come across the Altar for Watching the Plowing (观耕台 or *guan jing tai*). Originally a wooded platform constructed in 1449, the Altar was rebuilt in 1530 as a stone terrace with green and yellow tiles along its base. The emperor came to this altar each spring, along with municipal officials, to plough several furrows of land as an example of diligence and to emphasize the state's reverence for agriculture. The ceremony called for the emperor to plough eight furrows and plant rice seedlings. Princes and officials in attendance followed by plowing eighteen furrows and sowing millet. The harvest from these fields were stored in a round shaped granary in the middle of the courtyard of the enclosure directly to the north of the altar. These grains were used as sacrifices for rituals conducted at other temples in the city. Here also were the rooms where the emperor put on his robes for the ceremonies and where he received the congratulations of the empress for having managed to do a lick of work.

Other Asian countries have plowing ceremonies in recognition of the importance of agriculture. In Cambodia and Thailand, members of the royal family, to this very day, still conduct a ceremonial plowing every spring to the present day.

Leaving the altar, you return to Qian Men Nei Avenue and arrive at the east gate of Joyful Pavilion Park (陶然亭公园 or *tao rang ting gong yuan*), which is said to be an artificial lake first constructed in the Liao dynasty. In 1695, a scholar named Jiang Zao (江藻) built a pavilion overlooking one of the lakes. He entertained his friends with nighttime bouts of rice wine and poetry recitation. The phrase *tao ran* is taken from a poem by the Tang poet Bai Ju Yi (白居易): "Let us wait until the chrysanthemums are golden and our home-brewed wine matured, then with us all shall be intoxication and joy," (更待菊黄家酿熟，与君一醉一陶然。)

At the south side of the lake on the small island is the Temple of Mercy (慈悲庵 or *ci bei an*), which was first built during the Yuan. This current structure looks like a renovation from Qian Long's time. Inside the courtyard are Liao and Jin Buddhist pagodas and a hall dedicated to Guan Yin.

Another hall has an exhibition to the memory of various Communist martyrs. The exhibition suggests that the temple has a long history associated with political agitation. During the 1898 Reform Movement, Kang You Wei, Liang Qi Chao and Tan Si Tong held clandestine political meetings here. In the early years of the Republic, Sun Yat Sen came here to hold political rallies. In 1920, Li Da Zhao, Mao Ze Dong and Zhou En Lai attended night time study sessions in the temple on theories of Marx and Engels. The exhibition carries pictures of martyred revolutionaries Gao Jun Yu (高君宇) and his fiancée, Shi Ping Mei (石评梅) who bears an uncanny resemblance to Gary Trudeau's Honey.

A little to the west is the pavilion built by Jiang Zao, whose frivolous literary interests would probably have cut no ice in warming up Little Shi. On the larger island to the north east of the temple, Peking legend maintains that there used to be three graves. One of the graves is the final resting place of a parrot much beloved by a Manchu nobleman. It was said that the parrot could recite Tang poems endlessly.

Nearby was the resting place of the "Fragrant Concubine." This is a misnomer since Qian Long's captive Uighur beauty is buried in Kashgar. Rather, this is the burial ground for Sai Jin Hua (赛金花), a late 19th century courtesan who played an important role in preserving Peking from the worst excesses of the Allied Occupation Army.

Sai began her earthly journeys in Suzhou where she became the concubine of a Manchu prince. Later, they moved to Peking and then were sent off to St. Petersburg and Berlin as the Qing diplomatic envoy. During her time overseas, Sai learned German and charmed the Berlin diplomatic circle, including a young and upcoming officer named Waldersee.

Around this same time, an ambitious rival of the prince accused him of embezzlement. The prince had to return to Peking to refute these allegations successfully, though the political intrigue ruined his career and caused his death. With only a small inheritance, Sai returned to her former trade and opened a courtesan's house in the Heavenly Bridge District in the late 1890s.

After the Allied armies occupied Peking, a drunken Prussian soldier accosted Sai one night. Sai upbraided the cabbage head in fluent German. Her unique status as one of the few German-speaking citizens gave her entrée into the German High Command in Peking where she found her old acquaintance, Waldersee, who was overseeing operations. They revived their friendship and the Suzhou courtesan exerted her charms and skills to lessen Germany's desire for revenge. After the allied forces left in 1901, Sai dropped from sight and became a wizened old mama san. Upon her death, people in Peking remembered her efforts to save their city and raised a subscription to have her properly buried in Park of the Joyful Pavilion. The novel by Chang Hsin-hai, *The Fabulous Concubine*, sets out a dramatized account of Sai's life.

The third grave contains the earthly remains of the patron saint of modern Chinese journalism, a fellow called Drunken Guo (醉郭 or *zui heng*) who was buried here in 1900. Guo was a burly sort who probably would have gotten along like a house on fire with Prince Duan (and the author). He became something of a town crier because of his habit of standing on Peking street corners and lecturing crowds about the decay of the Qing empire and the need to rally support for China. He always seemed to have a full load on board, hence his sobriquet. After his death, Peking journalists took up a collection for Guo's burial, including a headstone. Alas, nothing remains of his grave.

On the north east corner of the park are several tall hills where the common folk of Peking could climb up to get a good look at the moon during the Mid-autumn Festival. This was a unique vantage point since only Manchu nobles could own two-storied houses and nearly all other man-made hills in Peking were off-limits in imperial parks.

The festival entails the exchange of moon cakes, round shaped pastries filled with nuts, fruits, egg yolks and other fillings. In past years, moon cakes could be as large as one foot in diameter and were made from molds that imprinted images of rabbits, which were believed to live on the moon.

Rabbits on the moon? The story is that while in disguise, the Buddha once begged several animals, including a rabbit, for food. While animals such as the fox and hound offered the spoils of a day's worth of hunting, the rabbit declared that he did not want to harm other sentient beings. Instead, he offered to kill himself for the Buddha's dinner. The rabbit's devotion to non-violence moved the Buddha, who rewarded the rabbit by letting him live on the moon, away from the violence of carnivores. (Ironically, these days rabbit-stamped moon cakes sometimes have meat filings — never mind.)

Another filling turned this harvest celebration into a momentous event in Chinese history. During the final years of the Yuan dynasty, the Mongols, fearful of an insurrection that would drive them back to the steppes, stationed a Mongol spy in every Peking household in an attempt to forestall seditious meetings. Someone hit upon the idea of placing secret messages in moon cakes, which were widely exchanged among friends and neighbors during the festival. These messages announced the timing of an insurrection in Peking that spread throughout the empire and eventually brought the Yuan dynasty to its end.

Returning to more sedate reflections, these hills simply remind me of families coming together to contemplate the moonlight and give thanks for the bounties of the harvest with a sip of rice wine and a taste of a pastry.

14

EASTERN SUBURBS

THE EASTERN SUBURBS OF PEKING were sparsely inhabited in the years before 1949. In the 1980s, it still felt as if you had left the urban section behind you and were entering farmlands. This rustic feeling has disappeared under a veritable tidal wave of concrete and steel. These days, this district is the major commercial district for foreign companies in China.

In the southeast part of the city, between the Second and Third Ring Roads, you will find the Pan Jia Yuan Morning Market (潘家园早市 or sometimes less respectfully called the "dirt market"). The market has come up in the world over the past ten years. Originally, a weekly flea market held in the open near a rubbish dump, the Peking authorities have spruced up the market, installed open-air roofing and systematized the process by which vendors peddle their goods. Inveterate curio hunters still get to the market at dawn in order to find bargains. In dark foggy mornings in winter, men cluster on the edges of the market, selling porcelain and other items from recently ransacked graves. Dashing Tibetans, with western hats set at a rakish angle, sell thangkas, bronze statues of Milarepa and prayer bowls made from human skulls. Row after row, you will see porcelain, scroll paintings, statutes carved from wood, metal and stone, walking sticks, door god posters, pre-Liberation cigarette advertisements, cabinets, furniture, jewellery, memorabilia from the Cultural Revolution, writing brushes, fossils, contemporary paintings, books, Victorolas, tools, farm implements, barrels, buckets, glassware, post cards, old black and white photographs and magnifying glasses. Men walking by bellow an ear-splitting yell "book bags for sale" (卖书包 or *mai shu bao*) which startle any shopper from his revelries. For the hungry, an egg pancake (蛋饼 or *dan bing*) provides warm nourishment on cold mornings.

Eastern Suburbs

1. Pan Jia Yuan Morning Market（潘家园早市）
2. Dong Zhou Canal
3. Altar of the Sun Park（日坛公园）
4. CITIC Building
5. US Embassy
6. British Embassy
7. Cuban Embassy
8. St. Regis Hotel
9. Russian Shops
10. Dong Yue Miao（东岳庙）
11. Agricultural Exhibition Hall
12. Dong Zhi Men Wai Avenue（东直门外大街）

Bargaining should proceed on the basis that the price paid is what you would pay for the curio even if it came off the production line yesterday afternoon. I savored once having a dirt market peddler try to sell me a "guaranteed" thousand-year-old piece of Ming porcelain.

Some items fit in nicely with the pages of this book. In one stall, I found a poster celebrating the first anniversary of the Cultural Revolution. At Mao's elbow is his then faithful heir-apparent, Lin Biao. Down a few stalls I discovered a medal issued by one of the Peking Warlord presidents, Xu Shi Gen, upon his accession of power in 1918. (He was the fellow whose inept representatives set off the May 4 Movement by acceding to Japanese demands at Versailles. His only laudatory move might have been permitting Sir Reginald Johnston to teach English to Pu Yi.) Elsewhere, a 1932 almanac, with Sun Yat Sen's picture on the cover, awaits a purchaser. A bound edition of the first volume of New China Review (October 1949 to October 1950) is on hand elsewhere.

A little further back in time? One vendor has documents written in Chinese and Manchu on yellow canvas. One little robber baron, knowing the value of his plain green porcelain, asks US$900 for a Ming ginger jar. Wooden statutes of Guan Yu, the Manjursi Buddha, Guan Yin and the God of Wealth are also for sale. (There are legions of wooden Gods of Wealth, reflecting his popularity both in the past and at present.) Elsewhere you will find old Lps called Long Live Chairman Hua Guo Feng and Japanese box radio sets manufactured in Manchukuo during the war.

Are you worried about the authenticity of the goods on sale? Dr. Rennie told a story about the curio vendor in the old Legation District in 1860, a fellow who had been afflicted with small pox: "Our pock-marked friend declared [the item for sale] to be 'numpa (number) one' and to give full effect to the declaration, he held up his thumb, as a material as well as verbal guarantee."[1]

On our way north, we pass by an unimpressive cement banked river. This used to be the Dong Zhou canal (东洲), which flowed into the Grand Canal to China's heartland. It was over these waters that barges laden with tribute rice arrived in the capital from the south. A small tributary once flowed from Chao Yang Gate to this canal. In a rustic setting that is hard to imagine today, ferrymen rowed boats from Chao Yang Gate to the Fox Tower in about an hour's time, with passengers enjoying tea and light snacks as the corn fields and cypress groves floated past. Foreigners in the 1920s used to seek out the banks of the canal for picnics, a quest that is impossible to contemplate now given the forlorn and polluted appearance of this once vital transportation artery.

After spending our Saturday or Sunday morning at the market, we can head north to the Park of the Altar of the Sun (日坛公园 or *ri tan gong yuan*). The site was originally owned by a member of the imperial guard. Court astrologers decided that the location was appropriate for rituals and recommended that the land be acquired in 1530. We enter the altar grounds through an entrance in the northwest through a *pai lou* inscribed with "gateway for the worship of the [sun] spirit" (朝阳门 or *chao yang men*). The courtyard containing small buildings immediately inside the enclosure were used for the emperor to don his robes. To the east were rooms where musical instruments and sacrificial utensils were stored. In the center is a red circular wall enclosing a low square altar made of white marble. The main imperial way was from the west, where a triple gateway stands. The emperor would attend ceremonies here on alternative years on the 15th day of the second lunar month, with a government official standing in for him at other times. A round red gem, symbolizing the sun, was held by the emperor during these ceremonies.

In the early 1980s, Pu Jie, the younger brother of the last emperor, used to come to the park to sell his calligraphy primarily to Japanese patrons. His was an interesting story. During the days that Johnston was the English tutor, Pu Jie had to attend English lessons with his older brother. (Arthur was Pu Jie's English name.) In the flight to the north lake mansion and then to the Japanese legation, Pu Jie accompanied his older brother. Likewise he went with Pu Yi to Tianjin and the mock-court in Chang Chun. He too was imprisoned by the Soviets and then carried on tending to his brother, both in captivity in Siberia as well as in the Fushun re-education center. After his brother's death, Pu Jie led a quiet life. He was a consultant to Bernaldo Bertolucci for the film *The Last Emperor*. He once commented dryly, "I saw the movie twice and lived it once." He finally joined his brother at the Yellow Springs in April 1993. A sample of his calligraphy can be seen at the restaurant Li Jia Cai in the Back Lakes district.

To the west of the Ri Tan Park stands the CITIC Building, a nondescript brown colored high rise that has the distinction of being the first skyscraper built in the city. China International Trust and Investment Corporation, a company that was formed by the State Council in the 1970s as one of China's first "window" companies for foreign trade and investment, owns the building. After its construction in 1982, the contractors had to test the electrical system. At precisely 9:00 pm, every light in the building was turned on as electricity flowed through the ducts, accompanied by a chorus of ooohs and aahhs (well, maybe mostly "waaahs"). Five seconds later, the entire Chao Yang electricity station blew out and the district was plunged into darkness for the next three days.

The Ri Tan Park is surrounded by one of Peking's embassy districts that was built as the city grew in size and made the former Legation District inconvenient. It is a pleasant area to cycle in, especially with the willows in bloom during the spring. Towards the south east side of the district is the American embassy which abuts Silk Street, a clothing and curio mall that is frequented by tourists seeking cut rate prices for silk clothes, down jackets and pirated beanie babies or other Western gimmicks. If you wish to discourage the relentless pirate CD salesmen, just tell them that you are only interested in classical music (most of their wares do not rise above the level of Britney Spears or the Backstreet Boys — they will back off). If one of them does produce a couple of dubious CDs of Beethoven concertos, you can whack the ball back into his court and say that you only want *Russian* classical music.

The American embassy was besieged, in a less threatening fashion than Boxer Debacle, after the bombing of the Chinese embassy in Belgrade. Embassy personnel were able to brass it out with rations from Pizza Hut, supplied through the courtesy of the friendly Irish embassy staff on the other side of the wall.

To the north is the pink colored building that serves as the British Embassy. A slightly more unnerving event happened during the Cultural Revolution when red guards stormed the gates and trashed the compound. Running for their lives, British embassy staff scaled the walls and jumped into other embassies. Those fortunate enough to land in the adjourning embassy were given sanctuary while the hapless fellow who landed in the socialist embassy was handed over to the Red Guards and bludgeoned to death. As the former ambassador from Cuba once explained to me with mirth: "The xenophobia was so palpable that I didn't dare go out and walk the streets of the embassy district. And I was a commie just like them!"

Incidentally, the Cuban embassy has an interesting collection of framed photographs of Che Guerva's visit to Peking in 1962. These can be visited by making prior arrangements with the Cuban embassy staff, who are extremely courteous and hospitable.

From the towers and office buildings in this area, the diplomatic compound retains a glimpse of the Old Peking view of the city from the old city walls; a sea of trees rather than buildings, a capital without a skyline. Although some bright light has put this part on Peking on the developmental drawing boards, you can, by looking over the compounds during the warm seasons and with a touch of imagination, understand how the city once looked from the heights of the city wall.

In this vicinity is the St. Regis Hotel (国际俱乐部饭庄), asserted to be China's only "six-star" hotel. The hotel also contains the facilities of the American Club, where you can have business meetings in fancy rooms decorated with pictures of Calvin Coolidge and dine off chinaware with eagle motifs that look suspiciously as if they were retrieved from the Third Reich.

I am not aware if the American Club has any portraits of President Herbert Hoover. It should. Hoover was a mechanical engineer with extensive experience in the Far East. He was caught up in the Boxer Debacle in Tianjin and spent many years in China. After World War I, he was responsible for delivering food supplies to Soviet Russia, at least until the foreign powers decided to intervene in the Russian civil war. Hoover and his wife were fluent Mandarin speakers. During White House soirees, they were sometimes overheard exchanging side comments in Chinese, presumably about things like when the soup should be served or whether a certain Republican congressman was in favor.

To the north of Ri Tan Park is Russian Town, so named because of the many shops selling clothes to Russian traders for import into that country. Signs in Cyrillic and Chinese will greet you as you stroll through the neighborhood. Russians congregate in the hotels nearby. At the northeast corner of Ri Tan Park are several Russian and Baltic restaurants serving up classic Slavic fare often with the music of Vladmir Vitosky in the background. In the evenings, the music is turned up loud and the Russians dance along with Mongolians, Chinese and other curious people from Central Asia.

In past years, the manager of one of the restaurants was a mysteriously attractive Asian woman who spoke Russian and Chinese fluently but did not seem to be from China. I recall the ultimate put down as one American tried to charm her. The icebreaking attempt was, "So, where do you come from?" Yawning, she replied, "I don't know."

Leaving the Ri Tan Park District, you travel north to the Temple of the Eastern Peak (东岳庙 *dong yue miao*), which is located on the north side of Chao Yang Wai Avenue. You will come across first a *pai lou* in green and yellow tiles, built in the mid 1700s. Across the way is the formal entrance to the temple, which used to be one of the main sights of Old Peking.

In the early 13th century, Taoism split formally into two major schools. The Northern School, which was headquartered in the White Cloud Temple in the western suburbs, advocated meditation and philosophical study. The Southern School had its headquarters in Jiang Su province and was ruled by hereditary Taoist Popes. This latter school, which was propagated in the Temple of the Eastern Peak, emphasized magic, elixirs, and exorcism. Blofeld's friend, the Peach Garden Hermit, was an adherent of the Southern School.

This Taoist temple was originally built in honor of Huang Fei Hu (黄飞虎) a rebel who killed a tyrant and was elevated to be a supreme god of the sacred mountain Tai Shan (台山) in Shan Dong province. The temple was first constructed in 1329 and has undergone many renovations in the past. The most recent has been the past several years. During the Cultural Revolution, the temple was especially targeted for vandalism because of its storehouse of "superstitious" statues and altars. For many years, the temple served as a club for communist cadres, and nothing would bring the security guards running like five foreigners, weaving back and forth on unsteady feet, holding open bottles of *er guo tou jiu* and asking if they could take a look around.

I recall one time, a teenage boy who lived in the surrounding *ping fang* came forward, and in surprisingly good and well-mannered English showed me a way to peer into the temple over a wall. While walking about, he pointed out many marble steles used as foundations for the *ping fang*.

All of this changed when the temple was open to the public again in 1999. Unfortunately, during the high season, most visitors are brought in with a guide, who gives an ear-splitting and inaccurate rendition of the history of the temple through a megaphone. You should try to arrive sometime between mid and late morning when these high decibel crowds thin out.

In the first gateway, there are statues of the Marshals Heng and Ha (哼、哈 二将 or *heng, hu er jiang*), two Taoist deities, attired in military outfits with fierce expressions, who are door guardians. They were two legendary generals who fought on behalf of the Shang Dynasty during its final years. Marshal Heng was the Chief Superintendent of Military Supplies for the last Shang king and was said to produce two rays of light from his nostrils with the sound of a great bronze bell, the effect of which was to decimate enemy forces. Marshal Ha's specialty was to blow a gust of yellow gas from his mouth, which annihilated anything it touched. Both marshals died in combat against the Zhou dynasty, which canonized them because of their military prowess.

To the west is a large abacus meant to remind visitors that all of their vices and virtues will some day be accounted for. Around the sides of the first courtyard are cubicles that hold recently (and clumsily) made plaster statutes of the deities of the Taoist pantheon. In a reflection of traditional bureaucracy, assorted Taoist deities are the functionaries in supernatural departments, or perhaps ghostly units, responsible for delivering rewards and punishments to mortals. Altogether there are 76 departments depicted with their supervisors, various second tier officials and human supplicants or victims. The departments span everything: wealth, longevity, health, betrayal, poisoning, lust, cruelty to animals, plagues, boils, suicide and the suppression of schemes. However, the supervisors of the 76 departments could not issue a verdict in their own right. The Taoist bureaucracy included an approval department that had to ratify each decision before the supernatural department supervisor could implement it. (It never ends.)

Many of the more popular cubicles, temples and trees are weighted down with red votive tablet offerings. My favorite offering is to the department responsible for helping people lead lives that comport with the Tao. Only two other fellow travelers saw fit to make an offering to this department prior to my arrival. See if you can find my votive tablet.

In the main courtyard stands a bronze horse, reputed to have magical healing powers. A petitioner can rub any part of the horse that corresponds to a physical pain that afflicts the petitioner. On the other side of the courtyard is a white jade horse of similar design and purpose.

In the north hall, in the first courtyard, is a shrine to Master Zhang Liu Sun (张留孙), the founder of the temple and tutor to the Mongol court. Carrying on to the second courtyard, you will see the Dai Yue Hall (岱岳殿), dedicated to the God of Mount Tai Shan, the general manager of the Taoist bureaucracy and one of the foremost deities of the alchemist branch of Taoism. By walking through the internal corridor after the second hall, you will pass to the Hall of Educational Virtues, which originally was the chamber of the spirit of Mount Tai Shan and now holds the shrine to the gods of water, earth and heaven.

In the last courtyard, the temples have exhibits on the history of the temple and Old Peking. Here is a small stage where sometimes actors perform the street theatre that once could be seen in the Heavenly Bridge. The desultory crowd normally pays only the slightest attention to the acrobats working their hearts out on stage.

The government has begun renovations on the temples on the west and east side of the Temple of the Eastern Peak. The building on the west once housed the Temple of Hell, with statues depicting the punishments that await evildoers in the next world. If the government plans to recreate these hellish spectacles, I respectfully request that we have a glimpse of the punishment awaiting the architect who placed the on-ramps for the Third Ring Road *in front of* the off ramps.

The scenes of hell have always been a favorite both of foreigners and Chinese. However this display does not seem to have much in common with Taoist philosophy. Blofeld put the question to one of the Taoist monks in the Temple of the Eastern Peak in the 1930s:

> "I have often wished to ask why the greatest of Peking's Taoist Temples has to be disfigured by that macabre spectacle of hell. Yours is a sublime doctrine; where is the need for such – may I call it 'crudity'?"
>
> He smiled roguishly, eyes puckered and lips curved on the brink of laughter.
>
> "Human nature. People like it that way. Tell them they are holy and beautiful, that every one of them is a living embodiment of the sacred Tao, and they will think you are a stupid fellow, or smell your breath to see if you are drunk. But

Votive tablets in the Temple of the Eastern Peak.

tell them they are worse than devils or hungry ghosts and only fit for hell, then they will respect your powers of perception and ask you privately to reveal the special tastes of hell's judges so they will know how to bribe them. Your honorable countrymen are, if you will permit my saying so, not better than our own people."

A good time to visit the temple is the Chinese New Year, when the government sponsors a revival of the old temple fairs. Leaving the Temple, we can travel north on the Third Ring Road, and look at several spectacular samples of modern Peking architecture in and around Dance Agogo, Brassiere Ho and Rainbow Plaza, which doubtless should be better placed in the Temple of the Eastern Peak display case of hell's tortures.

Near the Chao Yang Embassy District, the Third Ring Road shoots past the Agricultural Exhibition Hall, built in 1959 and yet another of the other buildings that sank Liu Si Cheng's boat. Further north takes us to the Chao Yang Acrobatic Theatre, where there are nightly performances at 7:30. Chinese acrobatics are a continuation of the traditional street art that received Chairman Mao's approval.

Xin Hua North Road (新华北路), which turns into Gong Ti Road (工体路), used to be the main thoroughfare for when foreign dignitaries or important government officials are brought into town. During those times, the road was unceremoniously closed off to commoners. In order to avoid a *bu hao yi si* (embarrassing) scene during Ronald Reagan's visit in 1984, the government built a blue gray traditional wall on either side of the road to hide the ugly, poor *ping fang*. Some of this cosmetic face lift still remains.

In some cases, government motorcades appear with little warning and traffic and pedestrians are violently hustled off the roads. I recall one event where the police had to push back a crowd to let Li Peng's entourage speed on by in secrecy. The police apologized to the people afterwards, explaining that he was just following orders and it couldn't be helped. This recalls an entry from Matteo Ricci's diary:

> The kings of modern times abandoned the customs of going out in public. Even formerly, when they did leave the royal enclosure, they would never dare to do so without a thousand preliminary precautions. On such occasions, the whole court was placed under military guard. Secret servicemen were placed along the route over which the King was to travel and all roads leading into it. He was not only hidden from view, but the public never knew in which of the palanquins of his cortège he was actually riding. One would think he was making a journey through enemy country rather than through multitudes of his own subjects and clients.[2]

Peking's second embassy district is in Sanlitun (三里屯), and here one can find a wide array of restaurants and bars for nightlife, ranging from Irish pubs to reggae hangouts to pretentious high-class dives. A bit further to the north is the area outside Kun Lun Hotel. The hotel is a joint venture in which Peking security officials have a stake. Accordingly, it is the largest cathouse in town, a fact that used to spill over to the streets in front of it, where most evenings the atmosphere felt like a stage set for the Three Penny Opera. Minority Korean merchants, shashlick vendors, hookers, Uighurs, and various other hustlers roamed these streets in between scams. I recall seeing a Korean kiosk-operator beaten senseless by several men wearing uniforms and left on the ground in an ever-widening pool of blood. Vicious *tu hua* arguments broke out among taxi drivers, usually leading to fisticuffs. Western teenagers hung out nearby with their friends, obviously bored of Peking and its international schools. Down on the corner, African exchange students used to gather in front of a small shop where they drank beer and listened to boom boxes of music by King Sunny Ade and Fela Kuti. Bars with the names of women hosted a combination of hookers and teenagers trying to avoid the trade. Occasionally, young kids walked by with the distant and stumbling gait of a junkie. Whenever a police car would turn into this street, the street vendors, hustlers and pimps jumped up as one and began to duck down the alleyways. I recall one fellow picking up a shashlick barbecue grill and agilely begin to run without having any of the kebabs fall off. As the police car passed on by, the crowds slowly moved back to the sidewalks and normal nightlife resumed. After a six year run, Three Penny Opera closed and this street is quiet once again, thus giving you an inkling about how quickly neighborhoods change in this city.

The presence of 21st century courtesans in the lobby of the Kun Lun Hotel is a convenient segue to a discussion about changing tastes in eroticism over the past 100 years. For centuries, Chinese women endured the practice of foot binding in order produce a crushed "lily foot." Even today, you might spy an elderly woman hobbling with a cane in the back alleys of the city. The swaddling walk apparently reflected some of the high points of traditional dance in the Song dynasty, during which this custom began. The kick in all of this, for men, was that the sight or touch of a deformed foot became an experience of intense erotic pleasure. This crippling custom has been replaced with silicon injections in contemporary Peking, thus illustrating the utter stupidity of the male libido.

While we are on the subject, it was the Chinese City, not the suburbs, where men sought clandestine sexual experiences from courtesans, both male and female. These houses were not simply knocking shops. Rather, the courtesans within were taught to play musical instruments, recite poetry and partake in engaging conversation, with the standard goal of making their customers feel important or interesting. In the "finer" establishments, coarse behavior was sharply discouraged, and a patron would need to make a series of trips before the courtesan might consent to a more intimate encounter. These days, it is cash on the barrelhead, as you can see by the trade being conducted in the hotel lobbies.

From here, we can go to the last bit of our tour of the Eastern suburbs by coming to Dong Zhi Men Wai Avenue (东直门外大街 or *dong zhi men wai da jie*). There is a mosque off to the north of this street. A gray brick structure originally built during Qian Long's time, it is a peaceful setting and perhaps a much-needed antidote to the district's nightlife. The imam is happy to talk with foreign guests.

Outer East Straight Gate Avenue also calls to mind an annual ceremony that once was conducted near the present location of the Second Ring Road. The mayors of imperial Peking welcomed the arrival of spring during the New Year's holidays with effigies in paper of Mang Shen (亡神), and Spring Ox (春牛), prophetic symbols of the coming year's weather. The mayor would return to the city, beating the paper ox to stress the need for diligence in farming to ensure a good harvest. Official astrologers would have prepared these paper effigies to represent their forecasts for the forthcoming year through symbolic colors of appearance. If the Spring Ox was black, epidemics will follow in the near year. If red, then fires; yellow for a good harvest; blue for war and white for floods. Mang

Mang Shen and Spring Ox carry on as weathermen.

Shen, if wearing no shoes, meant that there would be little rain while shoes would mean much rain in the New Year. If he has only one shoe, then the rain would fall in a moderate amount. A hat signified a cold winter while a hatless Mang Shen meant that extreme heat would be in store for the year. Though no longer having a household registration in Peking, it seems that Mang Shen and his ox were able to score Hong Kong identity cards. They can still be found on the first page of Chinese almanacs in Hong Kong, which continue a custom that has already seen 2,500 years.

15

NORTHERN SUBURBS

THE FACE OF NEW PEKING will be found in the suburbs to the north of the Old Tartar City. The authorities have selected these plains for the construction of modern apartment blocks for our friends displaced from the heart of the city, like Horn Rims. There really is not that much to see here, though there are a handful of sights that make the effort of a visit worthwhile.

About a quarter a mile to the north of the Lama Temple is the Park of the Altar of the Earth (地坛公园 or *di tan gong yuan*). When Yong Le built the Temple of Heaven, it was intended that heaven and earth would be worshipped together. In 1530, Jia Jing consulted his court astrologers who approved this site for a new altar solely for the worship of the earth. The altar is composed of two square-shaped terraces in white marble. Formerly, there stood robbing halls, bell and drum towers and storage rooms for sacrificial utensils, most of which disappeared in the 1920s. To the south of the altar is the House of the Imperial Gods (祭台院 or *cha tai yuan*) where a spirit tablet for the earth, mountains, seas and rivers along with imperial ancestor tablets, were stored until used as firewood by Feng Yu Xiang's troops. (Model reproductions of the ceremonies are now on display in the hall.) The ceremonies here were similar to those at the Altar of Heaven, though the sacred gem in this case was yellow and square shaped, representing the earth. The emperor wore yellow robes for the ceremony, which was held on the Summer Solstice. In recent years, the Altar of the Earth has been the site for revived temple festivals held on the Chinese New Year.

Returning to the Second Ring Road, you go north on An Ding Men Wai Avenue (安定门外大街) and take a left to Huang Si Avenue (黄寺大街). On the north, you come to the West Yellow Temple (西黄寺) built during the Ming. Originally there were eastern and western temples, but Li Zi Cheng razed them

Northern Suburbs

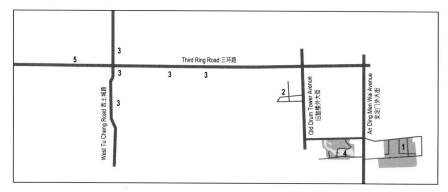

1. Altar of the Earth Park（地坛公园）
2. West Yellow Temple（西黄寺）
3. Earthen City Wall of Yuan Capital（元大都城）
4. Youth Park（青年公园）
5. Big Bell Temple（大钟寺）

both during his siege of Peking. Shun Zhi had them both rebuilt in 1651 as a temporary residence for the 5th Dalai Lama. In 1731, Mongol dignitaries were housed here and contributed to the reconstruction of the temple. In 1780, the Panchen Lama, on a visit to Peking, died of small pox while staying here. His body was returned to Tibet for burial though his clothing was interred under the white marble pagoda in the middle of the remaining west temple. The burial of a deceased's clothes is an old tradition whereby a temple can claim a connection with a deceased dignitary, albeit in a manner less grand than for a tomb containing his remains. The pagoda is a beautiful octagonal marble stupa, with scenes from the Buddha's life carved on each side.

The Yellow Temple is not open to the public, though a chat with the gatekeeper might persuade him to let you take a quick glance. You will notice that to the east of the temple are a series of three storied white stone buildings with brown windowsills. These are constructed in Tibetan style and are the dormitories for Tibetan students brought to Peking for special education.

Continuing to the north, we come to one of the remains of the Earthen City Wall of the Yuan Capital (元大都城废墟 or *yuan da du cheng fei xu*) which are found in the park that runs parallel to the south of the Third Ring Road. Other sections of the ruined wall can be glimpsed in the park by the same name that runs for some way along the west side of Xi Tu Cheng Road (西土城路), which becomes Xue Yuan Road (学院路). These earthen ramparts were built far to the north of the Ming stonewalls and enclosed a grassland where the Mongols kept their livestock. These days, the wall is a collection of tree-covered mounds of varying heights.

Old Summer Palace and Environs

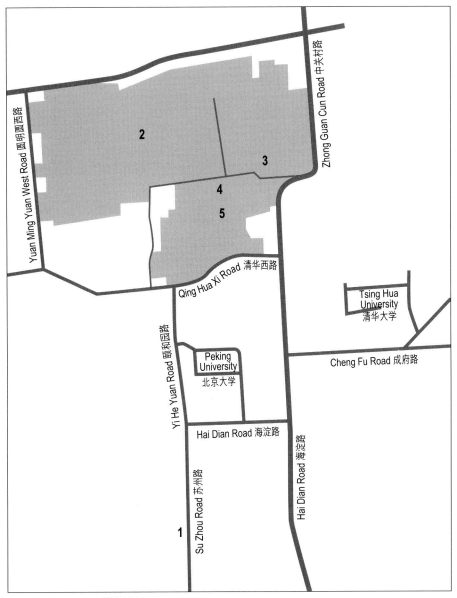

1. Hai Dian District Mosque（海淀清真寺）
2. Place of Perfect Brightness（圆明园）
3. Garden of Ever Lasting Spring（长春园）
4. Perspective Hill（线法山）
5. Outward Looking Temple（方外观）

To the northwest of the Yuan wall ruins near Xue Yuan Road is the Temple of Enlightened Life (赏生寺 or *shang sheng si*) commonly known as the Big Bell Temple (大钟寺 or *da zhong si*). The temple was built to house an enormous bell that was originally from the Temple of Ten Thousand Longevities. The bell, cast in 1406 at the Han Jing Foundry, just inside De Sheng Men, is seven meters tall and weighs 46 tons. (The Han Jing foundry was the former location of the Iron Dragon Screen that we visited in Bei Hai Park.) The outside of the bell is inscribed with 120 Buddhist sutras in Chinese and Sanskrit. The most significant of these is the

安 定 門 外 黃 寺 塔

A 1920s view of the Yellow Temple Stupa.

"Sutra of the Transformation of the Law" (法化经 or *fa hua jing*), a translation of the Sadharmapundarika Sutra, which was introduced to China by the Indian monk Kumarajiva sometime after his arrival in China in 401.

During imperial times, the emperors also came here to beseech the Dragon King for rain. In the early 20th century, many farmers, wearing willow wreaths, which were associated with water, came to the temple at the beginning of the Chinese New Year to pray for rain.

The rest of the temple has been converted into a bell museum, which reflects the long pedigree of bells in Chinese history. They were used for rituals and sacrifices as well as for muscial entertainment. One exhibit displays a set of bells that were retrieved from the tomb of Marquis Yi of the Warring States Period. The bells emit two tones, depending upon where they are struck, and can still be used to create music. The temple attendants will give you a demonstration if you ask.

While the temple is now a museum, it is pleasing to see folks leaving offerings of apples and peaches to the Guan Yin statue in the hall. The east side of the temple consists of an intriguing collection of gray brick courtyard houses, which have been converted into the offices of a law firm and Peking Sun & Sea Advertising Company. Renovation of old buildings is wonderful until the renovators become a little overwhelmed with the words "private property," especially when the buildings were formerly attached to a place of worship. You ought to consider strolling into the courtyards and taking a look, at least until someone chases you away.

Further to the northwest, you can visit the Hai Dian District Mosque (海淀清真寺 or *hai dian qing zhen si*) on Su Zhou Street (苏州街) to the north of the intersection with Haidian South Road (海淀南路). A large white Islamic archway leads into the mosque which was built sometime around the end of the Ming or the beginning of the Qing. I have especially fond memories of this mosque because of the graciousness of its imam, a gentleman sporting a wonderful henna-dyed beard and an effusive sense of hospitality, pushing into my hands cups of tea and chunks of nan straight from the oven.

The mosque has a single courtyard. Its main hall is built on a marble terrace and has a small enclosed observatory centered on the roof, not unlike a widow's-walk in old New England houses. The prayer room inside the hall is decorated in sedate green with quotations from the Koran in Arabic and Chinese.

Further to the north are the campuses of Peking University and Tsinghua University. The main entrance to Peking University is along the north on Haidian Road, a gate with two stone lions. The university stands on the former sites of two princely mansions, one owned by our old friend He Shen and the other by a poet, painter and calligraphist called Mi Wan Zhong (米万种), who lived during the Ming reign. Aside from the garden, nothing remains of the villas.

He Shen was responsible for the extraordinarily complicated arrangements for Lord Macartney's visit to Peking in 1792. After arrival in Peking in a boat bearing a tribute mission flag, the British delegation was housed in He Shen's villa. Eventually, Lord Macartney trudged to the imperial summer resort in Jehol only to be told to shove off. After a century of neglect, Harvard sponsored the establishment of Yen Ching University on the site of the two villas in the 1920s. After 1949, the communists appropriated the site and moved Peking University here from its crowded quarters downtown.

Across the main gate of Peking University, a road takes us to Tsinghua University which was established with funds remitted by the American government from the Boxer indemnities. The university excels in technical studies while Peking University is strong in the humanities.

Our last stop for the tour of the north suburbs is the Place of Perfect Brightness (圆明园 or *yuan ming yuan*), more widely known as the Old Summer Palace in English.

In its day, the palace was a wonder beyond words. It originally consisted of three gardens built starting in 1709. Later, these grounds included a classical Chinese garden with lakes and rockeries and over 140 pavilions along with halls for banquets, exhibitions, and libraries.

The Garden of Ever Lasting Spring (长春园 or *chang chun yuan*) is also known as the Western Palaces (西洋楼 or *xi yang lou*) because they were designed and constructed between 1747 and 1759 by Jesuits, under the supervision of the master Italian artist Giuesppe Castiglione. Castiglione helped to introduce Western techniques such as detail, shadow and perspective to traditional Chinese painting. While his works include such typically Chinese subjects as portraits of the emperor's horses, they also have a life-like three-dimensional appearance that is characteristic of European painters of that era. For a century or so, other Jesuits as well as their Chinese colleagues carried on his synthesis of East and West.

In their memoirs, the Jesuits declared that their "European buildings" were comparable in construction and design to those of Versailles. In the late 18th century, Qian Long directed the Jesuits to produce copper engravings of the palaces, which are our primary source in gleaning what they looked like. They were similar in appearance to the colonial buildings in the Spanish colonies or in Macao of the same era.

In 1860, Anglo-French forces burned down the Old Summer Palace in reprisal for the torture and murder of prisoners of war. Several British and French troops and clergy were seized during a truce and put to death, while other prisoners were subjected to death through torture, even after all combatants had declared a ceasefire. Lord Elgin, the general in charge of the British forces, sought to punish the Qing court in a manner that did not inflict any suffering on the common people. For this reason, the Old Summer Palace was selected as an appropriate target as it was the exclusive playground of the emperor and his government. Captain Charles Gordon, who later commanded a Chinese army on behalf of the Qing government against the Taiping Rebellion, implemented Lord Elgin's orders. The palace was looted of most of its transportable treasures by rank and file soldiers as well as local farmers who made off with whatever they could lay their hands on.

Other European memoirs cast doubt on the official rationale given for the sacking of the Old Summer Palace. David Rennie mentioned that the Anglo-French troops were not aware of the atrocities committed on the POWs until after the sacking had been completed. This view is supported by other contemporary accounts that say the troops carried out the orders in a dispirited manner as if they were aware of the irreparable damage inflicted upon the Chinese and their own reputations. In later years, British and French writers, reflecting a guilty conscience, point an accusatory finger at each other.

In subsequent years, Chinese builders carted away portions of the ruins for use in construction projects. During the 1970s, the ruins were infrequently visited and not closed off in a park. Students from the nearby language institutes could take solitary strolls through the ruins. One friend fondly recalls the calm of taking a nap on a grassy knoll in the autumn beside the marble ruins.

Entering the Old Summer Palace from the east gate, we first pass the Perspective Hill (线法山 or *xian fa shan*), which once consisted of European style archways built over a pool. On the archways, the Jesuits hung scenic oil paintings so realistic that they were said to be indistinguishable from the actual countryside surrounding the palace.

The ruins to the south contain carvings of early 18th century European crests, armors and cannons. A ruined fountain reveals a merging of a Western verandah with Chinese motifs. Nearby once stood a mosque called the Outward Looking Temple (方外观 or *fang wai guan*), which Qian Long reputedly built for the unyielding Fragrant Concubine. Ruined stele and columns are pleasingly reassembled and set out elsewhere in the park. Towards the west is a maze and pavilion built by the Jesuits. During the Mid-autumn Festival, Qian Long would sit in the pavilion and wait for his concubines to race each other, each carrying a lantern, in a contest to be the first to reach him.

The Old Summer Palace still stirs indignation among Chinese, as evidenced by the sign proclaiming that the palace is "the epitome of the fate of the Chinese nations [sic] in modern history." This indignation found expression in the 1980s when a Chinese delegation went to the Sudan to celebrate the 100th anniversary of Gordon's death on the banks of the Nile at Khartoum. Apparently, the head of the delegation was a poet who penned several missives in loving memory of Gordon's gory demise. In recent years, a Chinese arms manufacturer has stirred feelings of patriotic anger in its quest to purchase several artistically insignificant artifacts looted by the foreign troops.

The bodies of the British victims were buried in the Old Russian Cemetery, which used to be in the Northern Suburbs. David Rennie was critical of the sacking and burning of the palace. During a visit to the graves of the POWs, he jotted down the inscription written upon the memorial stone along with his own thoughts:

Lithograph of the Russian Cemetery from the 1860s.

"Sacred to the memory of Captain Brabazon, Royal Artillery; Lieutenant R.B. Anderson; Private Phipps, 1st Dragoon Guards; W. de Norman, Esq., Attaché to H.R. Majesty's Legation, T. W. Bowlby, Esq., and eight Sikh soldiers, who were treacherously seized in violation of a flag of truce on the 18th of September 1860, and sank under the inhuman treatment to which they were subjected by the Chinese Government during their captivity."

The expediency of having worded this record in terms calculated to excite feelings of permanent animosity towards the Chinese Government, with whom we are now at peace, and desirous of remaining for the future on terms of amity, appears to me to admit of being questioned."[1]

Some of my Chinese friends have argued that it is important to keep the resentment about the sacking of the Old Summer Palace alive to prevent a recurrence of such an event. With respect, I strongly disagree. Rennie takes the higher and less traveled moral path against jingoism, both past and present.

16

WESTERN SUBURBS

ON **W**EST **S**TRAIGHT **G**ATE **A**VENUE (西直门大街 or *xi zhi men da jie*), there is a relic from the time of paramount Russian influence in China. The Peking Exhibition Hall was originally constructed in 1954 as the Soviet Exhibition Hall. Its Russian motifs, inclusive of statues of Caucasian workers and farmers atop the main columns of the entranceway, make it seem more suitable for Moscow and other points further west. The design of the building earned Simon Leys' famous rebuke that the hall reflects Russia's condescending view of Peking as a "suburb of Irkutsk." Wreathed hammers and sickles and the Russian blue dome with white designs of flowers in the main hall have mellowed into an interesting image of time and place. These days, the exhibition hall is used as a shopping mall for high-end consumer goods. To the west of the hall is the Moscow Restaurant, a classic relic and once the only Western restaurant in Peking.

The Zoological Gardens (北京动物园) are slightly to the west of the hall and occupy the site of an imperial park built for one of Shun Zhi's sons. In 1902, the Empress Dowager rebuilt the park for a large collection of animals and birds brought to China by the Shan Xi provincial viceroy after a trip overseas. After the menagerie was placed in the park, its name was changed to the Park of the Ten Thousand Animals (万物公园).

All did not run smoothly at first. When the Empress Dowager visited the park for the first time, the director of zoo, who presumably came out fawning all over the old crow, was quizzed on the names and habits of the different inmates. The old boy didn't even get out of the starting gate as he drew a blank on the very first animal that she pointed to. He was duly cashiered on the spot. During the trying years before liberation, the collection at the Peking Zoo dwindled as hunger overruled biological curiosity.

Western Suburbs

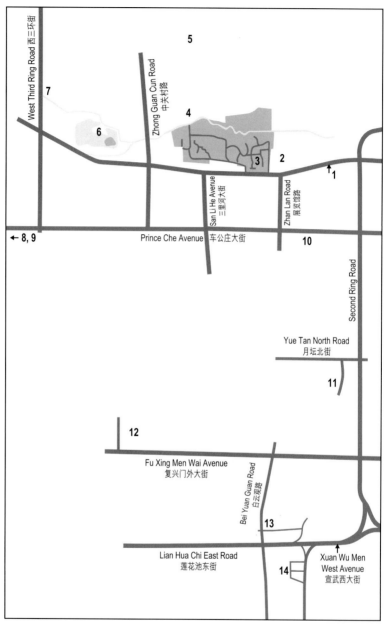

1. West Straight Gate Avenue (西直门大街)
2. Peking Exhibition Hall
3. Zoological Garden (北京动物园)
4. Five Pagoda Temple (五塔寺)
5. Temple of Great Kindness (大慧寺)
6. Purple Bamboo Park (紫竹公园)
7. Temple of Ten Thousand Longevities (万寿寺)
8. Temple of Benevolence and Longevity (慈寿寺)

9. Increasing Brightness Road (增光路)
10. Communist Party Cadre School
    (Grave of Father Matteo Ricci) (利玛窦墓)
11. Altar of Moon Park (月坛公园)
12. Military Museum of the Chinese People's Revolution
    (中国人民革命军事博物馆)
13. White Cloud Temple (白云观)
14. Temple of Heavenly Tranquility (天宁寺)

The gate at the entrance of the zoo is an interesting sample of Qing architecture, which is more appealing than the condition of the animals inside. The pandas are usually on strike with their backs turned to the crowd and petulantly munching bamboo trees. In the "petting zoo," children clamber up a visibly traumatized elephant. Further on, bears angrily eyeball their tormentors while waiting for a chance to break out and get even. A clinically depressed snow leopard escapes his lot by sleeping all day. Even the rabbits look outraged. They are probably wondering how they got swindled out of their safe harbor on the moon.

To the north of the zoo is the Five Pagoda Temple (五塔寺 or *wu ta si*), built in 1465 based on a gold model of the Temple of Buddha's Diamond Throne in Boddhgaya, India. An Indian monk named Pandita arrived in Peking in the 1440s and gave the gold model as a gift to the emperor, who decided to build a full-sized version. The Ming designers, however, could not leave things alone and added a Chinese circular hall on the roof.

The entrance way is flanked by statutes of various animals and spirits, in varying states of repair. Numerous bas-reliefs of the Buddha in the "calling the earth to witness" position decorate the square foundation of the temple. By climbing up the internal stairway, you come to a stone carving of a pair of feet, an ancient symbol of the Buddha's earthly wanderings and the first artistic depiction of the Buddha. It is said that the footprints are always cool, no matter how warm the weather. To the east of the pagoda in the courtyard are a collection of white marble steles, in Latin and Chinese, taken from the former French cemetery. They recall the lives of Catholic priests from Europe, China and Mongolia.

Further to the north in the Village of the Duke of Wei (魏公村 or *wei gong cun*) is the Temple of Great Kindness (大慧寺 or *da hui si*), built in 1513. It is said to be an excellent example of Ming timber construction. Only a single hall remains, but within are 28 clay statues of divine guardians as well as frescoes depicting the life of a virtuous man of good deeds. A huge bronze Buddha statute used to sit here, but was hauled away by the Japanese during the occupation of Peking. Now the hall contains a huge image of the Thousand Armed and Thousand Eyed Buddha, surrounded by bodhisattvas and arhats.

These days, the gatekeepers of the Temple of Great Kindness do not have too much kindness for outsiders wanting to view the temple's marvelous artwork. The temple is now on the grounds of the China Steel and Iron Research Center and assuming that you can make it through the main gate, the gate to the temple itself is perennially locked. On the rare occasion that the doorkeeper opens the door for you, after countless knocking, he will only let you view the temple from afar. I hope that you have better luck than me.

The Five Pagoda Temple.

Spring Festival at the White Cloud Temple.

Continuing back to the Central Guan Village Avenue (中关村 or *zhong guan cun da jie*), we go south and arrive at the Purple Bamboo Park (紫竹公园 or *zi zhu gong yuan*) whose lakes date from the Yuan dynasty. During the Ming and Qing, various structures were built here to accommodate the imperial family's trips to the Summer Palace. The only building of any age is the nine-storied Ming Pagoda.

The Purple Bamboo Park makes for a great early morning stroll on weekends to watch the folks of Peking spend their leisure time. Troupes of retired people practice *tai qi* (a traditional form of exercise, based on the martial arts and designed to enhance meditation and the flow of the body's humors) or participate in ballroom dancing, twirling under the trees. Others perform traditional rural fan dances (扭秧歌 or *pan ge*), first made popular after liberation, with a purely percussive musical accompaniment. It is pleasing to come across other folks jitterbugging to the tunes of Glen Miller.

Elsewhere, groups of people practice songs from youth as an accordion player squeezes out a tune. Others practice their calligraphy on the paving stones by using meter long brushes and water for ink. They write classical poems, which evaporate in a matter of minutes (as do all earthly possessions when you think about it). On the lakes, oarsmen row traditional Chinese boats and wave a gregarious arm as they pass by the shore. Both adults and children play a game of catch by kicking a shuttlecock to others gathered in a circle, an entertainment that enhances pleasure as well as blood circulation. In his description of sights in 19th century Peking, Dun Li Chen described "diabolo tops," which are still used by Peking folks: "The diabolo top is like the wheels of a cart in form, between which is a short axle. Children operate it by jerking two sticks to which is fastened a cotton string which is given a twist around the central axle, so that the top hums majestically with a sound like that of a morning bell beyond the horizon."[1]

About a mile further to the west is the Temple of Ten Thousand Longevities (万寿寺 or *wan shou si*). Built in 1577 by one of the eunuchs of Wan Li, it stands to the northwest of the same canal that flows by the Five Pagoda Temple and on to the Summer Palace. When the Empress Dowager traveled to the Summer Palace, she inevitably spent a night here and made offerings to the Buddhist deities, asking for felicity and peace of mind. In the 1930s, the monastery was converted into a university and during the Cultural Revolution a PLA platoon made its home here. In the main hall are fabulous statutes of the Three Buddhas. In the last courtyard is an artificial hill much favored by the Empress Dowager, who would rest here while taking in the view of the then verdant countryside.

Further to the west at Eight Mile Village Road (八里庄路 or *ba li zhuang lu*) is the Temple of Benevolence and Longevity (慈寿寺 or *ci shou si*) built in 1576 by Wan Li as an act of filial piety to his mother, who was a devote Buddhist. While the temple grounds have disappeared over the years, a magnificent octagonal pagoda originally called the Pagoda of Everlasting Peace and Old Age (长安万寿塔 or *chang an wan shou ta*) survives as an excellent architectural example of Ming pagodas. On each side of the pagoda, there are exquisite carvings of temple guardians in varying states of repair, some slowly decomposing to reveal their wooden skeletons. Along the base of the pagoda are Buddhist motifs, such as lotus petals and the eight Tibetan treasures of Buddhism. These eight treasures consist of a wheel (a symbol of the crushing effect of Buddhism upon delusions), a conch-shell (the voice of the Buddha), an umbrella (an allusion to the Buddha's royal birth), a flag (similar to Tibetan prayer flags), a jar (funerary urns for monks), a lotus (symbolizing perfection arising from the mundane), a pair of fish (freedom from the restraints of this earthly existence) and a mystic knot (reflecting Indra's knot, or the interconnection of all existence, now blasphemously used in an altered form as a service mark for some telecom company). The pagoda is situated in a park, which makes a perfect place for a picnic.

Coming back to the east, we find the remains of a small Uighur enclave on Increasing Brightness Road (增光路 or *zeng guang lu*). Urban redevelopment has left only a tiny portion of what was once a neighborhood overflowing with Xin Jiang restaurants and markets. The Uighurs are the original Turkish inhabitants of western regions re-conquered by Qian Long over two hundred years ago. They are a tough devotedly Muslim group whose culture has more to do with Central Asia than the Far East. Here you can see merchants selling stacks of *nan* or round bread, much like American bagels, and cooked in tandoori ovens. You can also pick up Hami melons as well as dried apricots and raisins here.

Given the close-knit nature of Uighur society, many Chinese view them with some suspicion. A slight air of lack of propriety hangs over a visit to this small enclave. Given the Islamic prohibition against alcohol, Uighurs are also known for growing hashish and marijuana, which deepens Chinese frowns. On one trip to Uighurville, I ran into an elderly man who, upon spotting me, called out the word "nasha" again and again. As I looked at him in some confusion, he followed these calls with an unusual gesture. He put his right thumb on his nose and then put his left thumb on his right pinky finger, with all the other fingers wriggling back and forth. I did not realize that this was the traditional sign language for hashish, which he had hoped to sell to me.

Still closer to town on Prince Che's Village Avenue (车公庄大街 or *che gong zhuang da jie*), you will come to the Communist Party Cadre School in whose courtyard is situated, with unintended irony, the remains of the Jesuit cemetery and the tomb of Matteo Ricci (利玛窦墓 or *li ma dou mu*) and other Jesuits.

Ricci exerted a profound influence upon the history of China's relationship with the western world. He was born in 1552 in Macerata, Italy and entered the Society of Jesus in 1571. In keeping with Jesuit practice, he studied a wide range of subjects ranging from theology to astronomy and science. Eleven years later, he arrived in Macao with the goal of starting a mission in China. He moved to Zhao Qing near Guang Zhou in 1583 and was never to return to Europe.

His first decade in China was tumultuous. Having mastered the spoken and written Chinese language, including classical written expression, he

The Jesuit Cemetery.

adopted the appearance of a Buddhist monk, wearing monastic robes and shaving his head. Gradually, it dawned on Ricci that the only viable way to convert the Chinese was a "top-down" approach directed at the literati. While the Ming court patronized Buddhism, he saw that acceptance of Christianity by the official classes would give his religion far greater legitimacy. At his urging, the Jesuits adopted the clothing of Confucian scholars in 1594.

Ricci had found that Western knowledge could trigger respect among the gentry. He produced China's first map of the world, which was widely reproduced (without royalties). He also wrote a treatise in classical Chinese about Christianity, using traditional philosophical methodologies. Since officials were keenly intrigued in Western goods, such as clocks, telescopes and harpsichords, he brought craftsmen from Macao to manufacture these toys.

While Ricci achieved some intellectual successes during his stay in south China, his mission was constantly beset by prejudice and violence. Locals attacked his church and its converts with impunity. Once a rabble attacked Ricci who walked with a limp for the rest of his life as a result.

In 1595, Ricci left south China for Nanjing. Among the literati, he astounded his Chinese friends by his acute memory, which was an intellectual trait much admired by Chinese, especially given its practical applicability for candidates of the governmental examinations. Once during a dinner, a Chinese friend challenged Ricci to read a lengthy poem and then to recite it by memory. Ricci met the challenge effortlessly. When other Chinese friends suggested that Ricci might have learned that particular poem elsewhere, Ricci offered a challenge in turn. He asked his friends to write down five hundred Chinese characters in no particular order and without any meaning. After one reading, Ricci recited the characters in perfect order and then recited them again in *reverse order.*

The Ming court permitted Ricci to reside in Peking in 1601 where he established a cathedral. Ricci managed to convert several Chinese officials and even some concubines and eunuchs. Always having to negotiate through the dangers of court intrigues, Ricci worked at a punishing rate in his attempt to overcome hostility in official quarters. He met and debated with Buddhist monks, wrote songs in classical Chinese, translated Euclid's treatises, assisted with the astronomical calculations of the imperial observatory and made himself available to everyone curious about his faith. Other Jesuits joined him and worked in Peking's foundry, casting cannons and making matchlock rifles. Ricci always seemed to prefer the company of Chinese farmers who had converted to Catholicism, sharing with them their simple meals and cherishing their good will. However, his goal condemned him to ceaseless rounds of social engagements with the official classes, at which he had to constantly prove his intellectual acumen and diplomacy. He never succeeded in meeting emperor Wan Li, let alone achieving his dream of converting him to Christianity. In 1610, the rigors of his work finally took their toll and Ricci died of exhaustion. Given the contributions in science and technology made by the Jesuits, Wan Li ordered a formal site for Ricci's burial.

Ricci was deeply aware of the universality propounded by the church and strove to combine Catholic teaching with Chinese culture. His tomb reflected this cosmopolitan view. Upon a stone altar in front of his tumulus, his confreres placed Buddhist symbols of reverence, such as stone carvings of an incense burner, candelabra and vases. Over the years, other Jesuits, such as Schall, Verbiest, and Castiligone were buried here in similar tombs.

The Jesuit presence in Peking continued after Ricci's death. When the Manchus seized Peking, the Jesuits demonstrated a realpolitik by dividing into two groups. One group stayed in Peking and cultivated close ties with the new rulers. Another group attached themselves to the court of a Ming pretender, which was constantly on the run as the Qing troops and their allies invaded south China. In the rump court, the Jesuits succeeded in converting the pretender's empress, who took the baptismal name Helen. Before the court disappeared in oblivion in Burma, Empress Helen sent a letter to the Pope, pleading for European assistance for a Ming restoration.

During the Qing, disputes between the Vatican and Kang Xi over the interpretation of ancestor rituals inaugurated the gradual demise of Jesuit influence in Peking. However, a small community remained attached to the court until 1827 when Dao Guang expelled foreign Catholics from the empire. For thirty years, the Russian ecclestical mission tended the cemetery of their brother Christians. Under the treaty signed with France in 1860, the Catholic Church returned to China. David Rennie records that the Jesuit cemetery was among the most beautiful vistas in Peking.

In 1900, the Boxers desecrated the cemetery. Though repaired afterwards, it never recovered its beauty. The next blow came in 1967 when the Red Guards tore down the graves for the construction of the Communist Party Cadre School. In the 1980s, the memorial steles were re-erected in the courtyard of the school, though in a much compressed location.

These days, no one objects to outsiders coming to visit the steles. The tombstones of Ricci, Verbiest and Schall are set apart from a stele forest recording the names of other Jesuits. The inscriptions are written in Chinese and Latin and the stones are decorated with carvings of roses, imperial emblems as well as the initials of the Society of Jesus. In front of Ricci's tomb is a small stone *pai lou* with a lamb statue symbolizing the Holy Spirit.

As you leave the main hall of the Communist Party Cadre School, there is an exhibition of newspaper articles about 20th century revolutionary Chinese luminaries, their contributions appropriately recorded on non-durable newsprint.

To the south on the west side of Li Shi Road (礼士路) is the Altar of the Moon Park (月坛公园 or *yue tan gong yuan*). The Altar of the Moon was erected in 1530 on a similar plan to the Altar of the Sun. A circular wall encloses a square white altar. The emperor came here to perform the lunar rituals on alternative years on a day in autumn and at an hour sometime between 6 and 8 pm. After donning a white robe and holding a white ritual stone, he ascended the altar from the east. Before him were the spirit tablet for the moon along with those of the pole star, the twenty-eight main constellations, the planets and other celestial bodies. Offerings were made of white jade, white oxen, sheep and pigs. Unfortunately, the Peking government installed a mammoth television antenna on these grounds. I have never been able to gain access to see if the altar is still there.

Chang An West Avenue (长安西大街 or *chang an xi da jie*) is the address of the Military Museum of the Chinese People's Revolution (中国人民革命军事博物馆), which is housed in a Soviet style building. If you come here on a weekend, you will see the disturbing sight of children admiringly gazing at machine guns, grenade launchers and bayonets. Peking has other military themed exhibitions, like a Tank Museum, all of which reflect a deep change in China's cultural landscape. Traditional China never glorified war and looked upon the military as a necessary but distasteful evil. An adage from the Tang dynasty held "just as good iron is not used for nails, worthy sons should not become soldiers." China's inability to overcome foreign encroachments compelled 20th century Chinese leaders to strangle noble pacifism for the warlike demeanor of other global powers.

With these thoughts and a sigh, you enter the main hall of the museum, passing by a granite statue of Mao and a series of large pictures of Mao, Deng and Jiang reviewing troops. There is a mural of the PLA triumphant in battle over Nationalist troops and another one painted in "socialist realism" and fictionally depicting a scene from the Long March. Just within this entranceway is the main hall, filled to bursting with tanks, airplanes, jeeps ships, as well as the official sedan cars for Mao and Zhu De. On the right hand side concealed by a MIG jet is a mural of the Chinese air force shooting down two American fighter planes.

The second floor of the main hall has a selection of statues of China's heroes. Asides from the usual suspects, there are busts of Kim Il Song, the King of Tonga, Zhang Zi Zhong and Norman Bethune. Outside the collection of statues is another serving of retail weapons of mass destruction, ranging from missiles to land mines.

In the west wing of the museum are two floors of exhibitions of oil paintings glorifying war. Only one picture actually alludes to death, and in this case, it is a heroically symbolic corpse with no gashes, blood or torn skull fragments. The third and fourth floors have historical exhibitions on ancient and modern Chinese military matters. On the third floor of the east wing is an interesting exhibition on China's side of the story about the War to Resist America and Help Korea. The exhibition shows the Chinese view of the Korean War, which is rather startling for Americans. Rather than a draw, the Chinese orthodoxy views the war as a victory of the North Koreans and Chinese over an American invasion of Pyongyang. The North Koreans and Chinese are presented as close allies (like lips and teeth, as the mainland propaganda described it). Most poignant is an oil painting of a Korean valley in wintertime, littered with the burned out hulks of American tanks and jeeps. A tattered American flag lies atop one of the tanks. Overall the painting reflects the same moral bankruptcy as any of Mel Gibson's propagandistic war movies.

Several miles further west on the same road is the Eight Treasure Mountain Revolutionary Cemetery (八宝山革命公墓 or *ba bao shan ge ming gong mu*). Within the cemetery are buried such luminaries as Zhu De, Chen Yun and, the American author Anna Louise Strong. The cemetery's location suggests a two-pronged continuity with pre-liberation China. On the one hand, many people were buried in the western part of the city as it was thought to aid them on their way to the Buddhist Western Pure Lands. On the other hand, the Eight Treasure Mountain was the site of a golf course and country club patronized almost exclusively by foreigners. I can picture no other earthly endeavor that more closely simulates death and burial.

Directly to the south is the White Cloud Temple (白云观 or *bai yun guan*) which, along with the Temple of the Eastern Peak, was one of the great Taoist Temples in Old Peking. In keeping with the geomantic principle of symmetry, they occupy roughly equivalent positions in the east and west suburbs of Peking.

The White Cloud Temple is supposedly the older of the two. It is said that in 1192, the temple was constructed on a Tang dynasty foundation. During the early Yuan dynasty, the temple became the sanctuary of Qiu Chu Ji (丘处机), a Taoist sage from Shan Dong province. He founded the Northern School of Taoism, or the Total Truth Sect (全真派 or *chuan zhen pai*), to use its formal name. The temple became the headquarters of the sect, which emphasized meditation and celibacy and rejected the practice of alchemy and magic potions as pursued by other Taoist groups.

Qiu was apparently a spiritual advisor to the Great Genghis Khan:

Genghis Khan was at that time engaged in his western campaigns and each day there was fighting. The Perfect One [*viz.*, Qiu Chu Ji], each time he spoke, would say that the person who wishes to make the world one, should not delight in killing men. When asked how to govern, he said that what was fundamental was to reverence Heaven and love the people. And on being asked the method for prolonging life and remaining a long time in this world, he replied that what was important was to purify the heart and lessen desires. Genghis Khan was greatly pleased and ordered [a historian] to make a record of what was said.[2]

It sounds like Qiu Chu Ji's advice came after Genghis turned the Jin capital into a grease stain, a fate that the Taoist master fortunately avoided, passing away peacefully at the temple in 1227.

Most of buildings in the White Cloud Temple date from the late Qing and stylistically are nearly identical to Buddhist temples. This is also home for Taoist monks, who wear their hair in the Ming fashion, uncut in a bun held by a silver or jade hairpin. In warm weather, they also tool about in traditional cotton clothing and straw sandals.

The present temple is constructed along a central axis with two parallel wings in the backcourt. We will first tour the structures along the central axis and then take up the side courtyards.

Passing through a three-doored gate, you will see black smudges on the right hand side of the main entranceway. It is believed that rubbing this spot on the lunar New Year will bring good luck, an act of faith that still motivates the folks of Peking to queue up for this extra bit of insurance. Once past the gate, you pass a pond spanned by a stone bridge. Under the bridge is a large copper coin at which people throw tokens. For those lucky enough to hit the coin, another tranche of good luck should be forthcoming.

The first main hall in the temple is the Hall of Ling Guan (灵官殿 or *ling guan dian*). Ling Guan was a warrior, as shown by the red-faced statue suited in armor holding a whip. He looks favorably upon acts of kindness and does not spare his whip on malefactors in this world. I sometimes think that he has been on a leave of absence for too long.

The next courtyard to the west is the hall for the Military and Civil Gods of Wealth. The military God of Wealth is a deified hermit from E Mei Shan in Si Chuan province, named Marshal Zhao Gong Min (赵公民). During a battle with evil spirits, a high priest of Taoism summoned him to fight on his behalf. Marshal Zhao rode into battle on his favorite charger, a black tiger, and hurled pearls at his foe with the same devastating effect as hand-grenades. Statues to Marshal Zhao commonly depict him astride a tiger with his right hand winding up to throw a pearl.

The Civil God of Wealth is Bi Gan (比干), a sage from the 12th century B.C. who remonstrated with the last emperor of the Shang dynasty to stop his vices, an appeal to virtue that prompted the Shang emperor to carve Bi Gan's heart out. He is regarded as the Civil God of Wealth and is usually (and anachronistically) depicted in Confucian robes.

Across the courtyard on the east side is the Hall for the Emperors of Water, Earth and Heaven (三官 or *san guan*) who represent the spiritual sources for delivery from evil, forgiveness of sins and happiness, respectively. These three deities also recorded the good and bad deeds of mortals. The central hall is dedicated to the Jade Emperor along with other allied Taoist deities. Kang Xi took a personal interest in the Jade Emperor and provided the statues that greet you here.

The King of Medicine (药王 or *yao wang*) is worshipped in the hall on the west side of the next courtyard. While deities such as the Yellow Emperor (黄帝 or *huang di*) were credited with writing treatises on health and healing, the King of Medicine was the universal favorite among Peking folks. As a mortal, the King was an early Tang dynasty pharmacist who compiled a thirty volume medical encyclopedia that dealt with acupuncture, massage, diet, exercise and love potions. While a shrine to his memory was set up in nearly every village and hamlet, they usually fell into disrepair, possibly because of the cost of upkeep and the uncertainty of the harvest. Western travelers often recounted the moving sight of a mother holding an ill child, beseeching the god in a broken down temple, with the wind whipping through collapsed beams and the robes of the god in tatters.

On the east side of the courtyard is a collection of lesser deities. In front of us is the Hall of the Venerable Law (老律殿 or *lao lu dian*). Its name is an allusion to the crossing from mundane to spiritual life. Inside are Ming era statues of the temple's founder Qiu Zhu Ji and other historical Taoist philosophers. Behind is another temple, the Hall of Ancestor Qiu (丘祖殿 or *qiu zu dian*), dedicated exclusively to the memory of Qiu Zhu Ji. The founder is said to be buried underneath the hall and that his statue is an accurate portrayal of the sage. The offering bowl in front of the temple is reputed to have been a gift brought from Xin Jiang by Qian Long.

In the next courtyard is the two-storey Hall of Four Great Men (四御殿 or *si yu dian*), dedicated to the four major protectors of Taoism, the Clear Emperor, the Emperor of the Four Directions, the Emperor of the South Star and the Emperor of the North Star.

On the second floor is the Hall of the Three Pure Ones (三清殿 or *san jing dian*), who are said to be a Taoist invention to match the Buddhist Trinity of Sakyamuni, Amida and Manjursi. These consist of the Clear Jade Primeval Deity (玉清元始天尊 or *yu qing yuan shi tian zuan*), the Dao Jun Deity (上清元始天尊 or *shang qing yuan shi tian zuan*) who is the controller of the yin and yang, and Lao Zi, here called the Great Clear Deity of the Virtuous Way (太清元始天尊 or *tai qing yuan shi tian zuan*). The sculptures all date from the Ming.

By taking the doorway on the west side of the courtyard in front of the Hall of Four Great Men, you enter the west wing of the temple. As you enter the western courtyard, a temple to the God of Literature, Wen Chang (文昌), greets us on the north and a temple to the south shelters a shrine to Confucius, reflecting Taoism's ability to absorb all gods and heroes.

Further to the west are temples to the Eight Taoist Immortals. These deities came into popular belief during the Song dynasty, an era that saw the rise of Neo-Confucianism. After centuries of Taoist and Buddhist influence, the apparatchiks of the empire launched an attack against these "unscholarly" philosophies and promoted Confucian ethics in a rather lifeless manner.

The devotion to the Eight Taoist Immortals flew right in the face of that orthodoxy. Here was a collection of eight iconoclastic oddballs who were quite fond of a dram and who could not give a hoot about the solemnity of age-old social conventions. The boisterous band of immortal humorists traveled through the material world, shaking up folks wedded to convention just like Ken Kesey's Merry Pranksters did in the 1960s.

The most famous of the band was Liu Dong Pin (吕洞宾) who was actually a relative of one of the Tang emperors. After Empress Wu usurped the throne, Liu escaped to the mountains, where he practiced meditational breathing techniques and began a long career of subduing evildoers while rewarding mortals who shared his dislike for conventionality. Liu's teacher and drinking buddy was Zhong Li Quan (钟离权) whose mortal career began in the military but, presumably like Hunter Thompson, he abandoned mindless regimentation and developed a reputation as an alchemist producing all sorts of mind-expanding elixirs. Li of the Iron Crutch (李铁拐 or *li tie kuai*) was an easily recognized deity. After an out-of-body flight through the heavens, he returned to earth to learn that his corporal counterpart had disappeared. Selecting the first body that had been vacated by a soul, Li awoke to find himself as a crippled beggar.

Zhang Guo Lao (张果老) was a native of Shan Xi who, like Zhuang Zi before him, rejected all invitations to be a court official. He appears to have been old from birth and traveled around the world on a donkey seated backwards. Han Xiang Zi (韩湘子), the nephew of the Tang era philosopher and poet Han Yu, was trained to be a lover of flowers and poetry and could produce plants with poems written in gold leaf amidst the veins of the leaves. He is often depicted carrying a jade flute and is the patron saint of musicians.

Cao Guo Qiu (曹国舅) was related to a black sheep member of the imperial Song family. After several years of a dissolute life, Cao took a vow to devote himself to the study of the Tao, which led to immortality. As in real life Cao acts as a go-between for people seeking an imperial audience and now carries a spirit tablet that acts as a passport to visit other Taoist divinities with requests from mortals. The sole woman member of the eight is He Xian Gu (何仙姑), a young Cantonese woman who acquired a powdered mother of pearl elixir from a spirit.

Finally there is Lan Cai He (蓝采和), a semi-crazed strolling musician whose gender was never clear. "A man but not a man" was the way he described himself, suggesting that he was gay. (Taoism would certainly pose no bar to admission on that account.) Lan Cai He composed verses that mocked the fleeting world of material grasping and dragged strings of copper cash behind him, not caring if they were there or not. A frequent imbiber of rice wines, he floated to heaven on their fumes, provocatively chucking a shoe at the world during his ascent.

The legends about the Eight Immortal Taoists could fill many volumes since they ceaselessly intervened in the mortal world on behalf of kindred spirits. As

Juliet Bredon aptly phrased it, the Eight Taoist Immortals appeal to the child that still exists in each person's heart and who has grown weary of the meaningless intrigues of the adult world.

To the north is a large courtyard with corridors, rockeries and an ordination terrace for acolyte monks. During temple fairs, the terrace becomes a stage for neighborhood Peking Opera troupes. Coming down the east wing you pass halls for the worship of the Emperor of the South Star (南极殿 or *nan ji dian*), the Emperor of the North Star (真武殿 or *zhen wu dian*), and the God of Thunder (雷祖殿 or *lei zu dian*), among many others.

Further to the south of the White Cloud Temple is the Temple of Heavenly Tranquility (天宁寺 or *tian ning si)*. The pagoda is the oldest building in Peking, having been constructed during the Liao dynasty. For many years, it was enclosed in the grounds of a record company and could not be visited. At the time of writing, the temple buildings to the south of the pagoda are under renovation and the maze of *ping fang* that obstructed access has been pulled down.

The pagoda is an octagon tower with thirteen stories, the most available to a pagoda according to imperial protocol. The best carvings on the pagoda, those of Buddhas and guardians, are seen from the south side. Once 3,400 bells graced the eaves of the pagoda and with the wind in the right direction, could be heard well within the city. Around the south entrance is an open-air market where vendors sell porcelain, kites, birds, crickets and goods for daily use. In August, you can buy peaches and pomegranates that make wonderful dry wines.

The area around Guang'an Men Railway Station has no existing buildings of historical interest but it nevertheless merits an entry in this book. This was the site of Peking's first beer-making experiment, the Shuang He Sheng Brewery (双和生啤酒厂) incorporated in 1914. Prior to that time, most beer consumed in Peking was imported from Germany or Japan. The outbreak of World War I disrupted the usual importation channels. A Peking local named Zhang Tian Ge and his Czech partner seized the opportunity and established the brewery, using barley from He Bei province and imported hops. The first batch of Five Star Beer was sold in 1916. Five Star Beer is still on sale, but is mostly found in the western side of the city. It is a refreshing lager.

Another sight long gone is Peking's horse racing stadium (跑马场 or *pao ma chang)* first built by the British at the turn of the century. Horse racing became an obsession for both foreigners and Chinese in Peking. Manchu nobles and Chinese officials, dressed in their finest robes, as well as foreign diplomats and businessmen, arrived in horse drawn coaches or by sedan chairs along with common folks delighting for a chance to bet on the races. Naturally, near the racetrack stood a temple for the God of Wealth, who could always be found in the city's Taoist temples but who naturally also had his own shrine built near this location.

The British love of horseracing resulted in race tracks built in nearly every coastal city in China. The horses were typically Mongolian ponies brought into China by an equestrian trading company run by a Canadian with an extensive network in Mongolia. He was the purchasing agent for the bourgeoise all throughout China.

Off the Jing Shi Highway is the walled village of Wan Ping (宛平) where the Marco Polo Bridge (卢沟桥 or *lu gou qiao*), built between 1189 and 1192, spans the Settled Water River (水定河 or *shui ding he*).

Wan Ping is a village of considerable age, having been incorporated into the territory under Peking's jurisdiction after Yong Le moved the capital from Nanjing. In modern times, the Japanese initiated its full-scale war against China here on July 7, 1937. Under the terms of the Boxer Protocol of 1901, Japan had the right to station a garrison in this vicinity. The precise ruse for the commencement of hostilities was a Japanese soldier who got "lost." When the Japanese demanded the right to search Wan Ping Village for the wayward soldier, the Chinese village commander refused. The Japanese responded by bombarding the village and then launching a full scale invasion of China proper. (It turned out that the missing Japanese soldier was hoisting pints of Five Star Beer at a nearly bar.)

An imperial era city wall surrounds the village where gray courtyard homes still predominate. If you can gain access to the wall, it makes a wonderful stroll for observing traditional life in the courtyards. At the south gate of the village we find the Marco Polo Bridge. Marco Polo supposedly visited the bridge in 1276. In his *Travels,* he says:

> When you leave the City of Cambulac [Peking], and have ridden ten miles, you come to a very large river which is called Pulisangkin and flows into the ocean so that merchants with their merchandise ascend to it from the sea. Over this river there is a very fine stone bridge, so fine indeed, that it has very few equals.
>
> The fashion is this: It is 300 paces in length and it must have a good eight paces in width, for ten mounted men can ride across it abreast. It has 24 arches and as many water mills, and is all of a very fine marble, well built and firmly founded. Along the top of the bridge there is on either side of parapet of marble slabs and columns made in this way: At the beginning of the bridge there is a marble column, and under it a marble lion so that the column stands upon the lion's loins while on the top of the column there is a second lion both of being of great size and beautifully sculpture. At the distance of a pace from this column, there is another precisely the same, also with its two lions and the space them is closed with slabs of gray marble to prevent people from falling over into the water. And thus the columns run from space to space along either side of the bridge, so that altogether it is a beautiful object.[3]

Marco Polo Bridge.

Polo's description has led to a longstanding debate on whether he actually made it to China. While he mentions stone lions, he does not describe the 140 balustrades each with its own lion, which is one of the most remarkable aspects of the bridge. Nor, for that matter, does he mention the stone elephants at each end. In addition, he refers to the river by its Persian name, Pulisangkin, from *pul* for bridge and *sang* for stone and not the Chinese or Mongol names. This has led some to speculate that the old boy never made it here and that he cribbed his memoirs from a Persian guidebook.

In 1698, Kang Xi had to have the bridge rebuilt and took a precautionary step of changing the name of the river to the Everlasting Settled River (水定河). This sophistry evidently did not impress the river gods for long as a flood devastated the region in 1890. Since then, the river has dried up and the bridge has lost its utility with the construction of nearby multilane highway bridges.

On the entrance to the bridge next to Wan Ping's south gate stands a stele erected with Qian Long's calligraphy, recognizing the bridge as one of the eight great sites of imperial Peking. In keeping with Yong Le's literary tradition, the Marco Polo Bridge is best viewed in the early hours of the morning on a day when the full moon slowly sets while the sun rises. Perhaps this is the most satisfying of the remaining eight sights. Once again the effort rewards the visitor with a brief second of timelessness.

17

THE SUMMER PALACE

NOT TO PUT TOO FINE a point on it, the Summer Palace (颐和园 or *yi he yuan*) has always underwhelmed me. Granted, the architecture is superb. My complaint is that this magnificent imperial park was designed for the visual delight of a small handful of people. More people flow through, well, actually are herded through, the gates of the Summer Palace than almost any other sight in Peking. Or perhaps that is because these imperial grounds were designed, after two sackings in 1860 and 1900, to recreate a sense of delicacy triumphing over raw force. In any event, the thronging masses following shrill loudspeakers and tour company flags cause more damage to the ambiance than French artillery ever did.

To grasp the cosmological grandeur of the place, David Kidd spins a fascinating (and perhaps fanciful) story about the Summer Palace and his inadvertent role in establishing the People's Republic. In Peking Story, he recounts how, in 1949, his aunt-in-law was talking about the rumors flooding Peking. The city was about to regain its traditional role as national capital. Auntie Chin, a traditional thorough-blood Manchu of noble stock, was a living archive of fact and legend about the city. She said she knew why the city has recaptured its proper status.

Auntie Chin explained that there are two major entranceways to the Summer Palace, the main gate to the east and a back gate to the north. The Western Hills were reservoirs of good fortune for the city, and such luck flowed along invisibly in currents down from the hills, entering the Summer Palace through the back gate and flowing out through Kunming Lake and into the city.

In 1911, the Peking authorities officially closed the back gate, a calamitous act for the city's *feng shui*. Like all other Peking old-timers, Auntie Chin knew that the city's fortunes could not possibly be reversed until the gate was reopened. At long last, this finally occurred in 1948. Auntie Chin steadfastly argued that

Summer Palace

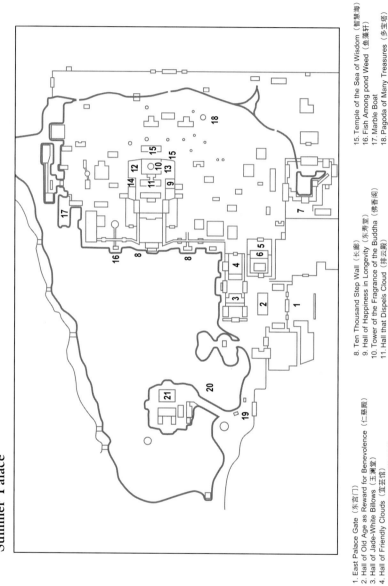

1. East Palace Gate (东宫门)
2. Hall of Old Age as Reward for Benevolence (仁慈殿)
3. Hall of Jade-White Billows (玉澜堂)
4. Hall of Friendly Clouds (宜芸馆)
5. Garden of Virtue and Harmony (德和园)
6. Hall of Pleasant Smile (颐东殿)
7. Garden of Harmonious Pleasures (谐趣园)

8. Ten Thousand Step Wall (长廊)
9. Hall of Happiness in Longevity (乐寿堂)
10. Tower of the Fragrance of the Buddha (佛香阁)
11. Hall that Dispels Cloud (排云殿)
12. Hall of Flowery Jade (玉花殿)
13. Revolving Archive (转轮藏)
14. Pavilion of Treasure Clouds (宝云阁)

15. Temple of the Sea of Wisdom (智慧海)
16. Fish Among pond Weed (鱼藻轩)
17. Marble Boat
18. Pagoda of Many Treasures (多宝塔)
19. bronze cow (铜牛)
20. Seventeen Arch Bridge (十七孔桥)
21. Temple of Dragon King (龙王庙)

the reopening of the back gate and the subsequent decision to reinstate Peking's capital status were intrinsically linked, signifying that China was on the verge of enjoying a strong and unified government.

Kidd has a shock for Auntie Chin. In 1948, Kidd had made arrangements to teach English to the director of the Summer Palace. The director had promised Kidd that in lieu of fees, he would arrange for him to live in one of the park's pavilions. Most of the villas had been assigned to important KMT officials (including Chiang Kai Shek, who spent only 3 days there). However, above the back gate was a whole upper floor, glassed in and facing the countryside to the north and the pine forest to the south. It was in a sorry state of repair, but the director had it restored and landscaped. As a couple of gatekeepers were hired for Kidd, the director also decided that the gate might as well be opened to the public.

"Auntie Chin listened with her mouth open through most of my story. 'The fate of Peking determined by a foreigner!' she cried when I had finished. 'The fate of all China ordained by my nephew-in-law!'" After several minutes of thought, Aunt Chin took her leave of Kidd. "She appeared tired, and perhaps puzzled, but no longer angry. 'I know you're not really to blame,' she said."[1]

The Summer Palace has clocked up many changes over time. The first imperial notice of the beautiful scenery came about in 1153, when a Jin emperor built a traveling pavilion here. The Mongols under Kublai Khan dredged the lake and created park grounds. The Ming rulers added their imprint by shaping the lake garden.

As Qian Long was very fond of the scenery in south China, he ordered his engineers to tailor the grounds to resemble the West Lake in Hang Zhou. In an act of filial piety, Qian Long constructed many pavilions and buildings to celebrate his mother's 60th birthday.

Alas, just like the Old Summer Palace, the Anglo-French troops leveled most of Qian Long's buildings in 1860. Only two famous structures, the Bronze Pavilion (actually the Pavilion of the Treasure Clouds 宝云阁 or *bao yun ge*) and the Temple of the Sea of Wisdom Temple (智慧海 or *zhi hai si*) remain standing. A late Qing poet alluded to the desolate sight of the grounds of the Summer Palace:

Jade fountain laments and Kun Ming mourns;

Alone, the bronze ox stands on guard amidst thistles and thorns.

In the hills of blue iris, the fox calls in the night;

Beneath the bridge of soft ripples fish weep at night.

玉泉鸣咽昆明塞，

唯有铜犀守荆棘；

青芒阁里狐夜啼；

綉漪桥下盘空泣。

The park enjoyed a renaissance when Empress Dowager ordered its reconstruction in 1886. She spent the warm seasons here, though this was to be short-lived. In retaliation for her support of the Boxers, the allied occupation forces destroyed the rebuilt palaces and desecrated Buddhist images and temples. Once the foreign troops withdrew from Peking, the Empress Dowager again ordered the reconstruction of the park in 1902 and enthusiastically threw herself into supervising the project. For this reason, the Summer Palace most reflects the traditional architecture of the late Qing on the eve of the invasion of Western design.

Under the terms of his abdication, Henry Pu Yi retained possession of the Summer Palace. After his assumption of official duties as English tutor, Reginald Johnston soon found himself saddled with the thankless job of supervising the maintenance of the Summer Palace. In order to defray costs, he opened the grounds to the public for a fee in 1924. However after Pu Yi's subsequent flight to Tianjin and the disarray of the Peking government, the Summer Palace became a much neglected sight well suited to the tastes of romantic poets like David Kidd and John Blofeld. In the 1950s, the People's Government renovated the Summer Palace.

Most people enter the Summer Palace through the East Palace Gate (东宫门 or *dong gong men*) through a *pai lou* inscribed with the words for water and hills. In imperial times, the imperial family alone could enter the grounds through this entranceway while commoners have to make their way to the North Palace Gate (北宫门 or *bei gong men*) where Kidd had his house. There are two bronze lions identical to those in the Forbidden City and cast during the reign of Qian Long. The large stone slab also dates from his reign and was brought here from the ruins of the Old Summer Palace. Bronze qilin also greet you as you arrive.

The first building is the Hall of Old Age as Reward for Benevolence (仁寿殿 or *ren shou dian*), which served as the audience hall for the Empress Dowager and emperor Guang Xu. Before the ill-fated Reform Movement of 1898, the Empress Dowager sat behind a yellow screen placed between herself and Guang Xu. After the Empress Dowager seized the reigns of State from Guang Xu, she herself sat upon the imperial yellow throne. In the courtyard are bronze dragons, lions, qilin, deer and phoenix. The hall is decorated in accordance with the taste of the Empress Dowager.

Behind this hall to the left is the Hall of Jade-white Billows (玉澜堂 or *yu lan tang*) where Guang Xu was confined during the Empress Dowager's visits to the Summer Palace. The hall once looked out upon a fine vista with the lake and far off temples with the effect of a traditional painting come to life. In 1904, the Empress Dowager ordered the view to be walled up, presumably to rub the emperor's face in his captivity. To the right of the hall is the Hall of Friendly Clouds (宜芸馆 or *yi yun guan*), which was the residence of Guang Xu's empress. They despised each other deeply.

Immediately behind the Hall of Benevolence and Longevity is the Garden of Virtue and Harmony (德和园 or *de he yuan*), which is a three-storied building where Peking Operas were performed. As with the Pavilion of Pleasant Sounds in the Forbidden City, the operas took place on the central storey while benevolent deities descended from the top floor and demons from the bottom. The Empress Dowager watched the plays from her golden lacquered throne in the Hall of Pleasant Smile (颐乐殿 or *yi le dian*), which is decorated with a phoenix, a symbol of the Empress Dowager, and a hundred birds paying homage to the phoenix. Nearby are several cages with clockwork birds. Princes and other Manchu nobility watched the performances from the side rooms. During the last years of the Qing dynasty, famous Peking opera performers, like Yang Xiao Lou (杨小楼) and Tan Xin Pei (潭鑫培) gave special command performances for the Empress Dowager.

To the northeast is the Garden of Harmonious Pleasures (谐趣园 or *xie qu yuan*), a separate garden within the Summer Palace. It was built in 1751 as a replica of the Ji Chang Yuan (寄畅园) at Wu Xi, again reflecting Qian Long's fondness for the landscapes of southern China. On the low white stone bridge at the eastern end of the pond, there are the characters Know Your Fish (知鱼 or *zhi yu*) in the calligraphy of Qian Long. This phrase refers to a famous exchange between Zhuang Zi and his friend Hui Zi. The two sages were standing on a bridge looking at fish cavorting in the waters below. Zhuang Zi mentioned casually that the fish looked happy. Hui Zi challenged his friend by saying, "You are not fish. How can you know if they are happy?" Zhuang Zi effortlessly replied, "But you are not me. How do you know that I don't know the fish are happy?"

From here, I suggest that you retrace your steps to the lakeside and continue in a clockwise fashion around the peninsula. The Hall of Happiness in Longevity (乐寿堂 or *le shou tang*) is where the Empress Dowager resided from spring to autumn. The courtyard once contained many magnolias, but all were destroyed in 1900 except for a single white one and a single purple one. The Hall is decorated with dark wood tables and stands. The western inner chamber was the Empress Dowager's bedroom and is kept as it was in her day. The eastern inner chamber is decorated with low wooden benches and low kang-style tables, which are said to be representative of Manchu interior design. The eastern courtyard of the Hall of Happiness in Longevity contains many peonies while the northern wall has a moon gate shaded by a wisteria that leads to the apartments of Li Lian Ying (李莲英).

Li was a corrupt eunuch whose position was unassailable as the favorite eunuch of the Empress Dowager. He is said to have been an impoverished street child. One day, he saw a group of soldiers laying into people with their whips so as to clear the road. Behind them was an elegant sedan chair borne by six men carrying a court eunuch to his palatial home. It was that moment that Li decided to swap his poverty and certain death from deprivation (as well as his family jewels) for the advantages of being a court eunuch. Once a servant at the Great Within, he seized the opportunity to rise to power.

There is a story that shows how Li Lian Ying handled the Empress Dowager. The Empress Dowager had first opposed the introduction of electricity into the city on the grounds that these foreign methods would upset the *feng shui* balance of the city. In particular, she believed that the electric lights and wires would introduce too strong of a *yang* influence. After receiving the customary squeeze, Li Lian Ying agreed to let a foreign electric company set up a generator on the grounds of the Summer Palace. They installed electric lamps with different colored light bulbs in the Hall of Delightful Longevity while the Empress Dowager was on one of her trips to the city. Upon her return, Li pointed out to the Empress Dowager one of the lamps hanging from the ceiling. "What color would you like?" he asked. Thinking little of this hocus-pocus, the Empress Dowager took the bait and said red. With a flick of a switch, Li turned on a red light bulb. This little game was then played with other colors. The foreign invention made the grade and she granted permission for other electrical lamps to be installed in the Summer Palace. (Electricity elsewhere in the capital did not arrive until 1920.)

Many tour guides go to great extremes about the luxurious habits of the Empress Dowager. It is said that at each meal, several hundred dishes were presented, usually with the Empress Dowager tasting only two or three. I agree that such waste is appalling but there is nothing new under the sun. I know a chef who was seconded to an army base for high-ranking officers. He was kept in virtual house arrest while being called to prepare dishes made from the finest ingredients in the world. "You would not believe the waste!" he said with amazement. "They would take only one or two bites of fine salmon or goose liver pate and throw the rest away." Plus ça change …

From here you enter the Ten Thousand Step Walk (长廊 or *chang lang*), a lengthy covered promenade. It was originally built in 1750 and has been reconstructed countless times. The beams of the corridor contain 1,400 different paintings of flowers, landscapes and scenes from Chinese history and literature. It is said that the promenade is so long that a couple could fall in love by the time they reached the halfway point and agree to be married by the time they reached the end. While not mentioned in the adage, I imagine that a separation and divorce settlement could be wrapped up on the way back. For couples, it's probably best to come to the Summer Palace in two cars, just in case.

At the midway point along the promenade, there is the entranceway that takes you up to the peak of Longevity Hill to the four-storied Tower of the Fragrance of the Buddha (佛香阁 or *fo xiang ge*). The buildings on Longevity Hill are roofed with glazed yellow tiles indicating a place for the imperial family. As a general guide, most of the timber framed buildings date from the Empress Dowager's reconstruction of 1886, while Qian Long erected the solid tile framed structures in honor of his mother's 60th birthday.

As you ascend Longevity Hill, you pass two *pai lou* and two bronze lions, cast during Qian Long's reign and said to be the finest in Peking. The first courtyard is in front of the Hall that Dispels Clouds (排云殿 or *pai yun dian*). In the next Hall of Flowery Jade (玉花殿 or *yu hua dian*), the Empress Dowager received congratulations on her birthday. Through the windows, you can still see her unopened gifts with their yellow paper slips signed by well-wishing toadies.

Going upward to the next level, you arrive at the Tower of the Fragrance of the Buddha. In the middle of the tower is a bronze statue of Avalokeitasvara with Tibetan style paintings of Chinese deities. On your right hand side is the Revolving Archive (转轮藏 or *zhuan lun cang*). The pavilions contain revolving sutra libraries that once held classical Buddhist texts. The main hall was for prayers.

On your left hand side in a courtyard surrounded by green pavilions, you can see the famous bronze Pavilion of Treasure Clouds raised on a high platform of carved marble (宝云阁 or *yu yun ge*). The pavilion was cast in 1750, possibly under Jesuit supervision and is a perfect replica of a timber pavilion with respect to its doors, end tiles, roof-ridge creatures and beams. In prior years, Lamaist monks prayed here on the 1st and 15th of every lunar month. The pavilion survived the sacking of the Summer Palace in both 1860 and 1900. Fortunately its luck still held out in 1945 when Japanese occupation forces tried to take the pavilion to Japan but only got as far as Tianjin.

Behind the Tower of Fragrance of the Buddha is the Temple of the Sea of Wisdom (智慧海 or *zhi shi hai*), which also dates from 1750. It is entirely covered with green and yellow tiles most in the form of small niches with seated Buddhas. On the roof, there are dragons and dagobas along with blue and purple tiles amongst the familiar green and yellow.

Returning to the east side of the lake, you continue on in the long corridor. In the Pavilion for Listening to Orioles originally dating from the 18th century but rebuilt in 1902, there is a restaurant that serves imperial cuisine of mediocre quality. At the end of the corridor, jutting out into the lake is a small pavilion called Fish Among Pond-weed (鱼藻轩 or *yu cao xuan*). Arlington and Lewisohn record that Wang Guo Wei (王国维), a Hanlin Scholar and the Dean of Peking University committed suicide here in 1928 in despair that China was "on the verge of going 'Red'." Wang was also a professor of German philosophy, which might explain things.

On the southernmost edge of the peninsula stands the Marble Boat, built by the Empress Dowager from funds taken from the budget of the imperial navy. The marble base was built in 1755 and originally had a Chinese style timber superstructure. This was destroyed in 1860, and rebuilt in 1893, in the style of a western style Mississippi paddle-steamer with stained glass windows. Many tour guides vilify her misappropriation of funds though they forget that if the Qing navy had access to such funds, this would simply have resulted in yet another Qing vessel at the bottom of the Yellow Sea during the Sino-Japanese War of 1895. At least the misappropriation of funds gives us something to shake our heads about now. If you turn to the west along the paved path, you come to the famous Camel-back Bridge, a frequent object of photography from the 19th to the 21st centuries.

The back lakes and western slopes of Longevity Hill were badly damaged in 1900 and have been less restored than the more popular sites on the east. Naturally, it has a more appealing air of desolate ruins and nostalgic sorrow. The Temple Where Clouds Gather (排云寺 or *pai yun si*) is not far to the west of the Sea of Wisdom Temple. Only one of three great bronze Buddhas in sculpted niches from the 18th century now remain. The temple courtyard is filled with pines and cypresses. To the north is a castellated gray brick wall with a pavilion on top. This is the Gate of Exuding Pleasure. Further north is the Pagoda of Many Treasures (多宝塔 or *duo bao ta*), a seven storied octagonal pagoda surrounded by ruins from the 1900 occupation.

There still remains the southeast section of the Summer Palace. Passing through the Garden of Harmonious Pleasure and arriving back at the entrance, you follow the east shore of the lake. You will pass the famous bronze cow (铜牛 or *tong niu*), which was cast and set on its present site in 1755 by the order of Qian Long. The ox is a symbol of both stability and flood prevention. It is said that after the Great Yu of 2205 B.C. had stemmed the floods in Anhui province, he set up an iron cow to prevent the recurrence of flooding and to ensure that sea-monsters would not get up to any mischief. Do ponder this for a moment. Here this statue, a part of living folklore, commemorates an event that occurred over forty-two centuries ago.

Across the Seventeen Arch Bridge (十七孔桥) you can see 500 stone lions carved on the marble balustrades, and, like the Marco Polo Bridge, apparently no two lions are alike. Once across the bridge, we find the Dragon King Island, so-called because it houses the ancestral hall of the Dragon King (龙王庙 or *long wang miao*), who governs rain and received the pleas of the emperors during times of drought. An image of the Dragon King, with blue face and imperial yellow robes, is to be found inside the temple. From the Dragon King Island we can enjoy a grand vista of the Summer Palace.

18

THE WESTERN HILLS

THE WESTERN HILLS HAVE GIVEN solace and delight to visitors for thousands of years. During the Jin and Liao dynasties, the ruling houses first sculpted the natural beauty of the landscape into an imperial park. Gradually, countless monasteries were built as a refuge for Buddhist monks. Later, as the Qing declined, many temples faded into nothingness. These days, the Western Hills are a fabulous place for hiking. Some of the old temples are reviving the custom of renting rooms to wayfarers.

You should first make your way to Fragrant Hills Road (香山路 or *xiang shan lu*), which runs to the north of the Summer Palace. While driving to the hills, you can get a glimpse of the Jade Fountain Pagoda of Wonderful Height (玉泉妙应山塔 or *yu quan miao ying shan ta*), a delightful white stone structure with Laotian touches in its stupa and spires. Behind it stands the Jade Peak Pagoda (玉峯塔 or *yu feng ta*). The entire grounds were first used as an imperial retreat during the Liao dynasty and were last revamped by Qian Long in 1752.

Banish any thought of visiting these sights or the Buddhist temple relics on these hills. Since 1949, high cadres have reserved the grounds for their private use. When the cares of the world prove too burdensome, Jiang Ze Min is said to take a stroll here. But do take a pair of binoculars along to view the forbidden fruit of Qian Long's architectural creativity.

Further to the west, there is a right hand turn that will take you into Village of the Goddess (娘娘村 or *niang niang cun*) which is a nice residential district for retired military personnel. Here you can find the tomb of emperor Jing Tai (景泰陵 or *jing tai ling*), the younger brother of emperor Cheng Zheng (the one who managed to get himself taken hostage in Mongolia). When Jing Tai died in 1460, people in Peking widely believed that he was poisoned by his brother in a new

Western Hills

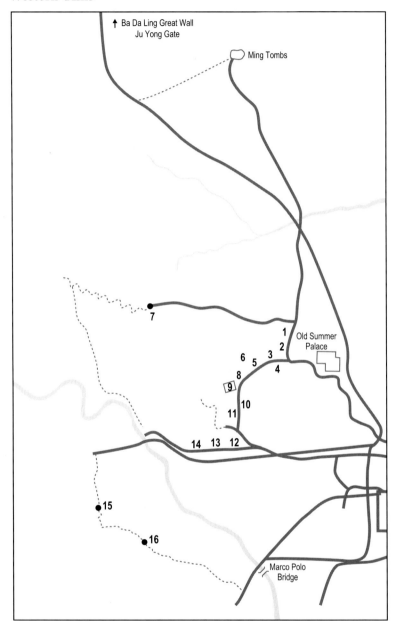

↑ Ba Da Ling Great Wall
Ju Yong Gate

Ming Tombs

Old Summer Palace

Marco Polo Bridge

1. Jade Fountain Pagoda of Wonderful Height（玉泉妙应山塔）
2. Jade Peak Pagoda（玉峰塔）
3. Tomb of Emperor Jing Tai（景泰陵）
4. Temple of Excellent Clouds（妙云寺）
5. Temple of the Sleeping Buddha（卧佛寺）
6. Garden of the Cherry Valley（樱桃沟）
7. Temple of the Great Perception（大觉寺）
8. Temple of Azure Clouds（碧云寺）
9. Fragrant Hills Park（香山公园）
10. Round City Martial Training Grounds（闭城演武亭）
11. Eight Great Sites（八大处）
12. Temple of Acquiring Grace（承恩寺）
13. Temple of the Sea of the Law（法海寺）
14. Tomb of Tian Yi（田义墓）
15. Temple of Clear Pools and Wild Mulberry（潭柘寺）
16. Temple of the Ordination Platform（戒台寺）

Fragrant Hills Park and Environs

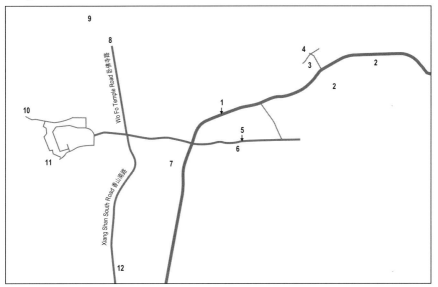

1. Fragrant Hills Road（香山路）
2. Jade Peak Pagoda（玉峰塔）
3. Village of the Goddess（姑娘村）
4. Tomb of Emperor Jing Tai（景泰陵）
5. Jade Springs Mountain Road（玉泉山路）
6. Temple of the Excellent Clouds（妙云寺）
7. Beijing Botanical Gardens（北京植物园）
8. Temple of the Sleeping Buddha（卧佛寺）
9. Garden of the Cherry Valley（樱桃沟）
10. Temple of Azure Clouds（碧云寺）
11. Fragrant Hills Park（香山公园）
12. Round City Martial Training Ground（闭城演武亭）

low of sibling rivalry. Jing Tai's grave was modeled on the simple format of a prince's burial site rather than an imperial tomb. In 1475, posthumous rehabilitation brought some imperial themes to his tomb, such as imperial dragons added to his stele and the tortoise statue. By following the path to the north, past a *pai lou* and a croquet court, you will come across the tumulus that encloses Jing Tai's remains. The south part of the tumulus is square; representing earth, while the north part is round, representing heaven.

Take any left hand turn onto Fragrant Park Road to Jade Springs Mountain Road (玉泉山路 or *yu quan shan lu*). On the south side of the road you come to the ruins of the Temple of the Excellent Clouds (妙云寺 or *miao yun si*), a forlorn and forgotten Buddhist temple built during Qian Long's reign. The main gate and hall, as well as the side halls, are shaded by ancient pine trees. However, now the temple serves as a ramshackle residence for local folk. Dogs and chickens amble about hungrily and washing dries on a clothesline strung between marble balustrades.

Eight Great Places

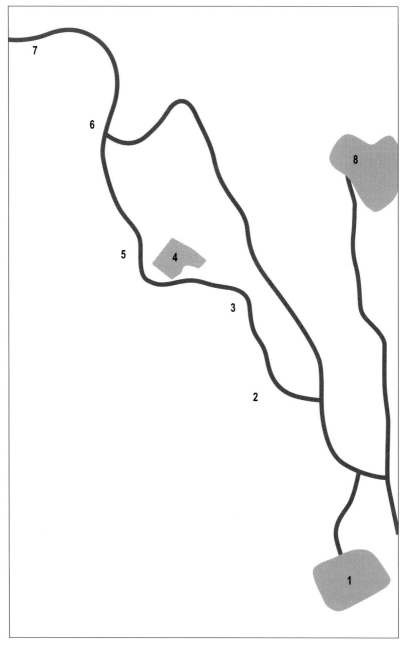

1. Temple of Everlasting Peace （长安寺）
2. Temple of Divine Light （灵光寺）
3. Nunnery of the Three Hills （三山庵）
4. Temple of Great Compassion （大悲寺）
5. Temple of the Dragon King （龙王寺）
6. Temple of the Fragrant World （香界寺）
7. Precious Pearl Cave （宝珠洞）
8. Temple of the Proof of the Fruit （证果寺）

Further to the north you arrive at the Peking Botanical Gardens (北京植物园 or *bei jing zhi wu yuan*), a pleasant park that is notable as the place where the rehabilitated last emperor, Henry Pu Yi, worked as a gardener before being hounded to his death by red guards. On the north end of the park is the Temple of the Sleeping Buddha (卧佛寺 or *wo fo si*). This temple's origins are as old as the Temple of the Origin of the Law in the Western Chinese City. Originally founded in the Tang dynasty, emperors such as Kublai Khan, Cheng Hua (成化) of the Ming and Yong Zheng of the Qing all authorized restoration projects. You approach the temple through an avenue of cypress trees leading to a green and yellow tiled *pai lou*. In keeping with Chinese tradition, the first hall contains a statute of the Maitryea Buddha and the second a Sakaymuni Buddha along with statutes of Guan Yin, temple guardians and disciples. In the third hall you will find the "sleeping" Buddha, reportedly cast in 1321.

It is something of a misnomer to refer to such statues as "sleeping Buddhas." They depict the last earthly moments of the historical Buddha as his spirit enters nirvana. While less frequently seen in China, this posture is common throughout the Theravada countries of South East Asia. The feet of the Buddha were said to have had 108 distinguishing marks, hence the representations of footprints in Buddhist temples and the gifts of shoes, some of which are said to be gifts from Qing emperors.

To the northwest of the temple is the Garden of the Cherry Valley (樱桃沟 or *ying tao gou*). In the early Ming, a Taoist monastery was established here, of which nothing remains except the park grounds. In the park is the Cliff of White Deer (白鹿园 or *bai lu yuan*) so named on account of a Taoist sage who made a landing here while flying on a white deer. Here you can see some caves where Taoist monks once meditated. The park is also dotted with pavilions, which make enjoyable picnic sites.

Further to the northwest is one of the loveliest monasteries in the Western Hills; the Temple of the Great Perception (大觉寺 or *da jue si*), originally built in 1069 and reconstructed both by Kang Xi and Qian Long. It is an exceptionally peaceful respite from the traffic, crowds and old crows of downtown Peking.

On our way in through the east-facing gate, there is an interesting botanical specimen, a "cypress tree adopting a wisteria." The inner core of the cypress, which was planted during the Liao, has become hollow over time. As trees age, they draw the primary nutrients from the outer rings of the bark, which continue to grow and expand while the inner core decomposes. In the case of this cypress tree, a wisteria took root in the hollow and now the two trees grow entwined, an appealing symbol of Buddhist pacifism and tolerance.

Inside the main hall are the life-sized Three Great Buddhas (三世佛 or *san shi fo*) made of wood with intricately carved backgrounds. These magnificent statues dated from the 15th century. Looking up, you see the inner roof with a dragon rotunda and about 30 wooden bodhisattvas.

The next hall contains more gorgeous woodwork. In the center is the Amida Buddha, seated upon an ornate throne and with a spirit screen to his back, decorated with elephants, dragons, bodhisattvas and a garuda at the very top. Two standing bodhisattvas flank Amida. The one on the right is Avalokitesvaras, the bodhisattva of great compassion whose other emanations include the Goddess Guan Yin as well as the Dalai Lama. On the left is Mahasthamprapta. The three statues date from Qian Long's day. The back of this hall was used as storage for Buddhist scriptures. Facing the back doorway is a clay statue of the bodhisattvas of the seas, earth and heaven.

The next hall is the Altar of Great Compassion (大悲坛 or *da bei tan*), which hosts an exhibition on Buddhism. In the next courtyard, you will come across a gingko tree planted during the Liao. By going through the door on the right and up the hill, you will find some Tibetan style funerary pagodas, the final resting place of monks who lived in the temple. Encased in a white brick structure is a Liao dynasty stele from the 11th century, recording the construction of the temple. In this area, a fresh water spring flows through dragon spouts into a white stone reflecting pool where lotus flowers grow abundantly in the summer. At the top is a temple to the Dragon King, whose command over water brings the mountain springs under his jurisdiction.

Returning to the south side of the temple grounds, you pass a number of buildings that have been converted into restaurants as well as overnight rooms, where visitors can enjoy the unfolding of the evening in the Western Hills.

Heading to the south, you find another religious sight inspired by Indian architecture. Do be careful when pronouncing the Chinese name of the Temple of Azure Clouds (碧云寺 or *bi yun si*) since a slip with the tones turns it into the Temple of Contraception. The temple was built in 1366 and has experienced many reconstructions since then. At various times during the Ming and Qing, court eunuchs misappropriated funds or extorted money from the citizenry in order to gain merit by renovating the temple. (This tendency to squeeze people for construction projects reminds me of the Peking Tax Bureau's "tax audit" in the 1990s when the municipal authorities were searching for additional funds for the construction of more ring roads. But I digress.)

We pass over a bridge flanked by two distinctively carved Ming stone lions and come to the Gate of Heavenly Guardians where Marshals Ha and Heng stand watch, with nostrils and mouths probably locked and loaded against evil demons.

The figures were sculpted in 1513. In the next hall a copper bronze of the Big Belly Buddha (or Maitreya Buddhas if you please) with a gaping navel, greets you. Unlike other depictions of this incarnation of the Buddha, this Ming era statue is intricately decorated.

By crossing another bridge you come to the Red Clear Tower (丹青阁 or *dan qing ge*) constructed during the Ming in accordance with the design of imperial palaces. Inside is a statue of the Sakyamuni Buddha giving his first lecture after his enlightenment in the Benares Deer Park. Murals depict the Tang Buddhist monk Xuan Zang, who spent more than a decade traveling through Central and South Asia in search of Buddhist sutras. His memoirs, a Record of Western Travels (西游记 or *xi you ji*) are an interesting account of kingdoms and customs long since disappeared from the rest of Asia. The travelogue itself spawned fables about a monk traveling beyond Tarim Basin in the company of a monkey and pig, each of whom could both reason and talk. Behind the Sakyamuni is a statue of Guan Yin.

The next courtyard contains a compound where Qian Long stayed on his visits to the temple. It is landscaped to resemble the gardens south of the Yang Tse River. A bodhisattva hall is the next structure along the temple's central axis and is followed by the Sun Yat Sen Memorial Hall, containing an exhibition on Dr. Sun's life. Photographs document when his coffin lay in state here waiting for the completion of his grand tomb in Nanjing.

Behind this memorial is an impressive marble *pai lou* that is unique among Peking's patrimony. The steps lead you to the Diamond Seat Pagoda (金刚宝座塔 or *jin gang bao zuo ta*) built in 1748. The foundation of the pagoda is square shaped and it is crowned with Indian and Tibetan style pagodas. When Sun's body was shipped to Nanjing, his clothes were buried in one of the vaults of the pagoda so that Peking could claim that a relic of the Father of the Country would always remain in the city.

Retracing our steps to the Sun Yat Sen Memorial, the doorway to the left leads to a spring fountain with bridges, rockeries, streams and juniper trees. The doorway on the right takes you to the Hall of the Arhats (罗汉堂 or *luo han tang*). Inside are 500 statues of Arhat, or disciples of the historical Buddha made from clay on wooden frames. Each arhat is in a different pose with a different expression, making this hall one of the most magnificent collections of Qing sculpture. Do try to arrange your day so that you can study and reflect upon the personalities of these sages as conveyed through the sculpture. What I find here is far more impressive than any number of SS troopers in terracotta stone at Xian.

Right next to the Temple of the Azure Clouds is the Fragrant Hills Park (香山公园 or *xiang shan gong yuan*), which was an imperial hunting ground from the

12th century until Qian Long's era. It was Qian Long who enclosed the park with a wall and then, for additional merit, built a number of the temples inside the grounds. Towards the east of the main entrance is the Glorious Temple (昭庙 or *zhao miao*) built in a Tibetan style in 1780 by Qian Long for use by visiting lamas. Nearby is the Glazed Tile Pagoda (流漓塔 or *liu li ta*).

To the north of the Glorious Temple is the Pavilion of Introspection (见心斋 or *jian xin zhai*) built during the reign of the Jia Qing emperor of the Ming. There is a semi-circular pool where water spouts from a dragonhead. To the south are the ruins of the Fragrant Hills Temple (香山寺 or *xiang shan si*), which was originally built in 1186 and then rebuilt in 1312 and then again in 1745 by Qian Long. The temple was another victim of the vandalism of foreign troops that occupied Peking in 1900. Only several terraces remain.

A long hike around the park brings you to Incense Burner Peak (香炉峯 or *xiang lu feng*), the highest peak in the park. It is best to make the hike in the autumn, on a week day, when the leaves of the smoke tree (黄栌树 or *huang lu shu*) turn red and the skies overhead are a deep clear blue. A weekend excursion is likely to result in seeing more people than scenery.

Returning to the Fragrant Hills South Road (香山南路 or *xiang shan nan lu*), you will see a fortress on the east side of the street. This is the Round City Martial Training Grounds (团城演武亭 or *tuan cheng yan wu ting*) built by Qian Long in 1749 to prepare his troops for his campaigns against the Tibetans. The training grounds include a circular structure with massive crenulated walls and a watchtower to the west from which Qian Long watched his troops practice archery. Qian Long anticipated long sieges against the Tibetans, whose traditional style multi-storey houses were formidable fortresses. With the assistance of Tibetan prisoners of war, Qing troops built mock replicas of Tibetan fortresses so that they could practice scaling typical Tibetan fortifications. These efforts proved successful, as Qian Long was able to reassert suzerainty over Tibet. In the general vicinity of the Round City, you can come across some of these mock replicas. (There is one on the north side of the Xiang Shan Road just past the turning to Jing Tai's tomb at the Eastern Happiness Apartment Complex.) Inside one of the halls of the Round City is an exhibition of swords, halberds, and matchlocks used by the Qing army.

Towards the south in a neighborhood with many residential complexes for military personnel, you arrive at the Eight Great Sites (八大处 or *ba da chu*) named after eight temples situated on the south side of the Western Hills. The Eight Great Sites make an outstanding destination to watch the folks of Peking enjoying their leisure time.

The first site at the park is no longer open to the public as it is being converted into a hospital. In the car park at the main entrance, you can see the gate to the

Temple of Everlasting Peace (长安寺 or *chang an si*), which was founded in 1504 in honor of Guan Yu and Guan Yin.

After entering the main gate and turning to the left, you come to the Temple of Divine Light (灵光寺 or *ling guang si*), which was originally founded in the 7th century and destroyed by foreign troops in 1900. In a showy advertisement for religious tolerance that simply did not exist in daily life, the PRC built a pagoda here to house a box containing a tooth relic of the Buddha. In the middle of the goldfish pond is a pavilion. Both now and in past years, Buddhist monks released fish in a symbolic ritual of gaining enlightenment and as an act of meritious kindness to sentient beings. Some of the fish are said to be over 100 years old. If they have anything like a historical memory, then these ancient fish must wince whenever they spy a foreigner lurking about the pond's edge.

At the foot of the pagoda, young devotees wearing Planet Hollywood t-shirts and Levis and elderly folks hobbling with walking sticks prostrate themselves on the stairway and gradually make their way to the incense burners. Monks with shaved heads and tawny yellow robes walk about busily taking care of the pagoda grounds while fingering their rosaries bead by bead.

The next sight up the hill is the Nunnery of the Three Hills (三山庵 or *san shan an*), founded in 1155 and reconstructed in the Yuan, late Ming and mid-Qing periods. Nowadays it functions as a carnival style house of mirrors. In little alcoves are games of chance. Its one notable connection with the past is marble stone called the Water and Cloud Stone because, when wet, the stone's veins become visible.

In walking up to the next temple, you pass vendors selling fruits of the season along with traditional and modern beverages. On the path there are more little stalls with games of chance as well as a small shooting gallery where the targets are Hitler, Mussolini, Goering and Tojo, which is an optimistic sign given that a few young Chinese, unaware of the implications, are said to write in praise of Hitler in internet chat rooms.

The Temple of Great Compassion (大悲寺 or *da bei si*), first established in the Liao dynasty, has a beautiful stone entrance carved with all types of mythical and realistic beasts. In the main hall sit the Three Buddhas. The arhats on the left and right are the work of the Yuan dynasty sculptor Liu Yuan (刘元). In the courtyard, an 800-year-old gingko tree, as ancient as the arhat carvings, is decorated with a myriad of red cloth lanterns.

After a turn in the path you come to the Temple of the Dragon King (龙王寺 or *long wang si*), more formally known as the Dragon Spring Nunnery (龙泉庵 or *long quan an*). A temple was first built into the side of the hill here in 916 and restored in 1425. Its name comes from a mountain spring that gushes through a dragon spout into a pool located inside the main gate. The adjoining hall contains a shrine to Guan Yin. On the temple grounds is a teahouse where you can rest before continuing with your ascent.

The next site is the Temple of the Fragrant World (香界寺 or *xiang jie si*). This is the main temple of the group, founded in 610 and restored continuously until the last major renovation by Qian Long. In the courtyard is a Tang stele with an early carving of Avalokitesvara as a man. The legend attached to the stele is that while traveling by this temple, Kang Xi suddenly had a premonition that a valuable relic was buried here. After a night of furtive digging, the stele was duly uncovered and installed here.

A steep climb takes you to the Precious Pearl Cave (宝珠洞 or *bao zhu dong*), which is approached through a Ming wooden *pai lou*. Here there is a stele set up in memory of the mad monk Hai Yu (海岫), who was an exorcist employed by Kang Xi to subdue enemy spirits. By working our way to the back of the temple, you come across a cave shrine in which a white plaster statue of Hai Yu can be seen. It is said that within the plaster is the body of Hai Yu, which formerly had been kept in Temple of Mercy and Kindness (慈善寺 or *ci shan si*) about one hour's walk from here.

After death, Hai Yu's corpse did not decompose, presumably as a consequence of his sanctity. The face of this "mummy" remained in tact and the body seemed to be full fleshed, thereby supporting the Buddhist belief that the body of a devoted believer will exist for all time. Accounts written in the 1920s say that the body was dressed in dusty imperial yellow robes and attracted considerable attention from both the foreign community (as gawkers) and the local community (as supplicants). According to legend, this was the body of Shun Zhi after he secretly abdicated the throne and withdrew to this temple after the death of his empress. The story seems to build on Shun Zhi's own attraction to Buddhism and his retiring nature.

In actual fact, Qian Long granted the posthumous title of "Ghost King" (鬼王 *gui wang*) to Hai Yu. The attendants in the cave say that the mummy began to decompose in the 1980s. When this was discovered, it was coated with plaster and removed to this dark and dry cave for better preservation. The plastering method is also claimed to preserve the actual features of the monk. It sounds more like a P.R. job for another casualty of the Cultural Revolution.

From the area around the cave you have a magnificent view of Peking. For those too tired to climb back down the mountain, a ski lift will bring you back to the base. From the main entrance, it is another twenty-minute walk to the last and possibly most peaceful site in the park. The Temple of Proof of the Fruit (证果寺 or *zheng guo si*), founded in 620 by a Taoist hermit named Lu, derives from a legend that two acolytes of a monk revealed themselves to be sons of the Dragon King, turned themselves into snakes and ended a drought. Through the Ming era, court officials came here to pray for rain.

To the southwest of the Eight Great Sites on Mo Shi Kou Avenue (莫市口大街), you pass the Temple of Acquiring Grace (承恩寺 or *cheng en si*) a Buddhist temple from the mid Ming but closed for renovation. From the road you can see a decrepit stone tower on the east side of the courtyard.

Further to the west is the Temple of the Sea of the Law (法海寺 or *fa hai si*) founded in 1439, which, like the Temple of Great Compassion in the Western suburbs, preserves Ming architectural motifs. In the years before the Cultural Revolution, photographs show that the temple was filled with statues, incense burners, altars, banners, candlesticks, incense coils and sacramental utensils. The Red Guards emptied all of these contents from the temple and destroyed them. However, in a typical display of a lack of thoroughness, they had fortunately forgotten about the walls on which were painted frescoes of the Buddhist spirit world. The Three Buddhas, Guan Yin and a host of other spirits float on pink and blue colored clouds, their poise calling to mind Serindian frescoes in Dunhuang, the Tarim Basin and the storerooms of the British Museum. Flowers, springs, mountains as well as cloud streams circle about the meeting of bodhisattvas discoursing on the way. This is a place to linger once your eyes have grown accustomed to the darkness and can pick out delightful images from the charming imagination of Ming court artists.

Returning to Mo Shi Kou Avenue, a little further to the west, an imperial marble *pai lou* announces the presence of the Tomb of Tian Yi (田义墓 or *tian yi mu*), the final resting place of the eunuch Tian Yi (田义), who was buried in 1605, and other colleagues. Upon entering the grounds, you find two Ming marble statues standing "on guard" face to face. On the right is a civilian official wearing the cap of a Confucian scholar and holding an ivory tablet. The other is a military official in formal robes and standing with a sword. These two guardians are an abbreviated version of the line of statues placed along the spirit way at imperial tombs. Behind the statutes is a marble *pai lou* with carvings of lions. Continuing on, you find the memorial stele to Tian Yi inside a circular pavilion and stele to two other eunuchs on each side.

At the far side of the cemetery is an assortment of marble steles, urns and pedestals with five small round shaped tumuli. Since one of the tombs has been excavated, you can climb down to see its chambers. The simplicity of this tomb structure will be a considerable contrast when you visit the Ming and Qing tombs. Returning to the main gate, there is a small walkway on the east with various stone animals and carvings with Buddhist motifs. On the west side is an exhibition in Chinese on the history of the phenomenon of court eunuchs.

Heading to the far southwest, you arrive at the Temple of Clear Pools and Wild Mulberry (潭柘寺 or *tan zhe si*). The foundation of the temple dates from the Han Dynasty (265–319) thereby giving rise to the saying that first there was the Temple of Clear Pools and Wild Mulberry, and then came the City of Tranquility (i.e., Peking). The temple was rebuilt during the Liao dynasty after a period of neglect. The existing buildings date from the Ming or Qing.

At the foot of the hill are the Upper and Lower Pagoda grounds, containing 75 stupas from the Liao, Yuan and Ming dynasties

A venerable gingko in the Temple of the Clear Pools and Mulberries.

set amidst a grove of pine trees. One of the pagodas is the tomb of Miao Zhen (妙严), one of Kublai Khan's daughters and a deeply religious person.

Ascending the path to the temples are wonderful scenes of mountain vistas and temple buildings. On the central axis, you come to the Hall of the Heavenly Guardians and then the main temple, housing a modern statue of the Sakyamuni Buddha. Beside the main hall is an imperial gingko, planted during the Yuan dynasty and conferred with an imperial title by Qian Long. On the other side is another tree, the emperor's wife, so-called because it grew a new branch around the time of the birth of each Qing emperor. No, I don't see the connection either.

The highest point along the central axis is the Vairocana Tower from which you have panoramic view over the temple and surrounding countryside. On the western axis are halls dedicated to Guan Yin among others. In the Hall of the Dragon King is a fish carved from a stone with high copper content. Striking the fish at different spots is supposed to produce different notes of the scale that were said to be a spiritual remedy for droughts and illnesses.

Qian Long built a palace along the eastern axis and frequently spent autumn evenings here. In the 1920s and 1930s, foreigners frequently rented halls for a weekend retreat and arrived with all sorts of material comfort and servants. George Kates describes a clash of cultures that arose during his stay at the temple. His friend, an elderly monk, came to him:

> "A large party of foreigners has just arrived below," he said. "Should we not together go to greet them?"
>
> We went quietly, he leading me literally by the hand — so great was his simplicity — and we were interrupted by a chattering group from my own embassy. Its members, well known to me, immediately and completely misinterpreted the scene. They had come here, with cocktails and crested china, napkins and ice, all the appurtenances of a traditional legation picnic; and white-robed servants were even at the moment laying a feast in a handsome yellow-tiled open pavilion, heavy with trailing festoons
>
> Soon my monk and I drifted away. There was nothing at the moment to hold me; and the temple was quite large enough for me to think only intermittently of my foreign friends that evening … . Finally I went up to my high courtyard of the four great trees, the doors were bolted, and slumber came early and was sweet … .
>
> My slumber was not to last for the rest of the night. After an interval, I became aware that my compatriots from the embassy were indulging in a prolonged celebration. Perhaps the voices were fewer, though by this time they were buoyant and happy, familiarly invoking Daisy, to give them her "promise true", all quite delighted at the mere thought of a bicycle built for two. The unremitting Buddhist clappers were still pounding away, the incantation, a little more rapid, going on endlessly. The priests, too, were apparently quite content. Surely the two worlds were not destined to meet that evening.

Nor are they likely to meet these days. Many Chinese merry-makers shout and holler at each other while walking about these sacred grounds. Happily more people come here to burn incense and pray before the gentle Buddhist gods than was the case a decade ago, though, sadly, a pervading sense of propriety has not yet taken root in all those who come here.

The temple is the site of the climax in *Peking Picnic*, a novel set among the presumptuous foreign members of the legations in the 1930s. Ann Bridge, the author and, in real life, the wife of Lord O'Malley, weaves a picture of such utter detachment from Chinese life that the narrative becomes almost compelling in its grotesque aloofness from its cultural setting. It is also a worthwhile read to gain some insight into the indignation that foreigners provoked among Chinese during that period (and now).

The Temple of the Ordination Platform (戒台寺 or *jie tai si*) is another one of my favorites in the Western Hills. Built facing the east, the temple was originally founded in 622. In 1070, a monk named Fa Jun (法钧) came to this spot for meditation and to teach the dharma. Given the clarity of his teachings and good-natured demeanor, many acolytes came to seek his instruction. In that year, he constructed a terrace for the ordination of monks. After his death, the temple fell into ruin until rebuilt in 1441 by Cheng Tung and then again by Kang Xi and Qian Long, all of whom were frequent visitors to these grounds. Generally most of the buildings are of Qing vintage while the ordination terrace dates from the Ming.

The temple did not develop proportionately around its central axis. For this reason, it is a wondrous collection of winding pathways built on the slope of the mountain leading to ancient pines and cypress trees, pavilions, pagodas, rockeries and prayer halls, all majestically overlooking the Peking plains.

A 1,000 year old scholar tree stands in front of the main gate where Marshals Ha and Heng again are on duty, guarding the temple with Tibetan swords. After giving a nod of recognition to these security guards, you pass into the first courtyard which is decorated with a 500 year old Dragon and Phoenix Tree as well as assorted stele and lilac bushes. The ensuing halls follow the usual pattern: the four heavenly kings with the Maitreya Buddha, the Three Buddhas and Avalokitsvara (or Guan Yin in this case). Between the Three Buddha Hall and the Hall of Guan Yin are the ruins of the Hall of Ten Thousand Buddhas, in front of which stand two dragon pines. The right hand tree is called the Sleeping Dragon Pine (卧龙松) since it suggests to the poetic mind a dragon in slumber. As the tree is over 1,000 years old, the dragon will be experiencing an ultimate Rip Van Winkle experience when he wakes, and not a pleasant one at that. Walking along the terrace to the north of the these pines, you come across two more famous trees, the Nine Dragon Pine (九龙松), consisting of a myriad of large trunks, said to resemble nine dancing dragons, and the Pine Embracing the Pagoda, an ancient tree held up with numerous supports as it reaches out to protect Fa Jun's funerary pagoda.

Continuing up the slope, you come to the Hall of the Ordination Platform (戒台殿 or *jie tai dian*) where Buddhist novices took their vows in the old days. Acolytes who passed scriptural and meditation training were ordained during an elaborate initiation ceremony. The abbot and other high-ranking monks took their seats on the platform while the monks meditated and chanted for an entire evening. Part of the ritual included placing burning incense on the shaved heads of the novices, who had to continue their meditations without any reaction to the painful burning sensation on their scalps. This part of the ceremony resulted in scars on which hair would never grow back. Such scars were the tangible proof of the initiation of a monk. (Similarly, the status of felons used to be recorded by the application of red hot iron brands on their arms or temples as eternal marks of their status, which were sometimes covered up with tattoos. This explains the on-going association of tattoos with gangsters and triads.)

In the niches of the platform are 113 Tianjin Zhang clay figures of gods, goddesses and heroes. This particular folk sculpture began in the late 1700s when the Shao Xing authorities cashiered a local magistrate called Zhang Wan Quan (张万全) for his outspokenness. Zhang fled to Tianjin with his family and attempted to make ends meet through

A gargoyle with Chinese characteristics.

several odd jobs. He eventually sculpted and sold small figurines based from real life. He incorporated colored clay in order to make his figurines life-like.

His son Zhang Ming Shan (张明山) took up the art and raised it to new levels, earning himself the nickname Clay Figure Zhang (泥人张 or *ni ren Zhang*) in the process. The Zhang family has entered its fourth generation of clay sculptors and the work of the family has come to be recognized as a national treasure. Interestingly, the artwork of the Zhangs took in the influence of soliders from the Eight Power Allied Army in 1900. One correspondent recalled seeing for sale clay figurines that replicated the uniforms and appearances of foreign troops so much so that individual officers could be recognized. In the 1960s, Zhang family members were introduced to leaders such as Mao, Zhou En Lai and Chen Yi.

Finally, situated around the Hall of the Ordination Platform are various shrines to deities from the Taoist pantheon, such as the God of Wealth and the God of the North Star.

The temple rents rooms for overnight visitors though at the time of writing, it has yet to obtain the license to rent to foreigners. Once this piece of administration is settled, the temple will make for another tranquil spot where you can sense the ghosts of Old Peking reappearing from the ether.

19

THE MING TOMBS

THE MING TOMBS, OR THE Thirteen Tombs (十三陵 or *shi san ling*) as they are called in Chinese, lie about 50 kilometers to the north of Peking, off the highway that leads to the Great Wall at Badaling and the Ju Yong Pass. The Ming Tombs and the Great Wall are commonly shoehorned into a single trip for tour groups. This is a big mistake as the grandeur of both sights merits more time.

In the past, the Ming Tombs accommodated independent travelers who wished to linger around the more obscure tombs and reflect on the impermanence of imperial grandeur and political glory. These days, a new imperial edict has been issued. Aside from three of the tombs, apparatchiks have locked the other tumuli behind iron gates and wooden doors. If you happen upon a tomb that has not been locked, someone will quickly scurry forward and slam the gate in your face unless you can make it inside before them.

It is said that the villagers near each tomb are the descendants of people who were hired to care for the final resting places of the Ming imperial line. Perhaps this imbues a sense of inherited nobility that results in the villagers arrogantly waving away the curious or even blowing smoke from their foot long pipes at a stray visitor lacking the power of a Hino bus behind him. Once, poetic romantics could camp overnight next to the tombs. Now unannounced visitors have to apply for permits from the unnamed Kafkaesque "relevant authorities."

Each imperial tomb of the Ming and Qing era were built on a similar design. A typical tomb consists of two portions: a front square-shaped courtyard symbolic of the earth, and a circular shaped tomb mound, representing heaven. The front courtyards contain above ground buildings used for the veneration of the emperor as well as the storage of various utensils and clothes for such ceremonies. The tomb mounds usually have a stele in the foreground and are surrounded by a

Ming Tombs

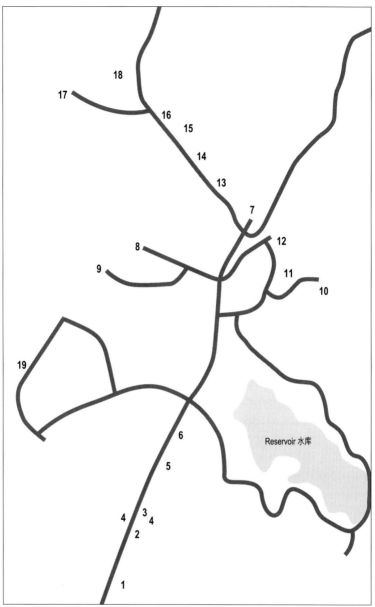

1. marble pai lou
2. Great Red Gate（大红门）
3. Stele Pavilion
4. hua biao（华表）
5. spirit road（神道）
6. Dragon and Phoenix Gate（龙凤门）
7. Chang Ling（长陵）
8. Ding Ling（定陵）
9. Zhao Ling（昭陵）
10. De Ling（德陵）

11. Yong Ling（永陵）
12. Jing Ling（景陵）
13. Xian Ling（献陵）
14. Qing Ling（庆陵）
15. Yu Ling（裕陵）
16. Mao Ling（茂陵）
17. Kang Ling（康陵）
18. Tai Ling（泰陵）
19. Si Ling（思陵）

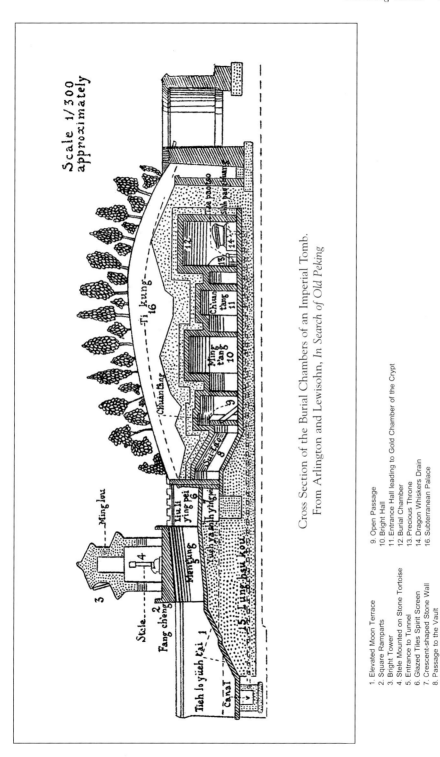

Cross Section of the Burial Chambers of an Imperial Tomb.
From Arlington and Lewisohn, *In Search of Old Peking*

1. Elevated Moon Terrace
2. Square Ramparts
3. Bright Tower
4. Stele Mounted on Stone Tortoise
5. Entrance to Tunnel
6. Glazed Tiles Spirit Screen
7. Crescent-shaped Stone Wall
8. Passage to the Vault

9. Open Passage
10. Bright Hall
11. Entrance Hall leading to Gold Chamber of the Crypt
12. Burial Chamber
13. Precious Throne
14. Dragon Whiskers Drain
16. Subterranean Palace

crenellated wall. A wall like a spirit screen marks the formal entranceway into the underground chambers that lead to three vaults. Many of the outer two vaults are carved with Buddhist motifs. The burial vault contains the coffins of the emperor and an empress or two. The tombs were constructed to replicate some of the structures from the Forbidden City as a symbolic bridge between life and death.

The founder of the Ming dynasty, Hong Wu, was buried in his capital, Nanjing. No one knows the final resting place of the second emperor, who was dethroned by his uncle Yong Le. Yong Le, of course, selected the site of his imperial tomb during the construction of the capital. As discussed in the chapter on the Western Suburbs, the unfortunate Jing Tai was buried in a forgotten and undistinguished vault designed in the style for nobles rather than emperors. In the valley containing the Ming Tombs, there are altogether the tombs of thirteen emperors as well as various empresses, concubines and their offspring.

Three Ming tombs are open to the public. These are Chang Ling (长陵) , the resting place of Yong Le as well as the first tomb constructed in the valley; Ding Ling (定陵), the tomb of the emperor of Wan Li which has been excavated; and Zhao Ling (昭陵), the final resting place of emperor Long Qing, which has undergone extensive renovations. The other tombs are behind lock and key and dismissive puffs of smoke.

On the way to the Ming Tombs, you sample another bit of historical irony. Sitting amidst the car fumes of the super highway is a statute of Li Zi Cheng on horseback. Li was the one-eyed "bandit emperor" who invaded Peking and brought about the collapse of the House of Ming. His own Shun dynasty lasted for only 100 days before he had to retreat from the Qing army and residual Ming forces who allied themselves with their northern neighbors. The Communist orthodoxy had declared Li to be the leader of a people's rebellion since some farmers flocked to his standard in the revolt against Ming corruption and inefficiency. As if deliberately flaunting the cause for the collapse of the Ming, Peking's city planners have put his enormous statue next to the off ramp for the Ming Tombs.

Once you have left the highway, you come to a marble *pai lou* built in 1540, which can be seen from some distance away. The marble has been carved to replicate timber roofing, and the columns are decorated with three dimensional lions and serpents. Further behind is the Great Red Gate (大红门 or *da hong men*), which is the official entrance into the necropolis. The valley has been beautifully landscaped in contrast to early 20th century photographs showing a dust-laden barren valley. The central gate was reserved for the processions carrying deceased emperors while living emperors entered through the right-hand side. All officials had to dismount at this gate and carry on by foot, which surely intensified the sense of power and grandeur of the deceased emperors.

Next, you come to the stele pavilion, with two roofs and four doors. The stele is inscribed with Yong Le's name and was built in 1425, but not erected until 1436. On the back is a poem written by Qian Long, describing each of the tombs in the valley. The pavilion is flanked on four sides by *hua biao* similar to those next to the Gate of Heavenly Peace in Tian An Men Square. These and other similarities were intentional so as to produce comparison between the locus of the ruling imperial power and the glory of the deceased emperors.

Further on, you will come across the famous spirit road lined with carved stone figures. At the beginning of the spirit way is a stone column (望柱 or *wang zhu*) which is an architectural innovation of the Song dynasty. In order of progress, you come across, in double pairs of kneeling and standing figures: lions, *xie zhi* (獬豸) (an animal with a lion's head and a horse's body), camels, horses, elephants and *qilin* (麒麟). Next, there are statues of four military officials, four civil officials and four imperial councilors, whose robes were embroidered with symbols of office and who wear flat hats representative of their ministerial status. The civilian officials each hold an ivory tablet (笏), which was used for ensuring that, in the presence of the emperor, their less pure spiritual substance, *viz.*, breath, was deflected from the emperor's presence.

Each sculpture was carved to reflect the ideal of each creature present rather than an actual animal. Some Western writers were sharply critical of the supposed lifelessness of the statues. The criticisms miss the point. As they served to represent symbolic spirits, each official and animal statue were designed to approximate the Confucian ideal of perfection for each creature.

Beyond the Spirit Way is the Dragon and Phoenix Gate (龙风门 or *long feng men*) which leads you into the tombs proper. In the Qing Tombs, each separate tomb has its own Dragon and Phoenix Gate whereas there is only one here for all the Ming Tombs.

Our next stop should be the first tomb in the valley, Chang Ling (长陵), the final resting place of Yong Le, who was buried here in 1424. You pass through a triple entrance gate and pass under another gate and enter the courtyard in front of the Hall of Imperial Favor (祾恩门 or *ling'en men*). The Hall and its courtyard are modeled on the Hall of Supreme Harmony in the Forbidden City. Off to the left and right ends of the courtyard are yellow porcelain paper burners where paper "gold and silver" ingots were burned as gifts to the deceased emperor.

In the Hall of Imperial Favor, the living emperors performed rites for Yong Le and sought his blessings. In establishing a new capital, Yong Le sought to make his tomb an impressive statement of imperial power and built triple terraces in marble, like those in the Forbidden City and the Altar of Heaven. The emperor walk way is carved with dragons and phoenixes. Inside the hall are 60 *nan mu* (南

木) wood columns each nearly 13 meters tall. All beams, brackets and window frames were made of precious *nan mu* wood.

Behind the hall is the Gate of the Lattice Star (灵星门 or *ling xing men*), consisting of a wooden gate with marble columns. Passing through, you arrive at a courtyard in front of a single stele tower, a square gray stone fortification bearing a red walled pavilion containing the memorial stele to Yong Le. Beneath the tower is a stone altar with replica of the five precious objects for use in funerary rites: a pair of candlesticks, a pair of vases and an incense burner.

The tower before the tumulus is built in the same manner as a city gate tower. On either side stand the crenellated ramparts that protect the grave area with its underground chamber and the coffin of the deceased emperor. By taking a tunnel in the center of the tower, you ascend stairs on the east or west sides to the top of the tower and view a memorial stele to Yong Le placed in the red pavilion. The top of the stele is carved with two dragons among clouds and two characters: Great Ming (大明 or *da ming*). The inscription on the body of the stele identifies the tomb as being the resting place of Yong Le by using the emperor's posthumous name.

In keeping with the symbol for heaven, the tumulus is perfectly round. It is richly planted with oaks and grass with the walkway along the wall providing grand views of the valley and mountains. Beneath the mound lies the body of Yong Le, who presumably has never been disturbed by vandals or thieves.

Back towards the Spirit Way is Ding Ling, the final resting place of Wan Li whose reign spanned 47 years of neglect and corruption. He died in 1620. Ding Ling is the only excavated tomb in the valley and tends to be thronged with tourists.

The archeological project for the excavation of Ding Ling owes much to sheer luck.

In keeping with imperial custom, the remains of Wan Li's empress were already buried in the tomb since she predeceased the emperor. Detailed instructions were needed on how to reopen the tomb for Wan Li's burial. These instructions were carved on a marble stele that was apparently left in the drainage tunnel by mistake rather than being kept under lock and key. In 1956, the tomb was undergoing routine maintenance repairs when several engineers discovered a hidden tunnel near one of the tomb's drains and found the tablet and hence the secret for reopening the tomb. (I can imagine some poor Ming official going through countless sleepless nights of worry on account of his misplacing this stone.)

An archeologist friend of mine once told me that upon opening of the main chamber, the sudden rush of oxygen and dampness supposedly caused the disintegration of frescoes, silks and other fragile artwork. If this story is true, it explains why the Chinese have been reticent in excavating other sites. Indeed, should the PRC government choose to do so, there could be a constant flow of exhibitions of dazzling ancient artifacts uncovered each year.

The general layout of the tomb is consistent with Chang Ling. When you descend into the burial hall, you will come across three chambers. At the entrance of the first chamber is a triangular shaped gate that leads to the throne chamber in the central vault. Here are three marble thrones for Wan Li and the two empresses buried with him. In the rear vault are three coffins set inside 26 lacquered wooden chests filled with yellow clay (to simulate gold) and jade. In a separate exhibition hall are various artifacts found inside the tomb.

The next tomb open to the public is Zhao Ling, the burial site of the emperor Long Qing, who reigned from 1566 to 1572, and his three empresses. You pass through a triple bridge beyond the tortoise stele and come to the tombs that had been in ruins until a restoration project gave the site a squeaky clean brand new appearance that is not to everyone's taste. However, few people come here and it is a restful place for meditation and reflection, especially after a snowfall when the bare trees and temples wear a crystal coat of ice. The troops of Li Zi Cheng destroyed Long Qing's memorial stele in 1644. In keeping with his committed renovation efforts, Qian Long ordered its reconstruction in 1787. A fine pine and cypress grove is thriving on the top of the tumulus. The dragon and phoenix marble slab in front of the Hall of Heaven's Favor is one of the most exquisite carvings of its type in any imperial tomb.

Your chances of gaining entry to the other imperial tombs will depend upon the luck of the road. Little villages, taking their names from the nearby tomb, have sprung up all throughout the valley. These are interesting farming villages where the people live in traditional courtyard houses made from tamped mud bricks. However, the villagers appear jaded from the tourist trade and resolutely block access to many of the tombs. If you are able to arrive here on a bicycle, you might be able to discreetly come across a tomb where someone has forgotten to bolt the gate. It is quite a shame since these other tombs, often in ill repair and shrouded in natural forest growth, are more pleasing than the ones that are officially open.

To the east of Chang Ling are three tombs. The furthest to the east is De Ling (德陵), which is the resting place of the emperor Tian Qi who died in 1627, and his empress Zhang, who was strangled on the orders of the last Ming emperor as Li Zi Cheng's troops breached the Peking city walls. Yong Ling (永陵) is the burial site for Jia Qing, who died in 1567 and his three empresses. Jia Qing's reign

Repository for expired achievements.

marked one of the low points of "Ming despotism" with 17 high-ranking officials slowly beaten to death. Perhaps Heaven showed its displeasure by using the elements to destroy the ceremonial hall in Yong Ling. Jing Ling (景陵) is the tomb of emperor Xuan Zong and his empress Sun. A village now surrounds his memorial stele.

On the road to the north of Chang Ling, there are six tombs. You first come to Xian Ling (献陵) the resting place for Yong Le's successor and sickly son Ren Zhong, who lasted on the throne for only nine months. It is one of the simplest tombs in the valley and has an unusual feature of a small hill intruding between the sacrificial hall and the tumulus.

Qing Ling (庆陵) is the tomb of the emperor Tai Chang, who ruled for less than a month in 1620. It is said that he was poisoned. Since Tai Chang did not have time to plan his burial grounds, his remains were placed in the vault originally intended for the emperor Jing Tai who was dethroned after his brother Zheng Tong, was released from captivity in Mongolia.

Yu Ling (裕陵) is Zheng Tong's resting spot. The hall over the memorial stele and the ceremonial hall collapsed long ago. Further north is Mao Ling (茂陵), which houses the remains of the indolent and passive emperor Cheng Hua who ruled from 1464 to 1487. The next tomb on this route is Kang Ling (康陵), the resting place of the emperor Zheng De (deceased 1521) and his empress. It is said the Zheng De was a wastrel who spent his years watching horse races and cock fights. Aside from the hall for the memorial stele, all other above ground structures have collapsed. This tomb provides lovely views of the valley and the surrounding persimmon orchards. Finally, off the main road you will find Tai Ling (泰陵).

Far off to the southwest side of the valley is Si Ling (思陵), the tomb of the emperor who was the end of the Ming line. The Qing regent Dorgon ordered that the remains of Chong Zhen and his empress be buried in one of the unfinished concubine tombs in the valley. Dorgon also made a bow in the direction of the eunuch constituency in the Forbidden City by burying Chong Zheng's loyal eunuch Wang Zhen En near his master. All that survives is the tumulus, the marble altar with its urn, candlestick holders and vases as well as a memorial stele. It is my favorite on account of its dilapidated and forlorn appearance that testifies to the impermanence of this world's vanities.

20

THE GREAT WALL

THE GREAT WALL OF TEN Thousand Miles (万里长城 or *wan li chang cheng*) is a destination that cannot be omitted from any trip to China. Boswell recorded the thoughts of Samuel Johnson about the signal importance of a visit to the wall:

> He expressed particular enthusiasm with respect to visiting the wall of China. I caught it for the moment, and said I really believed I should go and see the wall of China had I not children … . 'Sir', (said he), by doing so you would do what would be of importance in raising your children to eminence. There would be a luster reflected upon them from your spirit and curiosity. They would be at all times regarded as the children of a man who had gone to view the wall of China. I am serious, Sir.' [1]

Not all Englishmen were so persuaded. In the 1930s, Bernard Shaw gave these replies to questions posed by Hesketh Pearson after his trip to China:

> "Did you see the Great Wall?"
> "I flew over it in an airplane"
> "Interesting?"
> "As interesting as a wall can be."

With no disrespect to Shaw, the Great Wall *is* interesting. It commences from the seacoast at the Pass of the Mountains and Seas (山海关 or *shan hai guan*) on the Bo Hai Gulf and continues towards the Tibetan highlands passing through four provinces as well as Peking and Tianjin municipalities. The distance between these two points, measured in a straight line is 1,332 miles. But taking into account the various windings of the walls as well as reinforcing loops and arms, the wall has an aggregate distance of no less than 2,500 miles. The main wall, excluding the various appendages, would extend from New York to Denver or from London to St. Petersburg.

A winter morning on the wall.

While it conjures images of antiquity, the Great Wall also was the basis for a delightful urban myth in the 1980s. It was rumored that the Grateful Dead intended to hold a concert on the Great Wall, which presents to the wistful mind the pleasing picture of Jerry and the band performing Franklin's Tower with the backdrop of the Great Wall twisting through mountain ranges. It is also immensely satisfying to think about the encounters between Dead Heads and farmers and workers from the nearby villages. Alas, alas.

During the Warring States Period, the various kingdoms in China built extended walls as a tactical defense. After the unification of China in 225 BC, emperor Qin Shi turned his attention to the perennial military threat posed by northern nomads. He ordered the existing walls to be linked and extended across the northern boundary in order to prevent invasions by the Huns (匈奴 or *xiong nu*), a race who were sometimes described in earlier historical documents as red-haired and light skinned. (This latter point as well as archeological finds of graves of red-haired plaid dressed people raises many implications about a partial non-Mongoloid origin of the Chinese people.) The walls were made of pounded dirt, as was the case of the Yuan city walls.

Qin Shi implemented this construction project with a vigorous adherence to schedules and brutal treatment for infractions. For example, slow execution was the penalty for workers who failed to show up on time. One group of forced laborers, who were late because of floods and storms, spent an evening or two agonizing over their dilemma in the wilds outside the construction camp and decided "what the hell, let's launch a rebellion." Incidentally, it almost succeeded.

The wall required twenty years of construction, the deployment of over 300,000 troops and the forced labor of all the criminals as well as scowling literati in Qin China. Brutal work conditions resulted in countless casualties, thus giving rise to the grim saying that the wall is the longest cemetery in the world. It is said that the Mandate of Heaven evaporated because of Qin Shi's harsh policies. Qin Shi's successor and son lost power almost as quickly as Hua Guo Feng, with the result that after the collapse of the Qin, the wall became a decayed feature along the North Chinese border for several centuries. Chinese records indicate that it was repaired seven times between the 2nd and 7th centuries. Having rested political power from the Mongols, the Ming were keen to rebuild the 1,400 year old wall with bricks and stone. Once again, the construction sites were death camps where one human life was expended for every six inches. Bodies were simply dropped into the foundations of the wall.

As a defensive structure, history shows that the wall was about as successful as the Roman attempt to keep out Celtic barbarians with Hadrian's Wall. Armies from the north overthrew both the Song and Ming dynasties. On the other hand, the Great Wall does symbolize, rather emphatically, traditional Chinese introversion.

The main sites within reach from Peking date from the Ming, and occasionally you can spot a brick inscribed with a date from Wan Li's reign. Every 360 Chinese feet, watch and defense towers were constructed. Information was dispatched along the wall by smoke signals or by cavalry. A Tang era legend relates a story of a boy who cried wolf, where one emperor set off false alarms, in this case warning fires, along the wall in order to amuse his concubines. After being tricked like this several times, his disillusioned troops did not respond when enemy troops actually arrived.

The three most commonly visited portions of the Great Wall are at Ba Da Ling (八达岭), Mu Tian Yu (慕田峪) and Si Ma Tai (司马台). The Ba Da Ling sight is the closest to the city and can be easily combined with a trip to the Ming Tombs.

On our way to the Great Wall at Ba Da Ling, we come to the Ju Yong Pass (居庸口 or *ju yong kou*) which is situated in the Jun Du Mountains. The pass has been a key entryway into China proper. As far back as the Spring and Autumn Periods it was under the control of the Yan State, which had first erected a wall to keep out northern invaders. Various governments from the Han to Sui dynasties linked this wall with other sections of the Great Wall. The existing village and walls were built in 1368 just after Zhu Yuan Chang had forced the Mongols out of north China. Various Buddhist and Taoist temples were built throughout the pass, but were destroyed during the Japanese Occupation and the subsequent socialist purges.

The Tower that Straddles the Road (过街塔 or *guo jie ta*), also called the Cloud Terrace (云台 or *yun tai*), bears witness to the cosmopolitan culture that existed in North China. Built in 1345, the tower originally was the foundation for a large Lamaist temple, which burnt down in 1702. The tower now appears like a marble bridge with a hexagonal gateway underneath. Inside the tower are outstanding bas-reliefs of Buddhist deities. A garuda spreads his wings at the top of the gateway and is surrounded by two Naga serpents. The bas-reliefs consist of, going from bottom to top, the Four Heavenly Kings, four Buddhas and then the wheel of life at the crest of the tunnel. On each wall is also carved Buddhist prayers in Chinese, Sanskrit, Tibetan, Uighur, Mongolian and Tangut, which was a Chinese-based writing system of a Tibetan people who had an independent kingdom in the 11th century in Gan Su. Scholars have yet to decipher the language of this long vanished kingdom whose echoes can be felt in this tunnel. A stele set up outside the tower by the Qing announces it as "the first fortress of the world."

By climbing up through the main gate, you will come across a series of rebuilt temples with new statues inside, such as Guan Yu, the God of Horses, Guang Yin, the God of the North Star, Liu of the East Taoist Immortals and others memorializing military heroes from Chinese history. On the south face wall are rusted iron cannons, which perhaps are a legacy of Jesuit technology. Further to the north is the main entranceway to the Great Wall at Ba Da Ling.

Both Mu Tian Yu and Si Ma Tai entail a long day trip from Peking, and the trips themselves are worth the effort. As you approach the mountain pass, you will travel through delightfully rustic scenery. In these hills and valleys you can see traditional rectangular-shaped Chinese houses, made from mud bricks and topped with graceful wings on the gable ends. While the highway and its traffic sometimes create a misplaced sense of modernity, Chinese houses using this type of construction have existed on the Peking plains for over two thousand years.

Occasionally, the villages have an inspiring appearance when they are built along the sides of a stream flowing down from the mountain. On roadside stands, people sell fruits and vegetables in season. I recall one trip where the golden autumn light at sunset enhanced the hue of peaches, persimmons, almonds and walnuts stacked on the stands by the roadside while a crisp blue sky deepened in color overhead. Some of the farmers sold ring-necked pheasants that looked out regally from their cages. In mid summer honey taken from wooden stacks of beehives is on sale in quart jars. Scarecrows stand guard in yellow and green corn fields, and apples hang heavy on the branches in the orchards. Goats gambol on the hills while anglers try their luck with fishing rods in the rushing streams. In the winter, the snow shrouded villages look deserted but for the smoke rising from chimneys. The popular trees, which stand like exuberant green sentinels on the roads, seem like barren and forgotten exiles when winter winds whip through their branches.

After scenes such as these, the sudden appearance of the gray stone crenellated walls and towers will break into your reverie. Their ascent along craggy cliffs will hold your eye for quite some time before you begin your hike.

Some bright spark has thought to install ski lifts at these sites, which takes away the necessary exertion to appreciate the work that went into constructing the wall. Once you gain access to the wall, the walkways range from recently renovated to badly dilapidated. You can take along bedding or a tent and camp along the wall, or spend an evening in one of the towers imagining the ghosts of those stationed here so long ago.

In his memoir *Elegant Flower*, Desmond Neill describes a trip to the Great Wall at Ba Da Ling in November 1948. In those days, the wall was only accessible by train. Neill and his fellow travel partners clambered on board an unheated train at the old railway station near Zheng Yang Gate. In their carriage were Mongol and Chinese troops clothed in thickly padded green overcoats and fur hats being sent to fight the PLA beyond the wall. The passenger capacity of the train was stretched beyond the limit. Despite the intense cold, people were seated on the top of the carriages and on the platforms between carriages.

While Neill savored the sight of the wall in its winter glory, a Chinese soldier rode up on a Mongolian pony and appeared to be in an agitated state. When questioned about their intentions, Neill simply stated that they were there to see the Great Wall, an answer that relieved the soldier somewhat, though he then pointed out the dangers of "bandits" to the north. With dramatic gestures, the soldier also motioned to the grave of a comrade in arms near the wall. Off in the distance, Neill could faintly hear the thunderous sounds of bombs and artillery fire. It seemed that once again, strife and upheaval were coming down into Peking from the north.

Neill and his companions managed to catch a military train back to Peking. A well-nourished and self-absorbed general condescended to let them share his overheated carriage. Cups of tea were offered as Neill was whisked to a Peking where rank and file soldiers slept in the misty parks around the Altar of Heaven while their commanders contemplated routes of escape.

21

SIGHTS FURTHER AFIELD

To the North of Peking

A TRIP TO THE MING Tombs and the Great Wall can also include a visit to the Silver Mountain Pagoda Forest (银山塔林 or *yin shan ta lin*) in Chang Ping County (昌平县). Originally, the Liao rulers built a monastery here called the Temple of the Law's Transformation of Chan (法化禅寺 or *fa hua chan si*). In 1125, the Jin rebuilt the temples and the surrounding area flourished with 72 temples, which went into decline during the transition from the Ming to the Qing. During the Japanese occupation, the last remaining wooden temples were burned down. Nowadays the site is visited for the Liao and Jin stone pagodas that stand in the temple's courtyards and have somehow been well preserved.

The pagoda "forest" consists of seven pagodas built in a valley with a mountain range cradling them in the background. The mountains were poetically nicknamed the "iron wall and silver hill" (铁壁银山 or *tie bi yin shan*) because of the impression created by dark mountains rimmed with snow. The monks buried under the pagoda were all adherents to the Chan (or Zen in Japanese)(禅) school of Buddhism, which advocates meditation as a tool to reveal the limitations of dualism existing in linear speech and logic. Legend says that the first Chan monk in China was the 28th Chan patriarch named Bodhidharma who arrived in South China from India. He is usually depicted in paintings with a bushy beard and eyebrows and a quizzical frown. According to legend, he crossed the Yang Tze River on a single thin reed, thus giving us a parallel story of Jesus on Lake Galilee.

Chan Buddhism delightfully challenges the acolyte to break dualistic thought through a sudden flash of enlightenment (or *satori* in Japanese) that attends meditation on an impossible riddle. One Chan meditative technique well known in the West is the question "What is the sound of one hand clapping?" which has become trivialized from overexposure. A more salient example of Chan's irreverence of formality is the monk Rinzai who was upbraided by an abbot for taking a leak in front of a Buddha statue. Rinzai shot back: "As the Buddha nature is everywhere, where am I supposed to pee?".

Likewise, Chan monks stressed non-attachment in many of their parables: Ryokan, a Zen master, lived the simplest kind of life in a little hut at the foot of a mountain. One evening a thief visited the hut only to discover there was nothing in it to steal.

> Ryokan returned and caught him. "You man have come a long way to visit me," he told the prowler, "and you should not return empty-handed. Please take my clothes as a gift."
>
> The thief was bewildered. He took the clothes and slunk away.
>
> Ryokan sat naked, watching the moon. "Poor fellow," he mused, "I wish I could give him this beautiful moon."

Monks of Chan Buddhism spoke in riddles in order to break through subjectivity, which is the prison of each person's skull and its preconceived thoughts. A potent story tells of a university professor who seeks out a Chan monk named Nan-in to inquire about Chan.

> Nan-in served tea. He poured his visitor's cup full, and then kept on pouring.
>
> The professor watched the overflow until he no longer could restrain himself. "It is overfull. No more will go in!"
>
> "Like this cup," Nan-in said, "you are full of your own opinions and speculations. How can I show you [Chan] unless you first empty your cup?"[1]

With this sampling of Chan teaching in mind, let's go and pay homage to the Chan monks resting here.

The first two pagodas date to the Jin dynasty and are octagonal in shape, with decorations of floral patterns and bodhisattvas. Around these pagodas you can still discern the foundations of the original halls. Behind them is a pedestal that was inside a temple hall and supported statues of the Three Buddhas, which have long since vanished. The middle pagoda dates from the Jin as does the left hand pagoda in the back while the right hand pagoda is from the Liao. Further back are funerary pagodas in the Tibetan style. The openings of ancient wells can still be seen as well as a Liao pagoda on the far right.

There is excellent hiking through the nearby mountains. Along the way you pass ancient carvings of Maitreya Buddhas as well as caves that were once used as meditation centers by Chan monks. A wintertime visit is to be recommended in order to appreciate the contrast of colors between the "iron and silver."

To the East

Beyond the eastern suburbs of Peking Municipality are two sites that merit the time and effort to visit them. The first is the Temple of Solitary Joy (独乐寺 or *du le si*) in Ji Xian County, Tianjin Municipality and the centerpiece of the historical district in the heart of the county's main city. While the entire town deserves a day's leisurely stroll, the real treat is the temple located near the west gate. Built in 984, the Temple of Solitary Joy is one of the oldest wooden Buddhist temple in China. Entering the three-storied main hall, you are greeted by a 16-meter tall statue of Avalokitasvera (or Guan Yin) with ten heads. On the walls are Ming era murals depicting the Buddhist pantheon. On our way out of the main hall you pass a Liao seated Maitreya Buddha.

Continuing along the central axis, there is a small shrine to the god *Wei Tuo* (韦驮) who was given the task of fulfilling the Buddha's instructions throughout the universe. In the next temple is a reclining Buddha.

Further out in Zun Hua County (遵化县), He Bei Province, you arrive at the East Qing Tombs (东清陵 or *dong qing ling*), which are located about 120 kilometers from Peking. In all, it is a two to three hour drive to the main entrance of the tombs. You will have to travel through some of Peking's most unappealing suburban sprawl.

Before the conquest of China, the Qing emperors were buried in Sino-Manchu tombs in Shenyang. Once installed in Peking, the Qing court consulted with astrologers and geomancers to find a proper burial for the new imperial house. They chose this site, with the tall peaks of the Chang Rui Mountains (昌瑞山) serving to block malicious spiritual forces from the north. In all, five emperors, 14 empresses and 136 concubines are entombed here. The construction of the first tomb began in 1662 and the last burial occurred in 1909 for the Empress Dowager.

The tombs are modeled closely on the Ming Tombs, though they do not rise to the same level of exquisite design. While it is a speculative question, I sense that the Qing Emperors might have paid more attention to the details within the burial vaults. The tombs of Qian Long and the Empress Dowager have been excavated and provide us with a glimpse of the marvelous carvings in the inner sanctum as well as the pervasive influence of Buddhism, something that the more Confucian Ming emperors did not incorporate into their resting places.

Upon entering the tombs, you pass features which are already quite familiar from our tour of the Ming Tombs: a marble *pai lou*, a red gate, a pair of stone columns, a spirit road and a dragon and phoenix gate which bring you to a seven arch marble bridge. The statues along the spirit road are not as attractive as those in the Ming Tombs. This is perhaps a churlish criticism since they were constructed when the Qing throne had to marshal its resources for military campaigns against Ming pretenders and rebels in the south. Interestingly, the statues on the spirit path hold Buddhist rosaries rather than ivory tablets, perhaps reflecting Shun Zhi's devotion to the faith. At the end of the spirit way is the Phoenix and Dragon Gate (凤龙门 or *long feng men*) made of red bricks and containing bright green and yellow porcelain designs.

Behind this is the first main tomb, Xiao Ling (孝陵) for Shun Zhi. Two memorial steles, one in Chinese and one in Manchu, mark the entrance to the tomb grounds where you are likely to be assaulted by loudspeakers blaring recorded facts about the site. The structure of the tomb follows the Ming pattern. Behind the memorial stele is a gate leading to the Hall of Heavenly Favor where living emperors performed rituals for Shun Zhi. In the west hall in the courtyard is a painting of the fifth Dalai Lama's trip to Peking in 1652. Further to the north you will come across the funerary stele and Shun Zhi's tumulus. Some of the tumuli of the Qing Tombs are covered in gravel or asphalt rather than a grove of trees as found on top of the Ming Tombs. To the east is the East Xiao Ling (孝东陵 or *xiao dong ling*), the final resting place of Shun Zhi's empresses. Nearby 28 concubines are buried under smaller earth mounds

Shun Zhi's son and heir, Kang Xi is buried in Jing Ling (景陵), the imperial tomb to the east. The memorial stele, whose tower crumbled a long time ago, leads to a separate spirit path that ambles through a delightful grove of willows and streams. Jing Ling is constructed along the now-familiar pattern of imperial tombs. Only the Hall of Heavenly Favor is open to the public as Kang Xi's tumulus is off limits. However, the maintenance crew might be kind enough to unbolt the gate for you. If so, the spirit tablet is painted in black with green touches on the cloud carvings. Kang Xi's funerary name is carved into the stone in Chinese, Mongolian and Manchu.

Returning to the main spirit road, the next imperial tomb to the west is Yu Ling (裕陵), which is the excavated tomb of Qian Long. You approach Qian Long's burial place by way of another spirit way and over a three arch bridge with a stream that flows through the surrounding fields. It is a peaceful sight, with children and the elderly trying their hand at angling. Once through the ceremonial hall, you can descend into the excavated tomb. The vaults are covered with wonderful motifs of carved seated Buddhas as well as Tibetan and Sanskrit sutras. On the doors of the first vault are carvings of the Manjursi Buddha. On the walls of the vault you encounter once again our old friends, the four heavenly guardians, standing by to protect the emperor in his slumber. In the second chamber, the five senses are symbolized by carvings of a mirror (sight), a *pipa* or Chinese lute (sound), perfume (smell), heavenly fruit (taste) and heavenly robes (touch). The Buddhist teaching, which is that a sentient being must rise above these five senses, is symbolized by the nine-seated Buddhas that are placed above the carving of the senses. On the roof of the vault are carvings of the wheel of life and the trident, a glimmer of Shivan influences in Chinese art. The walls of the last vault are covered with Sanskrit sutras and contain the coffins of Qian Long and five of his consorts.

Proceeding from Qian Long's resting place to the west, you will come across the twined tombs at the Eastern Ding Ling (定东陵 or *ding dong ling*). Here rest the remains of the Empress Dowager and her sister concubine Ci An (慈安). The Empress Dowager's tomb was constructed over a thirty-year period ending in 1897. Immediately upon its construction, the Empress Dowager ordered her tomb to be rebuilt entirely, again at public expense, because she felt that the wooden pillars inside the Hall of Heavenly Favor were not impressive enough.

The carved marble slabs on the stairs of the halls in the Empress Dowager's tombs have an interesting feature. Usually, such slabs depict a dragon disporting with a phoenix, with the dragon *en ascendant* as symbol of the emperor's predominance. Here the phoenix is in the ascendant over the dragon, representing the Empress Dowager's vision of her own power over four emperors. The stone carvings on the marble balustrades also convey the same message through the carvings of phoenixes surging ahead of dragons while both gambol amidst the sea, air and mountains. In the ceremonial hall, the timber columns are indeed impressive, hewed from dark wood. A wax image of the Empress Dowager, attended by the eunuch Li Lian Ying and one of the princesses at court is in the hall. The burial vault is far less elaborate than Qian Long's. After an auspicious day was selected for burial of the Empress Dowager, a hundred bearers took four days to carry an enormous catafalque from Peking over a specially built road.

In 1928, a minor warlord and occasional Nationalist ally, Sun Dian Ying (孙殿英) occupied the territory around the tombs on the excuse that he wanted to protect them. Protection in this instance meant setting off bombs to break into the tombs of Qian Long and the Empress Dowager. Although the vandals dumped the bodies of Qian Long and the Empress Dowager out of their coffins, they must have been given the shock of a lifetime to see that the Empress Dowager's body was in a frighteningly life-like state. The rump Manchu court arranged to have the bodies encoffined again, though valuable jewellery had already disappeared. This event enraged Henry Pu Yi, who was by that time ensconced in Tianjin at the expense of the Japanese. His rage was fueled by a story that some of the pearls from the Empress Dowager's phoenix crown had wound up in Shanghai decorating Madame Chiang Kai Shek's shoes. This alleged insult was influential in turning Pu Yi into a cipher in service for the Japanese.

Further to the west is Ding Ling (定陵), the resting place of the emperor Xian Feng, who was buried in 1865. Xian Feng died in the imperial summer resort in Jehol after the Anglo-French troops had occupied Peking and forced a new set of unequal treaties on the Qing government. He is recalled as an indolent emperor, much drawn to sensual pleasures rather than the Confucian discipline necessary to rule an empire. His temple is remarkably simple and does not have the ornate carvings of clouds or dragons that characterize the other tombs. The statues on the spirit way are smaller but convey a more intimate feeling as a result. The stairwell leading to the top of the tumulus, sometimes called a castle crescent (月牙城 or *yue ya cheng*), also has a more intimate feeling.

Finally, on our way back to the main spirit way, emperor Tong Zhi, who was the son of the Empress Dowager and emperor Xian Feng is buried in the Hui Ling (惠陵). Tong Zhi assumed the throne at age 17, and he died two years later from small pox, though court rumors held that syphilis was the cause of his death. Certainly, both imperial and foreign officials in Peking were aware of his weakness for sexual desire with often-repeated stories of the young emperor visiting the brothels of the Chinese city, with the encouragement of his mother.

When Tong Zhi died in 1864, the Empress Dowager engaged in machinations so that Tong Zhi's cousin, Guang Xu, would inherit the dragon throne. Such a succession was a violation of Manchu and Confucian ethics since a relative of the same generation could not properly conduct sacrificial ceremonies for the veneration of a deceased ancestor. The Empress Dowager attempted to paper over this defect by having Tong Zhi posthumously adopt his cousin, which was a bit of legerdemain that did not appease the conservatives at court. A censor named Wu Ke Du (吴可读) protested the illegal succession by commiting suicide upon the tomb of Tong Zhi so that his ghost could always attend to the aggrieved spirit of Tong Zhi.

To the southwest

You can visit the site of the discovery of the relic of the Peking Man by taking the Peking-Shi Jia Zhuang Expressway (北史高速公路 or *bei shi gao su gong lu*), to *Zhou Kou Dian* (周口店). In the 1920s, Chinese and European archeologists excavated the caves in this region, eventually discovering in 1929 a molar relic of a Peking Man. Eventually, more bones, including a skull, of some 38 men were unearthed. These proto-humans lived some 300,000 to 500,000 years ago. It was clear from the site that fire was used. The remains suggest that the Peking Man walked upright, had a large brain cavity, used stone tools, hunted, cooked meat and ate nuts. The Jesuit Pierre Teilhard de Chardin was credited with the discovery.

After climbing up the steep road you will be greeted by (or perhaps startled) by a meter wide golden bust of the Peking Man. The site has a museum and walking trails that take you to his former residence.

A mystery hangs over the current location of the remains of Peking Man, a fact that is not mentioned at the exhibition. After surviving for half a million years, Peking Man has gone AWOL over the past sixty. The story is that on the eve of the Japanese attack on Pearl Harbor, the Nationalists and the Americans agreed to sneak the remains of Peking Man out of China for safekeeping in the United States. The American vessel carrying the assorted skeleton fragments ran aground in the Yang Tse River on December 8, 1941 and was seized by Chinese river pirates who looted the ship. Shortly thereafter, Japanese troops captured the Americans onboard. The relics were lost in the ensuing melee.

It seems probable that the river pirates might have simply tossed the fossilized bones into the Yang Tse River since they were of no apparent value. Others have suggested that the bones were carefully wrapped in velvet and stored in a varnished wooden chest, something that certainly would have aroused the curiosity of any pirate worth the name. In past years, rewards of up to US$10 million have been offered for the return of the remains but it would seem that the Peking Man is still at large.

The Temple of the Cloud Place (云居寺 or *yun ju si*) is located 75 miles to the southwest of Peking along delightfully rustic country roads that take you through the craggy mountains of Fang Shan County (房山县). During late afternoons, farmers sit together under willow trees, smoking foot long traditional pipes with cornfields unrolling to the foot of the mountains. Hundreds of dragonflies hover slowly in the humid summer air as the area near the temple gate fills with birdsong.

The temple was originally constructed in the 6th century by a monk called Jing Yuan (静琬), who borrowed the Confucian practice of carving classic texts on stone slabs. At one point, 4,915 stone slabs inscribed with Buddhist sutras were placed in and around the temple, though they were later removed to cave sites. During the Second World War, the Japanese air force bombed the temple and all that survived was a group of stupas. In the past ten years, the authorities have reconstructed the temple. There are five main halls built along the central axis. The first courtyard, whose trees are shrouded in red votive ribbons, leads to a hall housing black metal statues of the Threefold Buddhas. A Sakyamuni Buddha statue is placed in the second hall. The third courtyard leads to the Baisajya Hall (药师殿 or *yao shi dian*) where the Buddhist counterpart of the Taoist King of Medicine is worshipped. The fourth courtyard houses the Amida Buddha and the final hall has a Tibetan style Guan Yin with many arms. In the hall are fluffy stuffed animals and other gifts left by worshipers whose prayers were answered by Guan Yin.

On the south side of the temple is the series of pagodas built in 1093. You reach this by passing through a walk way through a bamboo grove. On the *cang jing* pagoda (藏经塔), a five meter tall stone structure, there are carvings of several winged bodhisattvas which look as if they were the result of Nestorfarian Christian influences during the Tang dynasty.

The North Pagoda (罗汉塔) is more impressive. Surrounding the pagoda at five points are small two-meter tall Tang towers. The oldest one dates from 711. Inside are carvings of the Sakyamuni Buddha attended by bodhisattvas as well as princes and princesses in Tang dress. In the center is a brick pagoda of the Liao dynasty decorated with pictures of heavenly fruit, along with Tibetan and Sanskrit symbols.

In He Bei province is the Western Qing Tombs (清西陵 or *qing xi ling*), the second burial ground, near Peking, for Manchu emperors, empresses and concubines. I find these tombs to be far more appealing than the Ming Tombs or Eastern Qing tombs. You are able to visit all of the tombs at this site and do not have to put up with noisy loudspeakers. The villagers living near the tombs are more hospitable and there are no high-pressure pitches to purchase a t-shirt. There are also guesthouses set in stone-built rustic farm villages so you can camp overnight near the tombs.

In 1730, Yong Zheng ordered the construction of his tomb far away from the Eastern Qing Tomb. This was an unorthodox move since Chinese custom usually required sons to be buried near their fathers. Subsequent Confucian historians claimed that Yong Zheng might have been embarrassed to be buried near his revered father Kang Xi because of the political intrigue and violence that attended his succession to the Dragon Throne. Later Yong Zheng's son Qian Long decreed that burial sites of emperors should be alternated between the two locations, least the tombs of the emperors Shun Zhi and Kang Xi became solitary and neglected. This decree was set aside by Dao Guang in 1840s.

The Western Qing Tombs follow imperial convention. Each tomb has its own spirit road, dragon and phoenix gates and tablet house. The imperial tombs and Lama temples are roofed in yellow tiles on red walls while those of empresses, consorts and princes are roofed with green tiles.

The main tomb here is Tai Ling (泰陵), the burial ground for Yong Zheng. There are five marble *pai lou* at the very entrance of the tomb. Passing under a great red gate, you come to another spirit road and a small hill intrudes before the Dragon and Phoenix Gate. There is a long walk from here to the Gate of Heavenly Favor (隆恩殿 or *long en dian*). Behind is the Hall of Heavenly Favor (隆恩殿 or *long en dian*) that is fairly weather-beaten. There are mock displays of typical sacrificial items such as an ox, two rams, various roasted meats, shrimp, rice cakes, nuts, beans, and fruits. The Hall creates a sense of height with its columns of peeling lacquer ware. In the courtyard, there are ovens for burnt offerings. Behind the Hall are stone copies of sacrificial vessels and the tower for the spirit tablet, leading to the tumulus.

About two miles to the northeast of Tai Ling is the Eastern Tai Ling (泰东陵 or *tai dong ling*) built for the empress Xiao Sheng Xiang, wife of Yong Zheng. The empress' life overlapped for a considerable time with the reign of Qian Long who repeatedly demonstrated his reverence for his mother, perhaps in a bid to impress the Confucian literati unimpressed with his devotion to Buddhism. He is said to have walked along side the sedan chair that would carry his mother on strolls along the imperial parks and built pavilions for her pleasure.

According to Manchu customs, an empress who predeceased the emperor would be placed in a temporary grave until the emperor died. Then the empress' remains would be placed in the same vault as the emperor. If the empress survived the emperor, she was entitled to be buried in a separate tomb. The empress Xiao Sheng Xiang lived for 39 years after Yong Zheng's demise. The Eastern Tai Ling is built on a grand scale and includes a gate and hall of Heavenly Favor, side halls and a walled tumulus with a spirit stele tower.

About half a mile to the southeast of the Eastern Tai Ling are the smaller tombs of twenty-one of Yong Zheng's concubines who are buried in brick tumuli within a red colored wall.

Striking off to the west is Chang Ling (昌陵), the final resting place of Jia Qing. It is a nearly identical copy of Tai Ling. The spirit tablet at Chang Ling is still painted with red and gold paint with inscriptions written in Mongolian, Manchu and Chinese.

The Western Chang Ling (昌西陵) is the tomb of Empress Xiao He Rui, who was the first wife of Jia Qing. A white brick round tumulus is enclosed by a large circular red wall with glazed yellow tiles. The tomb looks like a *yurt*, or the round shaped tents pitched by nomadic Mongolians.

On the west side of the Western Qing Ling is the burial place of the emperor Dao Guang, Mu Ling (慕陵). This is one of the more interesting tombs in the necropolis. According to Peking legend, Dao Guang had wanted to comply with the decree of his grandfather, Qian Long, and construct his own tomb in the Eastern Qing Tomb since his father was buried in the western tombs. However, the contractors delivered a faulty tomb that flooded one summer. Dao Guang was enraged because the flooding could be interpreted as his having a loose grip on the Mandate of Heaven. His decision to seek a second burial site in the west was taken as conclusive evidence of the convolutions that had unbalanced the poise of the Manchu emperors.

However, all these distractions at least allowed Dao Guang's architect to have some room to design a different tomb. Dao Guang asserted that he was mindful of the need for conservative fiscal policies and skipped the spirit road, the tower for the spirit tablet and other typical aspects of Qing tombs. However, the construction costs for the tomb wound up being the same as any other Qing tomb. In particular, the old boy splurged on his sacrificial hall, which is made of unpainted *nanmu* wood with exquisite carvings of dragons, many of which were vandalized during the Cultural Revolution. Dao Guang believed that construction on his failed eastern tomb was attributable to several dragons having been forced from their lairs. This might be the reason he overdid it will the dragons for his tomb. Because of the fragrance of the cedar wood, it was said that the hall is filled with the incense breathed out by ten thousand dragons.

There are no archways leading to Dao Guang's tomb. Rather a simple marble stairway leads to his resting place, which is a circular brick building. The tomb is topped with imperial yellow glazed tiles. Alas, Dao Guang never was able to remove the stains on his reign. His officials bungled the Opium War and seceded Hong Kong to the British. During his reign, the Taiping rebellion broke out. His successor was one of China's most ineffectual emperors, which, in Confucian terms, is an indictment against the father who raised the son. His temple is distinctive and perhaps justly suggestive of the dissipation of heaven's mandate.

Leaving Mu Ling, you go across the burial grounds to get to the tombs on the east side. On your way, you will pass a large stream flowing on the south side of the Tai Ling and other tombs. During summer, children escape the heat by cannonballing into the water. Elsewhere along the stream are anglers trying their luck to snare a trout. All of this bucolic recreation takes place in front of the monuments of imperial grandeur.

In the east is Chong Ling (崇陵), the tomb of Guang Xu, who died in 1908. Construction only began in 1909, and Guang Xu was laid to rest in 1915 during the Republican period. The workmanship of the tomb is quite poor, though you would not expect a Republican government to have lavished funds on the burial of an emperor. The empress Lung Yu is buried nearby, a bit of an irony as they hated each other in life and kept as far apart as possible. The grave of Guang Xu's favorite, the Pearl Concubine, is on the other side of the hill. In 1901, she was interred in a small grave outside of Xi Zhi Men, but the Republican government took pity and agreed to move her grave here in 1915.

The Chong Ling is the only excavated tomb in the Western Qing Tombs. There are Buddhist motifs on the doors of the tomb but the walls of the chambers have no carvings. The spirit tablet is still painted in red and brown colors.

The most moving tomb here is not designed with imperial intentions. If you take the road to the west of Chong Ling, you will come to the main entrance of the Chinese Dragon Imperial Cemetery (华龙皇家墓), operated by a Sino-Hong Kong joint venture company. The entrance is marked by a three holed bridge leading to a *pai lou* with five entranceways. This is a hard currency joint venture run for those, like most Chinese emperors, who believe that you can indeed take it with you, even if just for "face." Once you pass through a three gate *pai lou*, you should strike to the right. Flanked by two small cloud pillars is a three feet high mound marking the burial place of the emperor Xuan Tong or Henry Pu Yi. Juniper trees surround the grave and a small stone balustrade accentuates a simple tomb with words Ai Xin Jue Luo Pu Yi (爱新觉罗溥仪) 1906–1967.

To the west

The village of *Chuan Di Xia* (爨底下) is on the old road between Peking and Shan Xi province. It holds pride of place as one of the most spectacular sights for visitors to Peking. During the mid Ming, Shan Xi merchants needed a sanctuary to store their goods and silver while traveling to and from Peking. The village began as a fortified rest post for these merchants. Today, the village is a glorious collection of stone houses curling along the south side of a mountain. It will take you about three hours to make the journey from Peking by car. If you can arrange it, avoid the weekends.

On your way to the village, you will pass by craggy snow topped mountains as well as rope bridges spanning streams and rivers. Ruins of stone houses and garden walls decorate the route. In the summer time, you will see freshly hewn timber fences overgrown with morning glories and sunflowers raising their faces to the blue skies. There are miles of apple orchards where the farmers painstakingly wrap each apple on the branch in a plastic bag as a preventive measure against insects.

I find that the village of *Chuan Di Xia* leaves a far more satisfying impression than the Forbidden City, the Great Wall or any of the imperial tombs. It is a living receptacle of traditional Chinese culture. While it is a historically preserved site, it is home to rural villagers who still speak Mandarin with a Shan Xi lilt. They are exuberant and cheerful people. In the nearby hills, people keep beehives. Along the valley, folks grow corn and millet. Roosters crow from every corner and you can hear porcine honking from sties that are thoughtfully placed down wind.

As you stroll up through the village, each doorway and wall echoes memories from the past. Maoist slogans painted during the Cultural Revolution rub shoulders with Qing era paintings of Taoist saints seated in courtyards contemplating bamboos and birdsong. In the winter, villagers still wrap felt around their shoes so that they do not slip on the stone walkways covered with ice. In the spring, they plow the fields according to the auspicious lunar calendar dates set out in the almanac. In the summer, the folks tend to their crops, bees, goats and chickens. In the autumn, the farmers celebrate the harvest while awaiting the full moon with pastries made over stone heaths.

The villagers have thoughtfully set up a bar overlooking the valley. For the hungry, several courtyard houses offer to prepare nourishing northern dishes including even a whole roast lamb. As you lift up a glass of the local mountain hooch and listen with anticipation to dumplings cooking in the kitchen, you can watch sheep gamboling down from the mountainside. Pumpkin vines grow everywhere, with gourds in early August in a deep verdant color waiting the early October frost. Some enterprising folks are busily engaged in turning their rice into a proper (and delectable) moonshine.

I believe that there is no more fitting place to bring to close our wanderings in Old Peking. In many sections of the city, you have had to use your imagination to conjure the ghost of Old Peking. Here old China lives and thrives. You can rent a room of a rather large courtyard house for about 20 RMB a night during the week. Should you be a sensible person and elect to check in for three weeks worth of reading in Taoist and Buddhist texts, I am sure that the local proprietors are keen to work out a long term package.

22

FOOD

Whatever impressions you may have about the city, one thing is undeniable: Peking hosts a magnificent selection of regional Chinese restaurants. This aspect alone makes the trip worthwhile.

Food has occupied a central role in Chinese life for thousands of years, as can be gleaned by the role of serving various dishes to the spirits of the deceased. It is said that Chinese food reflects the country's tumultuous history. Famines would ensure that precious little ever went to waste. The need to conserve fuel also induced ancient Chinese chefs to slice meats and vegetables in order to reduced cooking time. While people could always buy food at inns and markets, restaurants, as social centers and culinary institutions, took root only in the Song Dynasty.

Nearly everyone coming to China will already have visited a Chinese restaurant in his home country. A Chinese saying maintains that wherever there is civilization, you will also find Chinese people. (一有文化的地方，就有中国人) and, implicitly, Chinese restaurants. With this diaspora arose the ubiquitous American Chinese restaurant, which has been exuberantly extolled by such down to earth actors — in character — as Jackie Gleason and Joe Pesci. Timothy Mo's unbearably tragic novel, *Sour Sweet* relates the struggles of an immigrant Chinese family to survive in Britain by running a restaurant. Throughout Europe, Africa and the subcontinent are Chinese restaurants, often run by terribly homesick families. I recall a Chinese restaurant in San Ignacio in Belize where the members of a small family restaurant were almost in tears of homesickness when my wife and I placed our order in Mandarin. I have been to Chinese restaurants in Guatemala, Liberia, Bombay, Moscow and Mandalay. As you might expect, the chefs in each of these places of exile have catered to local tastes and adjusted their recipes. Therefore, your prior experiences with overseas Chinese restaurants will not have prepared you for the astounding variety of Chinese cuisine available in the capital.

There is a debate among Chinese epicures about the precise number of regional Chinese cuisines. An old standard maintains that a region can only proclaim its own distinctive style if it can produce 108 dishes made from local products and spices. All agree on the existence of at least four schools. These are Cantonese (whose fame borders notoriety in many Western countries), Fu Jian/ Zhe Jiang (which is sometimes erroneously called "Shanghai style"), Shan Dong (again sometimes known by the misnomer "Peking cuisine") and Si Chuan. The disputed fifth school is He Nan cuisine. Other commonly known cuisines, such as Hu Nan, Tai Shan, Dongbei, Yunnan and Hakka, are regarded by purists as subsections of the major four (or five) schools of cooking.

Leaving aside these regional matters for the moment, we can divide traditional Peking restaurants into three main groupings: Shan Dong style cuisine, Chinese Muslim hallal fare, and restaurants run by Manchu bannermen.

Shan Dong province is close to Peking. Because of the frequent floods in the Yellow River, the province periodically tossed out waves of refugees seeking safety in the capital. As a consequence, Peking soon became the host of a large Shan Dong community who nourished themselves at restaurants serving their home cuisine.

Of these Shan Dong style dishes, perhaps the most famous is Peking duck, which is an extrapolation of a suckling pig recipe adapted for the specific species of ducks in north China and that, incidentally, are the ancestors of Long Island ducklings. The oldest Peking duck eatery name *pian yi kao ya dian* (便宜烤鸭店) was established in the Vegetable Market district in 1416, four years before Yong Le proclaimed Peking as the capital. Prior to the 20th century, most Peking duck restaurants operated simply as take-aways, with sit down parlors only becoming fixed in the culinary firmament in the early 20th century. For a while in the 19th century, there were nearly 30-competing Peking duckling restaurants using the name *pian yi kao ya*. Different shops would use different ingredients, such as molasses, honey, or plum sauce as well as charcoal from different types of trees. Apple wood charcoal is famous for giving a roasted duck the best smoked flavor.

Peking duck is eaten with wheat pancakes (饼 or *bing*), plum sauce, green onion slices and perhaps sliced cucumber. Though very rich, a properly roasted Peking duck is an indescrible pleasure. While not strictly Shan Dong in origin, another northern duck dish is *xiang su ya* (香酥鸭) where the duck is pressed and then roasted so that all of the fat drains away. The resulting dish is dry and tender, with morsels of the duck pulled away from the bones in tender chunks. Here again the duck is eaten with wheat pancakes, plum sauce and green onions.

With Chinese duck dishes on the mind, I cannot help but digress and tell the story of a summer associate at a large San Francisco law firm. The lad hailed from some god-forsaken state in the American Mid-west that knows of no Chinese restaurant. A senior associate dutifully took the hay seed to lunch at a Peking restaurant, only to be astonished at the sight of Farmer Brown mistaking the wheaten pancakes for hot towels and wiping his face and hands with it.

Shan Dong cuisine uses wheat and corn more than other Chinese cuisines. *Shao bing* (烧饼) are little wheaten loaves sprinkled with sesames, often eaten for breakfast or as a side dish for Mongolian hot pot. Corn flour dumplings stuffed with carrot shavings and bits of lamb and cold wheat noodle dishes with a spicy plum sauce and slivers of cucumber and beef are other snacks that echo of Old Peking. Garlic and scallions figure more prominently in Shan Dong cuisine than in other regions, as quickly discerned upon boarding the Peking subway. A spiced paste of eggplant is also a delightful local specialty. *San bu dian* (三不点) is sweet pudding made from egg yolks, flour and sugar and served as a filling dessert.

While adopted in many other parts of China, Shan Dong claims credit for the best dumplings. The stuffing, or *shaer* (砂儿) is usually ground pork with shredded cabbage or spinach, though other meats are sometimes used. When steamed, these are called *jiao zi* (饺子) while a lightly fried and steamed version is *guo tie* (锅贴), or "potstickers" as they are sometimes called overseas. Either variety can be dipped in a combination of soy sauce, vinegar, ginger and garlic.

Shan Dong has an open faced steamed dumpling called *shao mai* (烧卖) usually wrapped in wheat flour dough with pork, shrimp and fish. Recalling the northern landscapes, these are more basic than their Cantonese counterparts. They have a gray-white complexion that calls to mind the dusty northern winters. *Bao zi* (包子) are larger dumplings, which look like steamed bread and contain ground pork. Onion pancakes (葱油饼 or *chong you bing*) are wheat flour pancakes made with sliced green onions and fried like a latke. *Rou bing* (肉饼) are thin beef cakes enclosed in a wheat flour wrapper fried on both sides. *Yin si juan* (银丝卷) are white steamed breads that have been slightly deep-fried.

Though difficult to find, some Old Peking restaurants still sell *lao* (酪), a summertime refreshment. *Lao* is made by adding several drops of rice wine to sweetened whole milk brought to a boil. The wine turns the milk into curds, which are then thoroughly chilled. Yogurt, sold in attractive white porcelain bottles, seems to have replaced *lao* these days.

Although not solely a Peking drink, a "tea" made of sour plum juice (酸梅汤 or *suan mei tang*), thoroughly chilled, makes a satisfying thirst quencher in the summer months of Peking's "Great Heat."

Recommended Shan Dong restaurants

Du Yi Chu (都一处) is located at No. 36 Qian Men Avenue (前门大街36号) and was originally established in 1738. According to legend, Qian Long, whilst traveling incognito on a Chinese New Year's eve, was searching for a meal amidst the deserted streets of the Chinese City. The only restaurant open that evening was *Du Yi Chu*, where the patrons graciously gave the lonely sojourner their own dinner and their own specially distilled wine. Later, the emperor revealed his escapade to the proprietors by sending them a handwritten scroll declaring that the restaurant is the finest in the capital. *Du Yi Qu* used to have a plaque with its name written by Qian Long, though that seems to have disappeared. In its place is a plaque written by Guo Mo Ruo

Cui Hua Lou (萃华楼), located at No. 58 Wang Fu Jing Avenue (王府大街58号), was founded in 1940. Before 1949, it was one of the most famous Shan Dong style restaurants in Peking. They also serve Henan dishes such as the famous sweet and sour yellow carp and monkey head mushrooms, a delicacy that is as much sought after in Henan as truffles are in France.

Feng Ze Yuan (丰泽园) is another Shan Dong restaurant whose pedigree dates from 1930. It is located at No. 13 Dong Zhi Men Avenue (东直门大街)

Quan Ju De (全聚德) is one of Peking's most renowned duck restaurants, albeit rather commercialized as of late. The restaurant first opened its doors in 1864. Quan Ju De's name was written in a very distinctive and recognizable calligraphy by a minor Qing official who never rose above the county level (and was probably quite lucky for that). It is located to the south and east of Zheng Yang Gate, near *Du Yi Chu*.

Pian Yi Fang Kao Ya Dian (便宜坊烤鸭店) is the final survivor of the competition among Peking duck purveyors to claim the name *pian yi kao yao dian*. It is located at No. 2A Chong Wen Men Avenue (崇文门大街24号), and was founded in 1855.

Li Quan Kao Ya Dian (利群烤鸭店) is also located south of Zheng Yang Gate on Bei Xiang Feng Alley on Zheng Yi Road (前门东街正义路北翔风胡同) and serves Peking duck in a traditional courtyard setting in the back alleyways. It is advisable to book: 6705 5578.

Tianjin Gou Bu Li Dumpling Restaurant (天津狗不理包子饭压) is located at the corner of Di An Men West Avenue (地安门西大街) and Di An Men Wai Avenue (地安门外大街). The restaurant was founded in Tianjin in the 19th century with the curious name that means "dogs pay no attention." It is said that the chef, a wizard at making pork and vegetable *bao zi*, had a mug so ugly that even dogs ran away from him. Aside from the *bao zi*, the restaurant also serves highly recommendable Peking duck as well as other northern fare.

Hun Tun Hou (馄饨侯), on the north side of Dong An Men Avenue (东安门大街) near Wang Fu Jing, serves wonton dumplings in soup, which makes for a delicious breakfast before touring the Forbidden City and its environs. The restaurant opens at 6:00 a.m. Even when there is a power failure, the staff, wearing white sanitary caps and robes, continue to wrap the wontons by candlelight.

Given the long tradition that Islam enjoys in the city, it is not surprising that many famous *hallal* restaurants emerged to prepare delightful dishes for Muslim palates. Lamb figured heavily in the menus, though some of the Muslim eateries established their reputations for the production of (pork-less) Shan Dong dishes as well. One specialty of these restaurants was roast lamb meat (烤羊肉 or *kao yang rou*), broiled on a grill over a charcoal stove in the middle of the table. The grills were never cleaned, for such a proposition was a heresy. The accumulation of charcoal and burnt meat over the decades was believed to give the freshly roasted meat its unique flavor. Fried lamb (炒羊肉 or *chao yang rou*) , served with sesame and dried red pepper powder, is another hallmark.

Some Chinese Muslim restaurants specialize in "Mongolian" hot pot (涮羊肉 or *shuang yang rou*), which has spread to many other provinces in China. None do it as well as the *hallal* restaurants. Here you cook thinly sliced lamb or other meats as well as vegetables or frozen tofu in a samovar set in the middle of your table. Once the ingredients are cooked, you fish them out with a ladle and season them with a selection of spices and sauces that you have combined in a bowl.

Recommended Chinese Muslim Restaurants

Dong Lai Shun (东来顺), previously in a nicely rundown courtyard house in Wangfu Jing, originally started as a stall in the Dong An Market in 1903. It specialized in Mongolian hot pot, made with specially raised white tailed sheep from inner Mongolia. It now resides in the sterile splendor of the Dong An Plaza, and dozens of branches.

Kao Rou Ji (烤肉季) is on the north side of the Shi Cha Hai district near the Silver Ingot Bridge. It was established in 1848 and serves first rate *kao yang rou*.

Hong Bin Lou (鸿宾楼) was first founded in Tianjin in 1853 and moved to Peking in 1955. I always associate the restaurant with Dr. Li Zhi Sui's story about his family celebrating the arrest of the Gang of Four with a sumptuous Peking duck dinner here. It is located at No. 25 Haidian Avenue (海淀大街 25号).

Kao Rou Wan (烤肉宛) dates back to 1686 and was set up as primarily a grilled beef restaurant to serve the Chinese Muslim community in the Western Chinese City.

Bai Kui Lao Hao (白魁老号), first established in 1781, specializes in fried lamb (炒羊肉) and *gan shao yang rou si* (干烧羊肉丝). It is located at No. 158 Jiao Dao Kou South Avenue (交道口南大街158号)

Neng Ren Ju (能仁居) is another restaurant renowned for its Mongolian hot pot. Its main branch is at No. 5 Great Peace Bridge near the White Pagoda Temple in the Western City (太平桥5号).

Since the Qing legal system prohibited Manchu bannermen from owning land, retired soldiers often had to try their luck at the disagreeable world of commerce. Some of these retirees relied upon their contacts with the imperial government to procure the recipes or ingredients for operating a restaurant. The only unifying theme to this third type of traditional Peking restaurant is simply that they were set up by bannermen. Though the menus vary, the cuisine on offer is always northern. After the collapse of the Qing, some restaurants strove to present dishes made from "imperial" recipes from the Forbidden City.

Sha Guo Ju (砂锅居), located at No. 60 Xi Si Nan Road (西四南路60号), was founded in 1741 by a bannerman who was able to wrangle the concession for disposing of all the pork produced from the ritual sacrifices of pigs in the imperial city. At first, he set up a *chaucouterie*. After a few years of this line of work, inspiration led him to convert his butcher's shop into a pork-only restaurant where the art of cooking the swine reached its apogee. Pork products in all different styles and tastes are on offer. Many dishes are stewed in clay pots, from which the restaurant takes its name.

Li Jia Cai (李家菜) is located at No. 11 Yang Fang Alley (羊房胡同 11号). Mr. Li presents his customers with dishes prepared according to recipes learned by his grandfather who served as security inspector for the preparation of imperial meals in the Forbidden City. His restaurant is located in the back alleys near Shi Cha Hai. You will need to book a table in advance for a set banquet: 6618 0107.

Fang Shan (仿膳) is on the west bank of Hortensia Island in the Bei Hai Park. While not strictly a bannerman restaurant, it was opened in 1925 to serve imperial cuisines based upon the favorite recipes of the Empress Dowager. The light flour wheat buns with spiced ground beef are quite delicious. Lao She's calligraphy adorns the horizontal plaque with the Chinese characters for *Fang Shan*. (By the way, you eat better by ordering a la carte than going for a set banquet.)

We have not yet even begun to exhaust the gastronomic options available in Peking. On account of its regional guildhalls, Peking always had restaurants that served cuisines from other regions. As the capital of the People's Republic, this tradition has been fortunately reinforced.

As noted in our meanderings in the Chinese city, Old Peking hosted several guildhall restaurants for natives of Fu Jian and Zhe Jiang. In these regions, the temperature is less severe than in the north, with rice being the more prevalent grain than wheat. Here folks stew meats in locally made soy sauces of excellent quality. This type of stewing produces dishes that are called "red cooking" (红烧 or *hong shao*) which imparts a delightfully distinctive flavor of sweetened soy. Given the larger numbers of safe harbors, seafood is more prevalent, and accordingly, seafood dishes figure prominently on the menus.

This region has its own version of steamed pork dumplings called dragon buns (小笼包 or *shao long bao*), which are steamed in bamboo baskets. Large "red-cooked" pork meatballs, called lion's head (狮子头 or *shi zi tou*) are an improvement light years in advance of Western meat loaf, which it slightly resembles in appearance only. Stir-fried eel finds its way on to the menus for banquets along the coast. A special type of local green bean and pickled salty cabbage also reflect the considerable regional variation of Fu Jian and Zhe Jiang dishes.

The term "Shanghai cuisine" has eclipsed the designation of Fu Jian and Zhe Jiang, just as "Peking" prevails over Shan Dong. However, Shanghai is comparatively a very young city and restaurants serving its splendid cuisine are best classified in this section.

Recommended Fu Jian/Zhe Jiang restaurants

Lao Zheng Xing (老正兴), at No. Qian Men Wai Avenue (前门外大街) opened its doors in Shanghai in 1862. The Peking branch came along in 1956.

Lu Lu (鹭鹭酒家) is at No. 5 Xi Da Wang Road (西大望路北5号) and is said to be the best Shanghai restaurant in the city, though it is quite some way from the major sites.

Kong Yi Ji (孔乙己) is found near the south shore of the lake at Shi Cha Hai (什刹海后海南岸). Here yellow wine from Zhe Jiang is on sale as well as regional specialties like drunken shrimp and dong po pork.

Cantonese cuisine is the most familiar to Westerners and is considered to be less greasy and more subtle. Seafood and roasted meats are favorites as is *dim sum* (点心), which are Cantonese hors d'oeuvres made from shrimp, pork and vegetables. Cantonese *shao mai* (烧卖) are made from pork and shrimp, with a pleasing bright yellow cabbage wrapper and crab roe gracing the top. Beef meat balls (牛肉球) are steamed meatballs served with Worcestershire sauce, a delightfully incongruous mixture of East and West. Turnip cakes (萝卜糕 or *luo bo gao*) appeal to the Slavic tastes hiding in all our palates.

Recommended Cantonese restaurants

Da San Yuan (大三园) is located at No. 50 Jing Shan Xi Avenue (景山西大街 50号), convenient when visiting the Forbidden City or other areas in the heart of the Imperial City.

Full Moon Restaurant (福满楼) is in the Hua Du Hotel (华都) in the eastern suburbs and is known for fresh *dim sum*.

In my view, the champion of the four (or five) Chinese cuisines is Si Chuan. An inland province, Si Chuan has been long regarded as the rice basket of China. Its damp humid winters prepare the palate perfectly for its generous use of fiery chili peppers. Si Chuan peppercorns, added whole, are so spicy that they have a slightly numbing effect (麻辣 or *ma la*), which is another hallmark of the cuisine.

Si Chuan dishes include the awe-inspiring *ma la shui zhu rou pian* (麻辣水煮肉片), which is made by boiling thinly sliced pork in chili oil, peppers and garlic with a garnish of coriander. (For hallal or kosher friends, there is a beef version of this liquid fire.) *Ma po dou fu* (麻婆豆付), called pock marked bean curd is another spicy dish made with a generous dosage of chili peppers. *Gong bao ji ding* (宫保鸡丁) is sliced chicken stir fried with dried peppers. *Yu xiang qie zi* (鱼香茄子) is a stewed/fried eggplant with a spicy sauce often used for seafood. *Gan bian si ji dou* (干扁四季豆) is stir fried dried string beans. This recipe is sometimes adapted for spicy dried beef or *gan bian niu rou si* (干扁牛肉丝).

Si Chuan has a number of cold dishes that carry a fiery after-taste punch. Mouth-watering chicken (口水鸡 or *kou shui ji*) and garlic paste pork (蒜泥白肉 or *suan ni bai rou*) are unbeatable.

Just to show that there is mercy for palates that prefer less piquant dishes, stewed tea duck (樟茶鸭 or *chang cha ya*) is actually camphor-smoked duck that almost resembles the taste of a Smithfield ham.

Recommended Si Chuan Restaurants

Lao Si Chuan (老四川) is on the second floor of the Chongqing Hotel (重庆饭店) and one of the finest Si Chuan restaurants in Peking. If you have only one chance to eat out in Peking, then come here. I have never had a bad meal and would be pleased as punch to arrange to have my ashes interred here so that my ghost can partake in the kitchen preparations of the powerfully fragrant dishes.

Si Chuan Restaurant (四川) is located at No.14 Liu Yin Street (柳阳街) near the Palace of Prince Gong. Ousted from its original home now occupied by the loutish China Club, this restaurant was founded in 1955 and a favorite of Deng Xiao Ping's, who hailed from Si Chuan province. Unbeatable cuisine, though the staff seem to be overworked. Give them a big smile along with a tip.

Other Regional Restaurants

Of course, the foregoing list turns a blind eye to subgroups of regional cuisine. For *Shan Xi* cuisine, with its taste of wheat and inner China grit, the *Jin Yang Fang Zhuang* 普阳饭庄) at No. 241 Zhu Shi Kou Avenue (珠市口大街241号) is a delight given its setting near an old courtyard house. The restaurant first opened its doors in 1959. The *guo you rou* (过油肉) is pork "passed through oil" which is tasty and not as oily as it sounds. Pressed duck (香酥鸭 or *xiang sha ya*) is excellent as are "brains" (头脑 or *tou nao*) made from mutton, Chinese herbs, lotus root and rice wine.

For *Hunan* cuisine, the Makai Restaurant (马凯湖南餐厅) is on No. 3 Di An Men Wai Avenue (地安门外大街3号). Hunan cuisine is spicy in a way that tastes "deep-stewed" when compared with the numbing effect of Si Chuan cooking.

Xin Jiang cuisine has more in common with Central Asian than Chinese flavors. At No. 2A Hou Guai Bang Alley, off Chao Yang Men Nei Avenue (朝阳内大街后拐棒胡同甲2号) is a restaurant called Afunti (阿凡提). It has now become a much-visited restaurant, verging on the "touristy." I recall it starting life as a simple Xin Jiang restaurant with a statue of Afanti, a charater who appears in different forms in Islamic or Islamic-influenced cultures from Malta to Urumqi. He is a clever trickster who abhors formality and sanctimoniousness. Legend portrays him outwitting imams, merchants and officials. In its next incarnation, the restaurant tried to cater to the Russians, with a Russian menu and name cards. I recall one evening coming here around midnight with a couple of the usual suspects. I had in my bag a recording of a Pete Seeger and Arlo Guthrie concert, the first song being an Italian folk tune called the Tarantella. The CD somehow was placed into the restaurant's music system and before you could say Alice's Restaurant, the cooks and waiters were performing a folk dance in the nearly deserted restaurant. It was a spontaneous celebration that sometimes happens to you on the road. It also bespoke of folk connections that are so deep that the conscious mind lumbers unaware of them. Afanti went through one more metamorphosis, changed its name to "Afunti" (accent on "fun") and now caters to the Western crowd. While the food is still excellent, the place has devolved into foreigners dancing on the tabletops to Uighur folks tunes played on a Wurlitzer. The little restaurants in Uighurville are a better bet for exploration if your stomach has acclimatized to the local bugs.

Hakka cuisine (客家菜 or *ke jia cai*) is a subset of Cantonese cuisine. The Hakkas are the "guest people," a Chinese group originally from the north who moved to south China in the aftermath of the Mongol invasions. Unlike other Chinese, the Hakka men never developed a taste for women with bound feet.

The *Lao Han Zi* (老汉字) located on the Shi Cha Hai East Bank (什刹海东岸 offer superb Hakka food.)

In the south of the city, we come to Gong De Lin Restaurant (功德林素菜馆) at No. 158 Qian Men Wai Avenue (前门外大街158号), a place that specializes in Buddhist Lenten foods, though this might be controversial for those who have accepted a Kosher or hallal view towards meat flavors. Here we can sample mock meat dishes made with bean curd, mushrooms or turnips.

Tibetan dumplings and *chang* are on offer at Makye Ame (玛吉阿米) , located at 2/F Xiu Shui Nan Road

The most important part of Chinese culture.

(秀水南街) off of Jian Guo Men Wai Avenue (建国门外大街). At No. 14 Liang Ma Qiao Road (亮马桥路14号), King Gesar (格萨尔), named after one of Tibetan great monarchs, serves primarily yak as well as other dishes from the Snowlands.

Mongolian food is available at *Kehan Jiu Lou* which is next to *Kao Rou Ji* in the Shi Cha Hai district.

While not a regional cuisine of China, great Russian food is to be had in the neighborhood around the Altar of the Sun Park. The *Elephant* (大笨象) is at No. 17 Ri Tan Bei Road (日坛北路17号). You can sample *North Korean cuisine* at Pyongyang Haedong Raeng Myun (海棠花) at No. 8 Dong Da Qiao Road (东大桥8号). Its authenticity seems to be vouched for by the dour looking Koreans with Kim Il Sung pins on their lapels. Dining here is more of a cultural investigation than a culinary experience.

It is often said the Chinese believe that they have the most advanced civilization. I defy anyone to deny it in the afterglow of freshly made *guo tie*, followed by icy Chinese lager.

23

DRINK[1]

WHILE ANY FOREIGNER WITH a taste bud can learn to be adept at ordering
Chinese food, foreign connoisseurs of traditional Chinese wines and spirits are an
exuberant elite among Old Peking hands. We scoff at those weak-kneed fellow
foreign devils who make such a commotion about having to drink the spirits of
the land. We also know how to set our pace so that we can be back in the office
the next day, or, well, maybe sometime later. In any event, traditional spirits are
an integral part of Old Peking that cannot be avoided and, with some presence of
mind, can actually be enjoyed.

Springs in Old Peking produced a rough tasting water. People soon learned
that there was an exception to Peking's bitter waters in the mountain springs
flowing in the Western Hills. The Peach Garden Hermit distilled spirits from
mountain spring water and yellow flowers collected in the Western Hills. The
Five Star Brewery was built nearby in order to ensure a better source of fresh water.
During the imperial age, the varying quality of the city's water was attributed as
the cause for the erratic quality of Peking's spirits.

In traditional Peking society, drinking was encouraged and little stigma was
attached to someone who had taken a bit too much on board. On the contrary,
it was customary to force reticent folks to take a cup of wine at a banquet in order
to assist with creating the appropriate convivial atmosphere. Those who were
standoffish were described as "facing the wall" (面壁 or *mian bi*), which conjures
up the image of someone with their face to the wall while the rest eat and drink
in bonhomie.

Certainly, China's greatest poets never shrank from a drink. The great Tu Fu
drowned after reaching out of his boat in an intoxicated attempt to embrace the
moon. Liu Ling (刘伶)always had two servants travel with him, with standing

instructions. One of them was always to carry a pot of wine and the other a shovel to bury Liu Ling on the spot in case he died while partaking in too much drinking and good company.

Beer. The timid need not be fearful of the beer available in Peking. It always takes the form of a carbonated lager and usually comes in 16 ounce bottles. It is an excellent companion for all types of Chinese food and becomes indispensable when ordering spicy Si Chuan dishes.

Tsingtao beer, brewed in the successor of the old German brewery in Shan Dong, is well known and quite good. A bottle draft version of Tsingtao has arrived on the market and is good if indistinguishable from the regular brew.

Yanjing Beer is a widely distributed local lager that seems to have a high percentage of formaldehyde amidst the hops and malted barley. Drinking too much of Yanjing plain lager can lead to an unhappy morning. However, the brewery has introduced draft Yanjing beer in bottles that is a considerable improvement. Five Star Beer and Beijing (sic)Beer are relatively scarce but a better lager for those who like a bitter aftertaste.

Be wary of beer on tap from kegs. Some restaurants owners do not conscientiously clean their pipes resulting in the risk of bacterial infection. Peking's microbreweries should be approached cautiously for the same reason. In moderation, a microbrewery's ales are quite good although they should not be pounded one after the other all evening long, for the reasons stated.

Fruit Wine. Sino-foreign joint venture vineyards have been producing red and white grape wines for more than a decade, though records from the Yuan dynasty suggest that grape wine was a common, and potent beverage during the Mongol reign. These days, the three most common labels are Great Wall, Dynasty and Dragon Seal. After an extended stay in Peking, these wines will begin to seem to taste good, which is purely a symptom of a much-needed home leave. To be fair, the quality of these wines, especially the chardonnays and cabernet sauvignon, has improved considerably in the past five years.

Kuei Hua Chen Chiew (桂花陈酒) is a very sweet Riesling-like wine made from grapes and blossoms from the cassia tree. When very chilled, it is quite acceptable as a desert wine to be savored in rustic settings in parks, mountains and valleys. The English transliteration of its name is interesting in that a pre-1949 Romanization system is used, thus indicating that the trademark for this beverage, like Tsingtao beer, has a long pedigree in China.

For nostalgic old timers, there is China Benevolence Red Wine (中国仁葡萄酒 or *zhong guo ren pu tao jiu*), a heavy, syrupy wine that was the sole representative of fruit wines at banquets in the 1970s and 1980s, when it was usually mixed indiscriminately with beer and spirits at the bidding of the host.

This can only be considered as a beverage if you have run out of after-shave lotion or furniture polish.

Rice Wine. There are various types of Chinese rice wine. Most commonly, they come in black porcelain pots with a red label bearing the Chinese character for wine. The most well-known version is the *shao xing jiu* (绍兴酒), which is most famously fermented in Zhe Jiang province. There is a story that the local Zhe Jiang farmers would prepare a pot of rice wine on the birth of a daughter with the expectation that they would auction off the pot of wine in order to raise money for their daughter's dowry.

Shao Xing rice wine should always be drunk warm with perhaps a salted dried plum. I find that it is especially suited to Zhe Jiang and Fu Jian cuisine, though I recall an evening at the Tan Family restaurant in the Peking Hotel where the warm wine enhanced the flavor of the meal.

In addition to these "yellow wines," Peking families ferment their own rice wine with a bit of sugar and yeast. It is milky in appearance, like a Korean *makkoli* and very refreshing when chilled and served with dumplings and a sauce of soy, vinegar and ginger.

Spirits. Chinese spirits are best tossed straight back at one go, just as Russians drink vodka. I find their flavor to be well suited to hot pot cooking and lamb dishes accompanied by wheat cakes.

H.Y. Lowe summarized the sometime bewildering array of Chinese spirits (which he called white wine):

> White wine itself is subdivided into many kinds as it is variously scented with certain medicinal herbs, rose petals, bamboo leaves, young sprouts of the wormwood plant and so on. One special kind is supposed to be manufactured with tiger's bones as an essence and is said to be an effective relief to chronic rheumatism of the aged.[2]

The famous local spirit of Peking is *Er Guo Tou Jie* (二锅头酒), which literally means "two pot head wine." Despite first impressions, the name is not a reference to Cheech and Chong but rather to the fact that the spirit is passed through "two pots, viz., it is distilled twice. Among reprobates it is known by a nickname, "the Breakfast of Champions."

The standard issue Er Guo Tou comes in 16 ounce green bottle with a crimped cap and a basic socialist label in red, white and blue. A bottle sells for the equivalent of 60 United States cents. Like all Chinese spirits, it is distilled from sorghum, corn and rice and clocks in at a 64% alcohol content. For the man about town, *Er Guo Tou* is also sold in a stylish hip-flask bottle containing 8 ounces of the beverage.

The old adage is: "*Er Guo Tou*. If you don't respect it, it won't respect you." For safety's sake, make sure you have a bottle of mineral water handy. Unlike other spirits, it gives a boost to those who partake of it and in this regard generally exerts a tequila-like effect. *Er Guo Tou* is a coarse and fiery, with a slight coppery after-taste. As any Virginia moonshiner will tell you, a copper after-taste is no cause for concern. This simply confirms that the Red Star Distillery, purveyors of this fine beverage, use copper tubing, which is not toxic. Lead tubing or lead soldered joints are a different matter since lead causes brain damage and life-threatening illnesses. Since none of us would recognize the taste of lead because it has long since been removed from the world of Western cooking utensils, this raises the dilemma for us when sampling spirits distilled in China.

Moving on, the banquet halls at the Great Hall of the People serve *er guo tou*, but of a slightly higher quality. Its alcohol content weighs in at only 56% and comes in a clear white bottle with a twist off cap. There is also a high-end grade 12 year old *er guo tou* on the market, sold in a stylish black porcelain bottle and also with an alcohol content of 56%. A bottle will set you back about one dollar seventy-five cents. While it has less character than the cheaper stuff, some of the finer teahouses in San Li Tun sell shots of 12 year old *er guo tou* which are preceded by a lemon wedge sprinkled with sugar and instant coffee granules. The kick of this innovation is indescribable though for some reason it always reminds me of Keith Moon.

While we are on the subject of cheap but powerful tipples and long deceased madmen, it is only fitting to doff our cap to the Seven Sages of the Bamboo Grove and their leader Ruan Ji (阮籍). Unlike the mythical Eight Taoist Immortals, these seven renegades were historical personages renowned for their poetry, music and two fisted drinking capability. Their spirit is summed up with a great story. Once several Confucian scholars paid a formal social call on Ruan Ji. They were invited into his bedroom and found the Sage stinking drunk and naked. The Confucian scholars angrily rebuked Ruan for his lack of propriety. "What are you doing there lying naked?" Ruan propped himself up on an unsteady elbow and waived around his other arm: "As the universe is my clothing, this room is my trousers. So to you I ask in kind, 'What are you doing in my trousers?'" With a collapsing elbow, the sage passed out in front of his interlopers.

Moving all the way across the scale to the high priced firewater, my favorite is *Wu Liang Ye* (五粮液), a clear spirit distilled in Si Chuan province and retailing for prices comparable to Gordon's gin or Stolichnaya vodka. It has a 52% alcohol content with a slight rose flavor followed by a smoky aftertaste. It is the "cleanest" of all spirits since the high quality of the ingredients and the care taken in the distillation process makes for an easier morning. It also makes a well-received gift for Chinese friends.

Between these two are a spectrum of other Chinese spirits.

Mao Tai (矛台) is in the familiar white porcelain cylinder and is the scourge of signing ceremonies from Hei Long Jiang to Hai Nan Island. It has a taste similar to *Wu Liang Ye*, though less refined. Alec Le Suer, in his memoir *Running a Hotel on the Roof of the World* about his five years working in the Lhasa Holiday Inn, uncharitably asserts that *Mao Tai* tastes just like fermented cow dung. I don't suppose that cow dung can actually be fermented, lacking the required sugar content. But even if it could, I would much rather have *Mao Tai* than that, assuming that you can lay your hands on a legitimate bottle of *Mao Tai*. Some people claim that bootleggers make upwards of 85% of the *Mao Tai* sold in China. How can you be sure that your hooch is legitimate? If you wake up the next morning and you aren't blind, you were probably drinking the real McCoy.

Fen Jiu (汾酒) is a spirit much like *mao tai* in texture and taste though with perhaps a more subtle kick. It is also "cleanly" distilled and leaves little impact the next day.

Beijing Chun (北京醇) is a sorghum and wheat based spirit with a slight taste of anise. It is only 35% alcohol in content.

Jin Liu Fu (金六福) has a fruity after-taste with nice bouquet and 38% alcohol content. It is quite nice in moderation.

Liu Yang He (刘阳河) is an extremely coarse spirit with an overpowering sorghum taste. It is not a favorite even among the reprobates.

Jian Zhuang (尖庄) is a 50% spirit with a sorghum and rice base. It has a harsh taste with a syrupy texture.

Miscellaneous wines. In China, there are many medicinal wines made from rice and various animal parts, including deer antler, deer penises, whole lizards and snakes, as well as other representatives of the wild kingdom. If you can imagine in your mind's eye the distillery where these potions are fermented, you can understand why you shouldn't touch these with a barge pole. Some old timers swear by these unusual concoctions, which are indications an internal audit is overdue on the books in the office of this renegade who has gone way too local. If tempted or compelled to taste these unusual wines, you will find them to be slightly sweet or strongly flavored of Chinese medicinal herbs.

In the handful of Tibetan cafes and restaurants in Peking, you will come across *chang*, a barley beer with very low alcohol content and a grainy texture. The fermentation process for *chang* seems to depend on luck rather than a systematized recipe. Don't have too much as there may be bacterial complications.

In Mongolian restaurants, you may find fermented mare's milk, called *kusmis*, which resembles a slightly alcoholic yogurt drink. (Milk can be fermented because it contains the sugar lactose). Like chang, *kusmis* is made on an ad hoc basis and improves with quantity. Mongolian restaurants may also sell *arkhi*, which is Mongolian vodka that compares very well with high Russian vodkas like Stolichnaya or Mosovaka. You drink it neat with a toss of the head and neck.

Finally, the Chinese have embarked upon distilling local versions of popular Western spirits, like scotch, bourbon, vodka and gin. While most of these should be sensibly approached with caution, locally made *Four Roses Bourbon* is an acceptable alternative if Kentucky or Tennessee bourbons are not available. Local vodkas tend to be harsh and unforgiving. Special mention should be made of *Chinese Gin*,

A street side seller of strong drink in 1930s Peking.

distilled at the Tsingtao brewery in Shan Dong. An English classical musician resident in Peking as well as an old friend introduced it to me in the mid 1990s. It was every bit as good as Gordon's gin and cost ounce for ounce less than half the price of the tonic water. I am hopeful that it will make a comeback.

24

A NIGHT AT THE OPERA

I HAVE GROWN ACCUSTOMED TO incredulous stares when I tell people that I enjoy going out to see Peking Opera. After a startled second or two, my Western acquaintances will pull themselves together and launch into a standard critique, complaining of the art form's shrill, non-melodic quality and the imponderable gestures of the actors.

Alas, the reception is not always that much better from the descendants of the Yellow Emperor. One Chinese friend gave me a gazed look while pronouncing, "If I can't understand the story, how can you, a foreigner? Another Chinese friend, an elegant woman born and raised in Peking, just laconically muttered while yawning "I hate that stuff."

Yes, it takes preparation in advance to enjoy a Peking Opera, as it requires concentration that's a few notches above your standard Mel Gibson action thriller. Yes, it is hard to understand the lyrics but you can lay your hands on a libretto in Chinese or even a synopsis in English before the performance starts. Yes, it sounds strange to Western ears but this is only because Chinese music developed along a different set of music theories. With increasing exposure, your ear becomes adjusted to the different musical scale. But I wish to rush boldly forward with a few more observations. After you have begun to train your ear and eye, there isn't space for a piece of paper to be slid between Peking Opera and Jimi Hendrix. And if you are not able to grasp that point, then, with my heart breaking in regret, you haven't really *heard Jimi.*

Chinese drama began in the remote past as a form of spirit worship. However, by the Warring States Period, the state of acting had so developed that a court jester was talented enough to impersonate a deceased official that the flabbergasted king believed the official had come back to life. Most performances at this time were impromptu and had not developed beyond dancing and acrobatics. By the late Han, actors began to use masks, which were the precursors of the painted faces in today's Peking opera. Through the Tang and Song, the imperial house encouraged the development of opera.

A divide came about after the Mongols occupied northern China. Two schools, the *bei qu* (北曲) and the *nan qu* (南曲) or the Northern and Southern skills arose. The northern school reflected Mongolian tastes by adding string instruments to the primarily percussive orchestras. *Bei qu* plots were energetic with much action and narratives in addition to lyrics. The southern school was less exuberant and never absorbed the acrobatics of the north. Flute music predominated.

With the rise of the Ming, the imperial court viewed askance the *bei qu* on account of its Mongolian associations. The southern school gradually absorbed the northern school while Zhu Yuan Cheng poured cold water on the opera singing aspirations of his officials by ordering the tongues cut out of any official caught singing an opera aria.

Su Zhou became the center of an opera style called *kun qu* (昆曲). It is said that *kun qu* was so sophisticated and refined that its stories were accessible to only the most literate of audiences. Its premier status was gradually eroded as a new *bei qu* style of opera developed in An Hui province. In the 1780s, Qian Long discovered this type of opera and fell in love with it immediately. He moved various Anhui opera troupes to the capital where Peking Opera came into existence in the late 1700s.

In the 19th century, Peking Opera troupes were hard pressed to find rehearsal studios. By sheer happenstance, opera performers struck a deal with teahouse operators to rehearse in their restaurants, which quickly morphed into theaters. This also explains why audiences at Peking operas tend to be very "chatty." Just as you would expect in a teahouse, people's attentions wax and wane with the performance with people ignoring poorly performed bits and hollering their approval for virtuosos.

Some folks think of Peking Opera as a never changing element in Chinese culture. This turns a blind eye to the inevitability of change over time in cultures everywhere. For example, in the 19th century, a string instrument called *er hu qin* (二胡琴) was introduced into the orchestra. In the 1930s, actresses began to perform Peking opera. In the 1990s, some opera troupes began to introduce the innovations of stage scenery.

There were two influences in the aesthetic of Peking Opera. The first was minimalism. Few props are used. A whip with brightly colored tassels in an actor's left hand means he is dismounting the horse while in the right hand, it represents the actor mounting the steed. Two flags with a wheel signify a chariot. A simple wooden chair could symbolize a tower, a mountain or even a throne. Two bamboo poles with calico attached represent a city wall or gate.

Similarly, actors' movements convey a multitude of meanings. When an actor shakes the long sleeves of his robe, he conveys fear. Waving the sleeves like a fan means hot weather or exertion while thrusting hands into the sleeves represents winter. Anger, flirtation, happiness and surprise are all represented through an actor's use of his sleeves. Lifting a foot high indicates that the actor is stepping across a doorway. Hands slowly drawn across the eyes depict weeping. Walking with hands reaching out at each side represent the actor walking in darkness.

These gestures alone do not make for a virtuoso performance. Each movement must be accompanied by formalized mannerisms by each part of the actor's body. In Qing Peking, poor parents apprenticed their children to Peking Opera schools at a young age. The ensuing years of training for performance and song were brutally rigorous given the competition among opera troupes and the uncertainty of a troupe's income.

The second aesthetic influence is the primacy of suggestion over detail. As John Blofeld's friends admired the suggestion of the Altar of Heaven when shrouded in snow, so too the suggestion of an action is more pleasing than an accurate or detailed depiction. For instance, Dick Hughes relates a story where he attended a performance where a concubine was coughing as she slowly died, attended by the sounds of a Chinese violin. Hughes observed that nothing of the scene sounded like someone coughing a death rattle. However, a Chinese friend explained that the performance was superb because it conformed to the idea of a dying man's cough. Were the actor and orchestra to sound like a real cough, it would be lousy opera.

Until the 1930s, all Peking Opera performers were men on account of Confucian sentiments against women performing in public. During the apprenticeship, the opera master assigned a certain type of character to a student, and for the rest of the career of that student he only would portray that type of character. Given the years of training, it could scarcely be otherwise.

Connoisseurs of Peking Opera regard *dan* (旦) roles as the most demanding. A dan actor was trained to impersonate a woman in (almost) every detail. *Dan* actors further fall into three categories: a virtuous woman, a flirtatious woman or an elderly dame.

Sheng (生) were male roles, divided between youthful, mature and elderly characters. *Jing* (淨) were military characters whose faces were painted in various colors to indicate their personalities. The *clown* (丑 or *chou*) is usually recognized because he wears a white tag over his nose without any other accompanying face paint. Unlike the other characters, the clown often speaks in modern Chinese, making sly comments on the plot to the audience. For the foreigner struggling through the classical Chinese, the sudden burst of the clown's commentary can carry quite an impact. To find a Western parallel for this, picture, if you would imagine, a performance of Don Quixote with Peter O'Toole as the Don, reciting his lines in Cervantes' classical verse. Now picture Sancho performed by Danny De Vito speaking in colloquial English.

Just as traditional Peking court life was divided between civilian and military officials, Peking Opera drew a distinction between *wen* (文 or civilian) and *wu* (武 or martial) operas. The former tend to be poetic and, truthfully, tougher sledding for a foreign audience. The latter usually entails a dazzling display of acrobatics that can hold the attention of the most devoted Mel Gibson fan.

If you are inclined to see Peking Opera, I recommend the People's Theatre (人民剧场 or *ren min ju chang*) near Mei Lan Fang's former residence. The theatre was built in the 1950s and attracts only a handful of elderly Peking Opera fans, but these guys know their opera and you cannot help but be drawn into their enthusiasm. In addition, you should try to track down Elizabeth Halson's unparalleled book, *Peking Opera*. It is a short essay of only 88 pages but it does a superlative job of giving you all the information that you need to appreciate a night of opera.

25

EPILOGUE

No mosaic of Old Peking is complete. Least of all, this one.

The Italian diplomat Daniele Vare struggled with the dilemma of cultural relativism during his postings in Peking. Vare wrote novels set during the Qing and Republican eras. One day, he dreamed up a dramatic incident.

A Qing official remonstrates against the emperor's willingness to issue a decree for reform. The official submits a memorial protesting the contents of the decree. He is ignored. To persuade the Son of Heaven of the sincerity of his protest, the official mortally stabs himself in the courtyard of the Hall of Supreme Harmony.

Vare showed the chapter to his language teacher, an old-school Manchu, who sadly shook his head. "No Chinese would ever believe this." Vare, who already spent quite a few years in China, was taken aback. "Why not?"

His teacher said that no official would be so presumptuous as to commit suicide in the grounds of the Forbidden City. Only emperors and, by extension, his empresses and concubines, could do so. The traditional place for a protesting official to commit suicide would be at the foot of the Western Hills. Everyone also knew that an emperor would not pay the slightest attention to a memorial drafted by an official so lacking in a sense of propriety. And practically speaking, the imperial guards would not have let anyone with a dagger get close to the throne.

Stumped by his teacher's response, Vare asked him to think up a believable scenario. The old scholar agreed to do so. One week later, Vare's teacher trundled over to the Italian legation with the draft of a thoroughly understandable story — through a Chinese perspective.

The Chinese version was subtle. A Qing official is granted the privilege of visiting a highly positioned prince. During each visit, the prince offers sugared turnips as a symbol of his high regard for the official. One week, the prince receives the official but the turnips are nowhere to be seen. Taking this as a sign of his disgrace, the official goes off and hangs himself from a tree in the Western Hills. "A story such as this would be believable by all Chinese," said the teacher to a perplexed Vare.

After a moment or two, Vare protested. "If I wrote that story, no one in the West would believe it." "And no Chinese can believe your story," countered Vare's teacher.

There you have it, the great divide. As Stanley Karnow once quipped to fellow foreign devil Dick Hughes, "the Far East is a university in which no degree is ever granted." At that proposition, I am sure that the ghosts of Arlington and Lewisohn each lift a pint and say "Amen."

NOTES

CHAPTER 1

1. Osbert Sitwell, *Escape with Me*, p.182.
2. These were the terms used by the Boxers to describe Chinese Christians and Chinese purveyors of Western goods, respectively.

CHAPTER 2

1. It is also said that red symbolizes the blossom of the peach tree, which has been believed to have beneficial properties since time memorial. Sprigs of peach blossoms and canes made from peach wood are useful for warding off bad luck.
2. Quoted in Susan Naquin, *Peking: City Life and Temples 1400–1900*, p. 46.
3. An ancient remnant of this belief is to be found in 21st century Hong Kong. The "Lover's Rock" off Bowen Road is actually the continuation of worship of a fertility spirit that resides in a phallic-shaped (and thus *yang*-based) rock.
4. In keeping with traditional Sinologists, I use the traditional romanization of this Chinese word. It is pronounced "dowism."

CHAPTER 3

1. The Mongol word "Khitan" is the basis for the Russian word for China: "Kitai." In Western Europe Kitai metamorphosed into "Cathay."
2. Marco Polo, *Travels of Marco Polo — the Yule-Cordier Edition*, Vol. 1, p. 375.
3. Starting from the Ming, emperors used, confusingly, three different names. There was a personal name, given at birth and whose use became taboo once the emperor assumed the throne. Thereafter, the emperor was known by his reign name. Finally, there was a posthumous name that court ritual required in subsequent references to the deceased emperor. With a few exceptions, I will use the reign names of the emperors.

4. In written documents, it was customary to refer to Peking as [our] Capital City (京师 or *jing shi*). Beijing was only used infrequently until its rise in popular usage during the 20th century.

5. These Eight Great Sights of Peking were 太液秋风 (the rippling waves in fine weather on the three imperial lakes), 玉泉趵突 (the reflection of the rainbow in the Jade Springs at the Jade Fountain), 西山晴雪 (clear snow on the Western Hills), 金台夕照 (the reflection of the evening sun on the Golden Terrace, now no longer in existence but its name is preserved by a school nearby), 居庸迭翠 (the green ranges of Chu Yung, which is the Qing Long Qiao to the plains), 蓟门烟树 (the density of trees surrounding the Gate of the Reed, no longer in existence), 琼岛春阳 (the spring warmth on Qing Dao on Hortensia Island in the Bei Hai Park), and 卢沟晓月 (the reflection of the moon at dawn at the Marco Polo Bridge).

6. Jonathan D. Spence, *The Emperor of China: Self Portrait of Kang Xi*, p. 97.

7. In Chinese, her title was Ci Xi Tai Hou (慈禧太后).

8. Much ink has been used on speculations about the true Yeholona. Daniel Vare presented a more sympathetic account in *The Last Empress*. Sterling Seagrave's *Dragon Lady* takes the unconventional (and controversial) view that the memory of the Empress Dowager was intentionally blackened by anti-Qing Chinese and foreign accomplices. Like so many other people in Chinese political history, we are unlikely to ever have an accurate portrait of the Empress Dowager and her life.

9. Guang Xu's ascension to the throne caused tremendous controversy as Manchu custom did not permit an emperor's cousin to be his successor.

10. Peter Quennell, *A Superficial Journey Through Tokyo and Peking*, pp. 183–184.

11. Karl Eskelund, *My Chinese Wife*, p. 25.

12. David Kidd, *Peking Story*, pp. 195–196.

CHAPTER **4**

1. Jack Kerowc, *Desolation Angels*, pp. 284–285.

2. Simon Leys, *Chinese Shadows*, pp. 53–54.

3. Sidney Rittenberg, *The Man Who Stayed Behind*, pp. 245-246.

4. Lei Feng was a model worker famous for the statement that he wanted to be a screw in the great machinery of socialism. Indeed. He is said to have ceaselessly sought to serve the Party as well as the common people by doing good deeds like secretly washing his colleagues socks at night. Lei died at the age of 23 in 1962 and became an icon during the Cultural Revolution. However, evidence has arisen to show that the people's hero may have had feet of clay. A photograph in Fu Shun shows Lei wearing a wrist watch, a showy piece of extravagance that was officially denied to people of his rank. Maybe the old boy had some feudal notions of face. At any rate, the newly released photograph is just a storm in a tea cup as no one really cares about Lei Feng any more.

5. David S. G. Goodman, *Beijing Street Voices*, p. 95.

CHAPTER **5**

1. Reginald Johnston, *Lion and Dragon in North China*, pp. 125–126.

CHAPTER **6**

1. Daniel Vare, *The Laughing Diplomat*, p. 92.
2. George MacDonald Fraser, *Flashman and the Dragon*, p. 224.
3. Ai Xin Jue Ruo Pu Yi, *From Emperor to Citizen*, p. 121.
4. Quoted in Stanley Charles Nott, *Chinese Jade*, p. 1.
5. Elizabeth Crump Enders, *Swinging Lanterns*, pp. 189–190.

CHAPTER **7**

1. Derk Bodde, *Peking Diary*, p. 115.
2. Juliet Bredon, *Peking*, p. 179.

CHAPTER **8**

1. Marco Polo, *The Travels of Marco Polo: The Yule - Cordier Edition*, Vol. 1, pp. 364–365.
2. Derk Bodde, *Peking Diary*, p. 147.
3. Mrs. Archibald Little, *Round About My Peking Garden*, pp. 208–209.
4. Mrs. Archibald Little, *Round About My Peking Garden*, pp. 10–11.

CHAPTER **9**

1. I will discuss this further in the next chapter.
2. These clauses were the great diplomatic folly of the Qing court in the 19th century as they entitled each foreign signatory the same privileges granted to other foreign countries.
3. The exceptions to this observation are Russia and Japan, both of whom had territorial ambitions in Manchuria that could be furthered by retaining troops in Peking.
4. Quoted in *Spy Book: The Encyclopedia of Espionage* by Norman Polmar and Thomas B. Allen, pp. 110 to 11.
5. Harold Acton, *Peonies and Ponies*, p. 2.
6. Jenny Lu's is the name of a franchise established in Peking by a woman from the deep country in He Bei Province. She specializes in providing the highest quality produce for the expat community. Her employees, who are of the same rustic origins as Jenny, studiously learn the English equivalent of their inventory. A friend who was searching for a bottle of fennel seeds was astonished to see an elderly employee recognize the English words and hurried back, all smiles, with fennel in hand.

CHAPTER **10**

1. Father Ricci designed the first map of the world in China. By referring to the Western Hemisphere, Yang and others would have been aware of the reach of these two global superpowers.
2. Paul Reps, *Zen Flesh, Zen Bones*, pp. 16–17.
3. W.A.P. Martin, *The Chinese*, p. 89.
4. H.G. Creel, *Chinese Thought From Confucius to Mao*, p. 210.

CHAPTER **11**

1. John Blofeld, *City of Lingering Splendour*, p. 185.
2. John Blofeld, *City of Lingering Splendour*, p. 238.
3. Huthessing, *Window on China*, p. 56.
4. David Rennie, *Peking and the Pekingese* Vol, pp. 44–45.
5. "For You … " Ling Bing, quoted in David S. G. Goodman, *Beijing Street Voices*, pp. 122.

CHAPTER **12**

1. Taken from Juliet Bredon and Igor Mitrophanow, *The Moon Year* pp. 55–56.

CHAPTER **13**

1. Quoted in Naquin *Peking: Temples and City Life*, p. 631.
2. Juliet Bredon, *Peking*, p. 219.

CHAPTER **14**

1. David Rennie, *Peking and the Pekingese*, Vol. II, p. 21.
2. Quoted in Alan Samagalski; Robert Strauss, Michael Buckley, *China: A Travel Survival Kit*, p.

CHAPTER **15**

1. David Rennie, The Peking and the Pekingese, pp. 94–95.

CHAPTER **16**

1. Dun Li Chien, *Annual Customs and Festivals in Peking*, p. 78.
2. Dun Li Chen, *Annual Customs and Festivals in Peking*, p. 17
3. Marco Polo, *The Travels of Marco-Polo: The Complete Yule-Cordier Edition*, Vol. II, pp. 3–4.

CHAPTER **17**

1. David Kidd, *Peking Story*, p. 75.

CHAPTER **20**

1. Boswell, *A Life of Johnston*, p. 929.

CHAPTER **21**

1. Paul Reps, *Zen Flesh, Zen Bones*, p. 5.

CHAPTER **23**

1. The author wishes to acknowledge the valuable contributions made by Nicholas Smith and Jon Eichelberger during the research for this chapter.
2. H.Y. Lowe, *The Adventures of Wu*, Vol II p. 50.

BIBLIOGRAPHY

Harold Acton, *Peonies and Ponies*, (London, Chatto & Windus, 1941)

Aisin Gioru Pu Yi, *From Emperor to Citizen*, (Beijing, Foreign Languages Press, 1989)

Steve Allen, *"Explaining China,"* (New York, Crown Publishers, 1980)

Hikotaro Ando, *Peking*, (Tokyo, Kodansha International Ltd., 1972)

L. C. Arlington, *Through the Dragon's Eyes*, (London, Constable & Co., Ltd., 1931)

L.C. Arlington and Harold Acton, *Famous Chinese Plays*, (Peiping, Henri Vetch, 1937; reprinted: New York, Russell & Russell, 1963)

L.C. Arlington and William Lewisohn, *In Search of Old Peking*, (Peiping, Henri Vetch, 1935; reprinted Hong Kong, Oxford University Press, 1988)

J. Dyer Ball, *Things Chinese*, (fifth printing, 1925; reprinted, Singapore, Graham Brash (Pte) Ltd., 1989)

Jasper Becker, *Christmas Worth Half-century Wait*, South China Morning Post, January 1, 2002

Jasper Becker, *Hungry Ghosts: China's Secret Famine*, (London, John Murray, 1996)

Beijing Administrative Bureau for the Preservation of Artifacts 北京市文物事业管理局，北京名胜古迹辞典, [A Compilation of Famous Ancient Sites in Beijing], (Beijing, Beijing Yan Shan Press, 1989)

Beijing Arts and Photography Publishing House, *Hutongs of Beijing*, (Beijing, Beijing Arts and Photography House, 1993)

Beijing Arts and Photography Publishing House, *Quadrangles of Beijing*, (Beijing, Beijing Arts and Photography House, 1993)

Beijing Encyclopedia Editorial Committee 北京百克科全书编辑委员会，北京百科全书 [*Beijing Encyclopedia*], (Beijing Olympic Press, 1991)

John Bell, *A Journey from St. Petersburg to Peking 1719–22*, ed. J. L. Stevenson, (Edinburgh: Edinburgh University Press, 1965)

Terry Bennett, *Korea: Caught in Time*, (Reading, U.K., Garnett Publishing, 1997)

J. O. P. Bland, *Recent Events and Present Policies in China*, (London, William Heinemann, 1912)

John Blofeld, *City of Lingering Splendour*, (London, Hutchinson, 1961; reprinted, Boston & Shaftesbury, Shambhala, 1989)

Derk Bodde, *Annual Customs and Festivals in Peking*, (Peiping, Henri Vetch, 1936; reprinted, Taipei, SMC Publishing, 1977)

Derk Bodde, *Peking Diary*, (New York, Abelard-Schuman Limited, 1950; reprinted, New York, Fawcett Premiere, 1967)

M.L.C. Bogan, *Manchu Customs and Superstitions*, (Tientsin & Peking, 1928; reprinted, Taipei, SMC Publishing, 1994)

James Bowsell, *The Life of Samuel Johnson*, (Oxford, Oxford University Press, 1970)

Juliet Bredon, *Peking*, (Shanghai, Kelly & Walsh, 1922)

Juliet Bredon and Igor Mitrophanow, *The Moon Year*, (Shanghai, Kelly & Walsh Limited, 1927)

Emil Bretschneider, *Archaeological and Historical Researches on Peking and its Environs*, (London, Trubner & Co., 1876; reprinted, Boston, Elibron Classics, undated)

Ann Bridge, *Peking Picnic*, (New York, Little, Brown and Company, 1932; reprinted, New York, Berkley Publishing, 1964)

Ann Bridge, *Ginger Griffin*, (London, Chatto & Windus, 1934; reprinted Hong Kong, Oxford University Press, 1985)

John Stewart Burgess, *The Guilds of Peking*, (New York, Columbia University Press, 1928; reprinted, New York, AMS Press, 1970)

V.R. Burkhardt, *Chinese Creeds and Customs*, (Reprint, Taipei, Huang Jia Library Company, Ltd., 1976)

Fox Butterfield, *China, Alive in the Bitter Sea*, (New York, Bantam Books, 1983)

Nigel Cameron, *Barbarians and Mandarins*, (London, John Weatherhill, Inc., 1970; reprinted, Hong Kong, Oxford University Press, 1993)

Nigel Cameron, *The Chinese Smile*, (London, Hutchinson & Co. Publishers Ltd., 1958; reprinted, Hong Kong, Oxford University Press, 1990)

Nigel Cameron, & Brian Blake *Peking: A Tale of Three Cities*, (New York & Evanston, Harper & Row, 1965)

Cha Zhen Xing 查慎行，人海记, [*Account of the Sea of Man*], printed 1851, reprinted Beijing Guoji Press, 2000

Wing-Tsit Chan, *A Source Book in Chinese Philosophy*, (Princeton, New Jersey, Princeton University Press, 1973)

Chang Hsin-hai, *The Fabulous Concubine,* (New York, Simon and Schuster, 1956; reprinted, Hong Kong, Oxford University Press, 1992)

Chen Wen Liang, editor, 陈文良，北京传统文化博览, [*Compendia of Traditional Beijing Culture*], (Beijing, Beijing Yan Shan Press, 1992)

Chen Ying, editor, 陈英，北京名人官居, [*Residences of Famous People in Beijing*], (Beijing, Beijing Yan Shan Press, 1998)

China Esperanto Press, *Ancient Temples in Beijing,* (Beijing, China Esperanto Press, 1993)

China Esperanto Press, *Imperial Tombs of the Ming and Qing Dynasties,* (Beijing, China Esperanto Press, 1993)

Chinese Buddhist Association, *Buddhist in New China,* (Peking, Nationalities Publishing House, 1956)

Chinese Literature Press, *Sights with Stories in Old Beijing,* (Beijing, Panda Books, 1993)

Maurice Collis, *The Great Within,* (London, Faber and Faber Limited, 1941)

H.G. Creel, *Chinese Thought From Confucius to Mao Tse-Tung,* (Chicago, University of Chicago Press, 1953; reprinted, New York, New American Library, 1964)

Carl Crow, *Handbook for China,* (Shanghai, Kelly & Walsh, Limited, 1933; reprinted, Hong Kong, Oxford University Press, 1986)

Elizabeth Crump Enders, *Swinging Lantern,* (New York and London, D. Appleton and Company, 1925)

William Theodore de Bary, Wing-tsit Chan, Chester Tan *et al., Sources in Chinese Tradition,* (New York, Columbia University Press, 1965)

J.J. M. DeGroot, *The Religious System of the Chinese,* (New York, Macmillan Company, 1910)

Tillman Durdin, James Reston and Seymour Topping, *The New York Times Report from Red China,* (New York, Avon Books, 1971)

Nicholas Eftimiades, *Chinese Intelligence Operations,* (Annapolis, Naval Institute Press, 1994)

Karl Eskelund, *My Chinese Wife,* (Garden City Publishing Co., Garden City, New York, 1945)

Karl Eskelund, *The Red Mandarins,* (London, Alvin Redman, 1959)

John K. Fairbank, Edwin O. Reischauer, Albert M. Craig, *East Asia: Tradition and Transformation,* (Boston, Houghton Mifflin Company, 1973)

Roger Faligot and Remi Kauffer, *The Chinese Secret Service: Kang Sheng and the Shadow Government in Red China,* (New York, William Morrow and Company, 1987)

Peter Fleming, *The Siege at Peking,* (London, Rupert-Hart Davis, 1959; reprinted, Hong Kong, Oxford University Press, 1984)

George MacDonald Fraser, *Flashman and the Dragon,* (London, HarperCollins, 1994)

Fu Cha Dong Zhou 富蔡敦崇，燕京岁时记, [*Account of the Year in Yan Jing*], printed 1906; reprinted Guzhi 2000

Fu Gongyue, *Old Beijing in Panorama,* (Beijing, People's China Press, 1992)

Alice Getty, *The Gods of Northern Buddhism,* (Oxford, Clarendon Press, 1928; reprinted, Mineola, New York, Dover Publications, Inc., 1988)

Dru C. Gladney, *Muslim Chinese: Ethnic Nationalism in the People's Republic,* (Cambridge and London, Council on East Asian Studies, 1991, 1996)

John A. Goodall, *Heaven and Earth: Album Leaves From a Ming Encyclopedia,* (Boulder, Shambhala, 1979)

David. S.G. Goodman, *Beijing Street Voices, The Poetry and Politics of China's Democracy Movement,* (London & Boston, Marion Boyars, 1981)

Dorothy Graham, *Through the Moon Door,* (New York, J.H. Sears and Company, Inc., 1926)

A. E. Grantham, *Pencil Speakings From Peking,* (London, George Allen & Unwin, 1918)

Tenzin Gyatso, the Fourteenth Dalai Lama, *Freedom in Exile,* (London, Hodder and Stoughton, Ltd., 1990)

Emily Hahn, *The Cooking of China,* (New York, Time-Life Books, 1968)

Emily Hahn, *The Soong Sisters,* (Garden City, New York, Doubleday, Doran & Company, Inc., 1941)

Elizabeth Halson, *Peking Opera,* (Hong Kong, Oxford University Press, 1966)

Charlton Heston, *Beijing Diary,* (New York, Simon and Schuster, 1990)

Mary Hooker, *Behind the Scenes in Peking,* (London, John Murray, 1910; reprinted, Hong Kong, Oxford University Press, 1986)

Huang Shang, *Tales from Peking Opera,* (Beijing, New World Press, 1985)

Richard Hughes, *Barefoot Reporter,* (Hong Kong, Far Eastern Economic Review Ltd., 1984)

Richard Hughes, *Foreign Devil: Thirty Years of Reporting from the Far East,* (London, Andres Deutsch, 1975)

Michael Hunt, *The Forgotten Occupation: Peking, 1900–1901,* Pacific Historical Review, 45 (1979) 501–529

Raja Hutheesing, *Window on China,* (Bombay, Casement Publications Ltd., undated)

Immanuel Hsu, *The Rise of Modern China,* (New York and Oxford, Oxford University Press, 1983)

W.J.F. Jenner, *The Tyranny of History,* (London, Penguin Books, 1992)

Jin Shoukun 金受申，老北京的生活, [*Life in Old Peking*], (Beijing, Beijing Press, 1989)

Reginald Johnston, *The Cult of Military Heroes in China*, New China Review, Vol. III, No. 1 (1921) 41–64

Reginald Johnston, *Lion and Dragon in North China*, (London, John Murray, 1910; reprinted, Hong Kong, Oxford University Press, 1986)

Reginald Johnston, *The Romance of an Emperor*, New China Review, Vol. II, No. 1 (1920) 1–24

Reginald Johnston, *Twilight in the Forbidden City*, (London, Victor Gollancz Ltd., 1934; reprinted, Hong Kong, Oxford University Press, 1985)

George Kates, *The Years That Were Fat*, (New York, Harper and Brothers Publishers, 1952; reprinted, Hong Kong, Oxford University Press, 1988)

Jack Kerouac, *Desolation Angels*, (New York, Perigree Books, 1980)

David Kidd, *Peking Story: The Last Days of Old China*, (London, Aurum Press, 1988)

Ronald G. Knapp, *The Chinese House*, (Hong Kong, Oxford University Press, 1990)

Nicholas D. Kristof and Sheryl WuDunn, *China Wakes*, (New York, Random House, 1994)

U Kyaw Min, *Through the Iron Curtain Via the Back Door*, (Rangoon, Burmese Advertising Press, 1952)

Corrinne Lamb, *The Chinese Festive Board*, (Shanghai, Henri Vetch, 1935; reprinted, Hong Kong, Oxford University Press, 1986).

Kenneth Scott Latourette, *The Chinese: Their History and Culture*, (New York, The Macmillan Company, 1947)

Owen Lattimore, *Manchuria, Cradle of Conflict*, (New York, The Macmillan Company, 1935)

Alec Le Sueur, *Running a Hotel on the Roof of the World: Five Years in Tibet*, (Chicester, United Kingdom, Summersdale, 1998)

Louise Levanthes, *When China Ruled the Seas*, (New York, Simon and Schuster, 1994)

Simon Leys, *Chinese Shadows*, (New York, Penguin Books, 1978)

Li Xingjian, *Beijing Superlatives*, (Hong Kong, Hai Feng Publishers, 1989)

Zhisui Li, *The Private Life of Chairman Mao: The Inside Story of the Man Who Made Modern City*, (London, Chatto & Windus, 1994)

Mrs. Archibald Little, *Round About My Peking Garden*, (London, T. Fisher Unwin, 1905)

Liu Jilin, *Chinese Shadow Puppet Plays*, (Beijing, Morning Glory Publishers, 1988)

Pierre Loti, *The Last Days of Peking*, (Boston, Little, Brown and Company, 1902)

H.Y. Lowe, *The Adventures of Wu: A Life Cycle of a Peking Man,* (Peiping, Peiping Chronicle Press, 1940 and 1941; reprinted, Princeton, New Jersey, Princeton University Press, 1983)

Macao Museum of Art, *The Golden Exile, Pictorial Expressions of the School of Western Missionaries' Artworks of the Qing Dynasty Court* (Macao, 2002)

Madrolle, *Guide En Indochine,* (Hanoi, Ecole Francaise D'Extreme Orient, 1954)

Mao Zedong, *The Collected Works of Mao Zedong,* (Beijing, Foreign Languages Press,)

W.A.P. Martin, *The Chinese,* (New York, Harpers and Bros., 1881)

Robert Marshall, *The Storm from the East,* (London, Penguin Books and BBC Books, 1994)

Mei Lan Fan Exhibiton Hall, 梅兰芳纪念馆，梅兰芳表演艺术图影 [*Collection of the Techniques of Mei Lan Fan*], (Beijing, Foreign Languages Press, 2001)

James Miles, *The Legacy of Tiananmen, China in Disarray,* (Ann Arbor, University of Michigan Press, 1996)

Hedda Morrison, *A Photographer in Old Peking,* (Reprint, New York, Oxford University Press, 1999)

Michael J. Moser & Yeone Wei-Chih Moser, *Foreigners within the Gates,* (Hong Kong, Oxford University Press, 1993)

James Arthur Muller, *Peking, the City of the Unexpected,* National Geographic Magazine, Vol. 38, No. 5 (1920) 335 - 355

Officers' Morale Endeavor Association, *Information Pamphlet on Peiping (Peking),* (Peiping, August 1946).

Susan Naquin, *Peking: Temples and City Life,* (Berkeley, University of California Press, 2000)

Andrew Nathan and Perry Link, *The Tiananmen Papers,* (London, Little, Brown & Company, 2001)

Desmond Neill, *Elegant Flower: Recollection of a Cadet in* Cathay, (London, John Murray (Publishers) Ltd., 1956; reprinted, Hong Kong, Oxford University Press, 1987)

Stanley Charles Nott, *Chinese Jade,* (London, B.T. Batsford Ltd., 1936, reprinted Rutland, Vermont and Tokyo, Charles E. Tuttle Company, 1962)

Martin Palmer, *T'ung Shu: The Ancient Chinese Almanac,* (Singapore, Vinpress, 2000)

Ann Paludin, *The Ming Tombs,* (Oxford, Oxford University Press 1991)

Pan Rongbi 潘荣陛，帝京岁时纪胜，[*Famous Sites in the Annual Calendar of the Capital*], 1758, reprinted Beijing Guiji, 2000.

Pan Xiafeng, *The Stagecraft of Peking Opera: From its Origins to the Present Day,* (Beijing, New World Press, 1995)

People's China, Vol. II, Nos. 8–12 (1950)

Norman Polmar and Thomas B. Allen, *Spy Book: The Encyclopedia of Espionage*, (New York, Random House, 1998)

Bill Porter, *Road to Heaven: Encounters with Chinese Hermits*, (San Francisco, Mercury House, 1993)

Peter Quennell, *A Superficial Journey Through Tokyo and Peking*, (London, Faber and Faber Limited, 1932, reprinted, Hong Kong, Oxford University Press, 1986)

Walpola Rahula, *What the Buddha Taught*, (New York, Grove Press, 1959)

Rang Lian, 讓廉，京都风俗志, [*Essay on Customs of the Capital City*] MSS 1899, printed Guoji 2000

Red Pine, translator, *Songs of the Masters*, (Port Townsend, Washington, Copper Canyon Press, 2003)

David F. Rennie, *Peking and the Pekingese*, (London, John Murray, 1865; reprinted, Boston, Elibron Classics, undated)

Paul Reps, *Zen Flesh, Zen Bones*, (Garden City, New York, Doubleday Anchor, undated)

Matteo Ricci, *The True Meaning of the Lord of Heaven*, (St. Louis, Institute of Jesuit Resources, 1985)

Matteo Ripa, *The Memoirs of Father Ripa During Thirteen Years' Residence At the Court of Peking in the Service of the Emperor of China*, (London, John Murray, 1844; reprinted, Boston, Elibron Classics, undated)

Sydney Rittenberg and Amanda Bennett, *The Man Who Stayed Behind*, (New York, Simon & Schuster, 1993)

Tony Scotland, *The Empty Throne: The Quest for an Imperial Heir in the People's Republic of China*, (London, Penguin Books, 1993)

Sterling Seagrave, *Dragon Lady; The Life and Legend of the Last Empress of China*, (New York, Alfred A. Knopf, 1992)

Norodom Sihanouk, *Sihanouk Reminisces*, (Bangkok, Duang Kamol, 1990)

Osbert Sitwell, *Escape with Me!*, (New York, Macmillan & Co., Ltd., 1939; reprinted, Hong Kong, Oxford University Press, 1985)

Richard J. Smith, *Chinese Almanacs*, (Hong Kong, Oxford University Press, 1992)

Jonathan D. Spence, *Kang Xi: A Self Portrait*, (New York, Vintage Books, 1988)

Jonathan D. Spence, *Mao Zedong*, (New York, Viking, 1999)

Jonathan D. Spence, *The Memory Palace of Matteo Ricci*, (New York, Penguin Books, 1985)

Jonathan D. Spence, *To Change China*, (New York, Penguin Books, 1980)

Sir George Staunton, *An Authentic Account of An Embassy from the King of Great Britain to the Emperor of China: including Cursory Observations Made, and*

Information Obtained, in Travelling Through That Ancient Empire, and a Small Part of Chinese Tartary, (London: G. Nicol, 1798, 3 Vols., reprinted, Boston, Elibron Classics, undated)

William Stevenson, *The Yellow Wind: An Excursion in and around Red China with a Traveler in the Yellow Wind,* (London, Cassell, 1959)

Fr. Manuel Teixeira, *The Story of Ma-Kok-Miu,* (Macao, Centro de Informacao e Turismo, 1979)

Tizanio Terzani, *Behind the Forbidden Door: Travels in Unknown China,* (New York, Henry Holt and Company, 1985)

Sir Hugh Trevor-Roper, *The Hermit of Peking,* (London, Macmillan, 1979)

Daniele Vare, *The Last Empress,* (New York, the Literary Guild, 1936)

Daniele Vare, *The Laughing Diplomat,* (London Murray, 1938)

Wang Guo Zhen 王国祯，北京的桥，[*Beijing Bridges*], (Beijing, Beijing Yan Shan Press, 2000)

Wang Li, 翁立，北京的胡同，[*Beijing Hutong*], (reprinted Beijing, Beijing Yan Shan Press, 1997)

Wang Yong Bing 王永斌，话说前门，[*Talking About the Front Gate*], (Beijing, Beijing Yan Shan Press, 1974)

B. L. Putnam Weale, *Indiscreet Letters from Peking,* (New York, Dodd, Mead and Company, 1908)

Norman Webster, *Posters and Pedicarts,* (St. Paul, Minnesota, EMC Corporation, 1973)

Robert Welch, *The Life of John Birch,* (Boston and Los Angeles, Western Islands, 1960)

C. A. S. Williams, *Outlines of Chinese Symbolism and Art Motives,* (Reprint, Taipei, Tung Huang Books Co., Ltd., 1983)

Jan Wong, *Jan Wong's China,* (Toronto, Doubleday Canada, 1999)

Frances Wood, *Blue Guide To China,* (London, A&C Black, 1992)

Frances Wood, *Hand-Grenade Practice in Peking: My Part in the Cultural Revolution,* (London, John Murray, 2000)

Harry Wu and Carolyn Wakeman, *Bitter Winds,* (New York, John Wiley & Sons, 1990)

K.C. Wu, *The Chinese Heritage,* (New York, Crown Publishers, 1982)

Wu Zuguang, Huang Zuolin and Mei Shaowu, *Peking Opera and Mei Lan Fang,* (Beijing, New World Press, 1984)

Xiao Mao and Nan Tzu, *The Man With the Key Is Not Here,* (Dallas, Pacific Venture Press, 1990)

Xie Mu, Wu Yong Liang 谢牧、吴永良，中国老字号, [*China's Famous Traditional Stores*] (Beijing, Beijing Economic Daily Press, 1988)

Xu Chengbei, *Old Beijing: People, Houses and Lifestyles,* (Beijing, Foreign Languages Press, 2001)

Xu Chengbei, *Old Beijing: In the Shadow of Imperial Throne,* (Beijing, Foreign Languages Press, 2001)

Yao Ming-le, *The Conspiracy and Murder of Mao's Heir,* (London, Collins, 1983)

Henry Yule and A. C. Burnell, *Hobson-jobson, The Anglo-Indian Dictionary,* (Reprint, Herfordshire, Wordsworth Editions, Inc., 1996)

Henry Yule and Henri Cordier, translators, *The Travels of Marco Polo,* (London, John Murray, 1903; reprinted, Mineola, New York, Dover Publications, 1992)

Zhang Chang, *Chinese Clay Art: The Zhang Style Painted Figurines,* (Beijing, New World Press, 1989)

Zhou Shachen, *Beijing Old and New,* (Beijing, New World Press, 1984 and 1993).

Zhu Qixin and Yan Zhaohua, *Places of Interest in Beijing,* (Beijing. China Travel & Tourism Press, 1992)

ILLUSTRATION CREDITS

Todd Greenspan: 8 top, 11, 166, 352.

Hedda Morrison Archives, Harvard-Yenching Library: 3, 7 top, 77, 91, 215, 358.

Museum of Chinese Revolutionary History: 5 top, 58 top, 135 top, 147, 168 top, 185 top, 196 top, 266.

Christopher Smith: 12, 13, 33, 36, 53, 64, 88, 93, 106, 135 bottom, 157 top, 168 bottom, 187 bottom, 235, 258, 274 top, 322.

The author: 5 bottom, 7 bottom, 8 bottom, 58, 62, 121, 154, 157 bottom, 185 bottom, 210, 274 bottom, 277, 287, 310 313 326.

SOURCES FOR ILLUSTRATIONS

Arlington & Lewisohn, *In Search of Old Peking:* 212.

Bodde, *Annual Customs and Festivals in Peking:* 67, 75, 217.

Rennie, *Peking and the Pekingese:* 134, 167, 270.

MAPS

Hong Kong University Press

(Every effort has been made to trace copyright holders. We apologize for any errors or omissions in the above list and would be grateful to be notified of any corrections that should be incorporated in any future editions.)

INDEX